Two week loan
Benthyciad pythefnos

Please return on or before the due date to avoid overdue charges
*A wnewch chi ddychwelyd ar neu cyn y dyddiad a nodir ar eich llyfr os
gwelwch yn dda, er mwyn osgoi taliadau*

http://library.cardiff.ac.uk
http://llyfrgell.caerdydd.ac.uk

Purchasing for Health

Health Services Management

Series Editors:
Chris Ham and Chris Heginbotham

The British National Health Service is one of the biggest and most complex organizations in the developed world. Employing around one million people and accounting for £36 billion of public expenditure, the Service is of major concern to both the public and politicians. Management within the NHS faces a series of challenges in ensuring that resources are deployed efficiently and effectively. These challenges include the planning and management of human resources, the integration of professionals into the management process, and making sure that services meet the needs of patients and the public.

Against this background, the Health Services Management series addresses the many issues and practical problems faced by people in managerial roles in health services.

Purchasing for Health

A multidisciplinary introduction to the theory and practice of health purchasing

John Øvretveit

Open University Press
Buckingham · Philadelphia

Open University Press
Celtic Court
22 Ballmoor
Buckingham
MK18 1XW

and
1900 Frost Road, Suite 101
Bristol, PA 19007, USA

First Published 1995

A catalogue record of this book is available from the British Library

ISBN 0–335–19333–1 (hb)   0–335–19332–3 (pb)

Library of Congress Cataloging-in-Publication Data

Øvretveit, John, 1954–
    Purchasing for health : a multidisciplinary introduction to the
theory and practice of health purchasing / John Øvretveit.
        p.   cm. — (Health services management)
    Includes bibliographical references and index.
    ISBN 0–335–19333–1 (hb)   ISBN 0–335–19332–3 (pb)
    1. Health products–Great Britain–Purchasing.   2. National Health
Service (Great Britain)–Administration.   I. Title.   II. Series.
    [DNLM: 1. National Health Service (Great Britain)   2. Health
Services–economics–Great Britain.   3. Financial Management–
organization & administration–Great Britain.   4. State Medicine–
economics–Great Britain.   W 74 096p   1994]
    RA410.55.G7088   1994
    362.1'068—dc20
    DNLM/DLC
    for Library of Congress   94–27592
                                                                      CIP

Typeset by Graphicraft Typesetters Ltd, Hong Kong
Printed in Great Britain by Page Bros., Norwich

Contents

Foreword

I was very pleased to be asked to write the foreword for John Øvretveit's *Purchasing for Health*, which sets out the concepts and practical issues in purchasing for health. 1993 has taken purchasing to the top of the health care agenda and I believe that the NHS is now on its way to becoming a 'purchaser-driven' system which will improve health services for patients and the health of the nation as a whole.

Although there is still talk about the 'newness' of purchasing, there is also an ever growing awareness that purchasers can, and are beginning to, improve the health of their populations. GP fundholders, in particular, have been extremely effective in using the market to bring about change. Where fundholders have set the pace of change for quality improvements, this can lead to improvements for *all* patients.

Health care is changing in industrialized nations around the world and we can be certain that the pace of change will accelerate over the next decade. The UK's reformed health service is attracting interest in many of these countries. For example, many European countries are considering, or experimenting with, market reforms and are looking to us for understanding about the role that purchasing may play in any future systems. Similarly, the National Health Service reforms are contributing to current discussions of health care reform in the United States.

In conclusion, I support John Øvretveit's summary, that whilst structure and legal points are important, success in purchasing depends on effective joint working and strong relationships with others, i.e. GPs, local authorities, the voluntary sector and, of course, local people. I see purchasing as a major challenge and I am sure purchasers everywhere will benefit from the experience of North West Thames in seizing that challenge.

Sir Duncan Nichol
Chief Executive, NHS Management Executive

Acknowledgements

I would like to thank colleagues in Europe and the USA for their help in understanding purchasing and their health systems; in particular, Mats Brommels, Edgar Borgenhammer, Hans Maarse and Richard Saltman. My thanks also to colleagues at Brunel University, the Leeds Nuffield Institute, Birmingham Health Services Management Centre, and to Janet McKeown and Ron Kerr at North West Thames Region. I would also like to thank Chris Ham and Chris Heginbotham for helpful comments on the final draft of the book. Finally, thank you Mary for giving me the space to write the book.

1 Purchasing for health

Introduction

Purchasing for health is more than contracting the best value for money services. Contracting is one means to the end of improving health and preventing illness. Public purchasing is a new task and an emerging health management discipline. This book gives an introduction to the theory and practice of the subject, describes key issues and outlines concepts and practical approaches to purchasing for health. It judges different approaches to purchasing against a view of the purpose of NHS commissioning, and of commissioning organizations as service businesses.

The book is mainly for UK health purchasing managers working for health authorities and for primary care physicians or centres with a purchasing fund (in the UK, general medical practitioner (GP) 'fundholders'). It will also be of interest to private purchasers, such as insurance companies and large employers, in Europe and in the USA where health purchasing is a prominent part of current health reforms. Many such purchasers are taking a more proactive and long-term approach to contracting and to health promotion, and some are acting as purchasers using public finance. The book also makes available some of the experience of seven UK NHS integrated health purchasers (commissioning agencies) in forming and performing joint district health authority (DHA) and family health services authority (FHSA) commissioning. Parts of the book draw on a purchaser development programme for these agencies, and this accounts for the emphasis on practical problems and solutions in the later chapters.

This introductory chapter first lists some of the themes of the book, describes the sources and research methods, and gives an overview of each chapter. Then it puts public health purchasing in the context of recent changes in health services, and summarizes the issues for UK purchasers in the late 1990s. The chapter closes with a note on the emerging health management discipline of health purchasing.

Themes of the book

The themes running through the book include the following.

Purchasing is a service business

Both private and public health purchasers are service organizations and need to adopt modern service management and organization approaches to provide a better service to their populations. This is not to suggest that they use simplistic notions of 'the customer', or that there are not a variety of requirements which they have to meet. This is especially so for NHS commissioners, which are often caught between responding to local people's views and government directives. However, public commissioners need to establish their worth and be more responsive to the people whom they are serving. They can use modern service management techniques and concepts to do so, and to manage conflicting demands. Quality applies to purchasing as well as to provision.

The purpose of health commissioning

Many of the issues faced by public health purchasers are made more difficult to resolve by them not having a clear and shared sense of the distinctive purpose of public health 'commissioning'. The book continually returns to questions of purpose in examining different options, such as options for 'locality purchasing', approaches to coordinating purchasing for secondary and primary health care, and relations with GPs and others. It does not argue that purchasers must clarify purpose before acting, or the opposite, that action will itself create a sense of purpose. Rather, it emphasizes raising questions of purpose to help to decide how to act, and developing a sense of purpose through reflective action. The future of NHS commissioning depends on developing, within commissioning organizations, a shared sense of purpose and of a distinctive role in a changing health system, and on conveying this understanding to others, not least the public.

The terminology of health purchasing

Health purchasing is a newly emerging discipline, or perhaps more accurately 'multi-discipline'. It draws from experience in commercial purchasing and from the disciplines of public health, information sciences, health economics, management and organization science and other bodies of knowledge and practice. As with all new disciplines, people use new and different terms to formulate and to convey new ideas, and some terms become established as key concepts in the discipline. For example, in the UK 'purchasing' is being superseded by 'commissioning' to convey a sense that the role of NHS authorities is more than buying services.

A theme of the book is that people working in a commissioning organization have to have some common understanding of the terms which they are using in order to organize work and to communicate with others. The book does not seek to prescribe usage, but to describe how the terms are used in this book, and to draw attention to the different possible meanings of such terms as the 'primary care provision' and 'purchasing' roles of primary health care authorities (in England, family health service authorities).

Health strategy

We have already touched on this theme – that health purchasers, both public and private, must move beyond a preoccupation with contracting, to an approach which seeks health gain by a variety of means. Although buying treatment-only services will always be important, purchasers will need to pay more attention to prevention, health promotion and inter-sector collaboration with other agencies to prevent illness and conditions which harm health. They will need to decide how much time and resources they can justify putting into this type of work, given that many causes of ill health, such as poverty, are outside their influence.

Coordination

In the future, with a greater number and type of health and social care providers, health purchasers are the main organizations taking an overall and long-term view of the needs of a population and of all the services people need. They have a 'brokerage' role in ensuring that providers link with each other, and a coordinating role to require services to cooperate in their planning and provision, which they carry out through strategic planning and contracting.

A prerequisite for provider coordination is commissioner coordination. In England there are four main types of commissioners: district health authorities and GP fundholders commission secondary health services (mostly hospital health care); for primary care services there are family health service authorities; and for social care services there are local authorities. In other countries there are similar divisions, and often many purchasers for the same type of service. A theme of the book is the importance of commissioners cooperating with each other in a range of activities, especially in influencing markets, in planning the services which they will purchase and in needs assessment. We pay particular attention to cooperation in primary and secondary care commissioning, and to forming or developing organizations to combine primary and secondary purchasing finance (termed in this book 'integrated DHA–FHSA commissioning agencies', or just 'agencies').

Collaboration and relationships

Health commissioning is about working with other organizations and with informal community or patient groups. Legal or quasi-legal contracts are a minor part of the work: most of the work is done through forming and developing different types of relationships with providers, other purchasers, higher-level authorities, other government services, local patient groups and others. Purchaser managers and staff need to develop skills to work across internal and external organizational boundaries, manage conflict, develop networks and influence others. This way of working is different to managing provider units, and old attitudes and management styles will not work, although some provider and practitioner management skills and experience are still valuable.

Choices and justification

The gap between what is technically possible and what is affordable for both public and private finance is widening at an increasing rate. Both public and private purchasers have to decide which services they will not pay for, and to justify these decisions. Public finance will have to be targeted to certain populations and services, but it will still be necessary to secure broad population support for more selective purchasing.

Public and private

New mixes of capital and revenue finance, ownership and governance structures are being considered and developed for health care purchasing and provision. Purchasers are increasingly finding that traditional distinctions are a handicap to developing new approaches to securing services, and to health promotion and illness prevention. The increasing 'care gap' means that public commissioners may have to seek other sources of finance, and that private finance for health services may increase. In the UK and the Nordic countries, will it be possible to uphold NHS and public health principles with an increasing role for private finance, and how will these changes affect public health commissioning?

Information management

Another theme of the book is that health purchasers cannot do their work without the systems and skills to access and manipulate information about needs and about providers. New information technology (IT) allows fast transfer of information between purchasers, providers, primary care practitioners and other agencies. Electronic networks change relationships between organizations. Properly managed and appropriate IT reduces costs, and makes it possible to offer services and to undertake tasks which would not have been possible five years ago. Another 'information theme' of the book is purchasers' role in making available and interpreting information for the people they serve; for example, to increase choice by giving information about the quality of hospitals and of the performance of doctors.

Research sources and methods

The book draws on three sets of research material to give an introduction to public health purchasing. The first is reported research and the author's own research into the UK experience of NHS health purchasing, established in the NHS 'internal market' reforms of 1990. The second is the author's and others' research into health reforms and purchasing in Europe and the USA, conducted since 1990. The third source is a collaborative research and development programme with seven different integrated health commissioning agencies in the English North West Thames Region. The research was undertaken using a unique action research method developed at Brunel University and the Tavistock Institute of Human Relations (Jaques 1982; Øvretveit 1992b: Appendix 1).

The method is designed to apply and develop new knowledge to resolve practical problems and policy issues in organizations. It aims to construct answers, rather than just to raise questions. This method was appropriate for the purchaser development programme because there was often no established knowledge or experience to help with the issues that purchasing managers were facing. The collaborative and conceptual approach of the method made it possible to formulate the practical models which were needed, and to test them. Some of this work was published during 1992 and 1993 in a series of briefing papers for the agencies. The later part of this book draws more fully on this third source to present material which NHS commissioners will find of use to understand and address current practical issues. One such issue for English and Welsh authorities is how to merge DHAs and FHSAs.

My work with purchasing managers in the development programme emphasized for me the limited staff, time and finance available to purchasing organizations, and that they are evolving. For most, the issues were setting priorities: deciding what is most important, deciding how much time and resources to allocate, deciding what to do first and in which sequence, and ensuring that the different strands link together. The touchstone of the book is the practical issues raised by purchasing managers, and it aims to give practical ways forward for addressing these issues as well as an introduction and background to key aspects of purchasing and health reform. However, it also aims to develop conceptual and theoretical knowledge of purchasing, and to draw purchasing managers' attention to the research which they will need to apply to develop purchasing. One of the assumptions of the book and of the development programme was that lasting solutions to practical problems in commissioning require tested concepts and theories of commissioning.

The chapters of the book

Taking an overview we see that the next chapter starts with the purpose of NHS commissioning, and then we consider the role of commissioning in different types of market. Chapter 4 discusses centralized and local purchasing, and Chapter 5 the issues of rationing and accountability. The middle of the book examines specific issues, such as commissioners' relations with providers and with local authorities. It then moves back to the purpose of commissioning in describing the merging of primary and secondary care commissioning in integrated commissioning agencies. The final chapter broadens out to consider the future for NHS commissioning and health purchasing.

Chapter 2 considers purchasing in the context of a health care system and in relation to ongoing or proposed market reforms in different countries. A theme of the chapter is that a purchasing organization is part of a system, and that actions in one part affect all the other parts. In many countries purchasing is part of a system which could be described as a highly regulated 'market system'. In each country and region the system has specific characteristics – in the UK the system is a mix of planned bureaucracy and market, with a strong political dimension.

The chapter describes the three main system dimensions of (a) regulations and regulatory bodies, (b) types of purchasers and purchaser competition and (c) types of providers and provider competition. It gives frameworks and models for understanding health markets. The aims are to help purchasers to consider the purpose of their organization in the context of the system, to help purchasers to compare health purchasing in different countries and to give a background for Chapter 6, which covers contracting and local markets. It also summarizes the NHS 'internal market' reforms for non-UK readers.

The purpose of an NHS commissioning authority is to improve the health of a population and to prevent illness. But this is also the aim of a hospital, a GP and some private health insurers and providers. Is the difference that an NHS authority has this aim for a large and perhaps more stable population, and does not directly provide or manage any services, or is the difference that others have additional purposes? Are there any differences between the purposes of a commissioning agency, GP fundholders in their commissioning role and a private health insurer, and if so, are these differences of degree rather than fundamental ones? Chapter 3 encourages managers critically to examine views about the purpose of public health purchasing. It argues that a condition for stronger purchasing is a clear conception of purpose, which is shared among staff and with other purchasers. It puts forward a conception of purpose which is wider than contracting services, and which is based on the concept of health gain. This helps purchasing organizations to clarify the difference they make for their population, and to develop feasible health strategies. The chapter also shows how thinking of purchasing as a service leads to different strategies and relationships, and how different models help to translate different views of purpose into specific tasks and relationships.

Decentralized purchasing or locality commissioning is the first of a number of different approaches to purchasing which we consider. Chapter 4 considers different schemes, ranging from health authority 'locality commissioning' to GP fundholder purchasing. It gives an analysis of the purposes of different schemes and describes the options for authorities seeking to develop locality purchasing. We see that clarity about purpose lies behind choosing the right approach, and how ideas from modern service management can help to develop decentralized purchasing with devolved FHSA functions. The chapter presents models to help to assess which decisions and work should be undertaken centrally and which locally, and considers whether purchasers should have local offices or 'agents'.

If purchasers cannot explain the process by which they allocate resources, and give an acceptable justification for their decisions, then their own future is in question. Pursuing the theme of relating purchasing methods to the purpose of purchasing, Chapter 5 considers the link between resources and improving health. It introduces the 'rationing debate' and shows how attention is moving from the question of which services not to buy, to the question of how the bulk of health expenditure is allocated, and the rationale for these allocations. It shows how purchasers can make use of existing information about effectiveness, and how they can encourage providers to measure outcome on a routine basis. It describes practical approaches which purchasers can use to examine and alter their spending and gives guidelines for 'justifiable purchasing'.

Chapter 6 turns to purchasers' relations with providers, primarily hospitals. It is contracting which realizes many priorities, but in the past it has been contracting which has driven strategy rather than vice versa. One method for pursuing health strategy is to change contracts where there is provider competition. Another is to develop a relationship with a key provider and to use contract design to agree incentives for fulfilling health strategy aims. The chapter gives examples of contracting strategy and models of contracting which link health strategy to contracts. It shows how commissioners can make more use of different contract designs to give the right incentives and share risks.

Until recently, quality was considered a provider issue. Chapter 7 shows that the health of a population also depends on the quality of commissioning. The chapter defines quality in commissioning and considers how to measure and improve it. It then examines quality issues in commissioner–provider relationships and describes cost-effective and practical ways in which commissioners can work with providers in a partnership to improve quality.

If the aim of commissioning authorities is health gain, then their health strategy must address issues on the boundary of health and social care and involve working in different ways to create more healthy environments. Chapter 8 considers agency relations with local authorities, and how to establish relations for work that is wider than jointly planning which services to contract. It also considers relations with local authorities for community care planning, market policy development and service contracting. It describes one inter-authority structure for 'joint commissioning' and how this structure is evolving to manage purchasing budgets. The chapter shows that the purposes and interests of health commissioners and local authorities are converging, but that some financial and other considerations make it difficult for them to act together.

Chapter 9 considers primary care and the potential future role of GPs and community health services in the UK. It questions whether commissioners expect too much of primary care and GPs, describes GPs' current work and considers what commissioners and others need to do to develop the potential of primary care. To develop services outside hospitals, commissioners need to take steps to ensure that the increasing variety of providers coordinate their work for individuals and collaborate in planning. The chapter gives examples of different types of teams which show how different services can be coordinated, and describes the ways in which purchasers can ensure 'lateral linkage' between providers. Ensuring provider coordination in a market is an important service which purchasers provide, and a way in which they add value to the NHS.

In the UK FHSA relations with GPs are not well understood outside the primary care sector, or even, in some areas, by staff working in that sector. Chapter 10 describes the three main roles of the FHSA because staff in DHAs and others without a primary care background need to understand the work and culture of FHSAs. The chapter describes different views about the future for FHSAs and the meaning of the FHSA 'purchasing' and 'provider' roles.

Chapter 11 draws on the discussion of FHSAs to show how different commissioning agencies have approached integrating FHSA and DHA work and functions. It lists thirteen ways in which FHSAs and DHAs have integrated staff and systems, and outlines the reasons for doing so and the expected benefits. The chapter gives a model of four types of integration, and notes differences in approaches in North West Thames and in other areas. The chapter gives a checklist (reproduced in Appendix 5) which agencies have used to evaluate their progress in integrating.

A striking feature of DHA–FHSA commissioning agencies or authorities is that many tasks and projects cannot be undertaken within the boundaries of a directorate, however one defines the directorates: most activities span two or more directorates. This is not an organizational curiosity, but is fundamental to the nature and purpose of health purchasing as we see in Chapter 12. This chapter describes integrated agency structure and organization, first noting how different agencies have defined their directorate boundaries and structure, each of which is represented in the diagrams in Appendix 2. It then describes the two main aspects of agency matrix structure: project teams and dual accountability arrangements. The chapter finishes by considering how purchasers can ensure that their many different programmes of work are coordinated.

The final chapter moves away from the day-to-day practical issues of UK commissioning to look at the future for public health purchasing and returns to the question of purpose. It considers different options for financing, including those for purchasers to collect finance directly from the public. It considers how future changes could affect equity and choice, and the role of public purchasers in promoting certain types of equity and choice. It also questions the usefulness of the purchaser–provider and public–private distinctions, and considers some of the joint public–private schemes being developed for purchasing and providing health care in the future.

Health purchasing in context

It helps to view current changes in financing and health purchasing in an historical context. Purchasing health services is not a new activity. Since the dawn of time people have exchanged items of value in return for help in regaining health – often the exchange was with the gods or their representatives on earth. Throughout history, both rich and poor have purchased health care when they needed it. This has continued even in communist countries which prohibit private medicine.

The growth of organized modern medicine and of health professions was paralleled by a growth in schemes and organizations for paying for health care (Parry and Parry 1976). People grouped together to create funds which they paid into when well and working, and which paid for their health care when they needed it. The first of these schemes were non-profit cooperatives for occupations or towns which administered them, which have evolved in some countries into 'sickness funds' and social insurance schemes, for example in Germany, the Netherlands and France. In the past 100 years, private for-profit health insurance has grown, and insurers have introduced a variety of ways of paying practitioners and hospitals so as to contain costs and give incentives for efficiency. In the UK since the 1870s, and elsewhere, many insurers and social funds have employed doctors and owned hospitals, rather than contracting other independent health care organizations.

In the 1990s the bulk of health purchasing in both the developed and 'two-thirds' Worlds is 'collective purchasing' by non-governmental private, or not-for-profit, organizations. Second to this is individual private purchasing of medical and other health care, and of medicines. There is thus a considerable history and experience of health purchasing at both a collective and a personal level (Demone and Gibeleman 1989). There are also experience of and theories about commercial purchasing undertaken by large private and public organizations, of both goods and services, including professional and technical services such as computer, legal and engineering services, and basic services such as cleaning, refuse collection and laundry services (Scheuing 1989). In both public and private organizations in the 1970s and 1980s there was a trend to purchasing services which were not central to the organization's core business, rather than managing these services 'in-house'.

It is only relatively recently that, in a few parts of the world, governments have assumed a degree of responsibility for the health of their citizens and for financing health services for some or all of the population. In some countries, governments have assumed ownership of health service providers or created public provider systems. Even more recent is large-scale governmental purchasing of health care services; for example, in the USA with federal and state purchasing of health care for older people, the poor and veterans. Newest of all is public health purchasing in Europe, and notably in the UK, which separated NHS purchasing from NHS provision in the early 1990s.

This is not to suggest that public management and ownership of health services is an evolutionary dead-end. Some hold that, in the broad sweep of history, moving from private to public ownership and management of health services is a progressive trend, and cite the NHS as the most successful example. They claim that direct government management avoids the costs of a market superstructure and of market transactions and allows rational planning. This view holds that separating purchasing from service management is a regressive trend, and that the economic and choice arguments for doing so are a 'smoke-screen': that governments supported by private business advance business interests by opening up service provision for private profit. Others view this change as a positive evolution out of the centralized planned welfare bureaucracies of the 1970s and 1980s. They hold that regulated competition is a superior way of organizing public and private health services in the fast-changing consumer-conscious 1990s, especially with the lower cost of transactions and access to information in the computer age. From this perspective, the issue is not public or private ownership but the technical issue of which forms of regulation and competition are required to promote efficiency and preserve certain values in this specific type of market.

The general point is that, while public purchasing is new in public service management, it has to be viewed in an historical context, and in terms of the post-Second World War European welfare state. Like private purchasers, public purchasers face technical issues of contracting, but all their decisions are also political and value-laden and they are accountable for these decisions to governments and to the public they serve.

The focus of this book is public organizations using public finance to purchase services and to improve health – in particular, NHS health commissioners in the UK. Although such 'public health purchasers' can learn from the private and not-for-profit sector in the UK, Europe and the USA, their role is significantly different and more complex, being concerned more with health gain than with risk assessment and selection. The book argues that public health purchasers do have a distinctive role, and that they need to clarify and establish this role and their legitimacy. At the same time it also shows that there are similarities in the concerns, methods and strategies of public and private health purchasers. Examples are the health prevention and promotion programmes of private insurers and employer-purchasers, and public commissioners drawing on the contracting and quality assurance experience of private purchasers. Both public and private purchasers are developing the same types of 'partnership relations' with providers.

This book aims to contribute to an understanding of health purchasing as a new force in health systems, and of the role of health purchasers in health systems. It presents a different view to the two 'public versus private' views summarized above. The view it presents is that, in the developed world, similar problems and ideologies are leading to a convergence in many aspects of private and public health systems, and to the blurring of both the private–public and purchaser–provider distinctions. In the past, both private and public health purchasing was largely concerned with paying and contracting providers, and mostly with acute hospitals. In the future purchasing will be more strategic and less provider-driven. Purchasers will use knowledge about the cost-effectiveness of services and of other health-enhancing activities, and will stimulate new types of services and treatments outside hospitals.

Distinctions between public and private are already inadequate to describe existing arrangements or to conceptualize new directions. Competition between purchasers is one example of a trend which challenges these distinctions. There is competition not only for public purchasing finance between public purchasers, but also between public and private bodies, and between public and private organizations for individual citizens' finance, or for private collective purchasing finance such as employer funds.

Issues in UK public health purchasing

This section continues to set the context by describing issues faced by UK health commissioning organizations, and some of the changes since 1990. Two features of the 1990 NHS reforms were primary care purchasing of a limited range of hospital services by GP fundholders, and the re-creation of local health authorities as purchasers of health care for their populations of between 250,000 to 1,000,000. We consider the reforms and the justification for the 'purchaser–provider' split in more detail in the next chapter.

UK health commissioning in the mid-1990s

Ever since the NHS was established health authorities have purchased supplies, equipment and, more recently, non-clinical services. The 1990s reforms re-created health authorities and, by the mid-1990s, led to them becoming purchasers only (DoH 1989a; 1990a). This, together with the increasing number of GP purchasers, has resulted in NHS health purchasing for clinical and non-clinical services growing into a sizeable and varied business with distinctive methods and aims. Public finance of over £30 billion goes through public purchasers' hands, mostly to health service providers. How they direct and use the money is intensely political, not just in terms of hospital closures, but in terms of life or death for some patients, and in affecting the employment of one million NHS employees.

In 1992 and 1993 the government put more emphasis on strengthening NHS commissioning with ministerial speeches, development finance and a variety of initiatives (Mawhinney and Nichol 1993). NHS purchasing authorities continued to merge and to create larger 'commissioning agencies' to counter the dominance of large hospital or community provider trusts, and to adjust for their increasingly weakened position as more GPs assume control of finance to purchase a wide range of health services.

Health purchasing is new in the NHS, and many purchaser managers, staff and non-executive directors are new in post and 'finding their feet'. Provider managers are unsure of the direction or ideas of purchasers, and private insurers and hospitals watch on from the sidelines, ready to take the opportunities as they arise. Purchasers are at the centre of a number of highly political issues, including rationing, hospital closure, private charging, inequities in treatment between GP fundholder patients and others, local authority reforms and social services under-financing, and accountability and ethics in the new NHS structure. These and other issues which we consider below are testing whether purchasers, as 'champions of the people', will put their populations first, when there is a conflict of interests with provider hospitals.

In the early 1990s, many believed that the future for health purchasing in the NHS lay in larger health authorities. In some parts of the UK, authorities combined their purchasing power and reduced their costs by forming agencies and consortia. District health authorities (DHAs) merged, or formed common 'health commissioning agencies'. In some areas, DHAs and primary health services authorities (FHSAs) formed 'integrated commissioning agencies', before legislation allowed formal mergers between these authorities and the combination of finance for primary and secondary care. Later chapters of this book report how seven such agencies were formed in the North West Thames Region between 1992 and 1994, and Appendices 2 and 3 give details of these agencies.

Closer collaboration between primary and secondary purchasing was and is a key issue for all purchasers. Integrated agencies allow NHS commissioning of GP and other primary care services together with hospital and community health services, something which has not been possible in the past. This can create the conditions to develop a less acute illness driven health service, by developing primary care and health promotion and prevention services to avoid ill health.

The issues for NHS commissioners

Commissioning in the first years of the NHS reforms was driven by acute hospital issues and preoccupied with contracting. A critical view was that commissioners were hardly more than a channel for financing provider units, with no strategy of their own, either for contracting or for improving health. Many questioned what value they added to the NHS. However, during 1992 and 1993 commissioners developed alternatives to fundholding, and began to switch contracts and to take a more proactive role with providers. The *Health of the Nation* (DoH 1992a), referred to as the first real health strategy for the NHS, came on to commissioners' everyday agendas. A new language and set of ideas about health commissioning began to emerge. As part of the background for the rest of the book we note here some of the 'challenges' facing UK health commissioners in the late 1990s, many of which are also faced by health purchasers outside the UK.

Money, and the lack of it
It is easy to say that all problems stem from 'not enough finance', but there is no doubt that UK commissioning was born into a 'bracing' financial climate. First there is a change in financial allocation to commissioners from the Resource Allocation Working Party-based formula (DHSS 1976) to a weighted-population allocation formula. Although the change will take place over a few years, some of the urban health authorities will lose millions of pounds, with the hospitals in their areas also losing finance as distant commissioners withdraw their contracts. Second, as more GPs become fundholders, even the authorities gaining from the new capitation formula lose because fundholders' purchasing finance is taken from the authority's purchasing budget. Third, there are restrictions on commissioners' own operating budgets to an annual running cost of less than 1 per cent of their total budget, which means limitations to the staff they can employ. These and other operating constraints make it more difficult for commissioners to develop and pursue a proactive strategy.

Shared purpose and vision
A concept of the purpose of NHS commissioning as assessing needs and buying services is relatively easy for most people to understand. An issue for commissioners – both authorities and GP fundholders – is to develop a role beyond a narrow purchasing role, and to win support for such a role. A shared sense of this wider purpose is important for moving commissioning from a 'paymaster' to a 'proactive' and health promotional role. This shared understanding of purpose is especially important for

integrating DHA and FHSA staff and work, and for conveying the value of commissioning to the public and to others.

In one sense, integrated agencies or authorities are better able to define their distinctive role because they combine secondary and primary commissioning. Yet, beyond general statements of purpose, there are more options open to them for the future, and greater differences in view about purpose within the DHA and FHSA. We see in later chapters how purchasers develop their view of their purpose in parallel with making practical decisions about contracting, in considering options for localities, in their relations with GPs and in many other decisions.

Health strategy

For all commissioners a key task is to develop and pursue a strategy for health, which is more than a healthcare service strategy or plans for contracting providers. In integrated agencies, such health strategies have to make the most of combining DHA and FHSA staff, systems and finance. Many purchasers' initial health strategies outlined aims and methods for working more closely with governmental and other agencies to reduce ill health and to create health-promoting conditions, as well as plans for health promotion and prevention services. These strategies should give a basis for much of the work of commissioning and for directing contracting. Whether the strategies do so depends in part on how realistic they are and how widely they are known, shared and valued by all staff, and on internal organization to link strategy to everyday activities, and especially to contracting.

Needs assessment

Undertaking and using assessments of the health needs of a population is another challenge. In the early 1990s, the limitations of the information and of the processes for using it meant that needs assessment had little impact on commissioners' decisions. After the initial over-ambitious ideas, commissioners took a more pragmatic approach to assessing needs and recognized what could be done with the available information. Many now view needs assessment as both a political and a technical activity, and are developing needs assessment processes which combine different sources and types of information. This involves deciding how best to combine DHA and FHSA information with information from GPs and local authorities, and with people's views about needs. All are trying to establish needs assessment as a reference point and justification for many decisions. Further issues are how to link information about service and treatment effectiveness to needs assessment, and needs assessment to contracting.

Developing primary and community care

One service-purchasing part of health strategies is to contract and develop primary care and community services. In integrated agencies one set of issues concerns the agency's relations with GPs as providers, including how best to help them to improve and extend their services, and the agency's view about the future role of GPs. It is difficult, and some say inappropriate, to separate the role of GPs as providers from their role in influencing or undertaking purchasing, especially when considering community health services. An example is in commissioners' plans for developing primary health care teams, where GPs may or may not purchase other team members' services.

Health strategies have to link with those for social services and other local authority services. An issue for health commissioners is how to develop new relations with local authorities, which have their own priorities and are also undergoing purchaser–provider reforms. In the UK the term 'joint commissioning' now refers to a variety of types of relations with local authorities, relations which are becoming increasingly important.

Contracting

Most money for developing primary care will have to come from savings in the contracting of acute hospital services. In addition to using 'demand management' actions to reduce GP referrals to high-cost hospital specialties, commissioners are becoming more sophisticated in their contracting. They face a range of contracting issues, including how to ensure that contracting is driven by strategy rather than vice versa, how to subdivide block contracts, how to monitor contracts and how to contract for quality as well as for lower costs. Commissioners and providers are developing new types of partnerships and new types of contracts to share risks and give efficiency incentives.

The gaps

The warning 'mind the gap' in the London Underground evoked, for one American doctor, many of the problems facing the health commissioning agency he visited. One such gap is between what is technically possible and what is affordable with public finance. All purchasers face decisions about whether to refuse to fund certain treatments out of public money, and are having to be more explicit about what they are purchasing for their populations and why. The pressure to reconsider how the bulk of expenditure is apportioned to different client groups and services is growing. Crude rationing by refusal to fund certain treatments is being superseded by new approaches to prioritizing using information about cost-effectiveness. The idea of 'justifiable commissioning' is emerging in relation to these issues and to the next issue.

Legitimacy and relations with the public

Some of the larger commissioners in particular are concerned about losing touch with their public, and realize the need to establish their role as 'champions of the people'. One issue is getting public support for some of the difficult decisions which commissioners have to make about hospital contracts, when hospitals have a closer relationship with the public and can more easily establish their case. Another is the lack of formal local accountability of public health authorities, especially UK district health authorities made up of five non-executive directors and a chairman appointed by central government. Do they serve the government or local people, and can they serve both?

Locality purchasing

There are different ways in which commissioners can decentralize some of their work and 'get closer' to the populations they serve. Some are piloting GP-driven 'locality purchasing', and some are considering ways of involving local communities in purchasing decisions. All are examining potential locality boundaries, but with some uncertainty about the purpose and role of locality purchasing.

Information

A further set of issues concerns the poor information base for purchasing and the lack of skills, expertise and systems for information management. Information is critical for deciding where to place large and small contracts, and for monitoring provider activity. There are difficulties in getting information from providers, especially about outcomes, in checking accuracy and in making reliable comparisons between providers. One set of issues is how best to combine or merge different sources or types of information, for example 'hard' and 'soft' data about providers or about needs. All commissioners are investing in systems and staff skills to make use of available information, to improve databases and to access new information. Merging DHA and FHSA systems makes it possible to combine data from both to assess better the needs of different populations. However, there are difficulties in merging the systems and in manipulating the data for these purposes.

Commissioner organization structure and integration process

Last but not least of the issues to be mentioned here is what sort of management structure and organization is best for commissioners' evolving role. One issue is clarifying the core commissioning functions and considering which functions might be contracted out. Another is how best to group activities within directorates. The most important issue, however, is how to establish good cross-directorate working arrangements. All commissioners underestimate the skills and training needed for staff and teams to work successfully across directorates. There is a need to coordinate the many project teams and programmes within an agency to ensure that they reinforce rather than undermine each other.

These questions of structure and cross-directorate working have become more complex in the UK with the formation of integrated FHSA and DHA purchasing agencies or authorities. There are differences in culture between DHA and FHSA staff, and a poor understanding of each other's work.

There is also the question of how to manage the process of integrating DHA and FHSA staff and functions. Many have taken a cautious approach, identifying support functions which can be merged immediately, and each has formed directorates in a different way.

This book addresses these and other practical issues raised by commissioner managers. It also draws attention to other issues which will become more important in the coming years, to the research which has been done on the subject of health purchasing and to where managers may get further information.

Terminology and the emerging discipline of health commissioning

Purchasing management and public health commissioning are emerging as new health management disciplines. Both draw on experience from private health purchasing and from different health and management disciplines. As with any body of thought and practice, health purchasing involves terms and concepts to describe and to think about different aspects of the work, the purpose of the task and practitioner roles. The new terms include 'health gain', 'health strategy', 'locality purchasing', 'joint commissioning' and many others. As with any newly developing field, the meanings of many terms are ambiguous and changing – terms come and go, and some prove essential and are further refined.

In the UK it is inappropriate to prescribe definitions to these terms, with the NHS in such a rapid state of change, and with health commissioning at such an early stage of theoretical and practical development. However, for commissioners to organize their everyday work and for effective communication, staff within a commissioning organization have to have a shared understanding of the meaning of certain terms. This is particularly important for coordinating or merging FHSA and DHA tasks. To take one example, one problem in merging FHSAs and DHAs is different understandings of the meanings of the FHSA's 'purchasing' and 'providing' roles. It is right at this stage that there should be a variety of meanings because this is part of the process of exploring and developing different roles. However, to decide how work is organized within purchasers' directorates, and for DHA staff to understand FHSA work, it is important at least to recognize the different meanings, or to agree a common definition within an agency, and to make this meaning clear to others outside the agency. Another example is the different meanings to 'joint commissioning' and whether the term only refers to certain work undertaken with local authorities, and if so, which work.

One of the central concepts in the UK is 'commissioning' itself. The following makes a first general distinction between 'commissioning' and 'purchasing' and distinguishes both of these from 'contracting'. These distinctions correspond to the changing preoccupations and understanding of NHS authorities of their role since 1990.

Commissioning, purchasing and contracting

The purpose of public health commissioning as defined in this book is *'to maximize the health of a population and minimize illness, by purchasing health services and by influencing other organizations to create conditions which enhance people's health'*. Commissioning involves developing and pursuing a health strategy and committing both DHA and FHSA public revenue and capital to different activities and providers to achieve the maximum health gain, for those most in need, at the lowest cost.

This book refers to 'health purchasing' as an activity which is narrower than health commissioning. Purchasing is mainly concerned with buying health services from organizations which provide services such as treatment, rehabilitation, diagnosis, prevention, health promotion and long-term health care. The book defines health purchasing as *'buying the best value for money services to achieve the maximum health gain for those most in need'*. Health purchasing in public health services has much in common with health purchasing in private insurance companies and includes the work of assessing needs, planning services required, deciding purchasing strategy, contracting, managing withdrawals of services and dealing with complaints about contracted services.

'Health contracting' is narrower than health purchasing and involves selecting a provider and negotiating an agreement with them about the services they will provide in return for payment. It includes the activities of defining service specification for tendering, specifying a contract, monitoring the contract and reviewing contract performance. A contract can be for a single 'spot contract' or for services within a long-term partnership.

These distinctions introduce a particular view of the purpose and role of a commissioning agency. Chapter 3 further considers the meaning of NHS commissioning and the purpose of NHS commissioning agencies.

Summary

This book is about a new type of work in public health services, and about how this work is organized. The work is 'health purchasing' and the book is about how health purchasing managers can best improve the health of the populations they serve. Some of the work is not entirely new, as private insurance companies have for some time purchased health services, assessed the needs and health risks of their populations and initiated preventative programmes. What is new is public organizations using public finance to purchase services with the focus on improving health. Although public health purchasers can learn from the private and not-for-profit sector in the UK, Europe and the USA, their role is significantly different and more complex, being concerned more with health gain than with risk assessment and selection. Yet we see in the chapters that follow a blurring between public and private, and a convergence between public and private purchasing, for example, with more private insurers undertaking health prevention and promotion programmes.

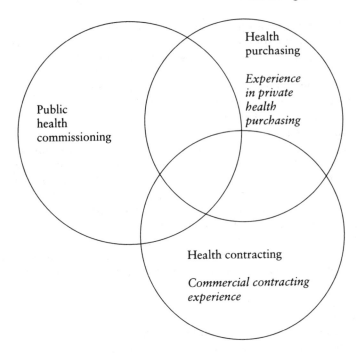

Figure 1.1 Subject domains: health 'commissioning' is broader than 'purchasing' and 'contracting' and draws on experience from the commercial sector.

In the past, both private and public health purchasing was largely concerned with contracting providers, and mostly with acute hospitals. In the future purchasing will be more strategic and less provider-driven, with a greater understanding of the cost-effectiveness of services and of other health-enhancing activities, and with new types of services and treatments provided outside hospitals. This book aims to contribute to an understanding of NHS health purchasing as a new force in health systems as well as the purpose and role of integrated primary and secondary commissioning agencies.

Key points

- This book is an introduction to public health purchasing. It aims to contribute to the theory and practice of purchasing in public health systems.
- In Europe, public purchasing of health services is a relatively new public service, and one which has developed out of the 'market' experiments and reforms of the late 1980s. Governments are investing in purchaser organization and management development to reap the potential benefits and minimize the disadvantages of market reforms.

- The themes running through the book include:
  - continually questioning the purpose of public health purchasing and relating purpose to different methods and approaches;
  - purchasing is a service business. If purchasers are to survive, they must think of themselves as special types of service organizations and use modern service management techniques;
  - precision about what terms mean;
  - health strategy is more than plans for contracting;
  - purchasers must account for their decisions – 'justifiable commissioning';
  - reconsideration of traditional distinctions between public and private;
  - coordination, within purchasing and to ensure that providers inter-link;
  - collaboration and relationships – the new management skills;
  - information management and reaping the benefits of IT.
- Research into NHS commissioning in 1993 found that NHS commissioners all faced similar issues, including:
  - lack of finance, and exploring possible new sources of purchaser finance;
  - developing a shared agency purpose and vision amongst employees;
  - developing and carrying out a feasible health strategy;
  - using a variety of approaches to make a more informed assessment of needs;
  - developing primary and community care;
  - becoming more sophisticated in contracting;
  - confronting the gaps between the technically possible and the affordable and developing systems for prioritizing;
  - improving accountability, legitimacy and relations with the public;
  - developing decentralized and locality purchasing;
  - improving access to and use of information;
  - combining or coordinating primary and secondary care commissioning.

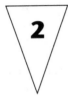

2 / Purchasing and 'market reform'

My local hospital trust in London has been recommended for closure by a regional planning group. Yet the hospital trust is financially successful, and market research predicts a significant increase in business for all specialties. Local GPs and GP multifunds have made clear their opposition to the closure. They and local people packed the large meeting hall which I went to the other night. The chairperson of the meeting, who was from the local authority, condemned the local purchasing health authority for refusing to attend to hear people's views, or to make any statements over the many months since the report had been issued. People were urged to write to the local Member of Parliament and to the Health Secretary to intervene, as she had done in other cases. Across London and in other parts of the UK there are similar situations. What sort of market is this?

Introduction

The actions and objectives of a purchasing organization depend on its part in a health system, and on the nature of that system. Public health purchasers are usually part of a particular type of 'market system' (termed a 'social market') which is similar to and different from other market systems, and from centralized national or regional public health bureaucracies. If health purchasing is to be more than paying bills sent by providers, then purchasers need to understand how these systems work. They need to understand how providers and other purchasers are likely to act, and the potential weaknesses of the system, in order to decide their own role and strategy and to influence future reform and regulations on behalf of the people they serve.

The aim of this chapter and the next is to help purchasing managers to define or reassess the purpose and objectives of their purchasing organization. This chapter shows how the initial national structure of the NHS 'internal market' determined the purpose of NHS commissioning. As this national structure and local structures changed, so did the purpose of NHS commissioning organizations. The argument of the chapter is that purchasing managers can shape market structure to make it easier for them to achieve their objectives, if they understand how health markets work, both in general and locally. An understanding of markets also helps to formulate realistic purposes and objectives for a commissioning organization.

An underlying question is: what is the purpose of a national public health system in the late 1990s? We find in the next chapter that, in the UK, there is no clear authoritative answer to this question, and this makes it more difficult to judge market reforms or other changes to the NHS. Where we can predict the effects of changes, our assessment of these effects is against a particular view of the purpose of a health system. One view is that the purpose of the NHS is to use resources to the best effect to improve health and to prevent illness. If this is the aim, what are the best means, or are there better ways than those we are using at present? We consider whether reforms such as 'contracting out', 'purchaser–provider split' or new regulatory or planning arrangements are better means for this end. We find that it is difficult to relate these and other means to such a general view about ends, and that we need intermediate aims against which we can judge specific changes, such as merging DHAs and FHSAs, or large system changes such as full market reform.

A theme of this chapter and the next is that we need continually to return to questions of purpose in making health purchasing decisions. Whether you agree with the views of purpose presented here is less important than whether you are provoked to examine your own views of the purpose of a health service and of health purchasing, and to consider the links between this view of purpose and different means. UK purchasing managers who are clearer about these issues will be more able to assess proposed changes, and to justify your assessments in terms of whether the change advances your view of the purpose of the NHS, and of an NHS commissioning organization. At a time of change, clarifying purpose helps to create stability, and is time well spent. However, purpose also has to be examined during action and in relation to experience; otherwise such examinations can become sterile and a distraction.

Markets and purchasing in an international context

We consider health markets from the point of view of health purchasers, and use frameworks to understand different markets for different types of health services. These frameworks also help purchasers to make more valid comparisons between their situation and those of purchasers in other regions, markets and countries. Purchasers in different countries face similar issues, not least the need to take a more strategic and proactive approach. For example, in The Netherlands:

examples of new strategic management activities are the creating of common health-purchasing units, the development of managed care activities, utilisation reviews and quality projects, the gathering of more valid information on costs of health, investments in staff development, critical appraisal of internal organizational structure, more specific and need-oriented production agreements, and selective contracting of physicians ... At present, health insurance in The Netherlands is at a cross-roads ... each [insurer] has to develop a strategic management approach to providers ... To what extent will the government eventually be willing to allow the health insurance agencies sufficient autonomy for a strategic management approach?

(Maarse 1993)

Emerging questions in the UK and elsewhere are whether, in terms of pursuing public health aims public or private ownership of a purchasing organization is less important than the source of finance, and how finance sources, public or private, control the way a purchaser uses the finance. Outside the UK there is more experience of governments allocating public finance to private and not-for-profit organizations to purchase health services for public ends. There is more concern about control of purchasing through mechanisms other than ownership and traditional accountability systems. There is great potential to learn from and compare practices in organizations such as social insurance sickness funds in The Netherlands, Germany or France, NHS health authorities and GP fundholders, and US insurance companies and Health Maintenance Organizations (HMOs), as long as purchasing by these organizations is put in the context of history, social values and the overall system. To draw valid lessons from research into the experience of purchasing from another country it is necessary to understand the system within which purchasing operates.

An overview of the chapter

The emphasis of this chapter is on public health purchasing in predominantly public health systems. To introduce the concepts it first distinguishes public health market reforms for 'contracting out' from those for 'purchaser–provider' separation which involve provider competition. It then distinguishes both of these from purchaser competition reforms. The arguments for each type of 'market reform' are different and need to be understood by public health purchasers for them to press for future reforms which advance the aims of public health purchasing.

The chapter then considers markets in more detail. It summarizes the theory of simple markets and shows the difference between this theory and health markets. It describes the three elements of market structure (regulation, purchasing and provision) and then different types of competition. It gives frameworks for purchasers to analyse different local markets for different services and simple models to help understand health market systems in different countries.

The last part of the chapter considers purchasing in one 'market system' in more detail: the UK NHS 'internal market' introduced in 1990. This description draws on the concepts of the chapter to characterize the particular type of market system in the UK. This introduces non-NHS readers to purchasing in the NHS ('commissioning') to allow them to understand better the more detailed discussions of NHS purchasing issues later in the book.

The chapter addresses some of the following questions raised by managers in public health purchasing organizations:

- *What is a health market, and what is the difference between an 'internal market', a 'managed market', 'managed competition' and a 'planned market'?*
- *How might a purchaser best plan, enable and regulate emerging markets in primary and community care?*
- *What scope is there for commissioners to lead the market, and what is their 'regulatory role'?*
- *Is not 'market management' a contradiction in terms? If we can manage it, it's not a market. Whatever it is, it's already too complex to understand, let alone influence.*

Market reforms in public health systems

Some services will always be provided in the public sector . . . Competition is as important for such services as it is for services which could be provided by either the private sector or the public sector . . . Managers in central and local government and the NHS have to account for their performance against financial and quality targets. This responsibility requires them to look for the best deal for the users of the services, whether the task is done in-house or bought-in from outside.

(HM Treasury 1991: 1)

In some systems there is little difference between private and public purchasing, and indeed one organization may do both. To introduce this chapter's discussion of different types of market, and of the purchasing role in each type, this section considers three types of 'market reform' to a public health system. We will see that health purchasing is a different task in three different types of 'health market reform': (a) contracting out, where a public service contracts out part of its work to an external organization; (b) purchaser–provider split, where a public authority ceases to manage direct service provision and becomes a purchaser only; and (c) a full market system, where there is competition between purchasers and a variety of other system changes are introduced.

Contracting out

Contracting out is a type of 'purchaser–provider split' but a public authority continues to manage many direct services and contracts out for specific services. A 'purchaser–provider split' involves reforming a public authority into a purchasing-only organization, as we see below. In recent years there has been a general trend for both private and public organizations to contract out 'peripheral' functions to external organizations. One aim is to seek better value for money and to introduce innovations from organizations which specialize in a particular service. Another is to enable the organization which contracts out to concentrate on its 'core business'. In a historical context contracting out can be viewed as a further extension of the decentralization trend in large organizations in the 1980s, and a reversion to a longer-term trend of increasing specialization.

Both decentralization and contracting out are the result, in part, of a view that centralized and planned bureaucracies are not able to respond to rapid changes and consumer demand or to give their staff incentives for efficiency. In the 1970s and 1980s many large commercial companies and public organizations reassessed their 'core business' and considered whether they were undertaking activities which could be better undertaken by other organizations. In some cases the in-house departments were re-created as semi-independent units or new commercial companies, in other cases the departments were closed and an existing external organization was contracted to do the work.

A result of this trend was a development of purchasing as a function within both private and public organizations. Some managers who managed large workforces found themselves managing one or more external companies through contracts. In some instances purchasing divisions were developed to undertake the new and increased amount of contract-management work. In public services, purchasing was done at different levels and in different ways: usually the higher levels of the public authority organized and oversaw a 'tendering' process, awarded contracts and monitored the contractor, sometimes involving service receivers, either their own hospital or the public, in all or some of the purchasing process. Sometimes purchasing was done at a lower level, for example from within a hospital.

Examples of contracting out

In the UK since 1981 local authorities have been required to invite tenders for managing leisure services and for certain services provided by manual workers. These requirements were extended to other services in 1988 and in 1991. The evidence is that, overall, savings of 6 per cent were achieved, with average savings of 40 per cent for refuse collection and 15 per cent for building cleaning (HM Treasury 1991).

In the UK after 1983 NHS health authorities were required to invite tenders for cleaning and catering services in the hospitals which they then managed. There was also 'enabling legislation' to make it possible to contract out a wider range of support services. The evidence is that savings of £626 million were made over seven years (Carnaghan and Bracewell-Milnes 1993). In 1991 there were further proposals and encouragement to contract out professional and management services and facilities management or site services (HM Treasury 1991). The final chapter discusses these in more detail. Since the 1990 market reforms some public purchasing authorities have agreed to NHS hospitals subcontracting clinical services.

Types of contracting out

Contracting out may be for an external organization to provide a service direct to the public (e.g. mental health services), or to provide a 'support' service, such as catering or laundry services to a public hospital. The most common model is for a public organization to invite 'bids' or 'tenders' from an external organization, which offers to provide a service currently provided by an in-house department ('market-testing'). The bids of both in-house and external organizations are compared against different criteria and a contract is awarded. In some cases contracting out may apply only to other public services, so that, for example, only other public hospitals are invited to bid to provide a service ('restricted public contracting').

We can distinguish types of 'contracting out' in terms of the different purchasing work involved for a public body:

1 *Open contracting*, involving invitations to public and private organizations to undertake direct or support services.
2 *Restricted public contracting*, involving invitations to other public organizations only to undertake direct or support services.
3 *In-house contracting*, involving the creation of an in-house unit as a distinct 'profit centre', and relating to that unit through 'contractual-type agreements' rather than through managerial relationships.

The third type is not 'contracting out', but one type of decentralization, often requiring the unit to secure income through 'internal trading contracts' with other units in the organization, as, for example, in some resource management programmes in UK hospitals. The UK government's creation of 'next-step' quasi-independent agencies in 1988 to undertake the executive functions of central government departments is a form of contracting out.

The arguments for and against contracting out

The arguments for and against public contracting depend on which of the above three types we are referring to, and also on whether we are considering direct services to the public or support services. In the NHS and for commissioning managers it depends on whether there is a clear link between this method and the purposes of the NHS. Is it a better method than current arrangements for advancing the purposes of the NHS? It also depends on whose perspective we are taking, and this brings us to the political dimension of contracting out. A government supported by public service unions is unlikely to require certain services to be contracted out, but might introduce legislation to allow public service managers to invite tenders for certain services. Conversely, a government supported by private

For 'open contracting' with private and public competition, usually for non-clinical support services.

The advantages and disadvantages (expected or proven) depend on whose perspective we take (e.g. government, workers, citizens, private business).

Advantages (*for whom?*)	*Disadvantages* (*for whom?*)
Efficiency incentives, and lower short-term costs to public sector	The UK experience for many workers has been lower wages, fewer jobs and worse conditions of employment
More scope for flexible and performance related pay in private contractors	Weakens collective bargaining and public sector unions
Productivity increases, from 'better management'	Harder work for employees
Potential for capital investment by the private sector without increasing public expenditure	Cost of contracting: tendering, specification, monitoring, payment
Faster service innovation	Higher risk for the public purchaser than with in-house services
Allows public service managers to concentrate on core services	Potential inflexibility: If contract is poor and long term, it may not be possible to change the service
Makes use of specialist expertise and experience in the private sector	Requires new contract management skills and systems
Contractor may be more responsive to user's requirements if future contracts depend on this	

Figure 2.1 Public sector contracting out: arguments for and against.

business and wishing to weaken public service union power is more likely to require many services to be contracted out only to the private sector, regardless of costs or quality. With these provisos, Figure 2.1 presents the common arguments for and against contracting out public services in 'open contracting'.

In the main this book is not concerned with the purchase of non-clinical and support health services. However, purchasers of clinical services do need to be familiar with the arguments and issues involved in contracting out, for three reasons. First, as for any other organization, a commissioning organization might choose to contract out rather than manage some of the services it needs, such as computer, legal, personnel or specialist public health services. To judge whether to do so a purchaser needs to be familiar with the arguments for and against direct management or contracting. Examples closer to clinical services are whether a purchaser should manage or contract for health promotion units or primary care development facilitators. Second, purchasers need to understand the implications for their populations if one of their contracted providers subcontracts clinical or non-clinical services. Should a purchaser allow or encourage a provider to subcontract for some services when waiting lists exceed a certain length, either routinely or when demand exceeds capacity? Would doing so advance the purpose of the NHS, or the purposes of a purchasing organization? Third, some of the considerations, theories and arguments for and against contracting out are the same as for reforms involving a purchaser–provider split, and for total system market reform.

We now consider one theory relevant to the economic and technical decision to contract out or to provide in-house.

The theory: Do-it-yourself or pay someone to do it

The first substantive theoretical discussion of the issues since Coase (1937) was by Williamson (1975). Williamson considered the conditions under which a firm would either contract out a function or create or absorb a function in-house, and the conditions for 'market failure'. These included the amount and type of competition between contractors, how complex contracts need to be and how they can be monitored. The theory was that firms seek to minimize the cost of transactions, and that if it costs more to specify and monitor a contract than to manage a function, then the firm will provide it in-house. Williamson proposed that the cost of transactions depends on: (a) bounded rationality: the difficulty purchasers have in judging future states so as to be able to write a contract protecting their interests, in part because of insufficient information; (b) opportunism: the potential for a provider to cheat a purchaser if the contract allows; and (c) asset specificity: the investment a purchaser, or more usually a provider, would have to put into a specific service, which would be of little value if the purchaser ceased the contract. Where all these are high, then management in-house is preferable to contracting out, from a transaction cost perspective.

Williamson's theory was a starting point for one strand of research into inter-organizational relations and network theory (Thompson *et al.* 1991; Alter and Hage 1993). It also provided a reference point for theories of quasi-markets in the public sector (Le Grand and Bartlett 1993). Williamson's 1975 book also considers a hybrid M-form organization, which is a type of internal market like an internal trading system in a hospital, and which combines some of the benefits of contracting with the lower co-ordination costs of in-house management. One weakness of the theory for public purchasers or providers assessing whether to contract out or provide in-house (if they do have the choice) is that it does not consider the political dimension. It is an economic theory about the behaviour of commercial firms. In public services, decisions to contract out are as much, or more, governed by political considerations as by economic ones. Political analyses of winners and losers, of stakeholders' interests and of the impact on equity and choice are at least as important as the economic considerations.

The purchaser–provider split

A second type of market reform is separating public purchasing from public provision. A government decision to separate public purchasing from providing clinical health services is of a different order to a decision to encourage or require contracting out of support services. Although some of the issues at stake are the same, it is important to recognize the differences and the different roles for public authorities in a purchaser–provider reform to their role in a limited contracting-out reform. In this section we consider the arguments for and against the 'purchaser–provider' split, the different types of limited and total separation, and the different roles of public purchasing in the types.

Types of purchaser–provider split

The purchaser–provider split is a term which usually refers to government legislation re-creating public authorities into bodies for purchasing health services, rather than organizations for managing and employing health service providers. The economic principle is to separate more clearly supply from demand for health services, and to use price mechanisms rather than planning mechanisms to relate supply to demand. The split may be total, where the public authority does not manage any of the health services which are directly provided to the public (e.g. UK district health authorities in the mid-1990s), or partial, where the public authority continues to manage some services and to purchase others. There are also many variations, one example being UK GP fundholders, where each GP has a contract to provide primary care services, but where the group practice (which is a private business partnership), administers a fund devolved to it to purchase secondary health services. There are even more complex arrangements in the USA, such as HMOs and Preferred Provider Organizations (PPOs), which have contracts for public Medicare and Medicaid programmes (Weiner and Ferris 1990; Patton 1992).

There are three types of purchaser–provider split, each of which has a different role for the purchasing organization:

1 *Total split*: a public purchasing authority does not manage any health services or employ any staff providing clinical health services. A total split may retain public providers in public ownership, and have them managed or overseen by another public body (e.g. the UK in the mid-1990s), or a reform may 'privatize' all or some public providers, as in some reforms in Eastern Europe.

2 *Partial split*: the public authority may be allowed or required to purchase some clinical services, but retain the management of other clinical services and the employment of staff in those services (e.g. UK in the

early 1990s, with DHAs managing some hospitals and community health services). Purchasing may be restricted to other public services only (some Swedish reforms in the early 1990s) or allow purchasing of private services (e.g. Stockholm).

3 *No-competition split*: the public authority relates to the provider service which it previously managed through a contractual agreement. It may or may not continue to employ the provider staff (e.g. some Spanish regional reforms).

The amount and type of provider competition decrease as we pass from 1 to 3. In market reforms of this type, purchasers may have a role in encouraging new providers to enter the market so as to increase provider competition and choice ('market-making'). As with contracting out, the advantages and disadvantages depend on which type of split we refer to, how this method advances the purposes of the health system and whose perspective we are taking. The most common type is 1, and the purpose is to introduce provider competition, either mixed public and private or public only (the latter is the usual meaning of 'internal market').

A purchaser–provider split: the arguments for and against
These arguments relate to a 'total' split with no direct patient services staff employed or managed by a public purchaser. Benefits and disbenefits depend on the perspective (government, health workers, citizens, etc.). Ultimately, the important questions are: does it advance or detract from the purpose of the health system, and what impact does it have on people's health?
   The advantages are:

- The balance of power to determine services shifts away from providers to purchasers.
- Allows purchasers to concentrate on needs and ways of meeting needs rather than on provider management.
- Can strengthen public health programmes.
- Incentives for public providers to increase efficiency and reduce costs to secure their income.
- Removes the efficiency penalties of some budgeting systems.
- Forces clarification of details of provider costs.
- Forces clarification of amount of finance allocated to different services, client groups and needs.
- Makes priorities in resource allocation explicit, and aids explicit rationing.
- The potential for capital investment by the private sector without increasing public expenditure (see Chapter 13).
- May increase patient choice, if purchasers also encourage new providers and increase the number of providers.

The disadvantages are:

- Makes planning more difficult, and may lead to provider duplication and worse coordination.

- Weakens collective bargaining for health professions.
- Hospitals popular with the public but failing to win contracts may be forced to close.
- Initial cost to set up the system and subsequent cost of 'market super-structure'.
- Cost of contracting lost to patient care investments: the cost of tendering, specification, monitoring and payment systems.
- Requires new purchasing and contract management skills and systems.
- Potential inflexibility: if contract is poor and longer term, may not be possible to change the service.
- Can reduce patient choice if a patient cannot use a provider which does not have a contract with the patient's purchaser.

Purchaser competition and market systems

So far we have distinguished public purchasing in a contracting-out reform from public purchasing in a purchaser–provider split reform, recognizing also that there is some overlap between the two. A third type of reform is one which involves competition between purchasers for public purchasing finance. This book refers to a 'health market system' as one which involves purchaser competition, as well as provider competition, and a variety of competing public and private health organizations.

To understand the different roles of a purchasing organization in different systems we need to recognize different types of purchaser competition:

1 Open mixed purchaser competition, involving a public body awarding a contract to a public or a private organization to purchase health services using public finance. Such purchasing organizations might or might not also act as purchasers using private funds, for example acting as a purchaser for an employer.
2 Limited public purchaser competition, involving public bodies competing with each other to act as public purchasers, using public finance to purchase some or all health services for a population. Public bodies may or may not also act as purchasers using private finance, for example acting as a purchasing body for an employer or an insurance company.

Some of the arguments for and against purchaser competition are similar to the arguments mentioned earlier for contracting out, including efficiency, incentives and, potentially, choice for patients. Again, the key issue is how purchaser competition advances the purpose of a health system – is there a form of purchaser competition which is better than current arrangements for achieving the purpose of the health system? One argument against is that changing contracts to purchase services for a population from one purchaser to another gives fewer incentives for longer-term health promotion and prevention programmes, whether through contracting or inter-sector actions. This is similar to one of the criticisms of annual contracting of HMOs by employers or by public funds in the USA: frequent switching results in neglect of long-term health programmes, even if they are stipulated in contracts.

Summary: the role of purchasers in different health reforms

One aim of the above discussion was to help purchasing managers to learn from the experience of purchasers in other countries. Understanding the type of market within which a purchaser is operating helps us to make valid comparisons. Raising questions about the purpose of health services in other countries and about the purpose of purchasing organizations also helps us to clarify our understanding of the purpose of the NHS and NHS commissioning.

The discussion also showed how the type of market determines the purpose and role of a purchasing organization. In contracting out, purchasing is limited and often confined to non-clinical services. In purchaser–provider splits, purchasing of health services is a significant body of work, whether or not the same organization also continues to manage some services. With purchaser competition and total system reform, purchasing becomes an even more complex activity, and involves the work of submitting tenders to win contracts to act as a purchaser in a complex system of providers and other purchasers. Regulation is a critical and expensive feature of such systems.

Another aim was to draw attention to the variety of types of 'market reform' in health services. Many debates have been about the advantages and disadvantages of health markets in general, and have not sufficiently recognized the different types of health market reforms, or the political dimension to public health reforms. These distinctions are particularly important in Eastern European countries where arguments for and against one type of market reform are often assumed to apply to another completely different type.

The discussion also introduced some of the theories and considerations for public health purchasers who are developing their role. Transaction cost theory helps purchasers to decide which of their own functions could be contracted out, and the issues for providers in making similar decisions. However, the theory does not consider the political issues, and public purchasers have to use political theories to analyse who wins and who loses from certain changes, and the impact on equity and choice. Finally, note that none of the market-type reforms we considered address a key problem in many health systems, the problem of coordination: ensuring that different purchasers cooperate and ensuring providers link to each other. Indeed, many market reforms make these problems worse and introduce major coordination inefficiencies. We return to the coordination issues in later chapters.

In the next section we consider the difference between health markets and simple markets, before looking at the elements of market structure and the NHS 'internal market' in more detail.

Market concepts and theory

We need an organization strategy which addresses the question so often heard these days: 'What sort of market do we want?' and which helps shape organizational arrangements to make it easier (not more difficult) to achieve our goals.

(Liddell 1993)

There is renewed debate in the UK, as in many other countries, about the amount and type of planning and regulation which are necessary in health system reforms. The need to make decisions about these issues has become more urgent in the NHS as competition intensifies, GP fundholding increases and the top tiers of the NHS are reorganized. The NHS cannot afford the duplication, waste and unethical practices that can occur in unregulated markets, yet the current mix of central direction and *ad hoc* political intervention neither allows the market to work for efficiency nor allows for effective planning.

Questions about the balance between equity, choice and economy are arising again in the context of debate about new sources of finance for the NHS and for health care, and with a greater awareness of European and US health system reforms. Purchasers in the UK and in other countries recognize that merger is one way to survive, and that to cope with the changes they will have to operate more strategically. Purchasers recognize that they will need to understand more about how the local markets for different services might develop, and how national changes will affect their strategies. Further, they will need to be aware of, and form a view about, changes to the market structure, such as new sources of finance, purchaser competition and an increased role for private purchasers and providers.

The following gives an overview of market concepts and their application to health care, and uses the NHS internal market as one illustration of the issues. The reason for doing so is to draw attention to some of the options which purchasers and NHS commissioners face and to give a background for discussions in later chapters about commissioner strategy in an evolving market.

Basic concepts: simple markets

A simple market is made up of two levels. At the exchange level, consumer purchasers exchange payment for goods or services from providers, after

LEGAL AND REGULATORY LEVEL

sets the context for the

LEVEL OF EXCHANGE

Payment
CUSTOMER/PURCHASER ⟶ PROVIDER

Service

Customers/purchasers *exchange* cash for the product/service which they chose as giving the *best value for money combination* of (a) quality features, (b) price and (c) quantity – the transaction is 'transparent', complete and fast.

Consumer choice is between options: each 'option package' has different combinations of:

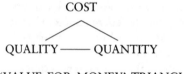

COST

QUALITY —— QUANTITY

THE 'VALUE FOR MONEY' TRIANGLE

Figure 2.2   How a simple market works.

searching for and deciding on a provider. An equilibrium between supply and demand is achieved through price: if demand is higher than supply, providers raise prices until other providers enter the market and competition reduces prices. In principle, there is no need for planning, as long as consumer purchasers and providers are free to enter and leave the market easily to correct for imbalances in supply and demand, and certain other conditions apply, such as easy access to complete information. The amount of planning which providers do depends on how long it takes them to make a product or develop a service to bring to market. Figure 2.2 shows how a simple market works.

A second level is needed for markets to operate, which consists of the laws and regulations which determine how exchange is to take place. Agricultural markets are examples of simple markets which need regulatory structures for planning and efficiency. They are also examples of how difficult it can be to regulate for efficiency, even with a simple product and production process. The laws and regulations influence the number of purchasers and providers – they rarely prescribe the number of providers and purchasers, but they do define conditions which are likely to result in there being more or fewer, and the way in which the exchange between them is to be conducted (e.g. contracting regulations).

It is within this predetermined setting that purchasers and providers make their exchanges. An issue in health (and social care) markets is how to ensure that there are providers in business for purchasers to contract and for patients to use: there are long 'lead-times' and complex regulations to meet to bring most health services and products to market. Small purchasers, such as UK GP fundholders, rely on larger purchasers to ensure stability of supply. We consider the practical issues involved in the chapter on contracting.

Many market economists believe that simple markets are 'efficient' (which can be defined in different ways) if there is maximum freedom for buyers and sellers, and that the following conditions exist:

- Consumers can judge quality, are well informed about alternatives and have clear preferences about quality, quantity and price.
- There are no 'transaction costs' (e.g. costs to process payment or to specify and monitor contracts).
- There are many buyers and sellers.
- There are no barriers to market entry or exit: that is, it is easy to enter the market to 'fill a gap' or challenge existing providers, and leaving the market does not incur losses because of a high investment to meet one purchaser's requirements ('asset specificity').

With these conditions, markets are economically efficient ways to match supply to demand. Providers compete to supply what consumers want at the lowest price, and there are incentives to be efficient and to provide what consumers want (choice and value for money options). In short, under these conditions:

Consumer choice + competition = low cost and responsive services

There are different views as to whether more or less regulation of different types in different markets creates more or less efficient systems. One view is that the proper role of the state is to create a legal and regulatory framework for the above conditions to exist and to ensure a 'free and fair' market. There are different views about how much and what type of state action is necessary to create these conditions, about which conditions are necessary for economically efficient markets, and about what is meant by economic efficiency (Reinhardt 1992).

Related to the question of state involvement to create efficient markets is the question of how much the state should 'intervene' to ameliorate the negative social consequences of markets. Many 'free-marketeers' believe that intervention, such as helping inefficient providers, over-distorts the system and is not helpful to anyone in the long term. Others hold that the concept of intervention suggests an original natural situation of no regulation, whereas a market can only exist because of some regulatory framework in the first place.

Markets for health services

Health service markets differ in a number of respects from the above caricature of a simple market. The following notes some of these differences and considers which market-type elements can be introduced to give incentives for efficiency and to ensure social goals. It considers how health markets differ in financing, in competition, in demand and supply, and in regulation.

Financing: users, purchasers and providers
The first difference between a simple market and health markets is that consumers rarely purchase a health service when they use it. There are three sets of parties, not two: consumers (or 'users'), purchasers and providers. People pay into a 'fund', and the fund undertakes to pay for services when the consumer needs them. We consider below the different types of fund, some of which are run by purchasers themselves. Often the fund distributes to local purchasing agencies, termed 'allocation' below. In the UK the fund is the national exchequer and people pay in through general taxation. There is no separate fund for health as in many other countries, and national allocations for health depend on many other factors apart from what people are prepared to pay in tax for health services. (There are proposals in the UK to introduce a separate 'health tax' or 'hypothecated tax', like the one introduced in France in 1991, which was soon increased from 1.1 to 2.4 per cent of a person's income.) In public systems, the government which administers the fund also takes steps to ensure that services will exist when the user needs them.

The purpose of this 'three-way', rather than 'two-way' market (i.e. the simple consumer/purchaser and provider market), is to insulate the consumer from the cost of using the service. All health markets are 'insurance' systems in one sense: we pay into a fund and draw on the fund. The fund evens out the finance which goes in, with the finance which goes out, across time and between high and low users. One of the underlying assumptions of the UK system was that people would 'not do what they should': look ahead and pay into a fund which would cover them for health and other 'social emergencies' (Beveridge Report 1942). It was in the interests of both the individual and the state to require people to pay into the fund, when they had the money to do so. Even the USA is moving towards this 'State paternalism' in its health reforms.

People pay for health services in different ways:

- by taxation, national (UK) or local (Sweden);
- by buying a private insurance plan (UK, most European, USA);
- by forgoing salary, because their employer buys health insurance for them;
- by compulsory contributions to a not-for-profit purchaser (e.g. German, Dutch and French 'social insurance' sickness funds).

We consider financing in more detail in the final chapter.

Purchaser competition for finance

The second difference from the simple market model is the type of competition which occurs in health markets between providers, and between purchasers. In some markets the consumer has a choice of purchaser, and there is a market between purchasers for individual or institutional subscribers. Many market system reforms introduce competition between purchasers for finance, either from individuals directly or from public or private funds (e.g. reforms proposed in The Netherlands (Dekker Report 1987)). In the NHS there is a type of limited competition for public finance between health authority commissioners and GP fundholders (but not regular competitive bidding).

There is discussion in the UK about allowing private agencies to compete with public commissioning agencies to manage purchasing funds for public finance (e.g. Ham 1993a). There is a potential for pilot schemes in 'border' areas in which public agencies compete with each other to cover patients living on geographical borders. There is also the beginnings of debate about allowing people to opt out of the NHS, and to choose whether to buy insurance from a public commissioning agency or a private insurer, as people over 60 can at present. We consider the future options in the final chapter, and provider competition later in this chapter.

Demand and supply

A further difference between simple and health care markets is how demand is related to supply. In the simple market this is primarily through a price mechanism. To some extent this also happens in health care markets. However, for specialist services, consumers usually do not drive demand: in the UK, GPs decide demand and drive consumption of hospital and most community health services. In health care, demand and expenditure are determined more by supply capacity than by any other single factor. Government and regional planning usually decides on the supply of hospital beds, facilities, medical training and employment. The latter is one way in which the second level of the market – the laws and regulations – affects supply, demand and prices, and influences the actions of consumers, purchasers and providers. Purchasers may or may not influence capital finance and markets for capital.

Regulation

A fourth difference between simple and health care markets is the complexity and amount of regulation in health care. Here we define a regulation as 'a directive or requirement, with sanctions for non-compliance' and they are often state regulations with the force of law. Regulations are set, monitored or enforced at national, regional and local levels, by government, not-for-profit agencies or associations (e.g. of providers) or commercial agencies (e.g. US Peer Review Organizations). Rules and regulatory agencies set the number of purchasers and providers, and their relationships to each other and to patients and payers (subscribers).

All markets are regulated in different ways, but health markets are the most highly regulated of all – the market for pharmaceuticals is one example. Three types of state regulation are, in order of degree of intervention:

- *Planning regulation* – to avoid wasteful duplication, or over- or under-production which a market for a particular service would not self-correct (e.g. of certain facilities, equipment, or training).
- *Competition regulation* – rules to ensure that there is competition, and of a type which is thought to produce beneficial results for the public (e.g. rules against price-fixing or mergers which are 'not in the public interest').
- *'Worst excesses' or 'ethical' regulation* – rules or laws to minimize any likely publicly unacceptable consequences of full market competition (e.g. refusing treatment to unprofitable patients or subscribers).

The amount and strength of a regulation depends more on the powers, sanctions and capacity of the regulatory bodies than on the rules themselves. For example, the US certificate of needs regulations governing hospital beds and expensive technology (Salkever and Bice 1978) are ineffective because the bodies upholding the regulations have few powers and a provider-influenced membership. A common way to strengthen or weaken existing regulations is to change the number of staff whose job it is to monitor and enforce the regulation.

In health, the most common types of regulation are of:

- capital expenditure (e.g. UK, for public capital);
- facilities/equipment (e.g. US certificate of needs);
- prices (some drugs or treatments, e.g. USA Medicare Diagnostic Related Group (DRG) pricing);
- services (e.g. registered nursing homes, ambulance services);
- professional practice, usually by professions (e.g. registration, training, discipline, and in the UK of siting of primary care contractors);
- service operation (utilization review and quality, technical specifications, e.g. X-ray machines/radiology, safety, health and employment regulations);
- required rate of return on capital for UK trusts is considered by some a regulation.

Other examples of regulations are those which

- prohibit private providers or purchasers;
- allow purchasers to own or manage providers, or providers to merge (e.g. US 'managed care' legislation);
- require patients to make compulsory direct payments, to providers or to purchasers (e.g. payment per visit or 'co-payments');
- govern how payment is made;
- restrict the supply of doctors, facilities and expensive equipment.

There are not just buyers and sellers, but patients, purchasers, regulators and providers

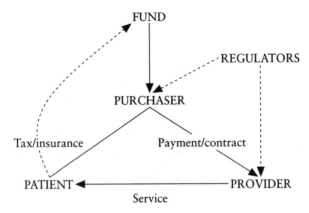

Figure 2.3 Health care markets: general model.

Summary: the difference between simple markets and health markets

We can contrast the model of the simple market in Figure 2.2 with the model of a health care market in Figure 2.3. Generally, in health care markets:

- Patients ('consumers') are not purchasers. They do not weigh up costs in choosing service, they have difficulty assessing value for money (as do professional purchasers), and value for money at the time of use is usually not important to them.
- Providers compete for contracts (and for referrals).
- Provider income depends on meeting many criteria, apart from perceived value to patients.
- There is usually little competition in rural areas.
- The information for purchasers and for patients is poor.

We note that one reason why simple markets 'work' is cost-conscious consumers. In health markets the purchaser, not the consumer, is usually the cost-conscious party. Systems differ in terms of whether the purchaser's or the consumer's choice of provider dominates, and how costs enter into the purchaser's or consumer's choice. For example, in Sweden people have direct access to and choice of hospital, whereas in the UK the purchaser's and the referring GP's choice of provider has a more dominant influence than the patient's choice, and possibly also the choice of the 'gatekeeper' – the referring GP.

Types of market competition

The above discussion of differences between simple and health markets gives a background for considering the most important feature of health

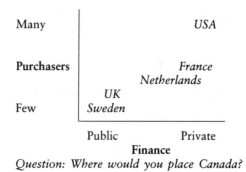

Question: Where would you place Canada?

Figure 2.4   Purchasers compete to attract individual or volume subscribers.

markets – competition. One of the aims of market reforms is to introduce economic incentives and competition to produce certain results, results which are supposed to advance the purpose of the health system. This assumes that it is possible to predict the effects, and that those who are to compete will in fact 'play the game', rather than putting their efforts into subverting the rules. These assumptions may be less valid than some of the assumptions underlying the rational corporate planning models of the 1970s, the defects of which markets are supposed to overcome.

The following builds on the earlier discussion of types of reform to give concepts to analyse different national and regional health markets. It distinguishes types and amounts of competition for finance and for patients, and the type of ownership of the purchaser or provider. It focuses on competition between purchasers and between providers. Purchasers can map markets for different services by considering the type and amount of competition between providers for finance and for referrals and the type and amount of competition between purchasers for provider capacity or for finance. They can also use these frameworks better to understand the part a purchasing organization plays in a health system in another country, and to judge if purchasing practices in other countries are translatable.

Purchaser competition

Purchaser organizations may be publicly owned and managed (e.g. NHS health authorities, Swedish counties), private not-for-profit (e.g. UK GP fundholder purchasing funds, Dutch social insurance funds), or private for-profit (e.g. UK private insurers and most US purchasers). Competition between purchasers is usually for finance, but the sources of finance are different in different systems – either direct from individuals, or from institutions such as government or private funds or employers (see Figure 2.4).

Provider competition

In the UK purchasers have found it useful to distinguish four broad types of market, with different types and amounts of competition between providers: market sectors for hospital services, for primary care, for community health services, and for social care services.

Hospital/specialist competition
In the UK, hospital competition is for finance from purchasers, through contracts and for referrals from GPs. There is also competition between hospitals for patients for direct access services, such as some therapy services. The amount of competition varies between specialties, and between areas – in many rural areas there is little or no competition. 'Boundary competition' occurs where hospitals compete with providers in other sectors for contracts or patients. For example, hospitals may compete with primary and community health services to provide mental health services. In some markets, only public hospitals can compete for public finance (e.g. Canada). In many health markets there is 'mixed competition' between public and private providers, and for some markets there is mostly private hospital competition (e.g. the USA). The latter is growing in the UK for certain specialist services, especially those which are not publicly financed, such as *in vitro* fertilization (IVF), cosmetic surgery and some mental health services.

Primary care competition
A second market sector is the primary health care market, where the type of competition and regulations are different. Primary care physicians or centres may compete with others for finance, or for patients (e.g. the UK and some Swedish experiments), or for contracts from purchasers to provide specific services. They may also compete for contracts to administer purchasing funds to buy hospital and other services. As well as 'same-provider competition' (e.g. GPs or private physicians competing for patients) there is 'inter-provider' competition between types of primary care providers for patients (e.g. between GPs and private alternative medicine therapists (e.g. homeopaths)), and for public finance (e.g. between GPs and a consortium of alternative therapists for a public contract).

Community care/social services competition
The third and fourth types of market sector are where there is competition between certain types of community care services for clients/patients or for contracts. Examples are competition between nursing homes, community nursing services (if not part of primary care) and social services or community care services. There may also be boundary or cross-sector competition (e.g. acute hospital units with 'outreach' home nursing services competing with community nursing services for patients or contracts).

Provider competition	*Ownership*	*For patients*	*For finance/contracts*
1 Between hospitals/specialties	Public Mixed Private		
2 Between primary care providers (e.g. GPs, Health centres, Dentists, Others.)	Public Mixed Private		
3 Between community health providers/social care	Public Mixed Private		
4 Between social care providers	Public Mixed Private		
5 Across-sector 'boundary competition' (between hospitals, primary care and community care providers)	Public Mixed Private		

Figure 2.5   The main types of provider competition.

Summary of types of competition in different markets
Purchasers need to recognize that the behaviour of different parties will be different in different market sectors, and to use their understanding of different types of market to develop their strategies. In different sectors competition is more or less fierce, there are different costs of entering and leaving the market, and different regulations. Figure 2.5 summarizes the main types of competition to help commissioners to assess the type of market for particular services and needs at present, and to consider how competition may develop.

Other market typologies

The above model of market structure and market sectors gives one way to analyse and understand different markets. We finish this section by noting two other market typologies. The first is one frequently referred to in discussions about European systems. Saltman and von Otter (1989) distinguish two types of market: public competition and provider market.

Public competition (internal market)
This type of market is a patient-led or 'demand-side' competition. Patients have a choice of primary care physician and of hospital. Incentives are based on patient demand and choice: payments follow patient demand.

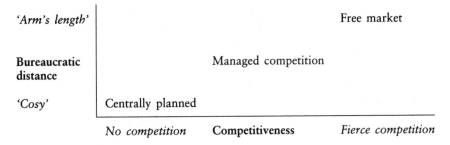

Figure 2.6 A simple market typology.

The advantages are said to be in empowering patients, in giving efficiency incentives for doctors and managers, and in forcing better balances between costs and quality of care. Examples are in reforms in Stockholm and Finnish GP experiments. The main problem is expenditure control because patients choose without regard to cost, and there are incentives for providers to generate demand.

Provider market (often mixed market)
This second type is manager-led or 'supply-side' competition. These types of markets put more emphasis on the role of purchasers, and involve competitive bidding by suppliers for purchaser contracts. Purchaser and provider managers balance cost and quality, and providers work to reduce costs to win contracts, or to compete on whatever criterion decides a contract award. Examples are UK hospital contracts with health authorities, and the proposals for the NHS by Enthoven (1985a,b). A problem with this type of market is that patient criteria are less important to purchasers than in the first type.

There are hybrid or mixed versions, which include the current UK approach with GP budgets, and systems with public and private providers, as discussed in Saltman and von Otter (1989).

A second and more simple market typology which is useful for understanding some reform proposals is that proposed by Tremblay (1993). He distinguishes markets in terms of the 'bureaucratic distance' between providers and financing authorities, and in terms of 'competitiveness' (see Figure 2.6).

Summary: market concepts and types of market

To summarize, the structure of a health care market is set by three elements: rules and regulatory organizations, purchasers and providers. Governments introduce market systems into public health services on the assumption that:

- it is possible to design and create a market structure to reward and penalize certain desired behaviours (e.g. increase cost-consciousness, productivity or health improvement);
- principles of equity can be upheld with the right type of regulation and competition;
- competition is more effective for most aims than bureaucratic direction and planning;
- the systems will produce certain behaviours, regardless of the culture and values of society and of health care personnel.

As a result of more research into the US system and experience elsewhere, it is now more generally recognized that all markets are and must be highly regulated, and none more so than health markets. In addition, the efficiency savings – of which there is little evidence in the UK – may not pay for the costs of introducing a market superstructure, and the new and higher transaction costs of contracting. There is a growing view in some parts of Europe that it is not necessary to have a radical, complete and fast reform to a market system to produce beneficial change: management development and selective incentives and rewards may be more effective than market competition. Within market systems there is also more recognition that, by cooperating, competitors can increase their chances of gaining scarce resources if they are prepared to make compromises. The threat of competition or closure may be more effective for some purposes than actual fast and cut-throat competition, if people believe that the threat is real. The fashion for markets amongst some politicians may be because it appears to absolve them from the responsibility of making difficult and unpopular changes. The experience is that, in most countries which have had a public system, and in others, the public expect politicians to take responsibility, and they have to intervene, often in systems which they then find to be out of their control.

We return to these issues and the future for public and private health purchasing in the final chapter. The following considers the 1990 NHS reforms from a purchaser perspective.

Purchasing in the NHS 'internal market'

Dear Sir,
Your review of private health sets out tables of subscriptions ranging from £113 to £1,194 per annum . . . My health authority has £354 per annum from the government to purchase, for each person in need, a wide range of hospital and community health care . . . the most cursory comparison with the private sector shows what fantastic value the modern NHS offers.
Yours sincerely,
J.R. Sully, Chief Executive, Eastbourne Health Authority.
                    ('Letters', *The Independent*, 3 June 1990, before the NHS reforms
                                                were introduced)

The purpose of this section of the chapter is twofold. First, it describes the particular type of market reform introduced into the NHS in 1990, using the concepts presented above. This helps UK health purchasers to see more clearly the similarities and differences between purchasing in the UK and purchasing in other countries. Second, it gives non-NHS readers an overview of the UK market system, so that they can better understand the discussion in later chapters of UK public health commissioning.

The initial reform proposals involved a mixture of 'patient choice' market reforms ('finance follows the patient') and 'purchaser choice' reform ('patients follow the contracts') (DoH 1989a). To some extent this mixture is still present, although the balance is certainly towards the latter – if a patient (and GP) chooses a hospital which is not contracted by his or her purchasing authority, the purchasing authority may not be prepared to pay (see the discussion of extra-contractual referrals in Chapter 6). The term 'market' does highlight the greater independence which UK commissioning health authorities now have to enter into different relations with both NHS and private providers. However, the term is misleading in suggesting that public commissioners can single-mindedly pursue the best value for money, without regard for the consequences for providers or for neighbouring purchasers. While the post-1990 NHS is different from the 'planned bureaucracy' of the 1970s and 1980s, it is not, and never will be, like any other market. The NHS and the Nordic countries are actively creating a 'third way', and regulation will be the key issue.

The United Kingdom is the 'nations' of England, Scotland, Wales and Northern Ireland. There are minor differences in NHS organization in Scotland, Wales and Northern Ireland, and these, together with the strong socialist and nationalist traditions in these regions and other political considerations, meant that the reforms were implemented slightly differently and less rapidly there. In Scotland and Northern Ireland, primary and secondary commissioning are undertaken by the same authority, whereas in England and Wales up to the mid-1990s they were undertaken by different authorities. About 12 per cent of the population subscribes to private health care insurance, but most people only use it for treatments with a long waiting list or not available on the NHS. Private insurers contract NHS hospital 'pay beds', as well as their own or other private hospitals. Privately owned hospitals and private medical and therapy practice account for a minor percentage of UK health care.

A plurality of purchasers and providers: how the NHS market developed

Legislation in 1990 (DoH 1990a) enacted the reforms proposed in *Working for Patients* (DoH 1989a). From April 1991 in England and Wales three types of NHS organizations purchased secondary health services: regional health authorities (which purchased some regional specialties), district health authorities and GP practices over 11,000 population (in 1992, over 7,000) which could opt to administer a fund to purchase some services (DoH 1989b,c). The early 1990s saw an increasing separation between state authorities' purchasing and providing roles. Health authorities established purchasing or commissioning organizations or executives, which, to begin with, agreed large 'budget contracts', mostly with their own directly managed provider units. Authorities then cooperated and formally merged, better to pursue their purchasing role.

The purchaser–provider separation increased with more provider units (hospitals and community health services) becoming NHS trusts, and with staff being employed by a trust rather than by the now purchasing authority. This reduced the bias which purchasing authorities had to retain contracts with their own provider units. It set the conditions for an increase in public provider competition, but significant competition did not occur during 1991 and 1992 for purchasing authority contracts because the government discouraged purchasing authorities from changing contracts, so as to ensure some stability during the other changes. There was, however, increasing provider competition for contracts and referrals from the small number of early GP fundholders.

The separation of purchasing and provision was largely completed by 1994, with the government encouraging the remaining NHS hospitals and community services to become NHS trusts. By the summer of 1994, 96 per cent of hospitals and community health services were trusts (419 in all). NHS trusts are corporate entities that are still tied to the NHS and publicly owned, and are managed directly by the Secretary of State. They have some independence to decide their organizational structure, to employ staff, to decide staff pay, to retain surpluses, to sell and buy land and buildings and keep the proceeds of sales, and to borrow capital up to a set limit (DoH 1989a). In 1991, 15 per cent of NHS beds were in trusts (41,000 out of 298,000 beds), which employed 13 per cent of the NHS workforce (110,000 out of 850,000 people). By 1994 over 95 per cent of NHS beds were in trusts, which employed most NHS staff.

During 1994 political decisions about the pattern of hospital service in London and in other cities gave an indication of how the future balance would be set between the market and rational planning. Another indication came from the reorganization of the top tiers of the NHS (DoH 1993b). The strength and type of regulation and planning changed with fourteen regional health authorities (RHAs) merging into eight in April 1994, with responsibilities for overseeing both purchasers and trusts. The replacement of the eight RHAs with a new intermediate tier of the NHS management executive in April 1996 introduced further changes to the type and strength of regulation and planning.

Reforms to social care and changes to local authority social service departments came in 1993. The same principle applied of the statutory local authority being an assessor, purchaser and 'enabler', rather than a direct provider. Some social service departments were divided into 'purchaser wings' and 'provider wings' to encourage comparisons and competition between providers.

The reforms led to providers being funded for their different services through contracts with purchasers. Providers (mainly NHS trusts, but also private and voluntary organizations) compete for contracts, and their contract performance is monitored by purchasers. To begin with, contracts were prospective, annual block budgets, based on the number and source of referrals from GPs and others in the previous year (people in the UK have little direct access to secondary hospital care – they are referred by GPs). Referrals outside these contracts were financed individually as 'extra-contractual referrals' (ECRs). GP referral-led purchasing continues, with DHA purchasers trying to influence GPs to refer to DHA-preferred services.

GPs as purchasers and providers

The reforms also introduced GP fundholding for larger GP practices. GPs can opt to become purchasers of a limited range of health services, mainly acute hospital procedures, consultant outpatient sessions and some diagnostic services, and, in 1993, community nursing and therapy services. In 1993 their purchasing liability was limited to less than £5,000 per year of the cost of care for any one patient – above this the health authority paid. Fundholding GPs can choose to provide some services themselves, or to buy in from non-NHS or NHS providers. As more practices became fundholders there were changes to the range of services they could buy. 1994 saw more experiments with GPs holding budgets for purchasing a wider range of services, and involving GPs in different levels of purchasing.

There is debate about whether health authorities or GP fundholders are the best purchasers of different services (Glennerster *et al.* 1992), which is focusing on the question of the 'quality of purchasing'. As we shall see in the next chapter, this debate is handicapped by the lack of a clear view of the current and future purpose of NHS commissioning. In 1991 there were about 300 fundholding practices (covering about 8 per cent of the population), in 1992 there were some 600 and 1,200 more applied during 1992. In 1993, about 25 per cent of the English population was registered with fundholding GPs and in 1994, 36 per cent. During 1993 and 1994 more fundholders formed 'multifunds' or 'consortia' – purchasing organizations which administered the funds and purchased services for a number of fundholding practices.

Summaries of problems from the purchaser perspective in the first years of the reforms are given in Harrison (1991), Øvretveit (1993c) and Freemantle *et al.* (1993). Fuller descriptions of the UK 'health market' are given in Ham (1991), Saltman and von Otter (1992) and Patton (1992), of the NHS in Levitt and Wall (1993), and of NHS principles in Seedhouse (1993). Figures 2.7 and 2.8 provide a summary of the key features.

People do not have direct access to secondary hospital services (apart from emergencies): they have to be referred by their local primary care physician (GP), the 'gatekeeper'.

1 *Patient choice* of primary care physician (GP) and the patient's views influence the *GP's choice* of hospital.

2 By 1994 nearly full *purchaser–provider separation* for district health authority commissioners. GP fundholders are purchasers *and* providers – they purchase some hospital and community services and provide primary care services.

3 Limited *purchaser competition* between DHAs, and between DHAs and fundholding GPs. But little private insurance purchasing. (There is evidence of fundholding GPs getting faster treatments for their patients.)

4 A 'mixed' *provider market*, although non-NHS providers are few (i.e. private and not-for-profit services).

5 *Provider competition*, certainly on costs for GP fundholder contracts.

6 Complex and fragmented *regulation* of purchasers and providers, with purchasers undertaking some provider regulation.

Figure 2.7 Summary: The NHS 'internal market': key features.

The results?

According to the NHS Finance Director, Gordon Greenshields, in the first financial year of the reforms,

> Both purchasers and providers have ended 1991/2 broadly in balance with some large cash deficiencies eliminated. Inpatient activity had risen 7 per cent overall: 20 per cent for day cases and 4 per cent for others . . . Directly managed units had increased activity by 6.9 per cent and trusts by 8.2 per cent. The number of patients waiting more than a year had fallen by 52 per cent and more than two years by 97 per cent. All with staffing levels 2 per cent below those planned.
>
> (Greenshields 1992: 12)

Was this owing to increasing productivity, and was it the first fruits of the reforms? It is difficult to say, for the government spent £154 million to reduce waiting lists, and a further £34 million in January 1991 for 1991–2: 'There was a warning that by the end of March 1992, no patient should have to wait more than two years for an operation' (*Health Services Journal* 14 February 1991: 12). The general election was held in the spring of 1992, after which the total waiting list rose to over one million people by June 1993, a rise of 15 per cent since March 1993 (*Health Services Journal* 12 August 1993: 4).

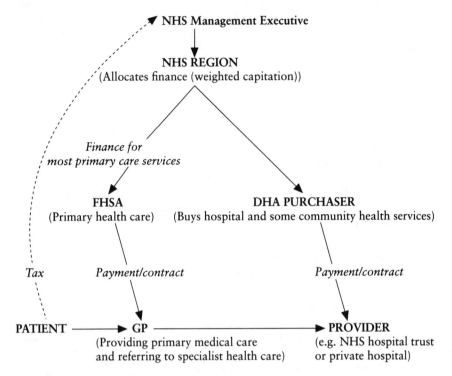

The GP chooses a hospital service and the patient follows the contract

Figure 2.8   The structure of the NHS 'internal market'.

It is difficult to draw definitive conclusions about the success or otherwise of the 1990 reforms, not least because of the lack of research, the contestable statistics and the difficulties of attributing any changes to the 1990 reforms rather than to other factors. No systematic evaluation was conducted, although one publication did draw together the research which was done on specific subjects (Robinson and Le Grand, 1994). Much depends on the criteria of success which we use and what we see to be the purpose of the NHS – one of the subjects of the next chapter. For the moment the reader is invited to choose between a pessimistic and an optimistic view of the future of NHS commissioning, and to consider what evidence they would use to support their view:

The system is now so fragmented and health authorities are so weak that any effective planning or regulation is impossible. The stock of goodwill built up over 45 years will no longer modify the market pressures and short-term interests which will now take hold. Political appointment and political intervention by a government supported by business interests is not the best way to ensure that the health of the population comes first. With pressure on public expenditure, the way is open for business to take advantage of the worsening situation under the guise of more choice.

Commissioners are now beginning to take the lead: we have reorganized and have the purchasing power. We now have health strategies to drive our purchasing strategies and our contracting, and we are planning the best provider configurations with other purchasers. We are establishing ourselves as the 'patients advocate' and more of our population are recognizing our value to them. Our experience with the internal market and our long-term and population health perspective means that we have an important contribution to make to the debate about the future of the NHS. We will keep health to the forefront and put the technicalities of financing and provision in their proper place – as the means not the ends.

Summary and conclusion

The purpose and role of a purchasing organization depends on the national and local market structure. Both follow from and also shape the purpose of a health system. Managers working in purchasing organizations need to understand market structures in order to define realistic objectives, to influence the market to serve their populations better and to draw valid lessons from the experience of other purchasing organizations. This chapter presented models and frameworks which can help purchasing managers to understand and analyse markets, and to clarify the role and objectives of their organization. It encouraged the reader to question how different 'market reforms' advance the purposes of the NHS (or their health system), and to clarify their view of the purpose of the NHS.

NHS commissioning followed on from earlier market reforms to public services, known as 'contracting out'. The purchaser–provider split market reforms of 1990 introduced NHS purchasing of health services and created NHS commissioning organizations. By the mid-1990s, public authorities were purchasers only, and entering into a variety of agreements with both public and private providers. With increasing competition between providers, there was also debate about introducing competition between purchasers, about new forms of regulation and further market reforms. The purpose and objectives of a commissioning organization are different in each type of 'market reform', as are the advantages and disadvantages for different interest groups. Critics argued that the aim of all these reforms was to take steps towards 'privatizing' public services, to give opportunities for the private sector to increase their profits, and to reduce employment and expenditure in the public sector. Advocates argued that the extra costs of the market superstructure would be recouped in time from increased efficiency, and that more choice would be available to people.

One conclusion of the chapter is that means have not tended to follow from a clear view about the ends. Means shape the ends: methods such as provider competition lead to changes in the purpose of a health system. Unless we examine purpose and ask how changes advance a favoured view of purpose, we may find that changes in means have resulted in changes in ends which were not wanted. This is not to underestimate the difficulties of defining and agreeing the purpose of a health system, but to emphasize the need to trace the links between particular changes and the purpose of a health system, rather than to stop at intermediate objectives such as efficiency.

This chapter drew attention to differences between a model of a simple market and particular features of health markets, such as third party purchasing, complex regulation, the nature of demand and supply, financing and types of competition. In general, for markets to be efficient there have to be a number of purchasers and providers, full information, low transaction costs, and easy market entry and exit. The absence of these features in most health markets makes untenable some assumptions about the effects of competition and incentives. These incentives do not always have the expected effects, in part because of the particular culture and values of the 'actors' in a public health system. To date, politicians in favour of markets have instinctively recognized these differences and the value and political issues at stake. This may change with the increasing 'care gap', and the public may be more prepared to support more private and mixed financing.

A key question for public health systems is whether either purchasing or provider organizations need to be in public ownership to ensure that they pursue public ends. If they are, do they need to be managed by public authorities, or can public ends be pursued through contractual relations with quasi- or fully independent organizations in competition? By comparing health systems we can make more objective assessments about whether mechanisms of control other than government ownership, employment and traditional accountability relations are necessary to ensure that public ends are pursued. Contractual relations and the purchaser–provider split raise the question of whether even public purchasing has to be carried out by a public authority. At least as important as the questions of economy and efficiency are the political issues, and the ethical and moral issues of profiting from purchasing or providing health services, subjects to which we return in the final chapter.

Key points

- In making purchasing decisions, NHS managers need continually to return to questions of the purpose of the NHS and of a commissioning organization.
- The purpose and objectives of a purchasing organization depend on the national framework for markets and the nature of the local market.
- Managers in purchasing organizations need to understand how markets work, their part in the system, and how they affect and are affected by

the actions of the other parts. Without this understanding they cannot influence local markets and national legislation on behalf of the people they serve.

- Market reforms in public health services may involve one or all of the following: contracting out, a purchaser–provider split or purchaser competition and total system reform.
- The arguments for and against each type of reform are different, and involve a different role for health purchasers.
- Most markets for health services are different to simple markets because patients are not purchasers, both patients and purchasers have difficulty judging quality, there are high transaction costs, there are often few providers or purchasers and there are high costs to entering and leaving the market.
- A framework of rules and regulatory organizations is necessary to create and sustain a market. This framework may allow for different degrees of planning and control, for example by regulating the number of doctors. In some markets purchasers may have regulatory responsibilities.
- In public health reforms the political issues of choice, equality and who gains and loses from a change are at least as important as the economic issues, and require purchasers to use political as well as economic analyses.
- The NHS reforms involve a mix of patient choice and purchaser contracting market, a particular type of limited purchaser competition and an increasing role for private sector capital and private clinical and support service providers. Current changes are making the purchaser–provider and public–private distinctions less useful for purchasers.

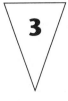

3

Health commissioning: purpose and work

Introduction

We all need to feel that we are doing something worthwhile at work. My impression working with commissioning managers in the early 1990s was that many were not sure of the value of what they were doing – of what it was for. The focus was on tasks, and on targets, but something seemed to be missing in the frantic activity. I assumed that this was an idle reflection of a researcher who had not yet understood what commissioning was all about, until one lunchtime.

Over lunch a purchasing manager was talking about the potential for commissioning to improve health, and her frustration was clear. It was not just overwork and late nights, but that many targets seemed to be getting in the way of the job and of the purpose of commissioning. This was heretical talk in an organization which commanded full 'commitment'. It became clear to me over the months that followed that this view was widespread, and that people were not committed to tasks and targets, but to their idea of the part which commissioning could play in the new NHS. Their ideas about the purpose of commissioning were not those of the commissioning organization, which had statements of values and objectives, but not of purpose.

Books have the luxury of starting with purpose, managers often do not. To some extent the lack of examination of the purpose of commissioning in the early 1990s was appropriate: commissioners started with statements of purpose describing needs assessment and contracting, and got on with it. We now have experience of commissioning, and need to review the early statements of purpose. We need to reassess what commissioning is trying to achieve, given the constraints and the conditions of the late 1990s. In this chapter we address the following questions:

- *What is the purpose of NHS commissioning?*
- *What work, tasks and organization follow from this conception of purpose?*

One aim of this chapter is to present ideas that commissioning managers can use to redefine the purpose of their commissioning organization. An updated and shared understanding of purpose gives a sounder basis for deciding priorities, organization, objectives and programmes of work. The second aim is to present the author's conception of the purpose of commissioning, which will be referred to in later chapters when we examine a variety of approaches to commissioning: forms of organization, policies, methods and models. We will ask how these approaches contribute to the particular conception of purpose presented in this chapter.

Why worry about purpose?

A sense of purpose is central to individual and organizational effectiveness. It is a source of energy and motivation for staff, and it is the basis for deciding organization and project timetables. A shared sense of purpose is the most effective 'coordination mechanism' there is. It provides a touchstone against which people judge what to do.

A suitable conception of the purpose of commissioning is essential to the future of the NHS, and to the health of people served by a commissioning organization. A conception of purpose which is too limited confines attention to contracting services, rather than acting for health. A conception which is too broad diffuses commissioning into a mission to eradicate poverty and unemployment. A 'suitable' conception is one which corresponds to current commissioning objectives and work, but which points to the future: there is a tension between the practicalities of the present and the ideal towards which commissioning reaches. It recognizes that commissioning is a service, albeit a complex one. Such a conception is necessary for commissioners to judge which type of commissioning organization is best in a particular area. It gives a basis for deciding how to structure the organization and the priorities and programmes for the coming years.

The approach this chapter takes is to work down a hierarchy of purpose, starting at the top with the purpose of the NHS. We consider:

- *The purpose and values of the NHS*, or a 'public health system' (shared by all NHS organizations), which *help to define*
- *The purpose of NHS commissioning*, or 'public health purchasing' (shared by all NHS commissioners and commissioning agents, and different from the purpose of NHS providers but sharing some common purposes), *which helps to define*
- *The purpose of an NHS commissioning organization*, or a 'public health purchaser' (health authorities, GP fundholders and other NHS commissioners have some common purposes, and some which are different), *which underlies*

- *A model of the work of health commissioning* (which helps to define the key work and tasks of a health commissioner, and the relationships through which they pursue their purpose).

The rationale for taking this approach is that managers can gain guidance from higher-order statements of purpose to define the purpose of a particular commissioning organization. We start by considering the purpose and values of the NHS, which in other countries would equate to the purpose of a public health system or strategy. We find that statements of the purpose of the NHS help to define the purpose of commissioning, but we then have to turn to other sources for guidance. We turn to government statements, which help to distinguish the purposes of commissioning from the health service provision. This sets the context for considering the purpose of an NHS commissioning organization, which is the bulk of the chapter. We consider ideas which can help commissioners to define and distinguish their purpose from those of other types of purchasers. We then consider the work and tasks which follow from these ideas and models of commissioning.

The purpose of the NHS

The principles which have guided [the NHS] for the last 40 years will continue to guide it into the twenty-first century.
(DoH 1989a: para. 1.2)

We ask ourselves, 'What is the core activity of the NHS?' It is not the management of hospitals – that is essentially a secondary activity. The core activity of the NHS is to secure a universal health care system available on the basis of clinical need rather than on the basis of ability to pay.
(Stephen Dorrell, financial secretary to the UK Treasury, presenting the government's 'Private Finance Initiative' for mixed public–private partnerships. (HSJ, 24 July 1993, p. 22)

What guidance can commissioning managers gain about the purpose of NHS commissioning from statements of the purpose of the NHS? One view of the purpose of NHS commissioning is to uphold and promote NHS principles and values. What are these?

The aim of the NHS as stated in the 1946 Act is to promote 'the establishment in England and Wales of a comprehensive health service designed to secure improvement in the physical and mental health of the people of England and Wales and the prevention, diagnosis and treatment of illness'. Commissioners searching for further guidance about their purpose and work face a half-century of government documents, reports and commentaries about the purpose of the NHS and its principles. As one of the more authoritative documents noted, 'The absence of detailed and publicly declared principles and objectives for the NHS reflects to some

degree the continuing political debate about the service' (1979 Royal
Commission review of the NHS). The 1990 reform statements were no
more specific.

To guide itself in its review of the NHS, the 1979 Royal Commission
derived seven objectives from the 1946 and 1977 Acts and from the history of the NHS. Underlying these objectives were three principles which
most commentaries and government documents have put forward as the
basis of the NHS. These are comprehensiveness, that the service will be
free at the time of use, and equality of access.

There are four ways of defining what 'comprehensive' means for an
NHS commissioner. The first is to refer to the details of Section 3(1) of the
1977 Act. This requires the Health Secretary:

> to provide throughout England and Wales, to such extent as he con-
> siders necessary to meet reasonable requirements:
> (a) hospital accommodation;
> (b) other accommodation for the purpose of any services provided
>   under this Act;
> (c) medical, dental, nursing and ambulance services;
> (d) such other facilities for the care of expectant and nursing mothers
>   and young children as he considers appropriate as part of the
>   health service;
> (e) such facilities for the prevention of illness, the care of persons
>   suffering from illness and the after-care of persons who have
>   suffered from illness as he considers are appropriate as part of the
>   health service;
> (f) such other services as are required for the diagnosis and treatment
>   of illness.

This statement allows a great deal of government discretion as to what
services are provided as part of a 'comprehensive service'. A second way
to define 'comprehensive' is by reference to resources: that a commissioner
purchases or otherwise arranges for as comprehensive a range of services
as possible, relative to the resources allocated to it. There is some support
for this interpretation in judicial reviews of NHS authorities refusals to
fund certain treatments for individuals. The judge found in favour of the
health authority that there was no statutory requirement to pay for the
treatment and that the duty of the authority was to secure services within
the available resources. Patients trying to enforce the statutory duties of
the Secretary of State under the 1977 Act have also failed – the finding has
turned on the statement in section 3(1) of the Act that the duty is to
provide 'to such extent as he considers necessary to meet all reasonable
requirements' (Dimond 1993). At the time of writing, the question of the
duty to provide long term care beds for different patients is under examination. We return to some of these issues in the section on rationing in
Chapter 5.

A third way to define comprehensive is relative to needs: that the role of a health authority is to purchase services which meet the needs of the population. Yet comprehensiveness in the 1946 Act (and the 1977 Act) is relative to improving health, which is different to the more ambitious 'meeting health needs'. The concept of 'health gain' discussed below is more appropriate to this former interpretation, even though reform documents (DoH 1989a) do refer to meeting health needs.

A fourth way is through reference to specific government policy guidance, one of the most relevant and recent being the 1988 guidance on planning and priorities (DHSS 1988). This sets out twelve priority areas for NHS development, and, like other similar priority statements, has been criticized for not ranking priorities or addressing issues of redistribution of finance or extra finance (e.g. Harrison *et al.* 1989).

With regard to the second principle of 'free at the time of use', the 1946 Act in fact states that 'The services so provided shall be free of charge, except where any provision of the Act expressly provides for the making and recovery of charges.' In general, no NHS purchaser or provider has the powers to make charges to the public unless covered by existing legislation, and then at set rates (e.g. prescription, dental, optical) or by new legislation. The more important underlying principle is equity: that there should be no direct or indirect financial barriers to poor people getting access to health care when they need it. As we see in Chapter 13, this principle is sometimes viewed in terms of equality of equal access, which refers to the equal right of people from different ethnic groups or geographical areas to have the same access to services – equity is different.

More recently, effectiveness and efficiency were upgraded in some discussions to equal status to the three 'traditional NHS principles'. In addition, the 1980s saw choice and consumer values being introduced as NHS principles, and these are currently in conflict with certain traditional population and utilitarian principles of the NHS.

From this short discussion of NHS principles we can draw the following conclusions for defining the purpose of NHS commissioning. First, with the increasing number of principles which NHS commissioners are expected to uphold, a key task is to resolve conflicts of principle in certain situations by deciding which principles are of overriding importance, and to justify the decision to their population and/or consult with their population. Second, GP fundholders administer a purchasing fund in trust, which is NHS finance, and their use of this finance should be governed by 'NHS principles'. If the principles of equity and equality have any meaning, then GP fundholders have as much responsibility for upholding these principles as DHAs and FHSAs. When GP fundholder patients get preferential treatment, then GPs have a responsibility for the inequities which they create. We can judge whether these principles have any meaning in practice by whether regions or others overseeing GP fundholders take action to reduce the inequities. Third, neither the original NHS Act nor subsequent Acts or government statements specifies that the NHS is to meet all needs or that there are to be no charges at the time of use, or defines equity. A compromise position for an NHS health commissioner is that their task is, 'to secure services sufficiently comprehensive to meet the most pressing health needs of those most in need'. This gives some recognition to resource constraints and equity principles. However, it is difficult to call upon authoritative documents to be more specific than this, and, I will argue below, health commissioners do not need to do so.

Implications for the purpose of NHS commissioning

These principles and values give some guidance for commissioners. Certainly one of the purposes of NHS health commissioning is to uphold principles referred to in legislation, but commissioners cannot define their purpose only in terms of principles or values. Values help to choose and guide purpose, but are not to be confused with purpose, which is a direction and an end result. Values give purpose a motive force and meaning, but they are not the same as purpose – we can achieve our purpose but we never 'achieve' our values.

Beyond a certain point discussion of values does not help to define the purpose of NHS commissioning, and neither does it help an NHS commissioning organization to define its purpose. Clarifying values and defining what they mean in practice is an important thing for commissioners to do, but it is of limited use in defining purpose. Values such as equity and choice do not themselves define the purpose of a commissioning agency.

It is the task of commissioning managers to define the purpose of NHS commissioning in their areas and for their commissioning organizations. To do so they need guidance from government about the general purpose of NHS commissioning itself. What guidance is there?

The purpose of NHS commissioning

The purpose and objectives of NHS health authorities in the 1990 Act

The 1990 NHS Act did not change the principles which guide NHS health authorities, but did change the way in which they pursue these principles (DoH 1990a). Their purpose is not to maintain hospitals but to secure the necessary health care for their populations. Some hold that this is the same purpose as before the 1990 reforms, but pursued by different means; others see it as a change in purpose.

The stated aim of separating purchasing from provision was to allow health authorities to concentrate on 'meeting the needs' of their population. This was said to be more difficult to do when health authorities' attention was taken up with the management issues of hospitals and community health services for which they were directly responsible. Their view of health needs could be over-influenced by providers' interests. Early statements of the purpose of district health authorities were to assess the health needs of their population and to purchase services to meet these needs. The implication is that they do not have responsibility for ensuring that a provider in their area continues to offer services, as long as they are able to purchase the services which their population needs from other providers.

We note that meeting all needs is impossible and was not the purpose of the NHS in the 1946 and 1977 Acts, which was to seek improvement in the health of the people. We note too that early government statements said little about the purpose of health commissioning, and did not give a statement of the purpose of commissioning organizations such as health authorities or of GP fundholders.

The 1993 'vision for purchasing'

A more specific view of commissioning was outlined by a government health minister in 1993 in three speeches (Mawhinney and Nichol 1993). He reaffirmed the importance which the government attached to purchasing for future improvements in the NHS. His vision of 'seven stepping stones to successful purchasing' was for health authorities to 'develop five year strategic plans; to secure tangible improvements in services in next year's contracts; to compile data on needs and outcomes, using central sources and local research; to implement the "local voices" guidance on community involvement; to build long-term "mature" relationships with providers; to seek wide health benefits by working more vigorously with other agencies; and to give urgent attention to their own management and organization development needs' (*Health Services Journal* 6 May 1993: 15).

For the minister, the new role of authorities as 'agents for people and their health needs' meant 'that they also need to be agents for GPs'. The speech did not propose that authorities' role should be strengthened at the expense of GP purchasing: 'We will not curtail the freedom of GP fundholders – quite the contrary.' The speech emphasized GPs and HAs working together to set priorities, pool skills and avoid duplication. It did not address how conflicts would be resolved or whether fundholders would have to come 'in line' with authorities to achieve strategic aims.

Although at this time it was clearly necessary to give a direction to purchasing, what was missing was a clear conception of the purpose of NHS commissioning. The earlier purpose of assessing needs and contracting services was appropriate in the first years where commissioners were required to give stability. But stronger commissioning required a new view of purpose, from which commissioning priorities could be derived. The answer to why each of these 'seven stepping stones' is important does not lead us as it should to a higher-order statement of a new purpose for NHS commissioning. Without such a conception the tension between GP and authority purchasing is greater. A common shared purpose has to be discovered locally, rather than flowing from a definition which governs all who act as commissioners with NHS finance. Without an analysis of the purpose of NHS commissioning it is more difficult to assess which type of commissioning organization – public or private – may be best for the purpose in a particular area, or to judge performance.

Towards a definition of the purpose of NHS commissioning

We established above that the purpose of the NHS in legislation is to improve health and to prevent illness, rather than to meet all health needs. We also saw that certain values guide how all NHS organizations fulfil this purpose, and that the 1990 Act makes it clear that NHS authorities are expected to assess needs and place contracts for services, rather than providing services directly. We moved from the purposes and values of the NHS to seven aims for health authority commissioners. This 'jump' reflects the 'jump' made by commissioners in the early 1990s: from discussions of NHS values to specific tasks and programmes with only a limited conception of the purpose of NHS commissioning.

It was the concept of health gain and the 'Health of the Nation' strategy (DoH 1992a) which 'filled the gap' in 1992 and 1993. Many began to use this concept to develop a broader view of the purpose of an NHS commissioning organization, and to rethink the task of needs assessment.

Health gain

The NHS and most health systems have long been criticized as being medical services for acute illnesses, or as being more concerned with health services than with health. The concept of health gain helped to shift attention from contracting health services as the end result of commissioning, to individual and population health, to health outcomes and to a variety of means for achieving these ends. In simple terms, health gain is an improvement in health. Health gain may be achieved by curing an illness, arresting or slowing a disease, or preventing predictable ill heath, for example by health education.

The concept of health gain in *The Health of the Nation* (DoH 1992a) builds on the WHO notion of 'adding years to life: an increase in life expectancy and reduction in premature death; and adding life to years: increasing years lived free from ill health, reducing or minimising the adverse effects of illness or disability, promoting healthy lifestyles, physical and social environments and, overall, improving quality of life'. One analysis of the concept proposed that commissioning for health gain involves three aspects: assessment of population health status and needs; evaluation of effectiveness of treatments and cost-effectiveness of services; and 'social value prioritizing', by understanding the importance the public attaches to certain treatments and services and the concerns they have about different health problems (Øvretveit 1993c).

There are advantages and disadvantages with the breadth of the concept for defining the purpose of NHS commissioning. The first is less serious: that it does not allow a distinction between the purpose of commissioning and provision; the purpose of both is health gain. The second is that the breadth of purpose can be too wide, and unrealistic for commissioners. There is a view that the NHS – both commissioners and providers – should concern itself with 'health care', i.e. health services, and that 'health policy' is a responsibility of a variety of governmental departments and organizations. NHS commissioners may have a leading role in formulating and coordinating 'health policy', but it is not one of their primary purposes.

An example of this view is presented in a document by the UK health managers' association on future health care options (IHSM 1993), which states that 'health policy, being much broader than health care policy, is properly the responsibility of the DoH (in collaboration with other departments of state), while health care policy is the responsibility of the NHS' (para. 3.7). This IHSM document views commissioners – as part of the NHS – as being concerned with health care services. In defining their purpose, commissioners might consider whether, in the following, the IHSM document is referring to provider services only, or commissioners as well: 'The purpose of health care is not to redress the inequalities endemic in society nor to be the principal focus for wide ranging programmes to improve health although it must contribute to such schemes' (para. 3.5). In the final chapter we consider the politics of the broader and narrower definitions of the purpose of NHS commissioning, the latter tending to be more compatible with philosophies which emphasize individual responsibility for health.

It is perhaps better to have too wide a breadth of purpose and to narrow it by focusing on specific health gain targets, such as reduction in coronary heart disease, than to limit the purpose of commissioning to that of purchasing services. The generality of the concept of health gain does mean that commissioners have to define intermediate objectives in their health strategy. This point takes us to the third disadvantage with health gain as the purpose of NHS commissioning: the problem of measurement. We consider the difficulties of measuring provider outcome in Chapter 5. The problems of measuring health gain achieved by a commissioner are even greater: what timescale should we use, and how can we unambiguously attribute changes in health to the actions of a health commissioner? However, the advantages of the concept outweigh the disadvantages in emphasizing the end results for the people commissioners serve. We therefore put forward the conception of the purposes of NHS commissioning shown in Box 3.1.

Box 3.1

The purpose of NHS commissioning is to make the best use of available finance to improve health and prevent illness, by influencing other organizations to contribute to these ends and by contracting health services.

We now turn to the purpose of a commissioning organization, and to concepts which help to define the purpose and tasks of such an organization.

The purpose of a commissioning organization: a service to the population

The next sections discuss commissioning as a service and health strategy. These ideas help commissioners to develop a shared understanding of what the organization is for and how to realize the purpose of NHS commissioning for a particular population.

NHS commissioning can be performed by different types of commissioning organization. The two predominant forms are health authority commissioners and GP fundholders. The latter may be smaller group practices or larger consortia or 'multifunds'. Some of the variations of the former are NHS commissioners, such as a DHA- or FHSA-employed commissioning organization, and an integrated DHA/FHSA commissioning agency, with or without DHA and FHSA merger. In theory a private organization could act as a commissioning organization for a DHA or combined DHA/ FHSA. The ideas we consider here help health authorities and regional organizations to assess which organization form is best in the local area for the purposes of NHS commissioning. They help to highlight any differences between these organizations in the purposes which they are likely to pursue.

One of the purposes of a commissioning organization is to translate the general purpose of improvement in health into specific and realistic health objectives for a population, and then to work to achieve these. This cannot be done by a health commissioner planning in isolation. Health objectives and health strategy have to be formulated with local people, GPs and local organizations to be realistic and to be achieved. This 'involvement' in formulating and realizing health gain will be superficial, unless we understand commissioning as a service and a commissioning organization as a service business.

Commissioning as a service

A health commissioning organization will not survive unless people working in the organization understand that they are in a service business. Just as important is to recognize the complex nature of the service, and the conflicts which arise in trying to serve different groups.

Something of the nature and complexity of the service is revealed by comparison with private health insurance purchasing. Both private and NHS commissioners ('public health purchasers') are service-giving organizations. The main service which private health purchasers offer to their customers is to pay for the health services their customers need, under agreed conditions. Most fulfil their service contracts with their customers by agreeing contracts with providers to give health services to their customers: they are 'third-party' services. The desired outcome of their service for customers is that they can gain easy access to a service when they need it. The purchaser does not agree a contract to 'improve health and prevent illness'.

UK NHS health commissioners are service-giving organizations which are similar and different to private insurance purchasers, and have a more complex 'customer'. Their purpose is to serve the public as individuals and as populations in the short and long term. We consider below what the outcome of their service should be, and whether some views of outcome are unrealistic, given the resources and powers available. Commissioners give service in the form of direct services to individual citizens, for example by dealing with a complaint, by registering a person with a GP or by giving information about a health condition or about a provider. Most of their work, however, is in providing an indirect service by purchasing other health services for individuals and for populations. In addition to contracting providers, they serve their populations by making sure that a range of health services are available, and by undertaking other activities to improve health and prevent illness (e.g. forming 'healthy alliances': DoH 1992a).

Features of public health purchasing services

There are four distinctive features of NHS commissioning as a service.

1 *Implicit contract with the public.* Unlike private health purchasers, NHS commissioners do not have a legally binding agreement with each customer to offer a service. Most UK citizens do not know that commissioners or fundholders act on their behalf, or even that they provide direct services such as information services. To clarify their purpose, commissioners have to examine and understand the distinctive nature of their implicit contract with the public as individuals and as populations, and the relationships through which they fulfil this 'contract'.

2 *The public health dimension.* The comparison with private health purchasers highlights this dimension. Some commissioner activities and some services they purchase are to improve the long-term health of their populations. Examples are health education and health promotion services. It is possible that the majority of the population may not want these services, or may prefer some or all of the money to be spent on other services. Unlike most private purchasers, commissioners have to strike a careful balance between the resources which they put into acute services and those which they put into preventative long-term services: they have duties beyond responding to immediate short-term concerns and a responsibility for future generations. Private purchasers acting as commissioners with NHS finance would also have these responsibilities.

3 *Relations with government, and with other bodies.* NHS health commissioners serve the government, as the term 'commissioner' implies.

Although they have a degree of autonomy, which is sometimes unclear, they have to comply with government directives which can conflict with population preferences. The analogy of the local public as shareholders in the commissioning organization is misleading under the current arrangements: commissioners are not formally accountable to them, but to the government. As a result they are required to provide information to central government, to cooperate with financial audits and to respond in other ways to central government requests. Some of these activities may be viewed as 'services' to the government.

4 *The service aspect of relations with contractors.* While the main beneficiary of their service is the public, it is also useful to understand some of the commissioners' activities as providing a service to their contractors. Commissioners provide a range of 'services' to their contractors, one of the most important being payment services to GPs, other primary care contractors, hospitals and community services. It is through providing high quality services of these types to contractors that commissioners secure contractors' ability to provide services to the public. If, for example, there are errors or delays in payments to GPs, GPs are less willing to cooperate with commissioners' plans, and in some cases a GP could go out of business.

Commissioning is a service, albeit a complex one. What are the services that a commissioning organization performs for a resident? What would not be done for that person if the commissioner did not exist, and health services were still financed out of taxation? Answers to these questions help to define the purpose of a commissioning organization, and to distinguish its purpose from those of other purchasers by degree or in absolute terms. Answers include: ensuring that there are providers which are accessible when the person needs them, using professional expertise to ensure that the services are of a high professional quality, using purchasing power to get the best value for money, taking action to reduce health-harming environments, and arranging registration with and of primary care contractors.

Thinking of the purpose of commissioning as giving a service can help in developing relationships with residents in an area. Commissioners have tended to neglect their relationships with the people they serve because they have not appreciated that they are service organizations. The notion of serving individuals and the nature of their relationship with individuals or with populations plays little part in many commissioners' thinking. If we consider commissioners as providing a service to their populations, we can move beyond more limited notions of 'consulting the public'. To fail to recognize commissioning as a service is a dangerous omission – people support organizations with which they have a relationship and where they understand the service that the organization performs for them. Providers and GPs have this relationship, and as a result are much more able to get public support to oppose steps which a purchaser may need to take, such as switching contracts resulting in the closure of a specialty or local hospital. This is not to underestimate the problems which arise because commissioners serve government and their population. However, commissioning organizations will not survive unless they can prove the value of the service they give to their people, as well as their other purposes. There is much to be learned from purchasing organizations in the USA about how to relate to subscribers and to establish the value of a purchasing organization in their minds. Pursuing this track helps us to develop the 'service concept' of a commissioning organization (Edvardsson *et al.* 1994) and to establish its role and relationship with a population. It helps to define what we mean by added value in the context of a public purchasing agency. It also helps to define the purpose of the agency with regard to GPs, and to consider to what extent the agency provides them and others with a service. We return to this conception of commissioning as complex service in Chapter 7, where we consider the quality of commissioning.

The purpose of a commissioning organization: formulating and realizing a health strategy

If the destination of NHS commissioning is health gain, then the vehicle is health strategy. It is through a health strategy that a commissioning organization pursues its purpose of health gain, and defines the part to be played by providers in achieving health gain. In this section we note approaches to needs assessment which are appropriate to the purpose of health gain. We also consider health promotion and causes of poor health to emphasize the broad approach to health strategy which a commissioner must take to fulfil their purpose.

Initially, commissioners' strategies were about hospital services and capital investments, and these concerns will not disappear in the future. However, if commissioners are to move beyond a reactive and provider-driven 'insurance fund' mode, they need to 'work back' to services from the end results of improvement in the health of their populations. It is clarity about these end results, and about targets for reducing ill health and for prevention, which allows commissioners to define the role and amount of different services in achieving these aims for their populations. One of the purposes of a commissioning organization is to formulate and pursue a strategy for health which is appropriate to the need of the local population and to the resources which are available.

A health strategy is based on,

- an assessment of needs,
- an understanding of the factors which cause ill health,
- an understanding of the conditions and behaviour which a health commissioner can influence to improve health,
- a decision about where a commissioner will invest their time and efforts with the prospects of the greatest health gain,
- an understanding of the part to be played by different services in achieving health gain, and of the consequences of changing contracts.

Needs assessment

The concept of health gain helped commissioners to rethink their approach to needs assessment. Needs can be defined in many ways, as can the task of assessing needs. If the purpose of health commissioning is to seek health gain and improvement in health, then this purpose helps to delineate and focus the task of needs assessment.

An early review by the DoH (1991a) noted three approaches, which came to be known as the 'epidemiological', the 'comparative' and the 'corporate'. The epidemiological assessment of need is of two kinds: first, the incidence and prevalence of disease and mortality, in a district, in localities and in different age or client groups; second, disease-specific studies which also consider treatment or service effectiveness. The comparative approach to needs assessment compares the use of services and providers' performance in the area with use and performance elsewhere. The corporate approach draws on views of different interest groups, such as GPs, local people, providers, other agencies, regions and the NHS Management Executive. A more recent and complementary approach is 'disease mapping' (DoH 1992c).

In assessing needs there is always the question of how much consideration to give to the methods and treatments for meeting a need. A 'pure' epidemiological approach to needs assessment only assesses mortality and morbidity in populations, without regard to treatments or services. A concept which links needs to an intervention is 'capacity to benefit'. One view is that a need does not exist unless there is a method for meeting that need, and that it is impossible and unhelpful to define need without reference to the method for meeting the need: 'There is only a need where there is a potential benefit, i.e. where the intervention and/or the care setting is effective' (DoH 1991b: Needs assessment project guidance to NHS).

Another view is that we can and should assess needs separately from methods for meeting the need. If we do not, we perpetuate in another form the disadvantages of not separating purchasing and provision and create a provider-defined view of needs. There may be no known treatment for a particular health need, but does this mean that a health commissioner should not assess the incidence and prevalence of that need in the population?

Probably one of the most urgent issues for many commissioners is how best to involve people in needs assessment, and how to deal with the conflicts between different types of needs assessment. The issues and methods are discussed in the 'local voices' document (DoH 1992b). We consider these issues further in the chapters on locality commissioning and rationing.

General points of note include, first, that it will take time to develop an information base of different types of needs, in different areas and for different client groups. Second, 'soft' information is available from GPs and providers and others (i.e. their estimates of need) which can give a sufficient basis for contract changes or other expenditure decisions. Third, there will never be an objective measure of needs, and needs assessment will always be a technical and a political process. Commissioners' task is to develop processes for combining different sources and types of information about needs for different purposes. Then, as more accurate epidemiological and 'technical' information becomes available, it can be fed into the needs assessment process. A fourth point is that health commissioners cannot wait for needs assessment information to make decisions. The task is for commissioners to develop their needs assessment to enable them to make more informed and justifiable decisions. Fifth, integrating DHA and FHSA data about needs is a priority for commissioners.

Later chapters consider these issues further, as well as how needs have to be considered in relation to service effectiveness. It is only by focusing the task of needs assessment in relation to the purpose of health improvement that commissioners can make the work more manageable, and produce more useful information for commissioning decisions. The more ambitious early approaches have largely proved irrelevant or impossible. 'It is about time we gave up on this notion of "needs assessment" . . . it's a joke . . . We should be honest and say that we are involved in a health care system rather than a health system' (a frustrated public health consultant, quoted in a Nuffield study of developments in purchasing in 1992 as a reasonably representative view of the difficulties of using needs assessment in purchasing: Freemantle *et al.* 1993).

We do not consider needs assessment in detail here because it is considered in a later chapter in relation to effectiveness and outcome, and discussed comprehensively elsewhere. Simple summaries are provided in Buchan *et al.* (1990), Bull (1990) and Stevens and Gabbay (1991), and a critique of the notion of infinite need in Frankel (1991).

Causes of poor health

In formulating strategy and defining achievable health targets for their population, commissioners need to understand the causes of ill health and how they may best act to improve health. Many factors contributing to ill health are difficult for commissioners to influence directly, and a realistic recognition of this helps to define the limits to the purpose of a commissioning agency. To illustrate the point that factors other than services affect health, Figure 3.1 shows a simple way of identifying and grouping these factors, and also helps commissioners to consider to what extent or how they can affect these factors.

The influence of factors is different for different illnesses, as is how factors interact: for example, a genetic predisposition may be more important for some illnesses, but people may still reduce their risks by self-diagnosis and early treatment. Even where health services are available, people's access to and use of them depends on education, cultural factors, personal finance and other factors. This is apparent if we consider health services as four

	Social factors (often outside people's control)		
Behavioural (psychological, genetic, cultural)	*Long-term life style* Smoking, diet, exercise, leisure, risk-taking, alcohol, drugs	*Health services* (access to and use of) Self-diagnosis, availability of health information, compliance with treatment, 'playing the system'
Individual factors		
Resources (wealth, income, employment, education)	Housing, overcrowding, sanitation, travel, occupational and environmental hazards	Finance to be able to make use of services and medicines (e.g. travel, time off)

Figure 3.1   Causes of poor health.

stages: diagnostic screening and preventative care, where a continuous relationship with one provider is important for routine check-ups; diagnosis and entry, including self-diagnosis and access; treatment effectiveness, which often depends on a person's compliance with treatments; and aftercare or fast readmission.

Knowledge of the prevalence and causes of ill health is the starting point for commissioners to consider a variety of ways of improving health and reducing inequities in health. For example, subsidizing exercise classes for retired people at a community centre may produce greater health gain and be far more cost-effective than some community health services. Under-fives in the West Midlands now have half the tooth decay of comparable areas, mainly because of fluoridated water. Inter-agency action is sufficiently important to require assigning commissioning staff or contracting others to work with other authorities and employers to improve health. Local authorities are major employers and can reduce accidents and smoking in public places, and improve occupational health for their own employees and in local industries. One part of a commissioner's health strategy will be health promotion, whether by specialist health promotion staff or as part of service providers' direct care work.

Health promotion

Health promotion is a variety of types of health education and actions which aim to get people to change their health behaviour. Health promotion also includes disease prevention, for example in screening, health checks and immunization, and may be thought of as: primary prevention, to stop a disease; secondary prevention, to stop a disease getting worse by early detection and treatment; and tertiary prevention, to reduce complications in an irreversible disease. Promotion is also health protection, which includes regulations, codes of practice or laws like health and safety at work, as well as tax policies which help to prevent poor health and promote good health (Downie *et al.* 1992).

Health promotion specialists can help commissioners to develop their health strategy, to form 'healthy alliances' and to evaluate health promotion programmes and provider services. Their own provision roles include giving advice and information directly to clients and to provider staff. There are questions as to how and where they are best managed, and whether units for more than one commissioner are cost-effective. The main options are: managed by a commissioning agency (e.g. within public health), managed by a provider (e.g. a trust) or managed as an independent unit or quasi-independent agency.

Commissioners should recognize that promotion and prevention should not be viewed entirely separately from diagnosis and treatment – for example, screening is also diagnosis. Providers such as GPs, community nurses and hospitals have an important preventative and health promotional role. Competition, market forces and problems in local authorities are making health promotion programmes more difficult, and threatening those 'health alliances' which have been successful (DoH 1993a; Ewles 1993).

Although the cost-effectiveness of many health promotion activities is not proven and is difficult to evaluate, more evidence is becoming available and there are useful guidelines for selecting programmes and priorities. For example, health promotion units (e.g. in Barnet, London) have criteria and models for deciding priorities: assessing whether the method of health promotion embodies certain key principles and could make a significant improvement in health, whether the target is a major cause of premature death or ill health, cost-effectiveness and whether others are working in the same area.

Summary: 'Can't buy me health?'

The ideas of commissioning as a service and of health strategy help NHS commissioning organizations and purchasers in other countries to develop a view of their purpose, and to distinguish their role from that of private purchasers. Although health depends on the amount and quality of health services, it also depends on housing, occupational hazards and a variety of other factors over which commissioners can have some influence. One of the purposes of a commissioning agency is to understand the factors which cause different types of ill health, and to work with and influence other organizations in a variety of ways to reduce the causes of ill health.

There are limits to how much time and energy commissioners can put into this wider purpose. The issue is more one of seeing activities other than purchasing services as legitimate for an NHS commissioner, and of using health gain ideas to develop a health strategy.

Box 3.2   Commissioning is not just buying services

The role of an NHS commissioning organization includes:

- Helping to create healthy environments, where this is within the influence of a commissioner, and where people cannot do this themselves.
- Ensuring that direct services are provided to those most in need: by primary, specialist community and hospital health services, and by social services, so that health is not impaired by lack of social care.
- Ensuring that different services are coordinated for people and their carers.

To do this, commissioning agencies need to:

- Know what the health needs are.
- Understand how health is affected by service provision and other factors.
- Decide the health priorities for the finance available.
- Work with local authorities to plan and commission services.
- Work with others to change unhealthy environments.
- Commission services, and ensure they are coordinated.
- Measure changes in health caused by service provision and evaluate how the population benefits from the service provided.

So far we have considered the content of a strategy for health gain, but have not considered how a commissioner formulates and revises a health strategy. In the next section on models of commissioning we consider the process of commissioning. (Further guidance about strategy formulation for health commissioning can be found in Eskin (1992), and a general text which discusses strategy formulation is Kanter (1983).)

The work of NHS commissioners: models and assumptions

In this section we consider how models of commissioning can help managers to translate a view of the purpose of commissioning into work, tasks and organization. A model simplifies and draws attention to what is important. Examples are:

- The IHSM/HFMA (1990) model of the contracting process.
- An early King's Fund model, focusing on the chief executive and the four activities of maintaining the vision for health, managing external relationships, managing the business and developing partnerships.
- Prowle's (1992) model of the purchasing process.
- The Audit Commission's (1993a) model of four groups of operational objectives for DHAs: improving current providers' quality and efficiency;

transferring providers; replacing or ceasing ineffective services; and objectives for working with other organizations and the community.

Most commissioning organizations use a model of commissioning to help to clarify the tasks which need to be done and the type of relationships which they need to establish. This model may be the one presented in the chief executive's vision for the organization. In this section of the chapter, commissioning managers are encouraged to reassess the model of commissioning which they and their organization hold. Consider which aspects of commissioning the model highlights and obscures. Consider the explicit or implicit conception of the purpose of commissioning behind the model – is this valid in the current circumstances? Consider whether the model helps to translate an appropriate view of purpose into the key tasks and relationships for achieving that purpose. Does the answer to the question 'why' any tasks or relationships are important naturally lead to a satisfactory higher-order statement of purpose?

Some models are useful for clarifying the work of contracting and other aspects of commissioning. However, as comprehensive models for deciding organization and work, many models have two limitations. They do not make explicit the conception of the purpose of NHS commissioning and of an NHS commissioning organization which underlies their selection of the things they highlight. In some cases it is difficult to see any view of the purpose and end result of commissioning which underpins the model. The second limitation is that, where there is a conception of purpose – explicit or implicit – it may not correspond to the view held in a particular commissioning organization. Some models which are presented as general models do not recognize a role beyond contracting, and view external relationships as primarily concerned with contracting.

This chapter presents a conception of the purpose of NHS commissioning which is broader than contracting services. Many models of commissioning have a more limited implicit or explicit conception of purpose, and managers need to judge which models are most suited to their own situation and which best help them to focus and organize their work. The following puts forward models of the process and structure of commissioning which are based on the conception of the purpose of commissioning as health gain and on a view of the strategic role of a commissioning organization. The first is a familiar process model, or more accurately a list of commissioning tasks in sequence, but one which recognizes a broader health gain purpose. The second is a model of levels of purchasing work.

A model of the commissioning process

Models of the commissioning process as a contracting cycle typically represent different phases in succession, starting from needs assessment, and moving to planning purchasing strategy, specifying services, negotiating contracts, monitoring and then returning to needs assessment. One weakness of such models is in not recognizing purposes beyond service purchasing

– typically needs assessment is to decide which services to purchase, and relations with the public and GPs are orientated to this purpose. A second weakness is in implying that each phase is undertaken in succession, when in fact work on each subject is continuous and interactive as emphasized in Figure 6.1.

The following list shows key commissioning tasks. While not offering a model of the commissioning process, it helps to link statements of purpose to the commissioning work to be done, and can show how different tasks inform each other. The work of commissioning involves:

- *technical assessment* of the health needs of the population (from public health epidemiological, DHA and FHSA and provider data);
- *seeking citizens' views* about priorities and services;
- ensuring that *'silent' citizens' needs* and interests are recognized and upheld in different purchasing decisions (e.g. the homeless, people in institutions, very old people);
- seeking and using *GPs' views* about needs and services in commissioning decisions;
- formulating local health *priorities*, within national policies and targets, involving resolving conflicts between competing priorities;
- formulating *health aims and strategies*, and a view of the role of other agencies in achieving these;
- *planning* which services to purchase to meet priority needs, using information about effectiveness and provider performance;
- *influencing providers* to plan and establish services so that the services are there to be purchased in the future;
- *coordinating* planning and contracting with other purchasing and providing agencies (e.g. fundholding GPs);
- *contract management*, i.e. negotiating and monitoring contracts to reflect the purchasing plan, and organizing payments;
- *evaluating the impact on health* and the cost-effectiveness of commissioned services and other activities;
- *'support work'* to the above work (e.g. commissioner staff training, recruitment, office systems).

The disadvantages of such task-list models of commissioning are:

- that they do not clearly distinguish authority commissioning from GP purchasing (fundholders claim that they do, or could, carry out most of the above for some or all needs and services);
- that they do not reveal conflicts between different influences, or highlight the work of managing conflicting requirements which is central to commissioning as a service;
- that lists of tasks often mix the methods for doing the work with the aims and objectives to be achieved, as well as mixing descriptions of work at different levels of abstraction (e.g. 'ensuring a comprehensive range of services are purchased' and 'contract management' – contract

Work	Examples of output	Sets limits to
Comprehensive health commissioning (Over 4-year perspective)	Health strategy	The role of health services, and health promotion
Strategic health service purchasing (2–4 year)	Purchasing strategy	The future pattern of services, which providers to contract
Systematic service commissioning (1–2 year)	Renegotiating volume contract, devising systems for different commissioning tasks, e.g. ECR payments	Where, when and with whom tactical purchasing can be undertaken
Tactical and situational service commissioning (1 month to 1 year)	Contract or authorization for an individual treatment, or handling a serious complaint	How clerical and other staff deal with a particular issue
Prescribed commissioning (timescale 1 hour to 1 month)	Dealing with invoices and billing, paying ECRs, GPs, patient registration	

Figure 3.2 Levels of decision-making and commissioning work.

management is, or should be, a lower-level task carried out to further a higher-level aim).

A model of levels of commissioning

This model (Figure 3.2) emphasizes the strategic purpose of commissioning. We noted that commissioners are developing a view of their purpose which is more than contracting services and which involves formulating a health strategy. This broader and longer-term approach is what some mean by 'stronger purchasing', although the test will be whether such strategies are carried through in practice. Commissioners have been able to take this approach because they have begun to undertake 'higher-level' work and to develop an understanding of what high-level commissioning work involves. Figure 3.2 outlines a model of levels of decision-making and of commissioning work according to complexity and time perspective.

Many of the tasks in the process list model above involve work at two or more levels. For example, contract management involves work to devise systems, as well as tactical and situational decisions, and also invoice payment work, for both hospitals and independent contractors. Each level of work sets the context for work in the levels below. For example, the work of comprehensive health commissioning defines health needs and the type of health service to be purchased. It sets the boundaries between health, social services and other services, and defines the purpose of health commissioning and health services in the area. It is this work which sets the context for strategic health service purchasing, which is concerned with which services to purchase over a two to four year period. This involves planning and managing the transfer of large contracts for specialties and the developments in primary care services, as well as planning specific joint projects with social services. This work, in turn, sets the context for the work of systematic service commissioning over the one to two year timescale.

This or some other model of levels of commissioning helps commissioners to make a bridge from general purposes and lists of tasks to how they organize the work. In theory there are arguments for a corresponding five levels of management structure, with staff at each level only undertaking work at that level, although they may do so in groups. In practice, staff will undertake tasks at two or maybe more levels, although their actual output may not be at the level required: for example, a purchasing strategy may not take a sufficiently long-term or comprehensive view, or be sufficiently realistic or thought through to be carried out.

A model of levels of commissioning also helps commissioners to form and examine options for locality purchasing, in particular which tasks should be decentralized. For example, in some options localities undertake strategic health service purchasing work, while in others they only undertake tactical purchasing. It also helps to distinguish the role of health commissioner authorities from GP fundholders, who would not undertake comprehensive health commissioning work. It helps to distinguish different fundholders according to the level at which they are operating: some only undertake tactical commissioning, others do systematic service commissioning. We return to these issues in the chapters on commissioner organization and locality purchasing.

Finally, such a model helps to clarify the information needs of different staff working in a commissioning organization. Commissioner information strategies aim to help their staff make more informed decisions. To develop information systems and strategy, commissioners need to clarify the different decisions to be made by different staff, using process models but also using models of levels of decisions. Davis and Olsen (1985) describe a model of four levels which can be used for developing management information systems for commissioning.

Summary and conclusions: from purpose to tasks

Foreign observers of the NHS may well be bemused by the way the English language is used in discussions of the NHS. One of the more peculiar terms, which native speakers who work in the NHS also found curious, was the term 'commissioning'. Certainly 'commissioning' rather than 'purchasing' does convey the idea that the purpose of NHS commissioning organizations is more than buying services. The ideas of patronage and art, which are also connoted by the term, are apt. Commissioning authorities are, in one sense, patrons of local hospitals and services, which are independent but depend on authorities' continued patronage. Placing a contract is more like commissioning a work of art than contracting in the commercial world: commissioners have little control over the outcome of the service or how professionals operate, and have difficulties in withdrawing their commission if they do not like the final product, assuming that they can tell good from bad.

For their part, some GPs and providers also consider that commissioning conveys another idea: of a hotel or cinema 'commissioner' – in the UK called the 'jobsworth', whose main reason for existence appears to be to police bureaucratic rules and increase costs for little benefit. This image goes to the root of the problem with NHS commissioning organizations: public suspicion about their function and who they are really serving. An NHS authority receives a commission from the Queen's government to carry out an important mission, and commissions others (e.g. service providers) to act on state business. Are the public the restless natives who do not know what is for their own good?

One aim of this chapter was to encourage commissioning managers and others critically to review the purpose of NHS commissioning: to use their own experience of what is feasible, as well as current thinking, to ask what is NHS commissioning for, what is it trying to achieve and what is the purpose of the commissioning organization for which I work? It argued that an understanding of purpose is the basis for deciding work, tasks and organization. A common shared understanding of purpose within a commissioning organization generates energy for the work, if it corresponds to people's values. Cooperation between commissioning organizations is easier if all share a common understanding of the purpose of NHS commissioning.

A second aim of the chapter was to present the author's conception of commissioning as 'making the best use of available finance to improve health and prevent illness, by influencing other organizations to contribute to these ends and by contracting health services'. This forms the yardstick for judging the approaches to commissioning discussed in other chapters. It allows us to question whether certain types of organization, policies, techniques or models help to advance this particular conception of purpose, either in practice or in the theory of commissioning. I would hope that many question the conception offered in this chapter, but more important is that the chapter provokes a critical review of the purpose of commissioning in the light of experience and ideas about what NHS commissioning is trying to achieve in the late 1990s, and for whom.

The practical theme of the chapter was that a clear idea of the purpose and role of a commissioning agency gives staff a reference point in the complexities of their everyday work and helps them to set priorities. Many of the problems and choices faced by health commissioners are made more difficult by managers and staff not having a clear and shared understanding of the distinctive role and aims of the organization. For example, decisions about shifting contracts or about the aims and structures for locality purchasing need to be guided by a view of the purpose of commissioning and of the work to be done. Decisions about investment in primary care and prevention will be pushed to one side by financial decisions about hospitals, unless commissioners have a view of purpose which extends beyond buying hospital services. An understanding of the purpose of NHS commissioning helps us to select more carefully from good practices in private health purchasing, and to judge the relevance of experience of purchasing in other countries and systems.

This is not to suggest that nothing can be done until purposes are clear and widely understood, a fallacy second only to the fallacy that one cannot act until one has complete information. Purposes are always clarified and understood in action: by looking at the direction in which the organization is going and at what different staff are doing with their time; by 'reading off' from actions the implicit purpose of everyone's efforts, and by stopping and questioning whether what one is doing is furthering the purpose of the organization. Neither is it to imply that this chapter gave a definitive statement of the purpose of NHS commissioning or of an NHS commissioning organization. Rather, the chapter aimed to raise the question of purpose, to outline current thinking and to consider what a commissioning organization is for in terms of the end results for the people it serves. It argued that an evolving and shared sense of purpose gives spirit and energy to the work of commissioning, and that agency strategy, structure and processes have to be consistent with this purpose.

Key points

- Stronger and more proactive commissioning depends on an understanding of the distinctive purpose and role of a commissioning organization. This understanding must be shared by all staff.
- The purpose and values of the NHS give some guidance for defining the purpose of NHS commissioning. Values are not the same as purpose, but guide how purpose is defined and pursued.
- The concept of health gain helps to redefine the purpose of NHS commissioning as seeking improvements in health, with contracting services as an intermediate aim.
- There are disadvantages with the breadth of the concept of health gain for defining the purpose of a commissioning organization – commissioners need to define the boundaries of their responsibilities for health.
- The central purpose of an NHS commissioning organization is to provide a service to a population. The service it performs is the difference it makes for the population.
- Commissioners need to make more use of concepts and techniques from

service management to clarify and publicize the value of commissioning for their population, to develop their relations with them, and to improve the effectiveness of commissioning.

- If the purpose of commissioning is health gain then the health strategy of a commissioning organization is to commission health promotion, to influence healthy environments and behaviour, and commission services for people who are ill.
- Models of commissioning can help commissioning managers to clarify the work and relationships of a commissioning organization, as long as the model is based on an adequate conception of the purpose of commissioning.

4 'Decentralized' or 'locality' purchasing

Introduction

The subject of this chapter is how to decentralize and devolve purchasing to be sensitive to local needs, yet also to retain the advantages of size and the strategic capability of a large purchasing organization. This subject is of interest to health purchasers and policy-makers in many countries, and involves consideration of the advantages and disadvantages of devolving purchasing budgets to primary care providers, and of how to regulate local purchasers. In this chapter we look at UK versions of decentralized health authority purchasing, or 'locality commissioning'. This term describes different ways in which health authorities organize commissioning work for distinct geographical populations within their area, which can involve basing staff in local offices.

As with other chapters, an underlying theme is how the method – locality purchasing – furthers the purpose of health commissioning as a service. Locality commissioning is a method which a service organization like a commissioning organization can use to be more responsive to its 'customers'. The chapter aims to help purchasers to develop an approach which is suited to their populations, to the issues which they have to tackle and to their view of the purpose of health commissioning. It emphasizes clarifying the purpose of decentralizing purchasing, and relating this to the overall purpose of a commissioning organization. In addition, it emphasizes that commissioning managers can learn from modern service organization and management theory about how large organizations can decentralize functions and create responsive service units.

The first two sections review the history and details of locality commissioning schemes (summarized in Appendix 4). They note different ideas referred to by the term 'locality', both in purchasing and in service provision. The next sections categorize different approaches in terms of their purpose, type of decentralization, and needs and services covered. The last sections of the chapter present ideas which UK commissioners have found useful in clarifying the work and purpose for localities, and give guidelines for examining the options for decentralized purchasing.

The UK context for decentralizing purchasing

In the first two years of the NHS reforms, district health authority (DHA) commissioning was dominated by acute hospital considerations, by providers' views and by the GP fundholder 'threat'. With more GPs becoming fundholders, DHAs became concerned that they were losing purchasing finance and their ability to purchase strategically, and any legitimacy which they had with the public. One response was to form larger commissioning authorities or consortia, but this increased their remoteness from GPs and their residents, especially when staff were centralized from smaller, merged DHAs. Another response, often by the same larger commissioners, was to seek ways to offer GPs some of the advantages of fundholding, and also to develop relationships with people and groups in local areas. A tension between 'localities for GPs' and 'localities for local people' exists in some schemes.

Fundholding is not a threat to family health service authorities (FHSAs) but involves them in a considerable amount of work. Regional health authorities required FHSAs to explain the scheme to GPs, calculate and negotiate a fund budget, advise on applications and oversee and administer a fund once it was devolved to GPs. During 1993 and 1994 there were three changes. First, as more DHAs and FHSAs formed closer links or agencies, existing and potential fundholders became concerned that they were now being monitored by their main purchasing 'competitor' – the DHA, even though FHSAs continued as statutory authorities. Second, some authorities began to view fundholders as less of a threat, and more of a potential ally, and fundholders recognized that they needed to cooperate with authorities: the term 'shared purchasing' embodied the wish for closer cooperation. This, in part, was the result of the intensive efforts of some authorities to improve their relations with all GPs. Third, authorities began to develop 'locality purchasing schemes' which gave GPs a stronger influence over commissioning for their populations.

An issue for purchasers is how primary care purchasing or fundholding can weaken or potentially strengthen their emerging strategic capabilities. Locality purchasing may offer a way of both responding to immediate GP concerns and advancing strategic aims. Locality purchasing is a more complex issue for integrated agencies or authorities than for DHA-only commissioners, but offers greater potential. As we see in the examples later, DHAs or consortia have developed a locality approach mainly to organize GP and community involvement in secondary care purchasing decisions.

This is an important aim for integrated agencies, but in addition there are opportunities to organize some FHSA work on a locality basis – perhaps the same localities and using the same staff – and to pool DHA and FHSA finance for localities. We consider these and other options later.

This chapter puts forward a concept of purchasing localities as a 'bridge' for resources between secondary and primary care, and as a support for improving primary and community care. This is an intermediate aim towards the purpose of commissioning for health gain. In some areas, integrated locality purchasing is possible, combining devolved purchasing budgets for both health and social services. It also notes the potential links between locality provision schemes and purchasing on a local basis, and the possibility of devolving integrated purchasing to a locality which also has integrated provision by health and social services (e.g. an integrated primary care team).

Issues raised by commissioning managers and addressed by this chapter include:

- *What are 'localities' for? Should locality commissioning be for improving relations with GPs, 'shared purchasing', community involvement, or all of these and more?*
- *How do we define localities for commissioning?*
- *What are the different options open to us for localities?*
- *Should we decentralize staff and offices to a locality?*
- *Is the cost of giving staff commissioning responsibilities for a locality worth the benefits, and can we afford to with a 1 per cent limit to commissioner costs?*

Concepts of 'locality'

History: locality provision, planning and purchasing

Over the years there have been many schemes for providing a coordinated range of health or social services, or both, to local communities. One of the earliest in the UK was the community health centre movement, which can be traced back to the early 1920s. In the 1970s and 1980s the concept was advanced by organizational theories of decentralization, which influenced social service reorganizations in particular, and by devolved general management in the NHS. More recently, locality provision schemes have been viewed as a way to organize for better customer service, as well as a way to increase community participation in running and planning services.

Locality provision schemes in the UK include the Norwich 'patch' approach discussed in Chapter 8 (Bailey 1987), Cumberlege 'patch' nursing (1986), changes proposed in the Edwards nursing report for Wales (1987), current 'patch' teams in Northern Ireland (Øvretveit 1991a; Tonks 1993), and experiments for integrated services arising from the community care reforms. There are also many similar reported primary health care schemes in other countries (e.g. the USA, Sweden, Finland, Australia, and in the two thirds World).

In the 1980s many DHAs also used local schemes to introduce local perspectives into planning services for different client groups, for example in mental health and learning disabilities, and for community services (e.g. in Exeter (King and Court 1984) and the Rhondda Valley (Øvretveit and Davies 1988)). Since 1990, the term 'locality' has been used with respect to purchasing, and to describe ways of making purchasing decisions more sensitive to local needs.

Box 4.1

Locality provision
To provide to a community of between 20,000 and 60,000 population a range of health and social services, which are continually reshaped to the particular needs of the population, from a base in a prominent and easily accessible position in the area.

Locality purchasing
Organizing commissioning work to ensure that purchasing is sensitive to local needs and views, typically by devolving purchasing decisions to a locality manager or group, or by reflecting a locality's needs and views in central purchasing decisions.

In some areas, all or some purchasing and provision can be organized on a locality basis, opening up new possibilities for local and responsive services.

Examples are locality based or orientated purchasing by health authorities, by GP consortia and, increasingly, by social services, who sometimes organize their purchasing on a locality rather than client-group basis, with purchasing locality managers and teams. Examples of the former are within North East Westminster and the DHAs of Dorset, North Yorkshire, Stockport, East Sussex, South East London, Bath, North Derbyshire and Northampton. Examples of social care locality purchasing are found in social service departments in Berkshire, Islington, Kent and Bedfordshire. Hillingdon is exploring joint commissioning on a locality basis.

From an FHSA viewpoint, localities are mainly a way of conducting service development and needs analysis, rather than for 'purchasing'. In 1993–4 the FHSA purchasing role (discussed in Chapter 10) was limited to contributing finance for practice staff and facilities, mainly because GP contracts are precisely regulated, but this may change. In examining options, commissioners will need to consider the scope for decentralizing and organizing FHSA work on a locality basis.

Advantages over GP fundholding

One question is how health authority locality commissioning differs from and compares with GP fundholding. The answer depends on the model, but, in general, locality purchasing:

- allows GPs to influence the full range of hospital and community services purchased by a health authority, rather than the more limited range of the GP fundholding scheme;
- saves GPs the time, trouble and expense of fundholding, but gives some of the advantages, albeit shared with a larger number of GPs;
- retains the purchasing power of large contracts but allows GPs' and others' preferences to be built into contracts;
- can allow community interests other than GPs to be represented in commissioning decisions;
- makes the best use of scarce commissioning staff expertise and contracting systems;
- counteracts the potential and perceived remoteness of larger commissioning authorities;
- provides one way of integrating a variety of FHSA and DHA activities.

The disadvantages also depend on the model, but, in general, are that GPs have less influence over secondary care purchasing, and less opportunity or fewer incentives to reinvest savings into their practice. This is not to suggest that health authorities or policy-makers only compare locality commissioning to fundholding; there are a range of options. We will consider how different types of locality commissioning advance the purpose of the commissioning organization and its role as a service. First we review some examples, and then we summarize these in terms of the different purposes served, and consider the lessons for commissioners from the experience to date.

Locality purchasing: some examples

The following considers the North Yorkshire and Stockport models, and a proposal for an integrated model. It then describes one GP-orientated model, showing the similarities and differences to fundholding, the work involved to establish the model and its future potential for GP resource management.

North Yorkshire

North Yorkshire provides an example of an approach for secondary care purchasing, and one based on local communities with which people identify.

It is a large authority (720,000 population), formed in 1991–2 from five smaller DHAs, within which some of the locality purchasing structure is organized. The authority did detailed research to identify local communities, and defined 24, each of between 20,000 and 40,000, which are similar to local electoral ward boundaries. North Yorkshire viewed these localities as the basic 'building block' and grouped them together in different ways for different purposes, for example to match local authority boundaries for some issues or to involve GPs. North Yorkshire has a decentralized management structure, with some staff from all directorates based in each of five local offices covering populations of 125,000. Each office also has some county-wide responsibilities, as well as responsibilities for localities which they serve. However, budgets are still centralized, and local staff are accountable to authority directors, not to locality 'leaders'.

Stockport

The approach taken by Stockport gives a practical illustration of the concept of levels of purchasing (Chapter 3) for different sized populations. It is also of interest because Stockport has a joint DHA–FHSA executive, a small population of 295,000 and a structure which combines a locality dimension with a care group (client-based) planning approach. Stockport has four 'tiers' of purchasing: 'neighbourhoods' of 10,000, six 'sectors' of 50,000, a DHA–FHSA tier of 295,000, and a 'consortium tier' for a population of one million. The neighbourhoods are based on electoral wards because it was thought that this, rather than a GP list, was better for commissioning work other than buying treatments, such as health promotion, public health, community care and planning primary and secondary care.

The sector or 'locality' managers (which Stockport calls 'health strategy managers') have, for each of their neighbourhoods, consultative arrangements, a neighbourhood plan and a public health advocate, for example a health visitor working on commissioning issues on a sessional basis. The locality/strategy managers work half-time for and in their sector, and half-time on cross-district care-group strategy work, such as mental health planning for the district.

The six locality/strategy managers are part of a management structure which combines their role with another 'wing' of functional directorates for the FHSA and DHA. The aim is to devolve DHA and FHSA purchasing budgets to the locality/strategy managers, and to offer GPs a variety of degrees and types of involvement in authority purchasing. Fundholders have the opportunity to 'piggy-back' on different authority contracts, or even to 'buy' a contract management system from the authority. Non-fundholders can take part in locality purchasing, in some cases with nominal locality budgets, or can opt for specific allocations to the practice for 'practice-sensitive purchasing'.

Appendix 4 compares summaries of the North Yorkshire and Stockport approaches to those of Dorset, East Sussex, South East London, Bath, North Derbyshire and Northampton. Ham (1992b) also provides details of different approaches. Appendix 3 describes the approaches of seven integrated commissioning agencies in the North West Thames Region with populations of between 240,000 and 992,000. Before we turn to the details of one GP-orientated approach, it is worth noting one integrated theoretical model.

An integrated locality purchasing model: 'social health and welfare centres and teams'

This speculative model is of a 'social health and welfare centre' (SHWC), which is allocated funds from an integrated commissioning agency to purchase some services directly for its population of between 10,000 and 20,000. Five to ten social health and welfare teams (SHWT) would cover the population of each SHWC. Each team of 20 staff, serving 2,000 people, would, in effect, be care managers, assess needs and 'refer to providers against predetermined contracts for services made by either the district or the SHWC'. The description of the model does not indicate whether they may also provide some services, or if budgets would be delegated to them (HSMU 1992). There are some similarities with the Swedish (e.g. Dalarna County) district purchasing and providing boards for hospital, primary and some social care (10,000–25,000 population) (Saltman and von Otter 1992).

The North East Westminster Locality Project

Kensington, Chelsea and Westminster (KCW) is an integrated commissioning agency in inner London. The locality scheme is a good illustration of the advantages and disadvantages of GP-orientated approaches. Plans for the scheme were laid in 1991 to involve GPs in planning and purchasing decisions made by this inner-London DHA. The aims were to make purchasing more sensitive to the needs of the population, as understood by GPs in the area, and, in the long term, to encourage GPs to take responsibility for managing a purchasing budget. It took until July 1992 to get the scheme running because of the considerable amount of work needed to agree representation and voting mechanisms with GPs. The scheme is different to fundholding in that the GPs in the scheme influence all DHA purchasing for people in the area ('a devolved mini-DHA'), and that the population is defined by an area, and not by GP lists.

The scheme covers purchasing for people in a defined area (including homeless people and commuters) who are served by GPs in and outside that area. The scheme covers the people resident in the locality (65,000: the OPCS postcode estimate for the area is 53,500), not those registered with the 33 GPs in 20 practices sited in the locality (42,500; 8,500 residents were registered with non-KCW GPs). The scheme thus involves 55 GPs, including one fundholding practice, and GPs based outside the locality but serving people living in the locality.

The commissioning agency employs a locality manager to 'coordinate all GP practices in the area to maximize their influence on the whole range of purchasing decisions'. The locality manager is accountable to the director of purchasing and 'steered' by nominees of the GPs, the DHA and the FHSA. There are monthly meetings of a 'locality group' which can be attended by any member (GPs in the locality). This group elects five GPs to an 'executive group', which also includes, as 'representatives', the locality manager, the director of purchasing and representatives from the other KCW directorates of primary care, finance and public health. The agency chief executive may veto any decision of the group. Surveys of GPs' views about services and their purchasing priorities for 1993–4 were carried out using a questionnaire by Bristol University. Further work on needs assessment is under way, as is consideration of the 'locality budget for purchasing'.

By the summer of 1993, after 18 months' of careful preparation, the scheme had won GP credibility, and produced some tangible changes:

- one contract for 50 gynaecology treatments was switched from one provider to two others, on cost and quality criteria;
- an ear, nose and throat services contract was changed to another provider because of GPs' concerns about quality;
- GPs and consultants agreed specifications for outpatient clinics for the locality with a dedicated time;
- one clinic was established in a GP's surgery and open to all in the area;
- a social service department liaison worker was appointed to the locality for care of the elderly/disabled.

Some of the issues involved in establishing and running this project included:

- *GP representation.* GPs were very concerned about fair representation, and a lot of time and effort was needed to work out and agree an acceptable mechanism, but the locality manager reported that this was time well spent. A fairly complex voting mechanism had to be agreed for issues which needed full voting (one vote per 700 North East Westminster residents, 78 votes in all). The membership of the locality group was changed as the scheme evolved to 31 practices and 55 GPs.
- *Mechanisms* for identifying a budget and for feeding locality views into agency contracts. It took time to develop both these mechanisms, and there are still questions of how best to influence strategy and contract negotiations. The aim is to move to all contracts for the locality being separate from the main district contracts.
- *GPs managing purchasing.* The scheme has involved GPs in purchasing, who are now developing referral-protocols with peer review, and learning how to manage a purchasing budget, although it is yet to be seen how

they manage cost/quality conflicts. The aim in the future is to integrate DHA/FHSA information about needs and services for the locality, and to educate GPs for a locality-budget-management role. The scheme has yet to work out incentives to carry-out more hospital work in practices or clinics, and to link with the role of GPs as providers – at present in this respect it is less effective than fundholding for developing primary care, although it holds the potential for such incentives.

Lessons for other commissioners

The KCW model, like many other decentralized purchasing models in the UK, is at present a GP-dominated secondary-care purchasing model, and it will be difficult to adapt it to involve other sections of the community in a wider range of purchasing issues, such as rationing decisions. It took a considerable amount of time to set up and to win true GP involvement: they were suspicious that the scheme was 'a token' and, when they did find they had influence, were very concerned about representation and 'fairness'. The locality manager emphasized the need to recognize that many GPs do not understand NHS management and how the NHS works. Many also tend to think that mistakes, even in a pilot, are conspiracies. The locality manager recommended being clear about what a commissioner wants from a locality scheme, what is in it for GPs and for others, and what the scheme cannot do. She stressed the importance in the pilot of good communications between the locality executive, other GPs, the agency, the CHC and users, and of reserving the right of veto for the agency chief executive, as well as being prepared to manage conflicts between what the locality wanted and the agency view.

In conclusion, it is notable that although GPs are very 'individualistic' in their concerns about their practice and individual patients (e.g. voting procedures), in this pilot they were ready to take a broad population view, were concerned about equality and 'spreading quotas' of homeless patients. This model does seem to be able to balance purchasing for individuals with purchasing for populations, but is GP-dominated and involves a considerable amount of work to set up and run. The tests are whether it can be developed to involve GPs in effective resource and demand management, how GPs in the scheme cope with some of the decisions the agency will have to make about large contracts in the London hospital reconfiguration, and how it can be linked to incentives for improving primary care provision.

Questions in developing locality purchasing

In my review of commissioners' different approaches, the following stand out as the common and central questions which had to be addressed by agencies developing a pilot or a policy for locality purchasing:

- What are the purposes and priorities of the agency, and can these only be achieved with a locality dimension to the agency's work?
- What purpose(s) is the model to serve?
- What work do you do or need to do on a smaller geographical basis?
- Do you need any of your staff or managers to be dedicated part- or full-time to work for, or in, this smaller geographical area (a geographical dimension in your management structure)?

The next section gives answers which some have found to these questions.

Models of decentralized and locality purchasing

The examples above show that there are many different approaches to locality purchasing. To help agencies develop their approach, the following summarizes some of the main purposes of locality purchasing. It then distinguishes centralized and decentralized models to give a framework for comparing different schemes.

Purposes, reasons and functions

The reasons why DHAs have developed locality purchasing, and the functions served, include:

- to *gather GP views* about services, to inform DHA purchasing decisions, typically about how much of which services to purchase, quality requirements and changes to services wanted by GPs;
- to *prove to GPs* that they can gain many of the benefits of fundholding and influence a wide range of purchasing decisions without the costs and risks of becoming a fundholder;
- to involve GPs in *managing budgets and demand* and to develop peer influence over 'excessive' referrals to hospitals or prescribing;
- a basis for *coordinating* health authority purchasing and planning with others' purchasing and planning (mainly that of local authority, and GP fundholders), both tactically (e.g. agreeing a common approach to standards or prices) and strategically (e.g. purchasing to develop certain services);
- a basis for organizing the *assessment* of the health needs of different areas within a purchaser's boundary (both 'hard' and 'soft' data);
- a basis for building *common databases* about needs and services among DHA, FHSA and local authorities;
- *politically*, a basis for organizing people and interest groups in a community to give their views and to involve them in purchasing issues and a way of increasing legitimacy and accountability (there are many purposes to, and types of, 'public involvement').

Some models aim to serve more than one of these purposes. We noted above that the KCW pilot was finding it difficult to add community involvement to its GP-organized arrangements. Few have as an explicit aim the purpose of giving a better service to the public. Commissioners can develop locality schemes and organization to make this purpose more prominent. They can draw on ideas from service management and organization to improve the service they provide and their relations with the public.

An analysis of models of centralized and decentralized commissioning

In simple terms, decentralized and locality purchasing approaches fall into two broad types: 'devolved budget' and 'central purchasing'. In the former the commissioning authority devolves a budget to a locality for the locality to use to purchase services. In its pure form, the locality could contract and purchase directly and entirely independently for some or all services, like a GP fundholder. Purchaser management cost constraints preclude this, even if it could be shown to be cost-effective – there would also be problems about cross-authority consistency between localities. In 'central purchasing', locality views and needs analyses are used to inform central contracting and planning. This may be more cost-effective, but also less responsive and may not give GPs or local people sufficient influence. In practice, decentralizing purchasing is about deciding which work and contracts are best handled centrally and which locally – we look at how to consider this issue shortly.

To examine the scope and options for decentralized commissioning we need to consider at least three elements. Decentralized purchasing involves:

- a locality budget, identifying a purchasing budget for a sub-population (for all or some services);
- devolving purchasing authority to those in the area to decide how some or all of the purchasing budget is spent;
- locality commissioner structure, purchasing staff working part- or full-time on commissioning work for the sub-population, and based in the area.

Some decentralized locality models involve only one of these. None at present have purchasing budgets devolved to a locality manager to agree contracts and purchase service independently, as do some social service models – all have centralized contract management and central veto over locality decisions. By decentralizing budgets, HAs can work out what regulations are required to constrain the scope of locality purchasing, without losing control as they have with fundholders and trying to build up controls.

In centralized locality models, no staff are assigned full-time to a locality or based in the area. In these models, staff at HQ may undertake some commissioning work on a 'locality basis', for example by doing needs assessment for geographical sub-populations using DHA and FHSA information, rather than for the whole population by care group or medical condition. The degree of decentralization depends mainly on how much

Central purchasing based on locality information	*Community consultation schemes (e.g. Dorset, SE London)*		*Some FHSA 'purchasing'*	
Degree of decentralization	*Practice-sensitive purchasing (e.g. Bath, N Derbyshire) NE Westminster*			
Devolved budgets and direct contracting by a locality	*GP fundholding*			*e.g. Berkshire SSD*
	Hospital care	Community health care	Family practitioner services	Social care
		Services purchased		

Figure 4.1 Types of 'locality purchasing'.

of what type of authority is devolved to the locality. Some authorities start with a centralized model and then decentralize one or more of the three elements listed above.

Locality approaches also need to be viewed in terms of which services are to be purchased. Most of the examples above are for DHA purchasing of secondary care services (usually only hospital services), but many are trying to link this with FHSA locality commissioning, whether or not there is an integrated agency or authority. Few are considering linking to social services commissioning, even if social services have a locality purchasing structure.

Thus, in summarizing the main options for authorities, we need to recognize that centralized or decentralized models can be used to plan and to purchase hospital health care, community health care (e.g. community nursing and therapy services) and family practitioner services, or all three. Purchaser–provider separation and care management in social services makes possible integrated health and social care locality purchasing.

For commissioners developing their own approach, the list of purposes above helps to clarify the purpose of decentralization, and to link this to the overall view of the purpose of the organization. The framework in Figure 4.1 helps to clarify the degree of decentralization and the scope of coverage.

Combining all DHA and FHSA responsibilities in one locality manager post may be cost-effective and allow GPs to relate to one commissioning manager, but there is a disadvantage: fundholding GPs may prefer to relate to a central FHSA group for fund-monitoring purposes. A more gradual approach is to devolve some FHSA functions to develop the service-giving role and relations with local people: for example, devolving responsibilities for patient registration and information services. We now turn to other ideas to help develop a suitable approach to locality commissioning.

Considerations in developing locality commissioning

A planned approach requires commissioners to clarify the work to be done and the main purpose which they need locality purchasing to serve. This, in turn, needs to be related to a view of the purpose of the commissioning organization and an understanding of commissioning as a service. Part of the problem is that commissioners often do not have a clear view of their distinctive purpose and work. Thus the following refers back to Chapter 3's discussion of the purpose and work of commissioning to help consider which work is best organized on a locality basis. The considerations and ideas which help are: resource constraints and priorities; purchasing process and tasks; levels of commissioning; decentralization; population size and epidemiological stability; and purchasing power.

Purchaser resources and priorities

Purchasing organizations have limited staff time and budgets to devote to locality commissioning. However, most locality models are for doing commissioning tasks on a locality basis. The issue is not one of 'taking staff away from commissioning work' for a 'special project', but the relative merits of organizing commissioning work on a different decentralized basis and of developing local relationships. The main consideration is the cost-effectiveness of different approaches. Some cost considerations tend towards centralization: certainly contract management is more economically handled on a central basis, and there are cost arguments against true decentralized commissioning, including retaining bulk purchasing power in large contracts. To make maximum use of staff capability, some authorities wishing to have high-level locality purchasing make high-level appointments of staff with both locality responsibilities and strategic cross-authority responsibilities for different care groups (e.g. Stockport). Another approach is to contract out some or all locality commissioning work, possibly to a local provider or voluntary organization.

The cost-effectiveness of different locality schemes also depends on the primary purposes and strategic priorities of a commissioner. Not having a locality dimension to purchasing may be economical, but it may not allow a commissioning organization effectively to pursue its priorities and might be a false economy. A commissioning organization needs to list the purposes which it wants a locality scheme to serve, and then clarify the importance of different purchasing responsibilities in its overall strategy. For example, if representing community views is considered the most important, then locality boundaries would be built on the communities with which people identify, rather than based on GP lists, or practice groupings, or district council boundaries.

This clarification of importance follows from a vision for the long-term future role of a commissioning organization. It will take time for commissioners to develop this vision, so one approach is to 'play safe' and build a locality approach which could be adapted to, or fulfil in part, a number of different purposes. This approach is the one proposed in the last part of this chapter, in part because it may offer the best way of defining localities to 'bridge' resources from secondary to primary care.

Commissioning process and tasks

Models and lists of the commissioning process also give some help in considering the work and purpose of locality purchasing. Are any of the following tasks more cost-effectively organized on a locality basis, or on an agency and authority-wide basis?

- *Technical assessment* of the health needs of the population, using epidemiological, FHSA and provider data.
- *Seeking citizens' views* about priorities and services.
- Ensuring that *'silent' citizens' needs* and interests are recognized and upheld in different purchasing decisions.
- Seeking and using *GPs' views* about needs and services in commissioning decisions.
- Formulating local health *priorities*, within national policies and targets.
- Formulating *health aims and strategies*, and a view of the role of other agencies in achieving these.
- *Planning* which services to purchase to meet priority needs.
- *Influencing providers* to plan and establish services so that the services are there to be purchased in the future.
- *Coordinating* planning and contracting with other purchasing and providing agencies (e.g. fundholding GPs).
- *Contract management*, i.e. negotiating and monitoring contracts to reflect the purchasing plan, and organizing payments.
- *Evaluating the impact on health* and the cost-effectiveness of commissioned services and other activities.
- *'Support work'* to the above work.

If we look at the earlier review of the purpose of different locality schemes we see that some authorities have decided that many of these tasks are better organized by locality, even if they have a centralized organization and base. However, for commissioners wishing to decentralize, these process, cycle or list models do not help to decide how to devolve authority, or to define the type of central control regulations and strategic direction which is required. Three further sets of ideas help with these issues: the concepts of decentralization discussed in the previous section (Figure 4.1); levels of commissioning; and population-size commissioning.

Levels of commissioning and locality organization

Better descriptions of commissioning work help us to consider options for locality purchasing. To decide an approach we need to go beyond 'involving GPs and local communities in purchasing decisions' to clarify which decisions need to be made, how best to 'involve' people and how to handle the conflicts that will arise. Such descriptions must distinguish levels of purchasing work and define the level of work to be undertaken by locality commissioning staff.

For example, monitoring contracts is lower-level work which follows from higher-level decisions about contract strategy and contract agreements: the higher-level decisions set the context for lower levels of work. What 'lower-level' purchasing work is best done on a 'local basis', and should a commissioner site staff in a local area to do this work? The model of levels of commissioning from Chapter 3 helps to answer this question (Figure 3.2).

This model does help us to decide which work should be devolved to localities, but we still need further ideas to help us decide what is appropriate in a particular area: some large localities in large authorities might well undertake strategic health service purchasing, and it is possible to set up different localities in the same authority to undertake different levels of work. The concepts of decentralization discussed in the section above help us to decide what authority to devolve to make decisions about different issues, as do the next set of ideas concerned with population size.

Population size: epidemiology and purchasing power

Although it is possible to undertake high-level commissioning work and to buy a full range of services for a small population (e.g. 10,000), it is not cost-effective to do so. The following discussion notes considerations of epidemiology, purchasing power and economies of purchaser resources for purchasing for different sized populations.

The first consideration is the epidemiology of different sized populations: over an average year, the probability of certain medical conditions and illness occurring increases with the size of the population. In a population of 10,000 we can roughly predict the average number of births, appendectomies, the incidence of schizophrenia, etc., but the larger the population the more reliable the prediction. In a population of 100,000, the chances of other rare conditions and illness occurring increase, as they do for even larger populations. We are referring here to a mixture of need and service requirements: some needs may not be presented or diagnosed. Thus, although morbidity rates vary significantly between areas there are two general principles: the larger the population the greater the likelihood of 'rarer' conditions occurring in the average year, and the more predictable the number and types of illness.

Health service staff are used to considering population size in relation to provider services, and to the notion that a population base or catchment area of a certain size is needed to support different services for primary, secondary and tertiary care. However, population considerations are different for purchasing. First, a provider does not need a large population catchment to support a specialty if a purchaser is prepared to pay a high price to have rare conditions treated locally. Although most rare conditions are not costly to treat, they do call for specialist services: they are only costly to treat if each area has a specialist service. However, outcomes are often worse for low-volume local specialist services than for high-volume regional or national specialist centres. Provision is usually more cost-effective for larger populations, and so is purchasing. Commissioning specialist services for rare conditions is best done for large populations, and using specialist purchasing expertise, possibly in a consortium or at a regional level. However, the population for purchasing services can be different to the population served by the provider.

Second, there are 'risk-spreading' considerations which apply for purchasers but do not apply for providers. The incidence of high-cost conditions, for example conditions requiring liver or heart transplants, or AIDS, would vary considerably year to year for a small population. The total annual purchasing costs would vary, whereas for a larger population the costs would be spread across the total costs for the population in one year – there is sufficient 'epidemiological stability'. The insurance and regulation literature considers some of these issues in detail (e.g. Van der Ven 1991), as does the US literature on optimum population size for health maintenance organizations (50,000 is proposed as a minimum by Weiner and Ferris 1990) and for managed care schemes.

Many locality schemes aim to set a purchasing budget for an area and encourage GPs and others to manage within this budget. The epidemiological and cost considerations mean that factors outside the locality's control, such as many high-cost conditions, make it difficult, and certainly unrewarding, to manage a purchasing budget for a small population. The GP fundholding scheme deals with this issue with a 'limited purchasing liability' of £5,000 for any one patient, and by restricting the scheme to purchasing certain diagnostic, elective surgery, outpatient and community services.

To take account of epidemiological stability in devising the details of devolved locality purchasing, we can take the following measures:

- place a limited liability on a locality for one patient or one treatment (central purchasing carries the cost above a certain amount);
- set the population size sufficiently high to spread risk for most conditions;
- define an exclusion list of conditions and treatments, which will be purchased at district level;
- allow annual budget variations for unpredictable high-cost conditions.

The general point is that, to decide the appropriate work and authority to devolve to localities, agencies need to understand the likely epidemiology of different sized populations, using normative and other data to make predictions for different populations in the area. This helps in deciding which services are best purchased for different sized populations, and in defining the purchasing work of a particular sized locality.

The final population-related consideration is 'purchasing power'. Here we mean both the amount of purchasing finance available and the capabilities of a commissioning authority in terms of staff expertise and time. A smaller locality will not be able to buy services in bulk, will be less able to get discount, and will also have less power to use contract withdrawal to force lower prices. Thus a further consideration is how devolving the purchasing of some services to localities may weaken a commissioning organization's purchasing power and bargaining position. If contracting is to be part of a long-term strategy, a commissioner will have to retain control over many contracting decisions, and will not be able to afford fully to devolve contracting.

For agencies wishing to decentralize as much as possible, we can summarize these considerations in the principle of 'subsidiarity in commissioning': that commissioning work and the purchasing of services should be undertaken for the smallest populations for which there is epidemiological stability for a defined range of conditions and services required. A final point has been made by one Chief Executive: 'It's a waste of time to decentralize functions in any organization unless you've got the capacity on the ground to manage them.'

Guidelines for developing locality commissioning

This section draws on the above review of experience and theoretical discussion to give guidelines for considering the options and for refining existing schemes. To develop an approach to locality commissioning an authority must consider:

- the resources available for undertaking the work, mainly staffing;
- its strategy and priorities;
- the purpose(s) to be served by localities in the short and long term;
- the commissioning tasks to be undertaken;
- levels of commissioning work;
- concepts of decentralization;
- the epidemiology of different populations and purchasing power.

A method for exploring options

A commissioning agency can define localities for different purposes, and then assess whether one approach can adequately serve many purposes, or whether one purpose is of overriding importance. For example, which geographical boundary and commissioner management arrangements are best for each of the following?

- Organizing GPs, for them to influence contracting and long-term purchasing plans.
- Collaborating with current and future fundholders over a variety of issues.
- Seeking the views of people in communities about the services they want, and other issues (which communities do people identify with and feel a loyalty towards?).
- Providing commissioner services to local populations (e.g. information, GP registration).
- Developing primary care provision.

We then need to consider:

- the geographical dimension to local authority service organization (e.g. locality social service purchasing and provision);
- areas in terms of 'health profile' and deprivation – which areas have 'poor' health, and what is the geographical map of needs developed by public health staff?

Drawing maps of localities from each of these perspectives and superimposing them may reveal locality boundaries which are similar. This is a method for thinking through the possibilities and for helping to clarify the purposes which a locality should serve. The result may be that a multipurpose locality approach is the best option, not just a compromise. The value of a locality approach may lie in it serving many purposes and being a way of integrating primary and secondary care purchasing, planning and service provision, something which has not been possible in the past.

Conclusions and issues for commissioners

Locality purchasing takes us to the heart of the theory and practice of commissioning. To decide on an approach to more locally responsive purchasing, purchasers have to confront many of the key issues of commissioning: what is the purpose of commissioning, what type of relations do we need with our population and with GPs, how do we improve our own services, how do we organize commissioning to make the most of integration and our scarce resources, how do we relate to social and other services, what are the needs and demands of different populations?

Different authorities have organized locality purchasing to serve different purposes, and to suit the circumstances of each area. In the early 1990s locality purchasing sometimes seemed like a solution in search of a problem, and discussion was often about the advantages and disadvantages of different models without sufficient analysis of what a purchaser aimed to achieve in the short and long term. In the mid-1990s there was still a tendency to develop locality purchasing as a reaction to 'the fundholder threat' and to prove to GPs that they can directly influence hospital contracts, rather than to consider longer-term and non GP-related issues. A long-term aim may be to develop primary care provision, with integrated DHA/FHSA locality budgets – structuring localities only for short-term aims may make it more difficult to realize longer-term aims.

While it is entirely appropriate that the early schemes clarified purposes as they evolved, there is now enough research and experience to decide purpose and to plan the best approach before making changes. Commissioners need to be clear about strategic and tactical aims, and then to consider whether a locality approach is a cost-effective way to achieve these aims. Why do they wish to develop a 'locality approach'? What would happen if they did not, and what are the alternative ways of achieving the same ends? A commissioning agency would define a locality and the organization and systems for localities differently depending on which functions it wanted to achieve and in relation to its strategy.

At present the evidence and arguments are against using a locality orientation to serve a number of purposes, but it may be that multipurpose decentralization is where the real advantages lie. A locality orientation can provide a way of 'bridging' primary and secondary care and a structure for transferring resources for developing primary care. If localities are defined in a way which favours both provision and purchasing functions, they can be a structure for creating incentives to drive primary care developments and to increase GP accountability. With GP 'indicative budgets' for secondary care purchasing, commissioners can create incentives to reinvest savings from secondary care into primary care developments – incentives which go beyond those of fundholding and which further strategic and health-gain aims. It is also possible to strengthen GP accountability, not just to the commissioning agency but also to the local community through 'locality health councils'. In this way commissioners can develop the service-providing potential of locality organization.

Considerations for commissioning authorities developing their approach include:

- the scarcity of staff with purchasing skills, if localities are to undertake higher-level commissioning work;
- the management cost limits for commissioners;
- the size of the commissioning authority (geography, population and budget);
- the actual and expected number of GP fundholders;
- the organization of other agencies (e.g. local authority purchasing, community services provision);
- mirroring current or future commissioner-preferred locality provision arrangements (e.g. locality managers in community services);
- ensuring consistency, equity and public health aims, while responding to GP and community views;

- ensuring that locality arrangements are compatible with long-term health strategy and contract strategies;
- balancing locality size with epidemiological stability for devolved budgets;
- how best to define a 'locality' for the purposes and functions identified (geographically and in other senses);
- the sophistication of information systems;
- the extent of integration between DHA and FHSA management and systems.

Key points

- 'Locality purchasing' is a term used to describe different ways to organize health authority commissioning work, and is part of the general subject of decentralized purchasing.
- Commissioners need to be clear about what they aim to achieve from a 'locality approach', about what is missing without such an approach, and about the costs and benefits of different approaches.
- To decide whether or how to decentralize, commissioners need to ask what localities are for. Can we develop our role as a service organization through this approach? Is it a cost-effective way to do so? Can one arrangement serve a number of purposes? Which purchasing work and decisions are best made at which level and for which size populations?
- There is a tension between the 'consumer purpose' and the 'GP purpose' in some schemes. In other schemes, locality managers have been able to develop commissioner services to the population, as well as shared purchasing with fundholders and other GPs. The customer service role of localities and relations with GPs can be developed by devolving FHSA functions to localities.
- Some difficulties in defining localities arise because of an unclear role and vision for an NHS commissioning organization and an uncertain view about its distinctive and overriding central purpose.
- A practical way to examine options is to define localities for different purposes and to assess whether most purposes are adequately served by one definition (i.e. to draw geographical boundaries for different purposes and superimpose them to see if common groupings emerge).
- Commissioners can learn from the practical experience of existing schemes and from concepts to define the primary purpose, the work and the degree of decentralization in a locality scheme.
- Larger authorities (over 300,000 people) may need different 'levels' of locality for different purposes, e.g. GP practice, neighbourhood (35,000), area (100,000).
- Localities can serve as a 'bridge' for transferring resources for primary care developments, if combined with incentives for GPs to save and redirect finance into primary care services. Localities would need to be structured carefully to serve this purpose.

5 Justifiable purchasing: rationing, priorities, effectiveness and outcome

[A key objective of the NHS Management Executive Business Plan 1993–4 was] to conduct a fundamental review of health expenditure to distinguish clearly between the essential costs of high priority spending which will continue to be funded and avoidable spending which cannot be afforded.

[The consumer view is that] People have a right to know what choices are being made in their names, to express their views and to expect that those responsible are held accountable for the decisions made.

(ACHCEW 1993)

Introduction

All health purchasers have to decide which health services they will purchase for whom, and how many resources to put into other health promotion and preventative activities. Private health insurers' decisions are driven by the market: consumers, both individual and institutional, influence the purchaser's choice of the range and amount of services to contract. Private health purchasers can offer different priced health plans, and get feedback from the market about preferred cost–coverage–quality combinations. They and their customers have the freedom to agree a service contract, and many can refuse to insure high-risk patients, although this is changing in some countries.

Public health commissioners are more constrained: they have a set financial allocation, and they have to ensure that certain services are available. They do not have a contract with their customers which limits their liability, and many of the people they serve have no alternative purchaser. However, they do have some discretion to decide the range and amount of services to match the most pressing needs of people in their area. Yet if they cannot increase their purchasing resources, and if needs will always be greater than the resources available, how are they to decide how much of which services to make available? What is their 'service contract' with their population, and by what right do they exclude certain interventions and invest in others?

This chapter is about relating resources to health gain. Most definitions of the purpose of NHS commissioning make reference to resources. The definition offered in Chapter 3 was: 'to make the best use of available finance to improve health and prevent illness, by influencing other organizations to contribute to these ends and by contracting health services'. So far our emphasis has been on health gain; in this chapter we consider how a purchaser decides how to allocate resources for the maximum health gain. We consider the public's role in these decisions and the ethical and technical issues which are involved.

The theme of the chapter is 'justifiable commissioning': how to decide resource allocation in a justifiable way, and decide which services to purchase as cost-effective ways to achieve health gain. It argues that if a commissioning organization is not able to justify such decisions, then it is acting unethically in directly or indirectly causing avoidable suffering. Without 'justifiable commissioning' the justification for a commissioning organization is questionable.

We consider the 'rationing debate' in the context of the purpose of NHS commissioning and of the view of health commissioning as a service. We consider rationing as restricting or ceasing to purchase interventions, and distinguish 'prioritizing' from rationing. The chapter argues that commissioning managers have to review the bulk of expenditure and ensure that it is not spent on ineffective services and is allocated in a justifiable way. The public holds it on trust that commissioners will do this, and has an implicit contract with them that they will do so. When individuals or sections of the community are denied services, the implicit contract with them and the rest of the population is broken if commissioners cannot justify the alternative use they are making of public resources.

The chapter shows how commissioners can use what is already known about treatment and service effectiveness and outcome to make better use of limited public finance and to justify their decisions. It finishes by proposing a practical approach to prioritizing for commissioners with full agendas and relatively few staff. This involves a five-step explicit rationing procedure, which combines different interest groups and information to exclude different needs and treatments successively according to agreed criteria. Such a procedure can be continually refined with new information on effectiveness, needs and outcome performance. The chapter addresses the following questions and issues.

- *How can we best set priorities across care groups and service sectors?*
- *How do we reconcile the conflicting priorities of the NHS management executive, region, providers, GPs, the public and politicians, and of individual 'rights' and utilitarian population responsibilities?*

- *What is the best way of involving the public in prioritizing decisions and preparing them for what is to come?*
- *How do we get and use accurate measures of outcome from providers?*
- *How can we pursue strategic priorities and ensure equity when we can't control extra-contractual referrals, tertiary referrals, GP referrals and fund-holders?*
- *How can we ration without jeopardizing patients' trust in providers?*
- *Should we be seeking information from medical audit: how do we engage hospital consultants in serious discussion about effectiveness and measuring outcome?*

Justifiable purchasing

Everyone agrees that health services are rationed in different ways, but few admit to doing it, outside a war situation or a medical school. No one wants to take responsibility for rationing, and none are prepared to be held accountable for it. Yet the increasing gap between resources and what can and needs to be done makes rationing public health services inescapable. More people are recognizing that there may be better ways of doing it, and that the larger the gap, the greater the need for fair and more effective approaches to deciding how much is allocated for different patient needs and services.

In the UK the 1990 NHS reforms and the purchaser–provider split made the issues more obvious, but did not allow politicians to escape their responsibilities, as some had hoped. Although there is public confusion about whether purchasers or providers are responsible for 'denying rightful care', commissioners are held accountable, at least by the media. Commissioners are having to justify their decisions to refuse to fund certain services and, increasingly, their choices about the proportion of resources which they allocate to different populations and services.

Box 5.1

Justifiable purchasing is giving an explanation of the basis for and process by which a commissioning organization decides resource allocations to different programmes and contracts providers. A feature of 'justifiable commissioning' is public involvement.

If commissioning authorities or their agencies cannot explain the process by which they allocate resources and give an acceptable justification for their decisions, then their own future is in question. If they cannot show that they commission fairly and effectively, then what is the value they add and the service they give to their population? Commissioners' concern about and ability to give an account of resource allocation priorities is an important way in which they differ from many fundholders, and is one tangible indication of whether they do in fact preserve equity and other traditional NHS values. Justifying their purchasing is a way in which authorities are legitimating their role.

The theory and the practice

Commissioners are already aware of the gap between what they should be doing and what is practical and possible – the difference between 'pure' and 'applied' purchasing. The amount of information about needs, outcome and effectiveness increases, yet their capacity to use it is not increasing at the same rate. It can demoralize commissioning managers to show what should be done and the arguments for doing it, without recognizing how much time and skills they have and the political dimensions of public health purchasing. Consequently the chapter emphasizes taking a selective approach, building up experience and frameworks to review systematically why resources are allocated in the way they are, and incremental approaches to changing the allocations. It considers how commissioners can identify which treatments or services to focus on, by deciding where there are the greatest gains to be made from questioning resource allocation.

In selecting services and treatments for review, commissioners also have to recognize the politics of public and provider change: time and energy may be better spent in areas where there is the potential for change. The chapter considers the role of the public and methods for involving them in deciding resource allocation, apart from expensive and often wasteful surveys. Figure 5.1 shows types of rationing and their justification.

A framework for 'justifiable purchasing'

Absolute rationing, or more effective use of resources?

The debate about which treatments should not be available has raised public consciousness about some of the issues, but it is a distraction from the more important question of how the bulk of public money for health care is spent. However, we note some of the 'absolute rationing' issues and approaches, before considering the wider question of resource allocation priorities and effectiveness.

Whatever the many criticisms of the 'Oregon approach' in the USA (e.g. Hunter 1993), it was at least an attempt at a more systematic and explicit approach to rationing public finance for health services. Professions and the public judged the priority of a long list of treatments, which the state was to use to decide which treatments would not be funded, depending on the final state budget allocation for health. The initial approach was to use cost–benefit analyses to prioritize, defined by diagnosis–treatment combinations. This was superseded by an approach which placed these diagnosis–treatment combinations in categories, and prioritized the categories according to the value to the community and the patient, and the necessity in a basic health coverage. Then the diagnosis–treatment combinations in each category were ordered according to 'net added value'. This

Rationing is often implicit, and by
• price
• queuing/waiting
• prioritization of need
• debarring rules
• restrictions on direct access
• according to likelihood of benefit
• personal opinion of provider
• restricting time on one case
• failure to publicize
• deterrent low standard of service (Rees 1972)
• or by deterrence, deflection, dilution and delay (Hunter 1993)

Justifications
For not purchasing, withholding or constraining services:
• generally, diverts resources from other services (benefit-opportunity cost)
• some needs/conditions are less life-threatening or painful than others
• unproven need, or capacity to benefit
• treatment/service ineffective, or unproven effectiveness, or benefits low for high cost
• little public support for contributing public finance for this purpose
• avoidable by more responsible individual behaviour
• the individual has an alternative to public service (private insurance, wealth)

Figure 5.1 Types of rationing and their justification.

is the difference between treating and not treating, in terms of the probable handicap, survival or cure. The final step was to revise the whole list according to criteria of 'reasonableness', which included cost, effectiveness, number of cases, social costs of treating or not treating and effect on public health (Oregon HSC 1991; *British Medical Journal* 9 March 1993: 549).

The state was prevented from acting on the list by the Bush administration in the summer of 1992, on the grounds that it discriminated against certain patient groups. No one could argue that this was not indeed what would happen, but one of the reasons was to make effective and valued treatments available to more of the US public who did not have insurance. The Oregon approach highlighted issues other than technical problems such as representation (only 0.14 per cent of the population): it highlighted the political sensitivity and the moral and ethical issues involved in explicit rationing, and this in a country where public health care has a minor role.

While it raised much interest in the early 1990s, the general consensus in the UK was that the Oregon approach was not suitable for the UK. However, UK health authorities carry out 'absolute rationing' according to various criteria. In 1991, a survey of 114 health authorities found that a number had planned not to buy certain treatments in 1992–3: tattoo removal (7), *in vitro* fertilization (6), sterilization reversals (4) and some cosmetic surgery (4). Two health authorities planned not to buy treatments of 'unproven value', but examples or criteria were not specified (Klein and Redmayne 1992). More recently North Essex Health Authority was reported as ranking treatments according to effectiveness and needs met. It now only offers 'low-priority treatments' in exceptional circumstances (such as cosmetic and gender surgery, infertility and sterilization), has cut back on homeopathy and is working to reduce referrals for 'high-cost' treatments for alcoholism, drug addiction and behavioural disorders (*Health Services Journal* 20 May 1993: 8).

Another area where implict or explicit rationing is undertaken is in refusing or questioning elective extra-contractual referrals (ECRs). Most ECRs are referrals by GPs to providers that do not have a contract with the GP's health authority. Because these individual referrals can be costly and because authorities try to keep within their ECR budgets, some have developed policies for questioning and refusing ECRs. Some are drawing on their experience in this area to review their explicit rationing policies, but in others there is a danger of creeping and unreviewed rationing through ECR management. The chapter on contracting considers ECRs in more detail.

Another approach is to rank patients on waiting lists according to explicit criteria agreed between purchasers, providers, GPs and the public:

> *Rationing scheme will exclude minor illness from NHS . . .* A waiting list scheme which ranks patients according to severity of their condition rather than how long they are waiting is running at Salisbury hospital . . . The scheme could eventually be used to ration care, according to Dr Lack [*sic*], 'If we've only got the funds to treat patients who score 2 or 3 or more we're not going to put patients with minor conditions on the list.'
>
> (*Health Services Journal* 26 September 1993: 7)

Prioritizing waiting lists in this way is more equitable and effective, for those who get on the list. It does not address the issue of how to decide the amount of treatments to purchase in a year, relative to other treatments or uses of finance. Neither does it address the question of whether the treatment is effective, or whether the provider's outcome performance is good – questions we consider below. It does, however, signal a movement away from rationing to prioritizing, which we now consider.

There are many examples of a trend among commissioners to be explicit about restrictions and to refuse to finance certain treatments. However, such 'absolute rationing' tends to be an *ad hoc* reaction to reduced funding, rather than the end-result of a more comprehensive review of priorities and of all expenditure. Figure 5.2 draws attention to the bulk of expenditure which often goes unexamined.

In examining their role in rationing as 'consumer representatives', the Association of Community Health Councils in the UK distinguished three types of rationing (ACHCEW 1993). One type is withdrawal of NHS services such as those described above, and another is through protocols and clinical guidelines which discriminate between patients, for example in

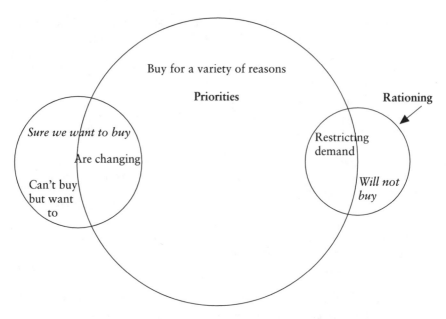

Buy for a variety of reasons

Priorities

Rationing

Sure we want to buy

Are changing

Restricting demand

Can't buy but want to

Will not buy

Figure 5.2   Purchasers' current service priorities are those that they buy.

terms of age. The third are systematic approaches to define how much of which services should be provided, including identifying low-priority services. We note this approach below, and return to it at the end of the chapter as one of the 'steps' in a practical and systematic approach for prioritizing for commissioners.

Box 5.2

Rationing: restricting supply by explicit or implicit means where demand exceeds supply, and where market mechanisms do not relate supply to demand in an acceptable way.

Prioritizing: deciding who goes first, or the relative proportion of resources allocated to a patient, patient group, population or service. It can be just for new finance or apply to the whole budget.

Systematic approach to resource allocation prioritization

Absolute rationing – denying certain treatments – is often called prioritizing, but so is deciding the relative proportion of resources to different client groups and services, or ranking which will come first for new finance. 'Prioritizing' is a general term, but this chapter uses it mainly to refer to the proportion of resources allocated to different groups or services. In fact, deciding 'which goes first' is often closely related to proportionate allocation. For example, if many people wait a long time because they have come last, an alternative to adding extra resources is to move allocations from other services with shorter waiting. However, prioritizing also involves considering service effectiveness as well as need: the concept of health gain encompasses needs and effectiveness. Systematic and justifiable prioritizing involves deciding the proportion of resources to allocate to different services on the basis of an analysis of need, and an understanding of effectiveness and cost which allows comparisons. Later in the chapter we consider different ways to prioritize in practice with limited information.

There are two principles to meaningful purchaser prioritizing with finite resources and limited information. The first is understanding what should and can be controlled by a commissioner, and then getting more control over how resources are allocated. This involves understanding how resources came to be allocated in the way that they are – the series of often unconnected decisions made by different individuals in the past which resulted in a particular resource allocation.

A second principle is stating where reductions will be made to supply the resources for the priority: the other side of the coin of priorities is the 'posteriorities', i.e. what comes last. With finite resources, something only becomes a priority when something else is made less important. The difficulty is that we are considering people and suffering, or even life and death. A decision not to buy an intervention (a treatment, screening procedure, service, etc.), or to provide some interventions to some patients and not to others, has to be justified and the end result of a cyclical process of planned resource allocation, hence 'prioriphobia'. The problem with many approaches to prioritizing, and especially some public consultation exercises, is that there is no consideration of what will be reduced to fund the higher priority, or comparison of the value of what will be gained against that of what will be lost. Priorities without posteriorities are meaningless.

Box 5.3

Posteriorities
Deciding who or what comes last or receives the smaller proportion of resources.
Prioriphobia
The inability to set and carry through priorities due to an awareness of the suffering which will be caused by denying care and a refusal to value one person's life or quality of life more highly than anothers.

Justifiable purchasing involves showing how the relative proportions which a commissioner allocates to different services and sectors are based on evidence of effectiveness and knowledge of the extent and severity of needs for the service. If there is no evidence or little information, then the allocations can and should be challenged. The real issue is how to make better use of limited purchaser finance, in cooperation with GPs, the public and providers, and by using the available information about effectiveness, provider outcome and needs. Commissioners face major challenges in reviewing, changing and justifying the bulk of their purchasing. We will return to practical approaches for doing so later in the chapter, after we have considered treatment and service effectiveness and routine outcome measurement.

In summary, some of the issues in rationing and prioritizing for health purchasers are:

• deciding how much of which interventions to buy, for whom and from whom;
• the best role for the public in different decisions, and the methods for involving them;
• collaborating with GPs (as referrers, purchasers and as providers) in deciding and implementing priorities;
• collaborating with providers in changing contracts, in agreeing protocols and in other areas (e.g. audit, outcome measurement).

Factors in local need and effectiveness

In this section we consider the practical task for commissioners, before reviewing effectiveness and evaluation research in the next section, and then routine outcome measurement. We return to practical approaches for commissioners in the final sections of the chapter.

Commissioners have an implicit service contract with their public. In exchange for their support, the public expects and trusts them to use their resources to the best effect to buy services and take actions to improve health and prevent illness. How do purchasers know that what they do spend public money on does improve people's health? Would other ways of spending the money produce greater improvements? How do they prove to the public that they have fulfilled the implicit contract?

Factors affecting the local cost–benefit of a service

Figure 5.3 shows the range of different issues which commissioners have to consider in order to judge the likely actual benefits to their local populations for the local costs of certain interventions. 'Effectiveness' means whether an intervention is known to produce the desired outcomes in most settings. A separate question is whether it is effective locally, which depends on how a potential or current provider applies the intervention, and on acceptability and uptake. Outcome measures are used by researchers to evaluate efficacy in controlled settings and to judge effectiveness, and by clinicians in audit.

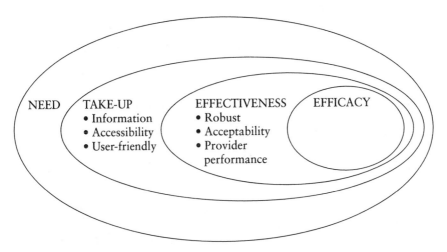

Figure 5.3 Factors affecting the benefits which an intervention may produce for a local population.

To decide how much to purchase, and from whom, to meet a particular need or condition, a commissioner has to consider the following.

- *Efficacy*: of an intervention in a controlled setting. Is there research evidence that the intervention can produce a desired result?
- *Effectiveness*: in most routine service settings. Is there research evidence that the intervention does produce the desired result in most everyday settings?
- *Provider outcome performance*: for treatments proven to be effective, what outcomes do potential or current providers get, compared to other providers?
- *Provider costs*: what is the cost/outcome ratio for different providers?
- *Acceptability*: to providers and to patients, which affects the next point.
- *Use* and take-up: also affected by accessibility.
- *Need* and capacity to benefit (involving selecting the right patients).

Commissioners have to consider similar issues in deciding how much of their time and effort to invest in activities other than contracting services, such as inter-sector actions for the *Health of the Nation* objectives (DoH 1992a). The general issue is understanding the link between the use of resources and improvements in health for people in the area. Although accurate information about all of the above is rarely available, even for one need or condition, commissioners have to make estimates about all of these, rather than just to consider efficacy or effectiveness. The following considers the 'needs' part of the process for rational resource allocation, before turning to the provider issues of effectiveness, costs and outcome performance.

Needs analysis

There is only a need where there is a potential benefit, i.e. where the intervention and/or the care setting is effective.

(DoH 1991a)

Is it possible or desirable for purchasers to assess needs separately from the means of meeting them? The above is one of many definitions of need, and the number increases when we turn to operational measures of need. This is not the place to discuss needs assessment, which we considered in Chapter 3. It is necessary to emphasize five points which are relevant to purchaser prioritization.

- Information about the incidence and severity of need is important to setting priorities and to justifiable purchasing.
- Information about needs will always be partial and disputable. There will never be a 'full picture', and purchasers do not need complete information to make more rational resource allocation decisions.
- Partial information can be worse than none, if it is assumed to be objective and used uncritically. The aim is to become better informed about needs and to recognize the limitations of both 'hard' data (e.g. epidemiological) and 'soft' data (e.g. GPs' opinions).
- Defining need in terms of capacity to benefit from treatments or services does make needs assessment more manageable, but, by definition, may not measure needs for which there are not curative or effective treatments.
- Purchasers can narrow their focus further to assess needs for treatments or services which are being considered for 'marginal purchasing' (see the HERG (1992) approach below).

It is difficult and, many argue, inappropriate to detach needs from the means of meeting needs (Øvretveit 1993b). It is useful to think of a needs–responses continuum ranging from the 'needs-only purists' at one end, through those that put the emphasis on capacity to benefit in the middle, to those that focus on the treatment/service response end of the continuum and define need only in terms of effectiveness – sometimes called the 'provider view' of need. Here is one view of where purchasers should put the emphasis:

Many purchasing activities have tended to focus on needs assessment – i.e. the invention of new demand for resources even when the existing activities cannot be financed. Obviously 'The Health of the Nation' and other 'wish-lists' can be helpful. But it is essential to identify the cost-effectiveness of these proposals relative to existing activities which give the biggest 'bang for the buck'. Unfortunately purchasers have paid too little attention to issues of effectiveness.

(Maynard 1993a: 23)

Effectiveness and evaluation research

While there is little outcome data from providers, and problems in making valid comparisons, commissioners do have access to information about the likely effectiveness of some interventions in an average setting. They also have access to evidence about cost-effectiveness from economic evaluations, and about comparative cost–benefit. Justifiable commissioning means using this research to decide resource allocation, on the assumption that it would apply to local providers.

The approach outlined below recognizes that it is impractical for a small commissioning organization to use all the information which is already available, and proposes that a commissioner does not need to. However, commissioners cannot justify *not* purchasing effective and low-cost services (e.g. some *in vitro* fertilization treatments) when they spend large amounts on interventions which are proven to be ineffective.

Effectiveness research

An increasing number of interventions have been or are being assessed for effectiveness. Commissioners have access to databases which list the studies. The national NHS *Effectiveness Bulletins* select certain conditions and treatments and summarize the main studies in periodic reports (Long *et al.* 1993). Reports issued include: screening for osteoporosis, stroke rehabilitation, sub-fertility, glue ear, depression in primary care and cholesterol-lowering strategies.

Outcome measurement

All effectiveness studies use outcome measures. The outcomes clearing house (Long *et al.* 1993), distinguishes between four types of measures.

- *Mortality*: total rates, number by age or populations (standardized mortality ratios), avoidable mortality or death rates in hospitals.
- *Morbidity*: a change in the incidence of disease which can be attributed to a service or intervention. The most common are negative outcomes measures of morbidity caused by the service (e.g. complications, re-admission rates, avoidable morbidity and adverse events).
- *Health status measures:* health-related quality of life measures (e.g. NHP, SF-36, Barthel (daily living), HADS, GHQ, EUROQUAL, QUALY, HYE, SAVES: see Long *et al.* 1993). These are either multidimensional or single-topic (e.g. mobility or pain).
- *Disease-specific measures*: for arthritis, chronic respiratory disease, depression, etc.

A later section considers which of these are useful for routine provider monitoring or audit. There are also many types of patient satisfaction measures which give measures of outcome, and indicators of poor process quality which are used for quality improvement and by US purchasers.

Table 5.1   QUALY comparisons

Intervention	Cost per QUALY produced (£)
Hospital haemodialysis for kidney failure	19,000
CABG (moderate, one vessel disease)	16,400
Cholesterol drug treatment	13,500
Heart transplant	6,700
Kidney transplant	4,000
CABG (main vessel disease)	1,090
Hip replacement	1,030
Cholesterol-lowering diet programme	176

Short-term or indirect outcome indicators and process measures are usually less expensive to collect, and some reliably predict long-term outcome and can be used as proxy outcome measures. Research measures for primary care are described in Wilkin *et al.* (1992), and a simple summary of the advantages and disadvantages of different types can be found in Shickle *et al.* (1993).

The main technical problems in using outcome measures are difficulties of being sure that the outcome is attributable to the intervention, and controlling for co-morbidity and severity of illness. In the USA, work has been done to develop and use risk-adjusted measures of outcome to compare providers' actual and expected outcomes: these are published annually in Pennsylvania (e.g. PHCCCC 1992).

Economic evaluation research

Economic evaluations attribute value to an intervention by using systematically gained information about costs and effects, and by comparing the intervention to nothing at all or to other uses of resources. Most evaluation studies measure costs and use outcome measures to measure effectiveness or benefit. Some assess effects other than those for the patient – studies differ in the scope of their effects assessments. Evaluations differ in how narrowly they define costs and benefits, and in the accuracy and the validity of their measures. The purpose of most evaluations is to compare the cost–benefit ratio or utility of the intervention with other uses of the finance. Some meta-studies draw together a number of evaluations of the same intervention to produce a synthesis evaluation, but there are technical problems in combining studies in this way.

Cost–utility evaluations use measures such as Quality Adjusted Life Years (QUALYs) to compare a 'unit' of benefit of different treatments for the cost. Table 5.1 (from the SMAC 1990 Report on Cholesterol Testing) gives an illustration of the kinds of comparisons which can be made. There are a number of criticisms of QUALY comparisons, some of which are important for purchasers to understand in order to decide how to use such comparisons (Smith 1992; Hunter 1993). These include: the small number of interventions which have been studied using this approach; technical flaws; the bias to giving greater value to duration of life than to life itself, and to valuing the young; that QUALYs do not distinguish between life-enhancing and life-saving treatments and try to equate them; and the impact which QUALY-based allocation would have on traditional rights of access to health care. However, where there is no other basis for re-source allocation decisions, commissioners are increasingly using these or similar cost–utility analyses.

QUALYs have served to encourage more debate about the merits and drawbacks of rational utilitarian approaches to resource allocation. From an economic perspective, purchasers have to maximize the benefit they can get from the total sum they have to spend. They should get and use information about costs and about outcome performance to decide bene-fits, for both national averages and potential providers. Buxton (1992) proposes that commissioners should purchase 'new' treatments only on condition that the provider evaluates them, and that commissioners should be prepared to contribute to the cost of evaluation.

Implications for justifiable commissioning

We can use the model in Figure 5.3 to summarize how commissioners can apply effectiveness and evaluation research.

Research and clinical practice
While research will show some interventions to be efficacious and some not, commissioners have to judge whether an intervention will be effective in the local context. This means judging whether providers can select patients appropriately and conduct the intervention in the right way, as well as local accessibility and acceptability.

Effectiveness and costs
Research may show that an intervention is effective, but commissioners have to judge its likely local cost-effectiveness. They need to add informa-tion about providers' costs, and consider the likely local benefits by assess-ing such things as likely maximum take-up. National reports may show some interventions to be efficacious, effective and cost-effective, but in a particular local setting they may produce few individual or population benefits for the cost. In principle, commissioners need to compare the local cost-effectiveness of different interventions and services and combine this with local needs assessment to decide how to change resource allocations between types of service or client groups. In practice a selective approach is more realistic.

A selective approach
This involves identifying high-volume and high-cost interventions, and, when evidence of effectiveness becomes available, using the evidence to

reconsider contracts. A later section of this chapter considers in more detail how commissioners use this information to develop a systematic 'step' approach to resource allocation prioritizing. There are advantages to a selective 'health gain approach' for targeted conditions and treatments.

Using information about effectiveness is part of 'justifiable commissioning'. However, an intervention may be effective and cost-effective elsewhere, but whether it should be purchased depends on the outcomes it produces for the cost in the hands of the local provider. The next section considers how providers can and should measure outcomes routinely, a different matter to how to measure outcomes for effectiveness or evaluation research.

Box 5.4   Technical and political questions for purchasers

Is the intervention effective, is the provider cost-effective? (Do not waste time evaluating interventions or providers where changes are not likely to be possible.)

Can we generate more benefit by using the finance elsewhere?

Is there public support for stopping or changing, and will this be sufficient to counter vested interests?

Outcome measurement and purchasing

Commissioning managers in Glasgow found that patient survival rates following surgery could vary widely. One factor was the surgeon: some were up to four times more likely to save their patients than others. The director of public health at Greater Glasgow Health Board has no doubt that purchasers have a responsibility for poor outcomes: 'Purchasing is about life and death . . . Purchasers are as guilty of killing people as inadequate surgeons. I am sure someone will die in the next year because I lacked the courage to make a service change that I thought was required' (*Health Services Journal* 22 July 1993: 7).

Towards purchasing by outcome

Most of the literature on outcome measurement is either for researchers or for providers, and usually for audit in the latter case. This section gives an overview of some of the issues, and shows where purchasers can find out more about routine outcome for their purposes. It considers how commissioners can use outcome measures and encourage providers to use measures and give routine reports of their performance. First, consider the value of outcome measures to commissioners in the simple example of total hip replacement.

Box 5.5 The value of outcome measures: the example of hip replacement

An outcome report proposes that there is in fact a finite and predictable need for hip replacements in an average district (Frankel *et al.* 1990). The basic conditions for effective treatment are also known, as well as the cost utility (average £1,030 per QUALY). An estimate of failure rate is that, over time, 14 per cent of all replacements fail and need to be redone, for various reasons. Outcome data from Trent Region show that the average reoperation rate per year is 6.5 per cent. The cost of reoperation is high, as are the likelihood of complications and the pain and suffering for the patient. Reoperation also increases the waiting list. The more operations, the more the waiting list lengthens, and the further commissioners get from meeting a need which may be finite.

Yet the ways to ensure low failure rate are known, simple and inexpensive: use proven replacement joints, reduce infection risks and use skilled doctors who do more than a certain number of operations per year. The result: a provider could approach one hospital's average total failure rate over 30 years of 1.1 per cent. The public is acting on this information, regardless of purchaser knowledge or action. Following a television programme on the subject, referrals to 'good outcome' providers rose dramatically. This will result in lower long-term costs for the home purchasers, who will not have to pay for reoperations and were saved from having to make the decision themselves. Is there a role for purchasers in making this information available to the public? Should purchasers take more responsibility for acting on the information? Providers are beginning to use this information in marketing their services.

Are hip replacements an isolated example of a 'simple' procedure, for which there are routine outcome data? Which other measures of outcome performance which also allow valid comparisons are, or could be made, available by providers? First we consider what we mean by outcome measures and their uses, before looking at one study which investigated whether outcome data could be used in a routine clinical setting.

Health service outcomes: definition and measures

Health service outcomes are the effect on a person or population which can be attributed to a health service treatment, service or intervention. Some definitions of outcome can exclude patient satisfaction and quality during the treatment or service process, and many exclude the costs to the patient as an outcome. Many outcome measures also do not adequately exclude the effects of other services, environments, or other factors affecting health. Figure 5.4 shows how outcome overlaps with, and is influenced by, other factors.

There are considerable problems and costs in measuring service outcomes on a routine basis, even if providers use a sampling approach.

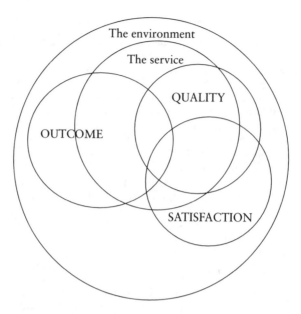

Figure 5.4   Outcome overlaps with and is influenced by other factors.

Simple measures like mortality provoke questions and rarely give answers. They can be misleading without other information about case mix, time period, severity of illness and other controls which are used in research studies. There are particular problems in making comparisons between providers. Many of these problems can be overcome, but at a high cost, and often only by regional or national action. Outcome measurement for research purposes is expensive and fraught with problems, and using similar techniques for all patients on a routine basis is not possible. Commissioners requiring providers to measure outcome will pay in higher prices, and the information produced would not reach the standards of those of a research study and could be misleading. The questions for purchasers are:

- have techniques been developed for measuring outcomes for different services on a routine basis which are cost-effective?
- have these measures been validated against more sophisticated research measures?
- would the information from such measures allow us to compare the outcome performance of different providers?
- are the benefits for us and the provider worth the extra costs of measurement?

A practical approach is to focus on identifying measures of poor outcome, to require providers to collect and record this information, and to track changes in provider performance on these measures. We now consider the use of more sophisticated measures.

The use of routine outcome data

Outcome data collected by providers can show variations and patterns of outcomes for one clinician at different times, or between clinicians in one hospital. If there is a standard system, as in some UK national audits, purchasers can make valid comparisons between services and clinicians, if there are adjustments for severity and co-morbidity (NCEPOD 1993). In the USA, patients make use of outcome data to choose their hospital or physician (PHCCCC 1992). In both the USA and the UK patients use outcome data with medical advice to choose between types of treatment, where there are different risk–benefit options. In the USA a drop of 44 per cent for surgical treatment for prostate problems was reported after patients used a video and computer to get full information about the risks and benefits of treatment for their condition ('informed medical decision making', a system being piloted for hypertension, back pain and breast cancer by the King's Fund at the Central Middlesex Hospital (MacLachlan 1992: 26)).

Doctors use outcome data to develop best practice guidelines and protocols. A protocol is 'practice guidelines for doctors or others to follow where rational procedures can be specified with a high probability of producing improved health for a defined illness or condition'. Protocols are used to help diagnosis, to improve medical care, to reduce costs, for legal protection, to decide where to refuse treatment and to decide priorities for treatment. However, protocols can increase costs, freeze practice on unsound treatment (especially where there is no consensus) and encourage litigation.

Outcome data are used in quality programmes in the USA with clinical (or critical) pathways (the anticipated flow of care after diagnosis), or with 'patient management paths', 'anticipated recovery paths', 'care profiles', or 'patient pathways' (Øvretveit 1992a). Outcome data are also used by managers to reduce costs, improve quality and plan investments. In the USA, purchasers make extensive use of routinely collected outcome data to select providers, monitor quality and encourage quality improvement.

In the UK, one study found that routine outcome measurement was feasible, and made a set of recommendations for future practice (the 1988 CASPE/Freeman Hospital (Newcastle) pilot: Bardsley *et al.* 1991). An example is the set of outcome measures for cholecystotomy surgery. This included: (a) death (perioperative mortality); (b) change in general health status (Nottingham health profile); (c) major adverse effects such as readmission or repeat surgery (measured by postal questionnaire at 3 months and 12 months, number of GP and/or accident and emergency visits); (d) relief of specific symptoms or problems (e.g. pain reduction, from 3 month and 12 month questionnaires); (e) complications of treatment (e.g. wound infection, by pro-forma on discharge); (f) rating of treatment success by the surgeon.

Summary for purchasers

Some of the conclusions from the 1988 CASPE study were borne out in later uses of outcome measures in routine settings. We can summarize these in terms of recommendations for purchasers.

1 Decide the purpose and use of the measure: clarify the decisions which are to be better informed with the data from the outcome measures or studies.
2 Clarify the detail and accuracy needed in order to make better-informed decisions (what is the additional cost and benefit of more detailed and accurate data?)
3 Choose outcome measure for the purpose and ensure:
   • reliability: same results if reapplied?
   • validity: does it really measure what it is supposed to?
   • responsiveness: sensitive enough to register small but significant clinical changes.
   • meaningfulness: data from measures allow comparisons between patients, populations or services.
   • the data are credible to potential users of data.

Guidance for providers and commissioners in agreeing outcome measures includes:

• Clearly define the treatment episode (e.g. 'consultant care episode').
• Control for variations in patient characteristics (sex, age, co-morbidity) and in service factors (case mix, isolate service effects).
• The scope of the assessment should be sufficiently wide to ensure that all the important effects are measured (time, size of sample).
• Do not use research measures for routine purposes: the costs increase for detail which is not needed for routine clinical or management decisions.
• Save time and money by first considering: why outcomes are to be assessed; search for the best measure (use others' experience – do not design a new measure); and pay attention to design so that outcome can be attributed to the intervention rather than to other factors.

Conclusions for commissioners: requiring and using outcome measures

There are six considerations for purchasers in deciding how to use outcome measurement:

1 *Outcomes part of 'quality'?* Purchasers need to decide whether they view outcome measurement and performance as part of a provider's

service quality or as a separate issue. In contract specification, will outcomes come under 'quality' or under another heading?

2 *Outcomes for some interventions.* Interventions and services differ. For some there are outcomes which can and should be measured on a routine basis, easily and at low cost. For others, we do not know how or what to measure routinely and cost-effectively. Most services are in between, where provider and purchaser have to weigh the cost of measurement against the validity and usefulness of the information to provider and purchaser.

3 *Routine measurement of a few negative outcomes.* The best general policy is to require that providers collect and use information about a limited number of negative outcomes (or 'poor quality outcomes') for all services and treatments, and to invite them to put forward their suggestions. The US literature has lists of these for every health service intervention, which are used routinely in audit and by insurance companies and regulators. Common UK 'adverse outcome' measures are discussed in Hopkins (1990). Chapter 7 discusses service quality in more detail.

4 *Outcome measures and provider development.* It is very expensive for providers to use a range of outcome measures devised for research purposes, on a routine basis. Whether purchasers should encourage or finance this depends on their judgement of the developmental role of measurement. Unless outcome measures are part of a quality programme for continuous improvement, they are not likely to be used by providers to make significant changes (Øvretveit 1992a, 1993a).

5 *Outcome measures and audit.* Commissioners should regularly review their policy about requiring access to outcome performance information from providers and to medical audit reports. They have to judge whether clinician and provider improvement is more or less likely if the provider is allowed to keep outcome performance confidential. Purchasers administer finance for medical audit and have a duty to raise questions about how it is spent.

6 *The public's right to know.* Commissioners have to consider how they might make information on effectiveness and provider outcome available to GPs and the public. People can only choose if they can get this information, and can get help to use it. There are arguments for provider confidentiality, especially concerning clinician performance. Commissioners also have to consider dangers of misinterpretation by the public, and balance these and other issues to decide what information should be made available, by whom and how. One option is an information service for the public and GPs, run by commissioners and giving expert advice about choosing providers.

The general conclusion for providers and for purchasers is that they should be selective about which services or treatments to concentrate on for collecting outcome measures. Where at all possible, they should use data already collected, using process and indirect measures, and recognize how much more it costs to measure a wider range of outcomes more frequently.

Box 5.6   Purchaser strategies for better outcomes

Steps for encouraging improved effectiveness through the use of outcome data, for specific services/treatments, or generally.

1   Require medical/clinical audit.
2   Require providers to use outcome data in their audit.
3   Require providers to take part in established national audits (e.g. maternity, NCEPOD).
4   Require that the audit uses systems allowing comparisons.
5   Specify which outcome data are to be collected.
6   Require the provider to share outcome information with the purchaser.
7   Specify outcomes standards in the contract.
8   The purchaser educates GPs and patients about the general effectiveness of treatment and what to ask providers about the outcome, and/or publicizes outcome information from providers.

Practical approaches to justifiable resource allocation

We now return to the question of how commissioners can make more use of information about needs, effectiveness, outcome and provider costs in their resource allocation decisions. The key is to pay attention to the process of implementation and to be selective. In practice commissioners have limited staff, knowledge and information for taking a systematic approach to rationing and resource allocation. They have to be selective and choose services where the above ideas can be applied, yet they also have to consider and explain how they allocate all finance between and within services. There are also problems of implementing change, including changes to GPs' referrals, the independence of fundholder purchasing, providers' difficulties and changes made by other agencies. In this section we review three practical approaches for 'justifiable commissioning' and in the next section propose a systematic approach which commissioners could adopt.

Approach 1: 'muddling through elegantly'

One review of rationing methods for purchasers (Hunter 1993) concludes that health authorities should be cautious about using QUALYs because of the technical criticisms and hidden value assumptions. Hunter also summarizes criticisms of the Oregon approach and argues that, to date, consultations with the public have not produced better informed decisions. He suggests that explicit rational procedures for rationing are vulnerable to subversion and highly costly. They are not necessarily better than implicit rationing, which, with all its disadvantages, does sometimes make more significant change possible. He proposes 'muddling through elegantly', or 'pragmatic sensibility backed by a set of procedural rights governing the way individuals are treated and informed about decisions affecting them'.

This view does offer valid criticisms of the dangers of an apparently objective approach and of the assumptions of economists and believers in rational change. However, it does not provide a clear way forward, or suggest how to improve democratic involvement or public education.

Approach 2: marginal change based on cost–benefit analysis ('pragmatic rationality')

At the other end of the spectrum to 'pragmatic sensibility' is an approach proposed by the Aberdeen health economics group which we could term 'pragmatic rationality' (Mooney *et al.* 1992). This approach combines systematic economic cost–benefit analyses with a practical recognition of the difficulties of change. It recognizes that commissioners only have enough resources to analyse and make informed choices about changes at the margin. The approach proposed is to judge the marginal costs and benefits of decreasing or increasing services, as well as of discontinuing and starting services. The process involves:

- Defining ten to twenty programmes (by client group or disease) and three to eight sub-programmes for each;
- forming 'programme management groups' (PMGs) for priority-setting within programmes;
- estimating programme budgets (how much is spent and outputs);
- PMGs then defining sub-programmes;
- PMGs then focusing on the margin (they do this by considering what changes will produce a high additional benefit, compared to the benefit of the same spend on other services. (This approach reduces the range of activities that will need detailed costing and evaluations of outcome);
- identifying incremental and decremental 'wish lists';
- costing the lists;
- examining the relative benefits of changes in spending (e.g. £50,000);
- deciding and implementing (Mooney *et al.* 1992).

This approach suggests a way of deciding what to buy less of, how to pace withdrawal, who to buy from and how to spend extra resources (released or newly allocated). The approach escapes some of the criticisms made by Hunter because it proposes using general cost–benefit principles and methods to consider incremental changes, using whatever information is available to assess costs and benefits within the areas under consideration. A few commissioners have made some limited use of this approach, one example being in deciding changes to a mental health programme.

Approach 3: targeted health gain approach and outcomes in contracts ('pragmatic targeting')

A third approach is to select a few specific conditions or treatments where the potential benefits of a more systematic and rational outcomes-based approach are high. One example is the Welsh approach, based on the WHO concept of 'adding years to life and life to years' (see the discussion of health gain in Chapter 3). The Welsh strategy targets ten programme areas, where there is evidence that further investment would bring measurable health gain and where some current practices are questionable, and which are priority areas for development (Welsh Office 1991). The *Health of the Nation* approach has some similar features (DoH 1992a), and each purchaser can use these principles to decide priorities in their health strategy.

The East Anglia Region used frameworks to outline how services may be purchased to achieve specified outcomes. Separate 'health outcomes frameworks' (HOFs) were developed for the region to review purchasers, and for purchasers to draw on in contracting providers. To date these cover road accidents, coronary heart disease, asthma, breast and cervical cancer. Each framework is developed by small mixed groups of ten staff from different services, using 'health outcomes grids'. These map the links between service inputs, outputs and outcomes for a disease in terms of primary, secondary and tertiary prevention. The grids identify the breadth of items to be considered, and show the links between process, outputs and contribution to individual and population health outcomes (Bardsley and Streeter 1992).

The features of this approach are: to select priority health problems, define the health outcome or health gain targets, analyse the factors affecting outcomes and draw on this analysis for contracting and contract specification. Although it leaves the bulk of health expenditure untouched, it is a practical way forward for priority areas and a way of developing a more systematic and outcomes-orientated approach.

A systematic 'five-step' process for purchaser prioritization

This section draws together some of the considerations discussed in this chapter to give a framework for 'justifiable commissioning'. The purpose is to show a way in which commissioners can move from an *ad hoc* withdrawal of treatments or services to prioritizing in a systematic and explicit way. It proposes the development of a process for continual review of resource allocation. This process encompasses three sets of issues:

- how and when to involve the key interest groups, mainly GPs, the public and providers;
- improving information about needs, effectiveness, provider outcome

performance and costs, and the proportions of total purchasing resources allocated to different populations, services and sectors;

- managing change, involving reducing services to switch resources to higher priorities and influencing GP referrals and public demand.

In practice, commissioners need to develop a 'step approach' which successively excludes certain needs, treatments and providers, according to explicit criteria. The aim is to allocate resources equitably, and in ways in which resources can do the most good for the least cost, and to ensure that providers do the same, where it is appropriate for commissioners to prescribe provider actions.

Step 1: needs-exclusion from publicly funded services. The first 'step' is excluding or restricting certain needs from being met by using public funds. The focus is on needs, and on social and moral views that, where resources are limited, public funds should not be used to pay for certain health needs. Examples are cosmetic surgery where there is no medical justification. Certain needs may also be excluded because no effective treatments are available. As with each step below, the list of needs and treatments excluded at this step is constantly reviewed, and has to include public and medical views, as well as development of the criteria used to justify exclusion.

Step 2: treatment exclusion or restriction, with poor cost-effectiveness. The second step is reviewing which treatments are known to have no benefits, or to have a low cost-effectiveness. This involves assessing the added value of different treatments, and considering the effect of treating or not treating. It also involves recognizing that there may be exceptions, and developing ways of authorizing providers to use certain treatments in certain cases, with or without commissioner agreement.

Step 3: provider exclusion, with poor outcome performance. The first two steps above exclude a range of needs and treatments from public funding in order to make more finance available for higher-priority needs and treatments. The third step concerns local provider performance. For the remaining needs and treatments to be publicly financed the issue for commissioners is to select the best provider, according to a range of criteria, including good outcome performance, low cost and public preference. This involves getting the relevant information, discussing the information with providers and GPs and consulting the public.

Step 4: deciding relative proportions of resources to allocate. Having excluded certain needs, treatments and providers, purchasers can then review the proportions which they allocate to different services, needs and populations, according to relative health gain ('horizontal allocation'). We discuss ways to do this shortly, one of the problems being that historical budgets are for services or specialties, not for conditions or needs. Once allocations are made for contracts for a particular service, treatment, or condition, purchasers can then consider with GPs and providers whether there should be protocols for prioritizing waiting lists ('vertical allocation').

Step 5: managing change. Commissioners are better at formulating than implementing priorities. The fifth step is to carry through any changes to resource allocations which follow from any of the above steps. This involves reducing or withdrawing contracts and transferring resources, influencing and agreeing changes to GP referrals (referral protocols), reaching agreements with fundholders and influencing public demand, in part by providing information about provider performance. It also includes reaching agreements with providers about protocols for selecting patients who can benefit from treatments, ECRs and tertiary referrals. We consider how purchasers manage such changes below and in Chapter 6.

Over time, commissioners would be able to develop criteria for decisions in each step. These will need to combine technical and value considerations and involve a range of interest groups, and the public in appropriate ways, but it is the responsibility of commissioners to develop the prioritizing process and criteria and to resolve the conflicts and justify their decisions.

More details about reviewing expenditure proportions (step 4)

At the beginning of the chapter we proposed that justifiable commissioning calls for a move from *ad hoc* exclusions to reviewing the bulk of expenditure. This means forming a more accurate picture of how the bulk of resources are allocated between care groups, sub-groups, services, sectors and treatments. Many commissioners are taking steps in this direction by disaggregating contracts and improving their financial and IT systems. A comprehensive picture then makes it possible to review allocations, and to consider different types of resource shifts and their effects. The following framework is one basis for a systematic review.

Meaningful prioritization has to consider how decisions about decreasing allocations can be implemented; otherwise the detailed work of formulating priorities and agonizing is wasted. Two difficulties commissioners face in taking a systematic approach to priorities are, first, understanding how different decisions resulted in the current expenditure allocation, and, second, recognizing which decisions they can and should influence in order to change allocations. Current allocations are the end result of a particular history of personalities, opportunities and many explicit and implicit decisions. The first step is to recognize the different decisions made (or not made) at different levels which result in resource allocations. Drawing on Klein (1992), we can distinguish three 'levels of rationing'.

- National: apportionment of public finance to health services (versus other services – other public services contribute to health).
- Local: apportionment *between* care groups, services or sectors, and apportionment *within* services/care groups.
- Individual: practitioners apportioning resources between patients they serve.

For each of the levels there are national and regional requirements which constrain the discretion commissioning agencies have over resource allocation (e.g. *Health of the Nation* targets, corporate contracts with the region, the Patient's Charter etc.). Distinguishing levels in this way also helps us to consider the scope for public involvement in certain decisions and how to involve the public.

Why prioritization is not so simple in practice

The above discussion emphasized review of current allocations, analysis of how these allocations came to be and where the scope was for commissioners to make changes. The point was to draw attention to implementing priorities and to making a comprehensive review because these two issues are often neglected.

Commissioners have difficulty in assembling the basic information needed to review their allocations, before they can consider effectiveness and the other issues discussed above. There are problems in deciding whether to consider allocations by care group, service sector, type of service or other category. Information systems which allow analysis by different categories are needed. There are problems in identifying budgets, and then manipulating the information in different ways to show the proportions of finance allocated for different care groups, services and sectors. This difficulty will be eased, in part, by disaggregating contract details and integrated information technology systems.

With information about relative proportions, commissioners can then make more meaningful decisions about changing proportions, drawing on their increasing knowledge about needs, effectiveness and provider performance. However, not only are budgets fragmented, but so are responsibilities within commissioning organizations for working on the different areas of needs assessment, contracting, etc. This makes it difficult to bring together these understandings in a comprehensive review, and, more importantly, to carry through changes in a coordinated way into contracts. Later chapters consider these 'vertical' and 'horizontal' linking problems in commissioning.

Does this mean then that a fully comprehensive approach to reviewing priorities and making rational change is not possible at present? It is certainly true that better information will become available about services, effectiveness, needs and outcome at different times, but for some acute treatments and needs we already have sufficient information to change priorities on a rational basis. There is a lack of even the basic information about many community and primary care interventions and needs. However, this does not mean that commissioners cannot take a systematic approach and develop ways to begin to recognize and justify their decisions.

A global review and assessment of changes has to be done, involving those who can support and block any changes. This means considering how different parties can and should be involved in the different decisions in the step process and in the different levels of the framework. It means working on ways to involve those who will have to implement or can prevent the changes (primarily GPs, providers and the public). It means developing processes and ways of resolving conflicts between interest groups and priorities.

A role for the public in rationing

In a survey of who should ration, the public put GPs first and then consultants, and third, managers (25 per cent). Only 22 per cent of the public thought that they should be involved. For their part, managers put GPs first, then consultants and then themselves – 52 per cent supported 'public involvement'. Doctors agreed that they should be involved (only 30 per cent supported 'public involvement') but few thought there should be any changes to how they ration at present.

(MORI/KF/BMA survey for BMA conference on rationing,
Health Services Journal 18 March 1993: 6, 16)

In this part of the chapter we return to the main theme: commissioning as a service to the public, summarized here as 'justifiable commissioning'. If commissioning is a service, what should be the role of the public in prioritizing? Other publications provide discussions of the purposes and methods of public involvement, especially those on 'locality purchasing', the NHS ME 'local voices' (DoH 1992b) and Sykes *et al.* (1992). Here we are concerned with how a purchaser as a service organization decides which services it will and will not provide, directly and indirectly. It needs to seek guidance about prioritizing decisions and to implement these decisions in a way which upholds its purpose in the eyes of the public as a service to them. While there are dangers in limiting the 'appropriate' role for the public, there are perhaps more dangers in expensive consultation exercises which produce information of little use.

A central issue for commissioners is to clarify the specific purpose of any relations with the public with respect to prioritizing. These can include educating and informing (e.g. about effectiveness and outcome), getting a representative view about priorities and 'posteriorities' (what to reduce in order to increase funding for priorities), giving an account of decisions made on the public's behalf and allowing appeals and challenges. Providing information to patients about effectiveness is one way to increase patient choice and to influence demand for more effective treatments. This can be done in collaboration with providers, by direct publicity by commissioners, by commissioners making sure that patients or patient pressure groups can get access to effectiveness information, or by a special expert advisory service. Commissioners can encourage the public (and GPs) to ask questions about outcomes and options, by providing general and condition-specific checklists. They can indicate for which treatments providers should give their outcome performance.

One consequence of viewing commissioning as a service is that commissioners have to be prepared to respond to demand for more effective but higher-cost treatments. What should be the purchaser's response to a public view that cosmetic breast surgery should have a higher priority than treating an open fracture of the femur, a finding from one consultation exercise (Klein 1991)? Commissioners have to be selective in how they consult the public, and over which decisions: they cannot afford to waste public money and raise expectations using approaches which provide contradictory, unrepresentative and unusable information. A practical way forward is to identify the areas of uncertainty, where the public can and should influence decision-making, and use cost-effective methods to seek public views.

The frameworks described above can be used to identify the areas for consultation and the purpose and methods of consultation. Consultation about priority allocation between different client groups and services is often less useful than consultation over lower-level issues of resource allocation within client groups and queuing criteria. People are more interested in client group and condition-specific issues than in general issues, and are more likely to have informed views about priorities within these areas. Finally, there is the question of how to respond as a service to patients or patient groups when the commissioner decides to discontinue services. A commissioning organization has to justify such decisions, and should have involved the public in the prioritizing process so that the decision is recognized as one made on behalf of and with the support of the majority. While there is debate about entitlement or substantive rights to different types of health care, there is more agreement about the importance of procedural rights, especially where fairness may be questioned. This means ensuring that patients and patient groups have procedural rights to:

- a fair hearing;
- equal treatment;
- unbiased decisions;
- providers and purchasers following explicit guidelines, where there is discretion and uncertainty;
- an explanation of the reasons and procedures for a decision;
- opportunity, procedures and information about appealing against decisions.

Conclusions: towards justifiable purchasing

Trust the public, lay it out in the open. Some argue that the problem is that everybody thinks there is infinite money. People don't think that actually; they have more sense. They know perfectly well that there is not infinite money and that some things are more important than others.

(William Waldegrave, then Secretary of State for Health, NHS ME Purchasing for Health conference, May 1991)

The public recognize that health services are rationed and have accepted the different ways in which this was done, assuming that doctors and others in authority did it fairly and competently. However, with a widening gap between needs and the services available, and a more individualist and rights-orientated society, many people are less willing to accept that they will not get the health care they feel they have a right to.

Rationing is acceptable to the majority, if it is fair and just, decided impersonally before the individual event, and appeals are allowed. The challenge to commissioners is to:

- give an account to the public about how they allocate finance, and why they make the decisions which they do, or fail to make them;
- explain exactly where they as commissioners have discretion to make changes;
- show the process by which they make decisions, and how the public may influence the process or appeal against the decisions;
- show that they are developing and introducing systematic ways to direct public finance to the most effective and needed treatments and services;
- develop commissioning processes which ensure justice and equity, and uphold the interests of the 'voiceless' and 'less noisy'.

This chapter gave a framework for developing a more rational approach to resource allocation. It showed how commissioners could make better use of finance by using information about effectiveness, cost-effectiveness and provider performance. Although there are major problems in getting information and making changes, commissioners can redirect at least some finance to better effect. This chapter also described practical approaches which recognized the current limitations.

Commissioners are increasingly controlling expenditure, which has grown in *ad hoc* and unplanned ways, by formal rules of resource allocation, in different ways at different levels. Some interventions are excluded because they are proven to be ineffective, some patients are excluded because their capacity to benefit is low, some providers are excluded because they have poor outcomes or high costs relative to outcome. For some interventions, the value to the patient of the benefit may be higher than a commissioner's evaluation, and commissioners may decide that the NHS should not pay.

While commissioners cannot intrude too far into clinical matters, they do have to take the lead in encouraging debate and agreeing changes with doctors and other interest groups. Unjustifiable commissioning means not being prepared to switch allocations of large amounts of public finance from costly services where the benefit is dubious. The onus should be on the provider to prove benefit, rather than on the purchaser to justify withdrawing when there is no proof of benefit.

More of the public are recognizing that, with limited finance, some high-cost interventions mean fewer, or no, low-cost but high-benefit services to others: that commissioning is political. Unless commissioners justify their allocations and show how they are to make better use of public finance, there will be less public support for the restrictions and changes that are coming. There will be little justification for public health service purchasing beyond a minor financial and administrative function.

Key points

- Rationing is restricting supply where demand exceeds supply. Prioritizing is deciding the relative proportion of resources to allocate to patients, patient groups or services.
- With limited finance and increasing demand, commissioners have to review the bulk of their expenditures, rather than excluding particular treatments in an *ad hoc* way – to prioritize, not just ration.
- Commissioners can develop their service role through 'justifiable purchasing': giving an explanation of the basis for, and process by which they decide resource allocation and contract providers, and involve the public in the process in an appropriate way.
- Commissioners are better at formulating priorities than implementing them. They need to pay attention to how decisions can be implemented, by involving interest groups and by developing a strategy for managing change.
- In deciding priorities, commissioners have to consider not only efficacy and effectiveness, but also local issues of provider performance, acceptability, preference, likely take-up, access and needs.
- Reliable and valid routine outcome measurement is expensive, and needs to be introduced and developed selectively. Initially, commissioners should focus on known indicators of poor medical quality or adverse outcomes.
- A realistic approach for commissioners is through marginal analysis and change: identifying services and treatments where investing small additional sums would produce a relatively high benefit (and reducing those where small reductions have a relatively small loss of benefit).
- A more comprehensive approach to prioritizing is through five steps which successively exclude certain needs, treatments and providers according to explicit criteria, before deciding relative allocations and managing change.
- Commissioners can offer an independent information service to the public and GPs to give expert advice about effectiveness and outcomes so that people can make more informed choices and drive change.
- Purchasers have to establish effective links within their organization between staff working on contracting and purchasing strategy and those working on needs assessment, information about effectiveness, information about provider costs and performance, global resource allocation, GP referrals and ECRs.

6 Contracting and contracts

I leave all that health needs nonsense to public health . . . it's irrelevant . . . I just place contracts and try to get more out of them [the provider] than they are giving us at the moment.
(A director of contracting, quoted in a study of health authority purchasing, cited in Freemantle *et al.* 1993)

Introduction

The principal means by which commissioners pursue their purpose of health gain is through contracting providers. In the 'pre-market' NHS there was a weak link between district planning and service operations: even well-developed strategies tended to disappear in the 'gaps' between district offices and hospitals and primary and community health services. With the purchaser–provider split the gaps widened, but formal contracts helped to bridge the gaps. The weak link was often within the commissioning organization: the gap between staff working on contracts and staff working on strategy and needs assessment.

This chapter considers how commissioners can take a more proactive role in contracting providers and ensure that their health strategy drives their contract strategy, rather than vice versa. The subject of this chapter is the relationship between a commissioning organization and larger providers, such as hospitals and community health service organizations. Although the focus is on the details of contracting and contracts, the theme is contracts in context: as an aspect of a deeper relationship and as linked to a health strategy. The purpose of the chapter is to help to strengthen the links. It does this by showing how contracts and contracting can be shaped by health strategy, and by giving commissioning managers not working on contracts an overview and an appreciation of what contracting managers need from them. We consider switching contracts in a competitive provider market, and how to influence a provider where there are no alternative providers.

The emphasis on hospitals and medical specialties reflects commissioners' preoccupations in the first years of the NHS reforms. Later chapters consider primary care and community health providers. This chapter starts with a summary of the evolution of service contracting in the NHS since 1991, and notes some of the issues for commissioners in the mid-1990s. It describes three practical examples of contracting practices and strategies: managing referrals outside large contracts, contracting medical specialties and reducing the number of contracts. It then describes the different types of contracts which commissioners can use, and considers how commissioners might change their type of contract to share risks better and to give providers incentives to reduce costs and improve quality. The chapter addresses some of the following issues raised by purchasing managers.

- *In effect there are no alternative providers for most services in our area – we're stuck with each other. How can we influence them in our contracting process?*
- *How can we pursue a contracting strategy, let alone a health strategy, when many providers and specialties are pursuing their own track, regardless, fundholders are acting independently, politicians chop and change, GPs refer where they like and we are not even prepared to refuse outrageous ECRs? It's already too complex to understand, let alone influence.*
- *How do we best identify the acute specialties where we can cooperate with other purchasers to drive changes?*
- *How do we balance the interests of our residents with the longer-term common good: if we agree to a common strategy for one or more specialties, our own 'local' provider may lose contracts to the point that their 'core' services become more and more expensive. We may end up footing the bill for others' economies and with a worse service for our residents.*
- *How do we bridge the gulf in our commissioning organization between public health, others working on strategy and those negotiating and managing contracts?*

The myth of the market?

The strength of health purchasing depends on the type of market and regulations, and on the local markets for different services. Chapter 2 summarized the NHS 'internal market' as introducing new types of economic 'market competition':

- separation between health authority purchasers and providers;
- providers not being assured income, and having to agree 'contracts' with purchasers to secure their finance;
- NHS trusts with more independence to borrow, set pay rates and decide the range of services to provide;
- limited competition between providers for purchaser contracts and GP referrals;
- limited GP purchasing of some services.

In the first two years of the NHS 'market reforms', commissioner contracting followed previous health authority expenditure patterns. Some commissioners changed contracts in 1993, for a variety of reasons. It was during 1993 that commissioners began to take a more proactive role, and to cooperate in 'managing the market' for a few medical specialties. In 1994, purchasers were getting more detailed information about costs and activity, and began to switch contracts to providers with shorter waiting times and lower costs. In many areas, GP fundholders were having an increasing effect on provider performance and viability.

In many areas of the UK and in other countries there is, and will be, little competition between providers or between purchasers. One subject of this chapter is how, with limited or no competition, a purchaser can influence providers to offer the services which the purchaser considers necessary and at the lowest cost. We concentrate on purchaser–provider relations and on contracting in these low- or nil-competition 'market situations', although we also consider how purchasers can influence the types and degree of provider competition over the longer term. The following section considers commissioners' relations with providers in the context of the NHS 'market'. This sets the context for looking at contracting and contracts in more detail in later sections.

The evolution of the purchaser–provider relationship in the NHS

It was only possible to introduce the 1990 market reforms in the NHS because of earlier management reforms and improvements to budgeting. During the 1980s, many authorities changed their accounting systems to form budgets for each provider unit. In the first 'steady state' years of the reforms (1990–2) this work was completed: in effect health authorities renamed their budgets for providers as 'contracts', and agreed broad descriptions of the providers' services ('block contracts'). These types of contract did not give providers incentives to increase productivity – they were paid the same regardless of the amount of work they did.

Most health authorities had one large block contract with their own directly managed acute hospital and community services, and a few small contracts with services in neighbouring districts. Referrals to services not covered by these contracts were treated as extra-contractual referrals (ECRs), discussed below. Some health authorities in urban areas had a greater number of contracts with the many providers outside the district, but within short travelling distance. More detailed contracts emerged during early 1992 and 1993. These involved more detailed descriptions of the different provider services covered by the one contract. An authority would contract a hospital to provide different medical specialties, and the contract would contain details of each medical specialty's services. More contracts specified the number of patients or treatments to be provided for a price, usually for a one-year period (cost and volume contracts).

There were exceptions. Contracts with community service providers (e.g. community nurses) often did not specify volume (e.g. 'patient contracts') or cost. Contracts were placed for different volumes and covering different lengths of time. Much depended on the purchasing authority predicting GP referral patterns, from information from previous years' referrals, and sometimes from discussions with GPs about their proposed changes. Generally, accurate information about past referrals was a good predictor of future patterns, but sometimes this information was inaccurate or not available.

The 1993 NHS 'market'

From the perspective of commissioning authorities, the main problems of the internal market in 1993 were:

- providers exceeding budget or contracted volumes;
- GPs referring to providers which were not covered by the commissioner's contract, and the commissioner having to pay a high price for an individual treatment (ECRs);
- GP fundholder purchasers getting faster treatments for their patients;
- the number of GP fundholders increasing, thus reducing the amount of purchasing finance available to health authorities;
- some health authorities' financial allocations being reduced – there was a change from RAWP allocation adjusted for cross-boundary flow (DHSS 1976) to, in 1991–2, allocations based on historical data of treatments received by residents in 'home' and 'away' providers (average specialty costs), and then over time to a weighted capitation allocation for the resident population.

The main market trends were authority mergers, more NHS trusts with less security, provider mergers and reconfiguration, and more small purchasers in the shape of GP fundholders. There was little change in private purchasing or provision. The contracting trend was from the original broad 'block' or 'budget' contracts to increasing detail and a variety of types of contract, and towards purchasers being more prepared to change contracts. In 1993, political and technical factors prevented purchasers from making major changes and from switching contracts to pursue better value for money single-mindedly.

The evolving 'market': post-1994

The maturity and efficiency of any market can be judged by the information available about provider costs, their potential capacity and their quality. The fourth year of the reforms saw an increase in the amount and quality of this information. There was an increase in the variety of types of contract and in details of contract specifications as purchasers and providers sought to minimize their risks. Beyond cost and volume contracts (described below), we see contracts including crude case-mix, and moves to healthcare resource group classifications (HRGs) and a few diagnostic related group approaches (DRGs). There was also a trend to specifying outcomes and quality, and towards a health gain approach which could involve a single contract with different providers. Purchasers and providers who had invested in information systems and resource management had a great advantage. For providers, detail about costs and past patterns allowed them to plan and control their activity, and to price competitively, even though the rules were that pricing was at cost.

Each year is hailed as the 'test of the market system', but 1994 was certainly a significant step for the NHS market. It tested cooperation between purchasers, GPs and providers, and relations with higher levels of the NHS. The contract negotiations for 1994 saw purchasers being more willing to change contracts, and the effects of these changes on providers being decisive in terms of their survival. While there is now a wish to ensure long-term purchaser–provider partnerships, rather than to pursue crude short-term gain, many purchasers are not able to continue to contract high-cost providers. Relatively small contract changes by purchasers or fundholders are having a disproportionate effect on some providers, who are forced to merge, rationalize or close unless purchasers are prepared to pay comparatively higher prices. Some trusts are forced back towards their 'home' commissioning agencies as other commissioners withdraw contracts. 'Home' commissioners, especially revenue losers with many fundholders, are not able to afford to maintain some local specialties or even institutions.

Contracting issues and models

In this 'market' or, more accurately, in these different competitive environments for different services, a purchasing organization has to develop ways to carry through its strategy and adapt it to the evolving situation. Here we note six sets of issues in doing so, and outline a model of the commissioning process which links health strategy to the contract cycle.

Six issues

The first issue is the need to continue to develop health strategy, and to ensure that this drives contracting and relationships with different parties.

Without such a strategy a purchaser is dominated by provider concerns and short-term contracting preoccupations. A key problem is ensuring that contracts staff and contracting processes link with other staff and processes within the commissioning organization. This involves getting the right internal organizational links at the right times, but also structuring categories for needs assessment and health gain objectives in ways which are relatable to services for contracting purposes. We consider the latter below under the subject of 'contract definition and grouping'.

A second issue is how to make the best use of staff time and experience. In most UK commissioning organizations, there are no more than four staff per 100,000 population working on contracts and purchasing strategy, and often fewer. This limits the amount of detail and sophistication which is possible in contracts, and the ability of staff to search for and negotiate value for money, especially with poor information. This limit to purchaser capacity is one factor which reduces the speed of evolution of contracting and of the NHS market. It calls for a selective approach, illustrated in one of the examples in the next section.

A third issue is how to influence GPs to refer to purchaser-preferred or contracted providers. Although commissioners can refuse ECRs (see below), such refusals make it more difficult to work with GPs to help them improve primary care and reduce their use of hospitals. Commissioner alternatives to fundholding are one way of influencing referrals and demand, and of keeping within expenditure limits, not least to be able to divert finance into primary care.

A fourth issue is developing and following a strategy with GP fundholders. Fundholders acting independently can undermine any strategies for planned specialty rationalizations. The faster treatment for fundholder patients is becoming more apparent, not just at year-end. In Hertfordshire the crude figures showed that, in 1993, waiting lists increased by 24 per cent for non-fundholder patients, but decreased by 33 per cent for fundholder patients (the hospitalization rate for non-fundholders was 34 per 1,000 population, and for fundholders 51). The inequities are not necessarily because fundholders are more astute purchasers, or because of the disproportionate effects which they can have on some providers. The development of 'shared purchasing' arrangements is necessary for future strategy and short-term contracting.

The fifth issue is getting and using reliable information about providers. The efficiency of a market as a system depends in part on easily accessible information about prices, quality and capacity. For commissioners to choose or switch contracts they need accurate information in a form which allows them to make valid comparisons. Having agreed a contract, commissioners need information about quality, provider activity and costs in relation to planned contracted levels. Skills in using the information correctly are also important – one view was that purchaser managers have been 'seemingly incapable of using routine data to interrogate clinical practices and inform purchaser and provider choices' (Maynard 1993b: 23).

The sixth set of issues solely concerns relations with a provider, mainly the scope to change contract design or to withdraw contracts:

• A small change in one contract can lead to a provider not being able to meet other contracts with the same purchaser.
• Uncertainty of the consequences of reducing or withdrawing a contract from a provider: the political repercussions and the effect on the provider's continued viability.
• Providers 'crying wolf': the difficulty of judging, without accurate information, a provider's claims that contract changes will threaten its viability.
• How to move from broad to more detailed contracts and how to approach case-mix costing.
• Whether to develop direct relationships with clinical directors within provider organizations.
• How to develop appropriate partnership rather than adversarial relations with providers.

Contracting models

For contracting to be driven by health strategy, a commissioning organization needs effective internal links between contracting staff and others (Chapter 12), and a shared understanding of the contracting process. Models of contracting simplify complexity and help us to focus on the key tasks: they help contracting staff to relate what they do to an overall process and timetable, and they can help other staff to see when and how they fit in with the process. There are many models of the contracting process or cycle, and purchasing managers need to judge which are most helpful for organizing their work, according to what the model highlights or ignores. Early models tended to view commissioning as a contracting process, with needs assessment at the front end. Some later models of the contracting cycle do not make links to a broader commissioner process of health strategy formulation and revision. More general models of the commissioning process sometimes do not give sufficient detail of the contracting cycle. The model in Figure 6.1 emphasizes the contracting cycle in the context of broader commissioning work.

Staff working in contracting will need more detailed models of the contract cycle or process, but these need to show the connections with other commissioning activities, and the critical 'link times' in the contract cycle. Some models are more suited to purchasers working with one main provider. Some are suited to situations where a purchaser has choice of provider, and where inviting tenders and selecting providers is an important part of the process.

Examples of contracting practices and policies

This section presents three examples of actions which commissioners have taken to address some of the issues noted earlier. It gives some illustration

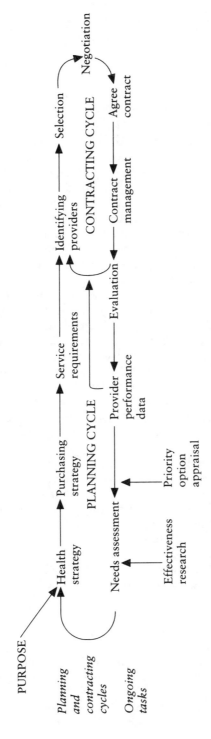

Figure 6.1 The contracting cycle in the context of a long-term planning cycle.

of the practical issues in contracting, before we turn to details of contract design in the next section.

Extra-contractual referrals (ECRs)

ECR management is not an administrative backwater but the front line of the market system. An ECR is a referral made to a provider, which is outside existing contracts between the provider and the patient's purchaser. Tangible evidence of how the market was working was first revealed in how commissioners dealt with ECRs, and ECR issues continue to foreshadow market developments. ECR management shows how commissioners have handled GP and patient choice, equity and budgetary constraints. In some respects the number of ECRs is an index of the quality of a purchasing strategy. In refusing to pay for ECRs which could be treated at an already contracted provider, but with a longer waiting list, commissioners are striking a balance between equity, choice and financial considerations, and shaping the type of market which will operate.

Initially ECRs were where GPs referred patients to hospitals outside the area with no contracts with the purchaser, and this still accounts for the majority of ECRs. Towards the end of the 1991/2 financial year some purchasers refused elective ECRs because they needed the finance to pay for emergency treatments. (In Sweden the opposite is the case: if a patient has to wait longer than three or twelve months for certain treatments, the county has to pay for treatment by providers other than its 'home' provider.) The cost of a single ECR treatment or care episode is usually higher than that of a part volume or block contract. In addition, the costs of ECR administration for a purchaser are high: Trafford HA estimated a cost of £41 to handle each ECR, and a total cost of £20,200 in 1991–2 (Sargent 1992).

Purchasers establish ECR budgets to pay for GP referrals which the purchaser cannot predict, or for which the purchaser has not established a contract for a variety of reasons, such as a 'tertiary referral' (to a second specialist provider: DoH 1992e). Increasingly, ECRs are not just to distant hospitals: more 'home' providers are excluding certain high-cost treatments from their large contracts and charging these as ECRs to reduce their average treatment cost. ECRs are a growing issue for all commissioners because their refusal to pay ECRs reduces GP and patient choice of provider. The choice may be because a distant provider has a shorter waiting list, but the higher cost of an ECR would mean less finance for other patients to be treated locally who have the same need, thus introducing inequities. ECR refusals also introduce rationing on an individual case-by-case basis.

The first of the two common ways for administering ECRs is for the provider to check with the purchaser before accepting the referral and agree a single 'ECR contract' with the purchaser. The second way is to do the work and invoice (i.e. 'charge' or 'bill') the purchaser in the hope that the purchaser will pay. Purchasers can refuse to pay for elective ECRs if they have not given prior authorization, but they can only refuse authorization if the referral was not justified on clinical grounds or there are 'equally effective' and acceptable alternatives. In the first few years of the NHS reforms, many providers were poor at identifying ECR patients or patients' 'home' purchasers. As providers improved their patient registration and invoicing systems, it became easier to check with a purchaser before treating even the more urgent cases. More cases arose where there were delays in patient treatment or transfer as providers sought authorization, even though emergency ECRs are automatically paid. Death resulted in one case – the inquiry commented that 'Phone calls to managers of purchasing authorities and provider units have no place in emergency transfer of patients whose lives depend on immediate action' (Inquiry Report, *Health Services Journal* 13 May 1993: 19).

It was not just better registration and administration by providers which increased the calls on purchasers' ECR budgets. As we noted above, some providers began to exclude high-cost treatments from normal contracts and to charge them at specific prices as ECRs, thus being able to reduce their average prices. As a result, purchasers increasingly found their ECR budgets heading for overspending half way through the financial year. One response was to cash-limit ECR spending for a provider with many contract exclusions, an example being Bloomsbury HA setting a £150,000 ECR cash-limit for Guy's and Lewisham Trust for 1992–3.

To keep within their budgets for ECRs, more purchasers began to refuse authorization for high-cost treatments. Guidance from the Department of Health in 1992 (DoH 1992d) reduced purchasers' scope to refuse ECRs: 'Occasions on which a clinician's choice of provider can be judged to be unwarranted are likely to be very rare.' The guidance was that purchasers could not refuse authorization only because an ECR would cost more than the same treatment under an existing contract with another provider. In practice, explicit rationing first took place through purchasers refusing certain ECRs and developing an ECR policy or protocol out of their case-by-case experience. An example is the Haringey protocol for elective referrals, which is to accept ECRs only when both patient and doctor are agreed on the need for the referral, and it can be supported on medical grounds (Whincup and Zahir 1993).

We now turn to two other examples of contracting in practice, to show the ways in which commissioners can influence markets and provider behaviour within the constraints of the system.

Contracting strategies: two examples

The following example illustrates the types of contracts and contracting in practice in the summer of 1993, as reported by commissioning staff in the North West Thames integrated agencies. It also shows that 'market co-operation' and a 'bottom-up' approach to influencing the market are possible. Commissioners can draw on such experience to formulate achievable commissioning strategies for specialties and hospitals.

Example A: contracts for hospital services
In July 1993 one commissioning agency (population of 300,000) had 20 main contracts of over £ 25,000 per year with 20 hospitals, and one main contract for community health services. The largest contract was for 65 per cent of the purchasing agency's expenditure (£32 million) with one provider. The second largest contract was for 20 per cent of expenditure, and the remaining contracts each accounted for less than 3 per cent of expenditure. The main contract with the local hospital covered 18 main specialties, and involved:

- a description of the services of each specialty;
- general and specialty-specific quality standards (e.g. waiting times);
- details of arrangements for monthly payment and monthly monitoring reports of activity, for day cases, outpatients and inpatients, for the hospital and for some specialties.

Other contracts were similar block contracts with the other 19 hospitals, for a number of specialties, sometimes with indicative cost and volume. Many of these contracts excluded some specialties within a hospital, where referrals were to be treated as ECRs. There were 'stand alone' specialty cost and volume contracts (i.e. just for a specialty service at one hospital) with two different hospitals (e.g. for paediatrics).

Most contracts specified, for each specialty, the proposed number of cases and the average price. The aim was to move to 'indicative' cost and volume figures for some specialties, such as orthopaedics, urology and ear, nose and throat. In a few instances a 'case-mix' distinction was made between minor, intermediate and major cases (e.g. orthopaedics). Two advantages of broad contracts which a commissioner manager cited were lower administrative costs compared to more detailed contracts, and allowing providers to transfer finance between specialties which under- or over-performed. The commissioner's contracting policy in practice was:

- to reduce the number of contracts, especially those with distant providers;
- to encourage more day surgery and non-invasive procedures, where quality was assured;
- to get GPs to refer to contracted providers and to reduce ECRs.

It was necessary to work closely with GPs to pursue this policy; otherwise GPs would continue to refer and a case would have to be paid for or refused as an ECR. One example of successful cooperation was persuading GPs to refer some patients to another hospital, with shorter waiting and lower costs. The GPs agreed, and a contract was made: after a time the GPs wanted to send patients to the other hospital routinely and asked for a change of contract from the original provider.

The purchaser was also increasing pressure on providers for more information about costs, and for information which would allow them to make reliable comparisons. They were taking a selective approach with 'troublesome' specialties with long waiting times, high costs or GP concerns. In some cases they combined with other purchasers to threaten withdrawal. More recently, the purchaser began to share price information with other neighbouring purchasers (e.g. one hospital was charging one purchaser double the price charged to a neighbouring purchaser).

Example B: reducing the number of contracts
A second contracting example is one purchaser's strategy to reduce the number of providers which it contracted. The aim was to save on the costs of purchasing, to get lower prices for larger volume contracts and to get higher quality. The approach the purchaser took was to work out the difference between contracting two or three providers, as opposed to seven or eight, in terms of the costs and quality of the options. These options were discussed with GPs, with other purchasers and with the providers. The result was that GPs agreed to refer to fewer providers, and fewer contracts were placed. This 'bottom-up' planning approach based on purchaser cooperation is possible with specialties which are not 'intrinsic to hospital viability' (examples are ENT, oral surgery and ophthalmology). The 'rule of thumb' used about viability was the type and amount of services needed in conjunction with a full accident and emergency department (e.g. general medicine, surgery, orthopaedics, urology). For other services and regional and national specialties, a 'top-down' planning approach is required.

In summary, to improve their purchasing strategy, commissioners need to draw on experience of successful contracting initiatives. Lessons from contracting are one part, but an important part of developing a realistic and achievable strategy. Such a strategy also depends on using the right contract design in order to share risks appropriately with providers and to give the right incentives, a subject to which we now turn.

Contracting and relations with providers

Selecting providers who will carry out the purchaser's objectives is one way of linking contracting to overall strategy. Another is for contracts managers to agree with providers a contract design which gives providers the right incentives. For some services, purchasers may have a choice of provider, and may be able to invite competitive tenders. They can stipulate or agree a type of contract, but need to know what the options are. They need to predict how the type of contract will influence provider behaviour, and how this will advance or detract from the overall strategy, rather than shape contracts only for short-term savings.

Many purchasers have little choice of provider, and need to develop their relationship with existing providers. Again, contract type and design is important for furthering the strategy. Purchasers can structure contracts in ways which make it more or less difficult for a provider to work to-wards a commissioner's objectives. This is especially so for smaller provid-ers in community and social care markets. In considering future contracts it is useful to draw lessons from past contracting experience, and to con-sider the advantages and disadvantages of different types of contracts for strategies in different market sectors. The following summarizes types of contract, describes ways in which contracts differ and discusses the factors which commissioners need to consider when deciding to change their type of contract, or which type to use with a new provider.

Contract definition and grouping

Most commissioners define and group contracts in terms of different pro-viders and mostly in terms of medical specialties, as we saw in the ex-amples above. Contract definition has tended to reflect provider boundaries and management structure, and this corresponds to a service-led rather than needs-led strategy. This is not to suggest that the other extreme – defining contracts by needs – is the best way forward even if it were practical. Examples of this approach would be to define and let contracts by patient or client group and/or patient condition, or by health gain target. For example, one could invite a tender from services to reduce death from heart attacks, which would involve provider consortium bids with a combination of health promotion, prevention, surgical, rehabilita-tion and community health services. A mid-way option is to continue to contract by service, but to emphasize outcome and health gain targets in the contracts. Another is to define and let some contracts for patient episodes or client pathways (Øvretveit 1993b), which cross different pro-viders, possibly allowing one provider to subcontract. Commissioners in the future are likely to use a combination of different ways of defining contracts, rather than defining all by service and concentrating on provider inputs and activity.

Contract definition is an issue for purchasers wishing to change from a provider-orientated to a needs-led strategy. Figure 6.2 depicts the 'translation gap' or 'matching problem' as one reason why needs assessment and health strategy have had little impact on contracting, even when a commissioner has good internal links between staff.

There are considerable problems in moving to defining even some con-tracts by needs rather than by services. For commissioners the key issue is how to relate categories used for needs assessment and health gain targets to the categories used to define contracts, such as by provider boundary and structure. Working out a way to do so makes it easier for contract staff to translate health strategy into contracts. It makes it easier for staff working on needs assessment and health gain issues to translate their work into provider actions. The main management tool is a matrix or concep-tual schema which relates types of needs to types of services. Over time we may see providers redefining their services to coincide more closely with

Needs (definition/categories)		*Contracts*

By care group
By condition or related
  conditions
By geographical area
By health gain subject
	←*The translation gap*→	By provider
		By medical specialty
		By provider's geographical
		  sector

Figure 6.2 Categorizing what to buy: a problem in relating health strategy to contracts.

the way purchasers conceptualize needs, especially where there is one main purchaser and one main provider. One example is agreeing the same geographical areas for needs assessment and community health service provision.

Contract type

Box 6.1 lists different types of contract, in terms of time, volume, detail and other aspects. In principle, commissioners have a wide choice of the types of contract which they can use, and need to be aware of the advantages and disadvantages of each. If the situation changes, a commissioner may need to establish a new type of contract with a provider, and may need to use a different type of contract in a different contracting process, such as tendering. The chapter later considers the factors which purchasers have to consider in deciding which type to use or whether to change.

The trend is towards differentiating large block contracts into smaller separate contracts. The reason for doing so is to agree better incentive and risk-sharing arrangements, and because it is required and recommended: 'The NHS ME has instructed HAs and trusts to end the use of block contracts after 1994–5, and negotiate "explicit agreement on sharing risks" if activity exceeded contract levels' (*Health Service Journal* 8 July 1993: 4). 'Health authorities should calculate the amount of neonatal intensive care they need and specify quantity and quality in separate contracts rather than rely on services being provided through block contracts' (Summary of a recommendation from a report by the Clinical Standards Advisory Group, July 1993).

In the next section we focus on changing contract design with an existing provider. Before this we look at one issue in selecting providers – how to make valid comparisons between providers concerning costs and types of services – and at new standards for costing and treatment and service classification.

Box 6.1 Types of contract

Contracts differ according to *what* is specified, in what *detail* and the *consequences* of not keeping to the agreement.

1 *Block contract*. Like a *budget for a defined service* – an agreement to pay a sum for a period of time (e.g. one year) in exchange for patient access to the service, but number of patients (volume) and costs per patient are not specified.

2 *Block, indicative cost and volume*. A block contract, with an agreed specification of the *total* number of patients to be treated by, e.g. a hospital, for a defined amount of money. Specification is guidance – an indication.

3 *Block indicative specialty cost and volume contract*. As for 2, but an indicative contract for one or more services or specialties within a provider organization.

4 *'Stand-alone' specialty cost and volume contract*. An agreement to pay x for y number of people to be treated by one specialty (e.g. a contract with a private hospital, for a service, to reduce waiting times).

5 *Case-mix 'stand-alone' specialty cost and volume contract*. As with 4, with different payments according to severity of illness and/or intensity of service, e.g. high, medium and low cost categories.

6 *Single item*. An agreement to pay a set amount for a defined service to one person (or a test), e.g. a single consultant episode, outpatient session, DRG/HRG category payment.

Standardization in provider contract costing and service definitions

UK purchaser's scope to change contract design was affected by new practices in costing and treatment classification. Guidance in 1992 (EL (92) 173) reaffirmed the general regulation which required providers to calculate prices in relation to costs, and prohibited providers from 'unfair' market competition through cross-subsidies. In 1993, guidance was issued for a standard approach to calculating average provider and specialty costs (e.g. apportioning overheads), in preparation for contracts in 1994–5 (EL (93) 16 (April)).

Later guidance in 1993 and 1994 was concerned with standardizing definitions of services, and this relates to the issue we considered above concerning contract definition by needs or services. This guidance is important for deciding how to separate certain treatments from general contracts because it sets how services and treatments will be defined. It is likely that the future guidance will be for a hierarchy of categories for contracting (Reeves 1993). At the bottom of the hierarchy are the current

10,000 ICD9/OPCS codes, which can be grouped into 250 'condition groupings'. About 80 per cent of total specialty costs are covered by these 250 groupings. The terminology used for healthcare resource groups (HRGs) will be used to give a common terminology for these 250 groupings. Each group is of conditions which consume similar amounts of resources, which are a high proportion of average total costs of a specialty and which clinicians view as sufficiently similar to be treated in the same way. These 250 condition groupings, or HRGs, will be aggregated into 150 contract categories. Thus each of the main 15 specialties is likely to be subdivided into 10 'contract categories'. The national steering group on costing is also working on definitions for community health services (Reeves 1993).

Value for money options

A final general point is that in agreeing contracts both purchasers and providers need to understand the relationships between price, volume and quality. A contract is an agreement about a service 'package' which is a combination of cost, volume and quality (see Figure 2.2, the 'value for money triangle'). Although commissioners will put pressure on providers to lower prices and increase volume and quality, this will often not be possible. Commissioners have a responsibility to state where they want the balance to lie. For their part, providers have to be able to offer different value for money combinations and to show, for example, how increasing volume will affect price or quality.

Contract design: the options

As commissioners either renew or change contracts with providers there are opportunities to change contract structure. Reasons for doing so are to give more incentives for efficiency, to change the balance of risk, to promote quality or for other purposes. One of the developing areas of commissioner expertise, and an area where the UK can learn from US and European purchasers, is how different contract designs affect the sharing of risk between purchasers and providers, and give incentives to providers to increase efficiency or improve other aspects of their service. There is probably even more scope and need for different types of contract for community and primary care services, especially with voluntary organizations or in collaboration with local authority purchasing. Box 6.2 summarizes the main variables in contract design.

In many parts of the UK, probably over 60 per cent of the services of most providers are covered by one local purchaser, and the contract has evolved from a previous management and budget-planning relationship. In considering new contracts, it is useful to look at how changing contract design will:

- favour the provider or favour the purchaser (e.g. balance of risk, incentives);

Box 6.2   Choices about contract design

1 *Contract structure*:

- Size (large numbers down to individual treatment episodes or specific aspects of treatment, e.g. rehabilitation therapy sessions).
- Time (e.g. 1 month, 1 year, 3 year).
- Subcontracts (how contracts are broken down into subcontracts for different services: client group basis, medical specialty, etc.).

2 *Payment arrangements*. Incentives and penalties, risk-sharing.

3 *Detail (degree of specification)*. How services are described and quality is specified, etc.

4 *Monitoring methods*. Verification/validation.

5 *Penalties and sanctions*. For exceeding target activity, or not meeting waiting times or patient charter standards.

What choices do you have? What is fixed in rules, nationally, regionally?

- affect costs and quality;
- be to the *mutual* advantage of purchaser and provider.

Contract size and time

The length of time a contract covers and the size of contract affects risk-sharing, incentives, cost and quality. Fundholders have many contracts for few patients and some single contracts for one episode or a few months. Providers are experiencing a trend to smaller short-term contracts, especially for some specialties, but it is unlikely that the UK will move to individual case contracting or billing. No generalizations can be made about whether commissioning for smaller rather than larger contracts is more cost-effective. Large contracts do give providers stability, but much depends on whether it is a block, cost and volume, or other kind of contract (see Figure 6.3). The subcontract structure is how a large contract with one provider is subdivided into specialties, care groups, and into case mix (for example, three levels of complexity for all cases in one specialty, or ICD9/OPCS4 or HRG/DRG categories).

The balance of risk, incentives, cost and quality is affected by whether a commissioner has one contract for a whole hospital, or one contract with one or two subcontracts, or a set of separate specialty contracts. It is also affected by how contracts are broken down into subcontracts for different services (client group basis, medical specialty, etc.). Normally contracts are based on provider services or provider organization (e.g. separate subcontracts for each directorate or specialty).

	Short-term	*Long-term contracts*
Low volume		
Item	e.g. ECR, one DRG	e.g. 2 year diagnostics
Case episode		
One service	e.g. GP fundholder 3-month	
High volume		
One service		e.g. 3 year obstetrics and gynaecology
Service 'bundle'		e.g. 3 year 'mental health services'

Figure 6.3 Contract size and duration.

Case mix

An issue within subcontract structures is case mix. We noted in the section above some of the issues in selecting providers. With a large contract the variation in the cost of cases can be absorbed or spread across the year. For example, in orthopaedics some simple procedures cost less than £100, whereas some hip replacements with complications can rise to over £5,000. If all procedures are included in the one specialty cost and volume contract then the balance of risk lies with the provider. If providers start to exclude high-cost procedures and charge these as ECRs, they can lower their average price and reduce their risks. A simple categorization of severe, medium and uncomplicated can be useful, but commissioners have to weigh up issues of risk-sharing and incentives, and the cost involved in specifying contracts, information collection and invoicing.

> The provider unit had run rings round the HA purchaser, having been paid for a contract to reduce a waiting list which had largely been achieved by treating more minor cases. The contract had not specified the case-mix and payment was made for an average case-mix. This failure of the purchaser to obtain value for money came to light only when a local GP fundholder scrutinised the provider's performance in more detail, noticed the change in case-mix and compared notes with the health authority. The HA had had the information on case-mix but had not analysed it.
>
> HSJ, 24 July 1993, p. 23, Huntingdon, J. summarizing the report of case five in Audit Commission (1993a)

Even a cautious view of the future predicts that, 'after 1994–5, most diagnoses would be grouped into case-mix groupings such as Healthcare Resource Groups (HRGs) conforming to nationally defined terms and underpinned by national accounting standards' (Colin Reeves, NWT RHA, director of Finance, Computing and Information; see also NHS ME 1992).

Commissioners have to weigh up which alternative subcontract structure is realistic, and which might do more to encourage providers to reduce

Advantages	*Choices*	*Disadvantages*
Low transaction costs	**Block contract** (payment to provide a service)	Few incentives for efficiency or for raising quality
Incentives for efficiency	**Cost and volume**	Higher transaction costs Sophistication of information systems Pressure on quality – unless precautions
Low transaction costs Incentives to reduce length of stay (efficiency)	**Per diem** (i.e. daily, prospective or reimbursed at cost)	Early discharge (to inappropriate services) Pressure on professional quality
Accurate costing structure (if treatment/service defined) Pay for what you get Can compare prices, if standard case classification (e.g. HRG/DRG) Incentives for efficiency Information usable for quality and resource management	**Cost per case**	High transaction costs Sophisticated information systems required (investment) Case classification for costing inaccuracies
Depends on how service is defined (e.g. C&V, or per case, or per item) Incentive to hold down costs to make profit on agreed price rate	**Fixed price** (pre-agreed rate for defined service, e.g. Medicare Prospective Payment Systems)	Risk-adverse providers do not bid (less competition) Low-cost patients selected Quality can suffer, early discharge Case classification inflation ('DRG creep') Unnecessary treatment/ utilization
For provider no risk Competition in bidding holds down price – reveals expected costs Could promote quality under certain conditions, e.g. with effective monitoring	**Cost-plus** (paid all costs plus a fee) (n.b. same as fixed price plus inflation agreement)	Purchaser bears risk Price provider receives not same as bidding price No efficiency incentives once provider wins bid

Figure 6.4 Contract type and payment arrangements.

costs, or increase continuity for patients, or improve outcomes (e.g. one contract for a care episode rather than consultant episode).

Payment structure and payment arrangements

The second set of contract design issues concerns how different payment methods affect risk, incentives, cost and quality. Figure 6.4 shows how payment per item, or per day, or by other methods, gives different incentives and penalties. Commissioners need to consider, for a particular service, which types minimize the costs to the purchaser and/or provider of bidding and payment, and which are better for quality.

Detail of contract (and degree of specification)

The third aspect of contract design is how services are specified in the contract and in how much detail. One aspect of contract detail is whether and how to describe specialty subcontracts and case mix. We noted earlier the standard categories which were being developed for defining services, based on HRG terminology. Contract detail also concerns how much the purchaser defines the details of provider organization and delivery. Initially some NHS purchasers specified details such as staff grades, operating theatre procedures and doctors' duty rotas. In preparing for the 1992–3 contracts, some purchasers issued service requirements which set out principles for service provision and some expected outcomes. This left it to providers to state how they would provide the service in their business plans, and the contracts were simpler, and referred to these separate purchaser and provider statements. One of the most problematic issues is how to specify and monitor quality – we consider this in the next chapter.

The purpose of detail in a contract with an NHS provider is not to cover all eventualities. It is true that for non-NHS providers there is a stronger argument for being able to refer to a contract if a purchaser decides to take the provider to court for not meeting the contract. However, for NHS providers the contract is not a legal document but a framework for developing the purchaser–provider relationship. In this context, and given the cost and diminishing returns of detail, the degree of specification and the items specified should be governed by what both parties find helpful to make explicit, and what helps each to review performance at a later date. Detail has its costs, and, if of the wrong things, distracts from the important issues.

Monitoring methods

A final issue in contract design to be mentioned here is to consider how the contract will be monitored, and what monitoring will take place of the items not covered by the contract. There are three approaches:

- first-hand, where the purchaser monitors the provider directly (e.g. authority non-executives visit, spot-checks are made by agency staff);
- second-hand, where the purchaser monitors the provider's records and checks their validity, or the provider supplies reports (e.g. monthly);
- third-hand, where an external agency audits or monitors the provider, and the commissioner uses the reports or data.

Commissioners use each of these approaches to monitor the provider's performance against the contract, and to monitor outcomes, especially complaints, patient satisfaction and poor medical quality. The next chapter considers each of these approaches for monitoring provider quality.

Another purpose of monitoring is to compare a provider's performance with national averages and other potential or current providers. During the year, commissioners and providers summarize monitoring data to build an end-of-year picture for the service evaluation phase of the contract cycle. Commissioners need to develop performance measures which allow valid comparisons. Examples are lengths of stay, percentage of day cases, outpatient non-attendance, days in hospital prior to operation, different waiting times and different costs. The frequency and type of monitoring depend in part on the provider's track record and history with the purchaser. As with other aspects of contracting, the costs of detail, accuracy and frequency in monitoring have to be judged against the likely extra benefit. Reducing these costs is one reason for developing long-term partnership relations.

Considerations in deciding contract type

In the UK, purchasers moved from block contracts to indicative cost and volume for some specialties, and into further detail in subcontracts and case-mix contracts. New information technology makes it possible to use different contracts, payment systems and monitoring arrangements which were not cost-effective or even possible in the past. Our purchasing examples earlier showed two early approaches to separating acute specialties from block contracts, and to using information to decide strategy. Commissioners need to develop the methods they use to identify the services and treatments where a more sophisticated contracting approach would be benefical. One simple method is to analyse their volume requirements, the provider's costs and predictability, as shown in Figure 6.5. Purchasers can then compare the cost and volume analysis to the predictability and variation in volume and cost. This approach helps the purchaser to assess the viability of a provider specialty, and to identify which services to separate from block contracts. It helps the purchaser to decide a contract design which shares risks appropriately, yet gives providers incentives to reduce costs, keep within targets and improve quality.

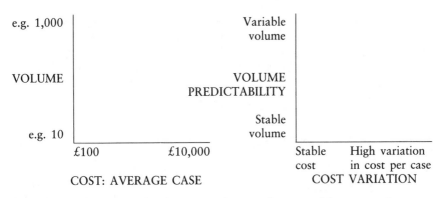

Figure 6.5 The relationship between volume and cost, and between volume predictability and cost predictability of cases.

Conclusion

A contract is the formal 'tip of the iceberg' of a deeper relationship. This relationship is shaped by history, the market structure, government directives and the immediate financial issues faced by purchasers and by providers. This chapter showed how it could also be shaped by a commissioner's health strategy. In the evolution of service contracting in the NHS the principal relationship between commissioners and providers evolved out of a management relationship. Most commissioners have small contracts with a variety of providers, but a limited choice of alternative services, and limited power to force change by threatening to switch contracts or introduce tendering. The chapter gave examples which showed how two purchasers used information and collective purchasing power to drive change in some acute hospital specialties. There is evidence that strategic considerations are entering into contracting, although the trigger to explore the options in the examples was the opportunity to make savings.

To change the emphasis in contracting from a provider-led to a health-strategy-led approach, commissioners need to pay attention to three things. The first is internal links between contract staff and other staff in the organization. The second is that staff have conceptual models which help them see and make the links at the right times. A model of the contracting cycle needs to be part of an overall model of the commissioning process, and to highlight opportunities for tendering (Figure 6.1). Commissioners also need a framework for relating the categories they use to define needs to the way they define contracts by service and provider (Figure 6.2). The third is for purchasing staff to agree contract designs which give incentives for providers to work towards health strategy aims (Box 6.2 and Figure 6.4).

For the most part 'market management' by individual purchasers is not possible. A purchaser can exert an influence over some services in the long term by collaborating with other purchasers with regional support. However, market management, like contracting, is a method, and may not serve the purpose of particular purchasers and their own health strategies. More important is using contract design as a medium-term method to influence local providers in the direction of the health strategy. Even if there is no choice of provider, commissioning managers have choices of contract type and contracting process which give opportunities to further their health strategy, or, if badly used, undermine their strategy. Some of the choices we considered were in:

- contract definition/grouping, e.g. defining some contracts in terms of health gain, or redefining a contract to cover more than one provider.
- contract type, moving beyond block and cost and volume contracts where appropriate, size and timescale.
- subcontract definition, defining specific services within a provider service or medical specialty.
- details of contract design, e.g. case mix, payment method.
- monitoring arrangements.
- contract renewal and renegotiation, how often and agendas.

For purchasers, 'market management' may not be possible in any real sense, but 'market cooperation' is feasible and necessary. The challenge in the UK is to use the remaining allegiances to the NHS and its values to counter short-term and overly self-interested behaviours. Commissioners have to strike a balance between ensuring the long-term stability of key providers for their resident population, promoting competition to reduce costs and raise quality, increasing choice and preserving equity.

As the pressures increase for commissioners, fundholders and providers to pursue their own short-term interests, there is growing need for pan-regional service strategies to decide the siting of specialties for the common long-term good. Such a strategy needs to be informed by each commissioner's health strategies. Within these health and service strategies, commissioners can develop their purchasing strategies for other specialties and institutions, and within this can clarify the role of locality commissioning and policy towards fundholders.

A danger is that commissioners will not put contracting and health provision issues in the context of health strategy and their primary purpose of improving health. Even with a strategy, reactive short-term contracting actions may produce a pattern of services which is of higher cost in the long term and of lower quality, and which results in greater inequities in health: a situation which no one wants but each is powerless to prevent as different parties respond to the incentives and penalties of the system.

Key points

- A purchaser and a provider enter into and renew their relationship within the context of a market structure. This structure determines the balance of power in the relationship, especially where a purchaser has a choice of provider and uses a tendering process in the contracting cycle for selecting providers.

- A purchaser's contracting cycle should be part of a planning cycle for reviewing and reformulating health strategy (Figure 6.1).
- For a needs-led purchasing strategy, purchasers need to link health strategy to contracts by internal organization, and by conceptual models and time-tables which are understood by staff in different parts of the organization.
- Most purchasers have one main provider, and little opportunity to switch contracts. They have to pursue their health strategy by developing the right relationship with their provider, as do purchasers who have a choice of provider.
- For most purchasers, contract design rather than competition will form the main method for influencing providers to pursue health strategy aims.
- To share risks with and create incentives for providers, purchasers need to use a greater variety of types of contract and become skilled in contract design. Providers have an important role to play in agreeing designs, as long as health strategy aims are at the forefront.
- As well as improving their information base for contracting, purchasers need to understand the choices in contract design of definition, service subdivisions, size and time scale, case mix, payment and monitoring, and the advantages and disadvantages of different designs for different purposes.
- Real savings and quality improvements can be made by developing a strategy for purchasing different specialties in collaboration with other purchasers and providers.
- Most purchaser-provider conflicts decrease in importance if both take a longer-term view and develop 'partnership contracting' (Øvretveit 1993d).

7 / Quality in purchasing

Introduction

The quality of provider services is a key issue for purchasers. Patients judge purchasers, in part, in terms of the quality of the services they purchase – they rely on their purchaser to check and ensure the provider's quality. Apart from reflecting badly on a purchaser, poor provider outcomes are a waste of purchasing resources which could be used for other health gain investments. Many believe that purchasers have forced lower costs and increased activity at the expense of quality, but there is little evidence because quality is more difficult to measure than costs and activity. Purchasers recognize that quality is the third ingredient in the 'value for money triangle' (Figure 2.2) and that they need to specify and measure quality, as well as costs and activity. But how can they do this, and in a way which helps providers to improve their quality?

These difficulties are minor compared to the problems of defining and measuring quality in purchasing. Apart from some research into quality in public health (Johnston *et al.* 1992) few purchasers, researchers or policymakers have considered quality in purchasing, which is a broader subject than the quality of contracted services. With further reforms to the top tiers of the NHS, more GPs becoming fundholders and concerns about purchaser accountability, there is a need to define what is meant by quality in purchasing, and to consider how to measure and improve the quality of purchasing. The public and the government ask the same value for money questions about purchasers as they do about providers: how do they know if they are getting value for money from a purchasing organization if there are no measures of the quality of purchasing?

The purpose of this chapter is to give an overview of quality issues in purchasing, and to offer guidelines and practical steps for purchasers to improve service quality – both their own and that of their providers. The first two sections define quality in purchasing using ideas about the purpose of purchasing and of purchasing as a service presented in Chapter 3. The next three sections concentrate on provider quality. They examine how purchasers can influence markets for quality and work with providers to improve the quality of health services. The chapter finishes with practical guidance for improving quality, which recognizes the limited resources and skills that commissioners have for the task. It addresses some of the following issues raised by purchasing managers.

- *How do we as a purchasing organization measure and improve our quality?*
- *Is there a better way of specifying and monitoring quality than the 'shopping list of standards' approach – what should we be asking of providers?*
- *If we are monitoring the quality of our local providers on behalf of other purchasers, how should we do it?*
- *How do we get information about clinical quality, outcome and costs, in a form in which we can make reliable comparisons?*
- *Is quality accreditation or registration a good predictor of future quality?*

Quality and the purpose of health purchasing

Chapter 3 proposed that the purpose of public health purchasing is to improve the health of populations and to prevent illness by making the best use of the resources allocated by government. Commissioners fulfil this purpose and serve their population by undertaking a number of activities, one of which is to contract health services. One indicator of commissioners' performance is the change in health status of their populations for the resources allocated which can be attributed to their actions: this change is the main 'difference that they make', or the value which they add.

As with measuring provider quality, outcome is one measure of the quality of commissioning: the change in health status of a population over time. There is an argument that higher levels of the NHS should select population outcome measures, and leave it to commissioners to decide the quality systems and actions which they need to improve outcome performance. As with measuring quality in provider services, there are theoretical and practical problems in relying only on outcome measures. First, changes in population health take place over long periods of time, and this reduces the usefulness of many such measures for quality improvement or performance assessment. Second, changes in population health status depend on factors other than those which a commissioner can influence, and it is difficult to attribute changes to commissioners' actions.

However, we do know that some morbidity and mortality can be directly attributed to a commissioner's failure to act: for example, failure to conduct an adequate needs assessment, or not switching contracts where there is indisputable evidence of poor medical outcome. There are also models of, and some evidence of, the inputs and processes which commissioners need in order to improve health, and we have considered these in earlier chapters. These involve assumptions which can and should be questioned as we gain more knowledge about the processes and purposes of commissioning, but there is now sufficient knowledge to justify starting to define some standards and measures of quality in health purchasing.

The third problem is that defining quality in purchasing in terms of the health status of a population is the same as a definition of the purpose of purchasing. It is useful to have a more specific definition of quality, at least at this stage in the development of purchasing. In particular, the role of a purchasing organization as a service organization needs to be recognized and the views of local people should form part of a judgement about the quality of the purchasing.

Purchasing as a service

We noted in Chapter 3 that both private and public health purchasers are service-giving organizations, and we considered the complex nature of the services of an NHS commissioning organization. NHS commissioners provide some direct services to individual citizens, but most of their work is in providing an indirect service by purchasing other health services. In addition to contracting providers, they serve their populations by assessing needs and deciding the balance and range of health services to be made available, and by undertaking other activities to improve health and prevent illness. Local people can make a valid judgement about some aspects of the quality of commissioning, but, as with providers, there are many other aspects where customer satisfaction is not a good measure of quality. We can use this analysis of commissioning as a service as a basis for defining and measuring the quality of commissioning.

A definition of the quality of health purchasing

The quality of commissioning can be viewed in terms of three aspects: the quality of the health services which a commissioner contracts, the quality of the commissioner's direct services to the public and to others, and 'population quality', which takes account of the quality of a commissioner's health strategy and its overall impact on health status.

Contracted service quality

Part of commissioners' service to the public is to ensure that the services which they contract on behalf of the public are of high quality, and, at a minimum, do not harm the people who use the service. People are not able to assess the professional quality of health services, and rely on commissioners to make such assessments on their behalf. Commissioners share responsibility with a provider for the quality of the provider's service, but they also have distinct responsibilities. It is important that both parties understand their different responsibilities, where responsibilities overlap and where the boundaries lie. Failure to do so results in commissioners either 'intruding' too deeply into provider quality issues or not paying sufficient attention to provider quality. We consider these issues later, but note here that commissioners' responsibilities for providers' quality include:

1 In *selecting* and deciding to contract a service
   - taking the past quality performance of the service into account (which may be difficult when authorizing some ECRs);
   - judging whether the provider's quality systems will continually reduce poor quality and are likely to assure the future quality of their services.
2 In *negotiating* and agreeing the contract
   - specifying appropriate quality requirements, including access, availability and aspects of patient prioritization;
   - agreeing responsibilities with the provider about who collects which information about quality.
3 In *monitoring* the contract
   - receiving providers' quality reports and checking the validity of these reports;
   - taking action on poor quality;
   - receiving complaints directly from the public;
   - getting feedback from the public about satisfaction with the service.
4 In *reviewing* the contract
   - reviewing quality performance;
   - agreeing changes to improve quality;
   - changing or proposing to change contracts if quality performance is unacceptable and there are alternative services.
5 In *long-term partnerships*
   - agreeing with the provider actions to continually improve quality;
   - ensuring contract design gives quality incentives.

Direct service quality

A second aspect of the quality of commissioning is the quality of the direct services which a commissioning organization provides to the public and to others. The quality of direct services to the public is assessed and measured in ways similar to those used in other public services: whether the required services are provided (e.g. registration with GPs, complaints services, etc.); whether a range of other services which are appropriate are provided, such as information services; and in terms of public satisfaction with these services

(Øvretveit 1993a). These types of services also include those to bodies representing the public, such as community health councils (CHCs) and patient groups (e.g. the quality of information to these groups).

With pressure on commissioners to reduce their staffing, many are considering contracting out direct services, and need to take account of quality issues and control in their decision to do so. Innovation in direct services is also part of quality: for example, innovations in the way a commissioner provides conventional direct services, or the introduction of new services such as an advice and information service on medical quality outcome to increase patients' choice of providers (Øvretveit 1994).

It is useful to think of some other commissioner activities as direct services, apart from those to the public or their representatives. Commissioners give a payments 'service' to their providers, they authorize ECRs and they give a support service to GP fundholders. All these and other 'services' can be assessed and measured in traditional ways, in terms of timeliness, accuracy and other criteria which are important to providers. Improving these services helps providers to give a better service and save costs, and is one way in which a commissioner develops a partnership relation with providers. Commissioners can use conventional methods to improve the quality of these services, for example by setting standards and improving their processes for providing these services (Edvardsson *et al.* 1994).

Population quality

This third aspect of the quality of commissioning is the broadest, and subsumes the other two. A commissioner could contract high quality services, and also provide high quality direct services, but the quality of commissioning could still be poor. There may be many people who do not get a service but need it more than those who do receive a service. There may also be people who do not currently need a service but will need one unless a commissioner takes certain actions, such as to encourage employers to prevent accidents at work or water companies to put fluoride in the water. A consequence of poor commissioner quality in 'population quality' would be that the health status of the population would be lower than it would otherwise be: there would be avoidable mortality and morbidity which could be attributed to poor quality commissioning.

In contracting providers, commissioners agree with providers the ways in which the service will be offered to ensure that those most in need get the service. Examples are systems for prioritizing waiting lists, convenient opening times and services offered in a range of settings. Many of these aspects of access and availability can be considered as part of provider quality, and would be addressed under 'contracted service quality' above. However, a provider may make services available in the way agreed in the contract, but the commissioner may not have taken account of different views about the prevalence or severity of needs, or related needs assessment to the contracts. Before negotiating contracts, a commissioner must assess needs, decide the range of services to contract and the proportion of resources to allocate to each, and develop a contracting plan.

To ensure a high population quality in commissioning, the contracting plan must be linked to a population needs assessment. Further, commissioners must engage in activities other than contracting services: they have to work with local authorities, employers and others to help create healthy environments and to avoid conditions which harm people's health. A commissioner's decisions about how much of which services to contract and which direct services to provide follow from a commissioner's health strategy. The quality of a commissioner's health strategy, and of the organization for formulating it and carrying it out, is fundamental to the commissioner's ability to achieve their aims, which are to improve health and prevent illness.

At a certain point population quality becomes indistinguishable from the general purpose of commissioning. Changes in population health status give some indication of 'population quality' in commissioning, but involve the problems noted earlier. A more direct assessment is of the adequacy of processes in commissioning which are thought to result in the desired outcomes: for example, the adequacy of the needs assessment and assessment of treatment and service effectiveness, how these assessments are related to service specifications and how specifications relate to actual contracts. It is possible to define quality standards and measures for these and other aspects of the commissioning process where we have confidence that these aspects result in high quality commissioner outputs and outcomes.

For example, what would be standards and measures of quality in the following activities?

- Needs assessment (does it identify the range and severity of need, and include GPs' and the public's view of need?).
- Prioritization and contracting plan (do these identify and justify the relative resource allocations between services, in terms of some assessment of cost–benefit; and are service specifications defined in a way which is related to the needs assessment?).
- Commissioning strategy (is there one, and does it cover commissioner activities to promote health and prevent illness, other than contracting services?).

The chapter now concentrates on commissioner–provider relationships and contracting services. This part of the chapter considers issues which commissioners have to consider in order to purchase quality health services. It discusses influencing the market for quality, defining quality, specifying and monitoring quality, and medical quality. It finishes with practical steps which commissioners can take to improve the quality of health services to the public, given their limited resources.

Box 7.1 Quality myths held by some commissioners and providers

- Health service quality is what happens to patients at the hands of providers, not whether the patients most in need get to the door, or the quality of commissioning.
- Quality always costs more.
- Providers need commissioners to pay for a computer system before they can collect any information about quality.
- Providers cannot allow access to medical audit minutes because they contain confidential information about patients.
- A provider's quality is good because it has many quality standards.
- Patients are only interested in menus or waiting times.
- It is difficult and too costly for commissioners to judge, specify or monitor primary and community services quality.

Market management for quality

Before they select services, commissioners have a responsibility to create conditions in the market which will give incentives for services to improve quality as well as to reduce prices, and for high quality services to survive or come forward. Commissioners have a limited influence over markets, but need to understand how they can exercise an influence and the factors which can lead to lower quality services over time. They need to be able to predict how changes to market structure could affect provider quality.

Chapter 2 described three aspects of market structure, and each has an effect on the long-term quality of services. The first is the number of purchasers and the type of competition between them: by acting together or merging commissioners can increase their influence over the market. The second is the number of providers and the type of competition between them: in some cases purchasers can act to increase the number of providers and promote quality competition. The third is the regulations and the strength of the regulatory bodies. Different combinations of these three elements of market structure give different incentives.

To date the limited competition in the UK has been in relation to waiting times and price, and few contracts have been changed or won on quality (Glasgow Health Board was an early exception in changing contracts on quality grounds: *Health Services Journal* Report 22 July 1993: 7). This is in part because of the market structure, especially the fragmented approach to quality regulation, and in part because of the lack of information or interest in information about quality. In some parts of the USA and for some markets, providers compete on quality as much as on price, and sometimes prices are fixed (e.g. for Medicare and Medicaid). Quality competition certainly happens where state regulations require the publication of hospital and physician case-adjusted outcome data (PHCCCC 1992).

The number and type of providers and purchasers in an area are probably a less important influence on provider quality than the regulations. Examples of regulations which have a significant effect on quality are those for accreditation, fixed prices and publication of outcome data. The UK has a variety of regulations about different aspects of provider quality, and many different regulatory bodies (see below under 'monitoring quality'). The number and complexity of these regulations, many of which do not deal specifically with quality, make it impossible for commissioners to check providers' compliance with all of them.

Some commissioners take the view that the UK should move towards a system for provider accreditation. Accreditation approaches, such as the King's Fund organizational audit (Brooks 1992), could integrate different quality regulations and give some indication of quality. However, many accreditation approaches do not require a provider to have a comprehensive quality system. Some such systems promote continuous quality improvement, rather than compliance with a set of specific and often unrelated standards. It is notable that the main US accreditation bodies have moved from 'external standards injection' to assessing a provider's approach to continuous improvement (e.g. JCAHO 1991; Øvretveit 1994b).

In the UK there is no consensus about which quality systems or accreditation approaches are most cost-effective or appropriate for different services, and little commissioner knowledge or expertise about different systems (Klein and Scrivens 1993). An alternative could be to require a 'total quality management' (TQM) approach, which includes continuous quality improvement. Some TQM approaches enable providers to integrate different quality initiatives in a cost-effective way, and ensure that attention is paid to attitudes and culture as well as to systems and procedures (Øvretveit 1992a; and Joss *et al.* 1994). However, commissioners would need to develop their knowledge about TQM to be able to judge between the image and the reality of a provider's TQM programme: is it cost-effective and sustainable?

In practice, individual commissioners can influence, and in some cases manage, primary and community care markets, but need to collaborate with other commissioners to influence many hospital acute services and specialties. There is a danger that the market-management role of regions will decline in the reorganization of the top tiers of the NHS, and may not be counterbalanced by commissioner collaboration. Market management has to address quality issues explicitly, or cost considerations will dominate.

Quality and contract design

One specific way in which commissioners can influence markets before contracting services, or in negotiating contracts, is by using a different type of contract design. Purchasers can work with providers to design contracts to share risk and give incentives to providers to improve quality (Watkinson 1993). Many current cost and volume contracts give incentives to reduce costs and length of stay. Cost and volume contracts, with no other stipulations, can encourage a provider to increase throughput to clear capacity for resale. Different types of contract and payment systems can promote or reduce quality. Whether they do so depends on the level of demand and on the commissioner's quality specifications, monitoring and other regulations concerning quality. Commissioners need to consider how the different contract designs described in Chapter 6 influence provider behaviour with respect to quality.

Defining and specifying provider quality

Turning to the relationship between a commissioner and a provider, it is notable that many difficulties arise when commissioners do not clarify for providers what they mean by quality, and what they want providers to achieve. If an outsider were to look at quality standards and statements in a contract, would he or she get a good idea of what a commissioner understood by quality and expected of a provider? In the UK in the early 1990s, many commissioners' definitions of quality were the sum of the standards in a contract.

More commissioners are recognizing that they need to clarify their definition of provider quality, and decide whether it should include or exclude such things as types of choice, equity considerations and medical outcome. Definitions of quality range from narrow customer-service definitions (quality is 'customer satisfaction') to broad definitions (Maxwell's (1984) six features of accessibility, relevance to need, equity, acceptability, effectiveness and efficiency), and some focus on improving processes and outcome (e.g. Øvretveit's (1992a) patient, professional and management quality). There is a bewildering array of definitions, frameworks and approaches. Too broad definitions of quality cover everything which a provider does. If commissioners use such a definition, they must then give more specific expectations and prioritize areas for attention.

Commissioners need to decide what they will include and exclude in their definition of provider quality. Such definitions should not be so prescriptive that they make it impossible for a provider to choose a quality system or framework which is appropriate for them. The broad definition should form part of all specifications for services to be contracted, and each individual specification would then add any details of quality which the commissioner views as necessary for that particular service. A commissioner's quality definition and policy then provides the context within which it conducts relations with a provider, and within which it specifies quality in standards.

Specifying and monitoring quality: standards or systems?

Some commissioners believe that specifying more standards in a contract is the way to ensure that a provider offers a quality service. This leads to lists of standards, which neither the commissioner nor the provider can monitor without great expense. It directs providers towards a fragmented approach to quality, and can involve purchasers in making detailed judgements which are not justified about what providers should do to offer a quality service. There is evidence that some treatments are ineffective and that certain protocols improve quality of care, and, where the evidence is sound, there is a case for the commissioner using this evidence in specifying standards. However, there is a danger that in their concern to 'do something about quality', commissioners become overly prescriptive.

Probably the single most important thing that commissioners can do to improve quality is to require a provider to have an appropriate quality system, and to have access to the system documentation (Øvretveit 1993a, d, 1994b). In simple terms, this approach is like requiring providers to do medical audit and to follow established guidelines for doing audit, rather than specifying detailed medical standards and protocols which the commissioner thinks they should observe. This is not to suggest that commissioners should not set a few key standards, but rather that an appropriate provider quality system would ensure that providers formulate the critical standards, which include those of concern to the commissioner: commissioners then only need to ensure that the system is working.

The reasons for taking this approach are that it is in the provider's interest to have a quality system in order to survive in the market, and that commissioners do not have the expertise to set standards beyond a certain point, and cannot and should not monitor them all. More importantly, an appropriate system moves the provider towards making continuous improvements, rather than aiming only to meet minimum standards (Øvretveit 1994b). Commissioners need to move from specifying an ever-lengthening list of unconnected standards to requiring providers to have an appropriate quality system. They need to develop their knowledge of quality systems, and to be able to judge which systems are appropriate for a particular provider. In evaluating quality systems or frameworks, commissioners (and providers) need to ask:

- Is there any evidence that high rating on the quality audit or system assessment is related to levels of service quality at later dates?
- Which systems are more suited to particular types of service?
- What is the definition of quality underlying the system?
- What assumptions are inherent in the framework, for example about what it takes to assure and improve quality, about organizational change or about motivation?
- Can or should an audit method or system be adapted to build on experience about what is critical for service quality in a particular service, or would 'tailoring' invalidate the internal coherence of the system?
- Which approach is the most cost-effective?
- Once a contract is agreed, would using an audit method enable a more focused monitoring of potential weak areas?

An appropriate system will incorporate the standards which the commissioner specifies at present, will measure and record quality performance, and will integrate medical and other professions' audits into one approach. Examples of quality systems are the BS 5750 which is appropriate for some services, systems based on the USA Baldridge award and the Brunel 'WelQual' system (their use for purchasers is discussed in Øvretveit 1993d).

Monitoring provider quality

If a provider has an appropriate quality system, then monitoring quality is more manageable for a commissioner. Commissioners can monitor some standards directly and some indirectly, by monitoring the provider's quality system documents and by using other 'third party' quality monitoring.

Box 7.2   Monitoring quality

First-hand: purchaser direct
Of providers' processes, patient views and outcomes. Selective and ongoing, or the purchaser uses an audit framework for a comprehensive audit at regular intervals.

Second-hand: of providers' quality system records or other records
Do they have a quality system?
Is the system appropriate and cost-effective (a commissioner will pay in higher prices if it is not)?
Does it capture and record what purchasers want (medical quality)?
Does it correspond to what happens (validity, reliability and accuracy)?
Does the system promote continuous improvement, or only require compliance with static standards?

Third-hand: external body assessments
External body contracted by the purchaser or provider.
Independent/ongoing (e.g. Audit Commission).

External assessors/regulators of quality or of aspects of quality
Community health council, local authority inspection, nursing home registration, market research (patients, staff), safety, hygiene. Professional: registration, accreditation for training, disciplinary bodies. National Audit Office, Audit Commission, Patient's Charter, Ombudsman. Quality systems: BS 5750 (British Standards Institution), King's Fund Organisational Audit and others.

Medical quality

The last aspect of provider quality to be considered here is medical quality, the most important aspect of which is poor medical quality or adverse outcomes. To date UK purchasers have only required providers to have some form of medical audit, but have not taken an interest in the cost-effectiveness of audit. Neither have many purchasers made use of information about variations in provider outcome quality, or used recommendations and protocols from national audits (e.g. NCEPOD 1993).

Public concern about medical quality is fuelled by media coverage (e.g. BBC *Panorama* 28 June 1993; *Sunday Express* 21 November 1993). There is a growing view that commissioners have a duty to inquire into medical quality, to use medical quality as one criterion in placing contracts and to monitor medical quality for their residents, or ensure that another commissioner is doing so.

Box 7.3   Purchaser policies to improve medical quality/outcome

For specific services/treatments, or generally.
1 Require audit.
2 Require that audit be conducted according to established guidelines.
3 Require providers to use outcome data in audit.
4 Require providers to take part in established national/regional audit (e.g. maternity, NCEPOD).
5 Require that audit uses systems which allow comparisons.
6 Specify which outcome data are to be collected (e.g. poor quality).
7 Require the provider to share outcome information with purchaser.
8 Specify outcomes standards in contract.
9 Purchaser educates GPs and patients about general effectiveness of treatment and what to ask providers about outcome, and/or publicizes outcome information from providers (based on Pollitt 1990).

Commissioners need to use the available information about medical quality from national audits and other sources, and to require access to medical audit records or reports about audit activity. One approach is to require providers to collect and use information about a limited number of negative or adverse outcomes for all services and treatments, or to invite them to put forward their suggestions for which negative outcomes data they will collect. The US literature has lists of these for most health service interventions, which are used routinely in audit and by insurance companies and regulators (Blumberg 1986; Des Harnais *et al.* 1991), and a useful UK summary is given in Hopkins (1990). There are problems in making valid comparisons between providers, but this should not stop purchasers from requiring a provider to collect the data, and from monitoring trends over time for that provider.

Purchasing for quality: a practical approach

In practice, commissioners have limited time and expertise, and recognize that some approaches to quality specification and monitoring are costly with no evidence of improvement or patient benefit. Taking these and other factors into consideration means that purchasers need to take a selective approach, and to collaborate with other purchasers to assess and improve

---

Box 7.4   Commissioning for quality: ways forward for commissioners

Define quality and develop a quality policy
- Define quality in commissioning and propose standards and measures of quality in direct services, in commissioning processes and indicators of poor quality in commissioning.
- Decide how broadly or narrowly to define provider quality, and make clear to providers what your definition encompasses and excludes (choice, equity, medical quality).
- Recognize the few instances where there is a cost/quality trade-off, and decide where the balance should lie.

Influence market structure for quality
Stimulate competition (where possible) between existing providers on quality criteria:
- Ask providers for information about service quality.
- Ask providers for information about what they are doing to improve quality.
- Ask providers for information about their quality system.
- Actually choose or change contracts on above three quality criteria.

Commissioner–provider relationship
Where there are no or few alternative providers, commissioners can:
- Use a contract design to give incentive to improve quality.
- Consult with other commissioners using your main provider(s) about which aspects of quality they are concerned about.
- Move from setting standards to requiring a provider to have an appropriate quality system, and auditing the system.
- Pay more attention to medical quality, get and use the available information, ask for information about poor quality, question variations and probe medical audit.

---

quality. One approach is for a commissioner to conduct a 'shared audit' with one or more provider. This involves the following.

1 Develop a policy for selecting specialties (or services) for quality assessment. This involves deciding the criteria to use for selecting specialties for quality attention: for example, GP concerns, known quality problems, provider interest and willingness to consider quality with a commissioner, or likelihood of being able to encourage improvement.
2 Formulate a programme to work through each specialty (e.g. three to six months per specialty), with flexibility to focus on one specialty if problems arise during the year.
3 Decide a method for working with specialty: a 'shared audit' approach which considers patient, professional and management quality (Øvretveit 1992a). Decide the aims of shared audit, and the methods to be used to assess quality.
4 Work with provider staff to assess current quality status, compare this

with other providers and establish routine quality measurement and improvement systems.

5 Finish with an action plan to improve quality, with targets.

Smaller commissioning organizations may not even have the resources for this selective approach. An alternative is for commissioners in an area to collaborate in undertaking selective shared audit, and agree which commissioners will audit which specialties or providers. Generally there are advantages to commissioners pooling their resources and agreeing which commissioner will lead on quality with each provider, or across providers for one specialty. Commissioners forming a 'quality consortium' can agree with their GPs and others to channel quality concerns to the lead commissioner for a particular provider, and agree what each lead commissioner will do to specify, monitor and promote quality.

Conclusions

As service organizations, purchasing organizations have to pay attention to the quality of their services to different groups and of their own internal work processes. They can use modern quality methods to reduce their costs and improve their relations with the public and with providers. The starting point is defining quality in commissioning, and specifying work processes and standards. Commissioning organizations need a quality policy which defines quality in their own activities, as well as their expectations of providers. The chapter proposed a definition which included:

- *contracted service quality*: the quality of services which the commissioner contracts;
- *direct service quality*: the quality of the commissioner's direct services to the public and to others;
- *population quality*: whether the priority needs of the population are met.

The chapter drew on models of commissioning which propose inputs, processes and structures of commissioning that are thought to avoid poor quality commissioning. Although knowledge of relations between process and outcome in commissioning is even more limited than for provider services, the chapter proposed that there is sufficient knowledge to define quality standards and measures in commissioning as a basis for improving and assessing the quality of commissioning organizations.

Commissioners can influence markets to offer high quality services if they cooperate with other commissioners, and if they make information about quality available to GPs and the public. The chapter argued that commissioners need to pay more attention to quality performance in contracting services, and to develop their knowledge about provider quality systems and TQM. It put forward a practical approach for commissioners to work with providers to improve quality by selecting specialties for a programme of shared audit.

Key points

- Quality in purchasing is more than ensuring the quality of contracted services. It also involves purchasing organizations themselves providing high quality services, as well as 'population quality'.
- Modern quality methods help purchasers to define their 'customers' and their different and sometimes conflicting requirements, improve their services and reduce the costs of poor quality in their own activities.
- Market pressures act to lower quality, unless purchasers specify and monitor quality in contracts and use other methods to help providers to improve quality.
- Purchasers need to decide how they will define quality in their own organizations and services, and what their definition of provider quality encompasses and excludes.
- For providers to improve quality continuously and in a cost-effective way, they will need an appropriate quality system. Purchasers need to develop their expertise to judge whether the system is cost-effective and appropriate.
- An appropriate system will incorporate the standards which the purchaser specifies at present, will measure and record quality performance, and will integrate medical and other professions' audit.
- Commissioners need to use contract designs which give incentives to raise quality, as well as to increase activity and lower costs.
- The most important aspect of quality is medical quality: commissioners have a duty to their populations to investigate medical quality and assess the cost-effectiveness of medical audit.

8 Collaboration with local authorities

The intolerance you often find among NHS people and social services people of each other is a real impediment to effective purchasing . . . what we want are educated purchasers who understand the world in which local government works.
(Andrew Wall, *Health Service Journal*, 19 August 1993, p. 20)

Introduction

In many countries, social care services are purchased or managed by a different organization to the one purchasing or managing health services. A client or patient often needs a range of health and social services, and will not get them unless the different agencies coordinate their planning, purchasing and provision. Both health purchasers and providers need to cooperate with other social welfare agencies to fulfil their purpose, even with a narrow conception of health as the absence of acute medical illness. If a purchaser holds a broader conception of purpose, such as health gain, the need to cooperate with other agencies will be greater. Health gain depends on intersector action to improve environments and change life-styles, and this requires that health purchasers initiate and lead programmes which involve actions by other organizations and groups.

The aim of this chapter is to help UK purchasing managers to review and improve their relations with local authorities, in order better to pursue the purpose of health commissioning. Many of the issues are similar in other countries. In the UK the health and social service 'market' reforms and the purchaser–provider separation disrupted already fragile links between health and social care services, and called for new links between agencies. This chapter considers UK health commissioners' relations with local authorities as purchasers and providers of social care. It considers the issues for which collaboration is necessary or most beneficial and the different ways of working with local authorities.

The chapter starts by summarizing the implications for health commissioners of three aspects of the community care reforms introduced in the UK in 1993. It then discusses why, and when, commissioners need to relate to local authorities, before defining 'joint commissioning' – a general term used to describe many types of collaborative relations with local authorities. The chapter then gives an example of a joint commissioning structure in one area, and finishes with principles to consider in reviewing and developing formal and informal joint working arrangements. The chapter aims to help commissioning managers to find answers to the following questions.

- *What is the experience of other commissioners in collaborating with local authorities?*
- *To what extent are local authorities jointly commissioning with health for the bulk of their services, rather than for small and occasional joint projects?*
- *How do health purchasers deal with the role of politicians in local authorities, for example overturning decisions, delays in decisions and financial controls?*
- *How do we plan with social services how to care for people in a private nursing home which becomes bankrupt?*
- *How can we best integrate health and social care when local authorities can charge for care but health services must be free?*
- *With purchasing decisions being devolved to care managers, how can we know what services local authorities are planning, and where? Which services should be purchased locally and which in blocks under long-term contracts?*
- *How do we mix a locality approach with a care group approach to needs assessment, planning and possibly purchasing?*

Welfare agencies in the UK

In the UK the separate organization and financing of welfare services has long been a source of criticism and problems. Secondary health care is the responsibility of district health authorities and primary health care the responsibility of family health service authorities. Both authorities are financed from national funds, and have little local representation. Social welfare payments are dealt with by the local offices of a national social security service, and social care, education, housing and other services are the responsibility of local authorities. These local authorities are governed by elected local representatives, and are financed by local revenues raised through property and business taxes, and grant support from central government allocations. In many areas the DHA, FHSAs and local authority have different geographical boundaries. In addition, there are many local and national independent voluntary and charitable organizations.

From health commissioners' point of view, the social services department of the local authority is the most important of the government agencies. To improve health, commissioners need to plan and purchase services in collaboration with local authority social service departments. They also need to work with other local authority departments to create more healthy and less harmful environments in their area, and arrange health education in schools and local settings. However, as in other countries, the history of intersector collaboration in planning and in service provision has not been encouraging: a few isolated examples of successful projects, some cross-agency consultation and mostly informal 'common sense' agreements between operational managers and practitioners. Where plans were developed jointly, they were often not implemented, for a variety of reasons: the finance was not allocated to carry them out, the plans were overtaken by changes in one authority or the management process operated independently and in isolation from the joint planning process and structure (Øvretveit 1993b).

Managers from the commercial sector tend to regard such failures in implementation as being because of poor planning: long-term joint ventures in the commercial sector have to contend with a more turbulent and unpredictable environment. Others see the problem as being because of differences between the NHS and local authorities, mainly the different sources of finance and local political direction within local authorities.

With markets developing in health and social care, the need for closer and more collaboration has never been greater. The NHS reforms in 1991 and the local authority community care reforms in 1993 made collaboration more difficult, with purchaser–provider splits, reorganizations and staff changes in both health and social services. With fragmentation and more independent providers, collaboration at all levels became more necessary, but more difficult and complex. After the next section we consider different approaches to collaboration.

The UK community care reforms

This section reviews three aspects of the UK community care reforms which are of most relevance to health commissioners.

> Community Care means providing the right level of intervention and support to enable people to achieve maximum independence and control over their lives.
>
> (DoH 1989b)

> The rationale for this reorganisation is the empowerment of users and carers.
>
> (SSI and SOSWSG, 1991b: para 6)

> For the user, the care reforms appear to be mainly about increasing rationing of social services, tighter eligibility for assessments, and highly

restricted choices of care. A truly needs-led service offering genuine and equitable choices across the nation requires a community care charter to underpin the principles behind the reforms.

(*Community Care* Editorial 22 July 1993, echoing the
Commons Health Select Committee's review,
'Community care: the way forward')

The three most important changes for local authorities in 1993 were: new financial arrangements for social security payments; the emphasis on the 'enabling' role and a 'mixed economy' of social care; and assessment and care management.

Finance

Before 1993, acute and long-stay hospitals were able to discharge people into private and nursing homes, and social security paid for their care. Now, local authorities administer an annual cash-limited allocation for paying for these services, and have to ration them. The total sum allocated to local authorities in England for 1992–3 was £400 million. Local authority staff assess a person's needs and financial means before hospital discharge, and arrange residential or home care. Nurses are increasingly being asked to assess financial means, to avoid duplication in the new 'care management' arrangements.

Most people now have to pay a contribution for many local authority community services (e.g. charges for 'meals on wheels' or 'home help' services), and also may not be eligible for income support for residential care. For social care, the proportion of personal financing is increasing relative to public finance. For some clients, these social services are important for regaining health after a hospital stay or for avoiding ill health. One significance of the definition of what is health and what is social care is that the former is free to the patient, and the latter is often paid for by clients: people are learning that it does matter whether a service is provided by health or social services.

Local authorities also received special transitional 'start-up' payments in 1993 to cover the costs of new assessment arrangements and other changes (£140 million in total for England). These special transitional grants ('STGs') will decline over the years. Both the income support allocations and the lower transitional grant for the next year are announced in November of the preceding year.

The enabling role

The government did not require local authorities to separate their purchasing and provision management, as it did for the NHS in 1990, but encouraged them to do so. It did require local authorities to spend 85 per cent of the transferred social security finance on non-local authority providers.

In 1993 about 5 per cent of this sum was spent on private domiciliary care services, rather than on homes, which was less than was hoped. The aim is to increase domiciliary services as an alternative to residential care, but so far it has proved difficult to encourage independent agencies to offer these services. Indeed, all voluntary and private organizations, and especially the smaller ones, found the new tendering and contracting process expensive, time-consuming and in some cases a barrier to offering services.

NHS community health trusts are counted as 'independent providers' and can be contracted by local authorities to provide domiciliary social care. There are great advantages to forming integrated health and social care teams, in terms of ease of coordination, reducing duplication and lower costs (Øvretveit 1991a). However, these developments were not taking place, mainly because community health trusts cannot charge for services. Some trusts are setting up 'independent' social care organizations to get over this problem, but many are more interested in investing in professional health services, and in 'going for the high end of the market', as one trust chief executive put it.

A number of local authorities have introduced purchasing divisions, some of which manage decentralized purchasing 'care management teams'. A few have contracted out most services, or are planning to: in 1993 Westminster contracted for £8 million of its £55 million of services from voluntary organizations, and planned to put out to tender £12 million of care services by the end of 1994. This tender is to be followed by learning difficulty services, mental health and elderly services (Marchant 1993).

Assessment and care management

A third aspect of the reforms is individual client assessment and care management. One of the aims of the reforms is to increase choice and client participation, mainly through individual needs assessment systems. 'Care management and assessment lie at the heart of this new approach – "the cornerstone of quality care"' (SSI and SOSWSG 1991b: para 2). 'All users and carers should experience the process of care management, whatever the type or level of their needs' (SSI and SOSWSG 1991b: para 56). These new systems currently focus on social care needs, but there is a trend to form combined health and social needs assessments, and this is necessary for some people with complex needs. For this to happen, improvements in teamwork, communications and record systems will be needed. There is the potential to aggregate individual assessment information about service shortfalls for better planning, but it will take time to develop the computer systems to do this. Local authorities are concerned that the recording of 'needs shortfalls' will lay them open to litigation by clients who do not receive the services which they are assessed to need.

The purpose of care management is to make sure that a client has one person who coordinates the other people involved in his or her care. There are different views about whether this should be the same person who does

Many purchasers e.g. *care managers and GP fundholders*	• Low choice • Easy provider coordination • More difficult purchaser coordination	• Maximum choice and variety • Coordination most difficult
One purchaser	• Lowest choice • Easiest to coordinate	• High choice • Provider coordination difficult
	One provider *e.g. LA SSD or community trust*	Many providers *e.g. Range of private and voluntary services*

Figure 8.1   Coordinating purchasing and provision, and variety and choice for clients.

the assessment, and whether a care manager should have a budget for some, or all, of the client's care and purchase services. There are many different models (Øvretveit 1993b), but the trend is to increase local purchasing of social care, with the attendant difficulties in planning and market regulation similar to those which commissioners have found with GP fundholders: decentralized purchasing can undermine strategic purchasing if it is done independently, and can work to everyone's disadvantage in the long term.

It is far easier to stimulate competition between social care services than in health by encouraging new providers because the 'start-up' costs are far less than for many health services. However, increasing clients' choice by increasing the number and variety of providers often makes service and purchasing coordination more difficult. This causes problems in planning and providing for clients who need many types of service. Gains in choice and variety are offset by losses in ease of coordination and higher administrative costs. Is choice and variety only possible through many different organizations, and is there a balance to be struck between choice and costs? Should it be left to the market to strike this balance, and how can local and health authorities influence the market in joint market management policies?

Figure 8.1 provides a summary of the changes and shows that the concerns of local and health authorities are becoming similar. It also shows the advantages of collaboration in a number of areas. How might they best collaborate in the future?

Joint commissioning

This section concentrates on health commissioner collaboration with local authority social service departments, and on the concept of 'joint commissioning'. It describes how joint commissioning grew out of joint planning arrangements in one area: the London Borough of Hillingdon (where Heathrow Airport is situated). It draws on this research and others' experience to consider how a commissioner might review and improve current arrangements. First, what is 'joint commissioning'?

Definition

There are many ways in which authorities can usefully cooperate to carry out their separate and common responsibilities. 'Joint commissioning' is a general term to cover a range of activities, defined here as in Box 8.1.

Box 8.1

Joint commissioning: arrangements and agreements between agencies for commissioning services, where each agency has a partial responsibility for commissioning services to meet the needs of a client group or population (Øvretveit 1993e).

Joint commissioning is sometimes taken to mean true pooling of finance and handing over purchasing responsibilities to a separate agency. In the UK statutory public authorities cannot give up control of finance to another body in the full sense. However, the use of the term joint commissioning rather than, for example, 'collaborative planning or purchasing' does suggest a wish to move beyond aligning purchasing plans to finding ways of working together more closely.

Purposes

The purposes of joint commissioning are:

- to share assessments of need from different perspectives;
- to align plans or forge a common plan;
- to agree priorities and shared and separate responsibilities;
- to avoid the duplication or gaps in services which can occur when each agency commissions services in isolation;
- to ensure that contracting decisions further agreed plans.

Generally the aims are to strengthen commissioners' capability to meet the needs of the population at the lowest cost by pooling experience and knowledge, and agreeing joint strategies, for example for encouraging new providers. In terms of the organization of joint commissioning work there are two main dimensions: 'horizontal' and 'vertical'. The horizontal grouping of work is usually on a care or client-group basis, for different client groups, such as for children and families, for older people, for mental health clients, etc. Within each grouping there are different levels of work: for example, decisions about individual clients which require a joint agreement, or about provider systems and policies, or about longer-term strategy. Frequently, joint commissioning groups get involved in the wrong levels of work because there are no other arrangements for joint decisions.

Some assume that the ideal is an integrated health and social services authority, and that joint commissioning is a 'second best' arrangement. That is, it is a way of minimizing the problems which occur when two or more organizations assess needs and commission services for a population or client group, and where separate and shared responsibilities have to be agreed. However, an 'integrated commissioning agency' would still need to cooperate with other agencies. Further, the agency itself would have to divide its assessment and purchasing responsibilities internally: the cross-agency coordination issues simply shift to issues of coordination within the same organization. Experience in merging FHSA and DHA organization and staff demonstrates that division of responsibilities and coordination problems are not overcome just by forming one management organization. Placing previously separate staff and functions under one manager does not of itself solve problems of coordination, as we also see from experience of integrated Health and Social Service Boards in Northern Ireland.

The following section gives an example of one approach to joint commissioning before considering how commissioners might improve cooperation with their local authorities in the future.

The Hillingdon approach to joint commissioning

Although health and social service boundaries in Hillingdon (240,000 population) have not always been the same, there is a history of good collaboration. Arrangements for joint planning in the 1980s centred on seven client-based joint planning groups. Confidence in joint working was increased by a successful transfer of all learning disability services from health to social services in 1988 (Spenser and Macdonald 1989).

In 1990, the old planning groups were replaced by seven smaller joint commissioning groups (JCGs). The groups were made up of health purchasers (DHA, FHSA), health providers (community health, two acute, GPs), social services divisional directors (who managed both purchasing and providing), social services provider team managers and representatives from voluntary services, housing and the community health council (CHC) (8–16 people on each group). The groups started one-by-one over a 14 month period, and although community care was viewed as mostly concerned with adult services, it was decided that a group for child services was also needed.

The work of the JCGs in 1994 was to review and update community care plans and to advise the local authority about how the local authority special transitional grant should be spent. Future joint commissioning arrangements will involve a locality dimension, and take into account the changes in the local authority purchaser–provider reorganization. The terms of reference for each JCG included:

- assessing needs of the client population;
- describing current service provision;
- clarifying how much is spent on services for the client population and by whom, including both 'new' community care grant finance and 'old' finance (i.e. what resources are 'available' for the client population, and what resources the JCG can influence);
- formulating the community care plan for the client population;
- considering and reporting on providers' and purchasers' plans for changes to services;
- proposing changes to services.

Some JCGs spent a large proportion of their time on provider operational coordination issues. The chairs of each group met monthly in the Joint Chairs Working Group (JCWG). This group recommended allocations of the community care grant to the JCGs and reported to the chief executives' group. In addition there was a borough forum for voluntary organizations and a parallel set of voluntary groups 'shadowing' each JCG. More details are available in Øvretveit (1993e).

Summary

The Hillingdon JCGs do not in any way 'purchase' services, but are rather 'joint advisory groups' advising on the use of the community care grant and contributing to the community care plan. Each JCG had difficulties in clarifying exactly how much each authority spent on services for its client group, and how this was spent in different contracts. There was a question about how JCGs can best influence commissioning which uses finance other than the 'new' community care grant finance. One measure of their effectiveness is whether they have been able to change 'old' contracts to target needs better, and ultimately whether the needs of their client population are 'better met' as a result of their work.

The new chief executives undertook a review of arrangements in the summer of 1993. Their review, and a report on the arrangements (Øvretveit 1993e), identified a number of difficulties. Because there was no clear purchaser–provider split in social services, some social service managers in the JCGs were both purchasers and providers. In addition, all groups had health service providers as members, and two groups had provider managers as chairs. Although this mix is effective for planning, it did have a potential for groups to be biased towards current services. This was noted by some private and voluntary organizations, but because there had not been serious financial cuts and competition it had not emerged as such a serious problem as in other parts of the country. Other issues included, how to get better information about needs and service costs, how best to influence 'main-line' health and social service budgets and commissioning beyond the relatively small transitional community care grant, and the lack of a strategy for creating and managing a social care market, or even contingency plans for residential home bankruptcies.

Joint commissioning in Hillingdon: future options

The joint commissioning groups in Hillingdon are a way of coordinating needs assessment, planning, provider operational changes, contracting and other functions, for clients who have similar special needs (e.g. mental health problems). Whether JCGs performed any one of these functions well and whether combining functions in this way is the best way forward were questions considered in a review in 1994. Future arrangements are likely to separate purchasing and provision functions, and to introduce a locality dimension into the client-based cross-district perspective. One option was to limit the role; another was to extend the purchasing role to one in which the JCGs became true purchasers of most services for their client populations.

Limited role for JCGs
One view was that, in effect, JCGs are the last vestiges of joint planning groups, for the purpose of sharing accountability for deciding how to spend the community care grant. This view saw them as having an increasingly limited influence over most health and social services commissioning as the divergent pressures on the two authorities increased. One option is to limit their role to an advisory one, and look to other ways for developing a joint community care plan and for coordinating purchasing and provision.

Extended role for JCGs
Another view was that JCGs have hardly had time to 'find their feet', and that advice about the CCG grant is – like joint finance projects – a specific task that they have been able to apply themselves to, before going on to greater things. The view was that their capacity to assess needs and monitor services should be developed with support staffing and information systems, and that the two authorities (and perhaps fundholding GPs) should view the JCGs (or future equivalents) as the main 'purchasing bodies' for the future. In this model each authority would commission some services separately from JCGs, but budgeting and most purchasing will be through JCGs, and this opens the way to devolving some joint purchasing to care managers and/or localities.

General implications for health purchaser collaboration with local authorities

What are the lessons from Hillingdon and others' experience for how health commissioners can best collaborate with local authorities? First, many existing arrangements which mix purchasers and providers will become more problematic. Related to this is the need to separate levels of purchasing and provider work and to develop different collaboration arrangements for different levels of work: for example, to develop structures for providers to agree operational decisions which need to be considered across a range of services. However, provider expertise is helpful in planning, and some links between purchasing and providers will be necessary to ensure coordination.

Second, although one structure for all client groups is useful for formulating a community care plan, it may be better to have different joint planning or purchasing arrangements for different client groups. For example, it might be better to have separate purchasing and planning groups for client groups where many providers are involved.

Third, it may be more realistic for some health commissioners not to have a full range of client planning groups, but to take a selective approach to joint commissioning. This involves identifying particular areas for collaboration where there are disputes, problems or advantages in joint working.

Fourth, money divides or unites. If it was joint finance which gave purpose to joint working in the 1980s, it is financial cuts which can make or break joint working in the 1990s. In Hillingdon, local authority cuts were decided without consultation with JCGs, because the cuts plan would have made staff redundant (including possibly some staff on the JCGs) and reduced finance to voluntary services – the local authority could not afford 'leaks'. This affected confidence in the JCGs. Elsewhere, however, a local authority chief executive wanted the cuts package discussed in joint planning teams, and a confidentiality agreement was followed which added to the teams' credibility.

Fifth, future arrangements will need to involve voluntary organizations, clients and carers more fully. A strength of the Hillingdon model is a borough forum group and 'shadow' groups for each JCG (called 'special interest groups'). Involvement is real and mature, but has been developed over time. Elsewhere, partly as a result of cuts, voluntary organizations and CHCs have an adversarial relationship with the two authorities, and this makes real involvement difficult.

Reviewing collaboration

Most NHS health authorities reviewed their working links with local authorities after the NHS reforms. Many are again reviewing their relationships as a result of local authorities reorganizing and developing their purchasing role, and of health authority mergers. The key to establishing more effective arrangements is being clear about why working links are required, the purpose such links should serve and what work needs to be done jointly. The Hillingdon example shows one way of working with a social services department, where the authority boundaries are the same and where there is a history of good relations with voluntary organizations.

For others in a similar situation, the five lessons noted above may be helpful for reviewing their arrangements. Questions for others which arise from the Hillingdon experience include:

- For each area where collaboration is required, are groups like the Hillingdon JCGs the best arrangement for doing the collaborative work?
- What is the proper role for providers in arrangements for commissioner collaboration?
- What are the separate and common policies of chief officers with regard to social care market development and management (especially support for new entrants, and agreed approaches to planning market exits, e.g. private home failures as the 'care gap' widens)?

We now broaden the discussion to look at general principles and considerations in forming effective working arrangements with local authorities for the future. Many commissioning agencies inherited joint planning and consultation structures which evolved during the 1980s. But times have changed: health authorities have established their purchasing role and are pursuing health strategies, and local authorities have been or are restructuring, many with purchaser and provider divisions. These changes and the new tasks facing the authorities call for review of existing arrangements. With the emphasis on collaboration in purchasing, what arrangements should purchasers establish to ensure that providers collaborate? Do they need to establish structures for provider collaboration? We now consider issues and options for commissioners undertaking such reviews.

The purposes and benefit of collaboration: why collaborate at all?

Joint meetings, which are one method of collaborating, are expensive and time-consuming. Not only do they divert scarce time from other work, they are bad for morale when decisions are overruled or the situation changes in one authority to make all the work irrelevant. The question must be asked: why collaborate, when the results for all the time and effort seem so meagre or non-existent?

The first reason is because it is a government requirement that authorities inform or consult with each other over a variety of matters. These may be infrequent issues, where a special time-limited working group may be needed, or predictable and recurring tasks, such as the annual community care plans. At the other extreme, there are many tasks which health commissioners can do without needing to consult with or inform a local authority, and to do so is costly, introduces unnecessary delays and wastes everyone's time.

In many areas chief executives of health and local authorities meet regularly to deal with particular issues which arise. The question is: what other structures and processes do the chief officers need to establish between the authorities? This depends on their view of what work is best done jointly or shared. A simple starting point is to draw up and keep up to date a list

	Required to inform	*Required to consult and consider responses*	*Optional, but in our interests to reach agreement*
Tasks/subjects	e.g. hospital closure	e.g. community care plan e.g. discharge arrangements e.g. assessment	e.g. decentralized locality commissioning proposals e.g. care management arrangements

Figure 8.2 Reasons for consultation over decisions.

of the subjects and types of decision where authorities are (a) required to inform each other and (b) required to consult and consider responses, and (c) where it is in their interests to reach agreement. This list also needs to note if the task is recurring or infrequent (see Figure 8.2).

The second reason for collaboration is that the health and social service reforms have made it more necessary for authorities to have closer links in order to meet their responsibilities. Chapter 3 drew attention to the part local authorities can play in carrying out the objectives of *The Health of the Nation* (DoH 1992a) and in providing social care services for people coming out of hospital. From the local authority point of view, health services withdrawing from 'social care services' (e.g. long-term 'chronic care' services) put more demands on local authority services. We now further consider the benefits and purposes of collaboration, before outlining principles for deciding the best arrangements.

The benefits and purposes of collaboration

Any review or forging of new relations must start with the purposes and aims of collaboration. Collaboration is particularly important for:

* *Planning hospital closures* and new community services, especially client groups requiring linked health and local authority services (e.g. mental health, learning difficulties and geriatric hospitals). The experience of the 1980s shows the importance of joint planning for a range of community health and social services for people leaving long-stay hospitals. Building up community services for 'new' clients who would otherwise use hospitals also requires close health and social services collaboration.
* *Agreeing market strategy*: less residential and nursing home care could delay hospital discharges, reduce throughput and increase health commissioners' expenditures and waiting lists. Health commissioners need to know about and influence a local authority's market-management

strategy for homes and home care. Both need agreed contingency plans for home bankruptcies. Both need to work out what is best purchased locally and what is best purchased on a district, borough or county level.

- *Contracting and monitoring*: there is potential for sharing skills and knowledge in contracting some services, and in having a common approach to specifying and monitoring quality. Health commissioner quality staff concerned with non-hospital care often have more in common with their social service counterparts than with experts in hospital service quality, and there are benefits to forming joint quality teams and inspectorates and to joint appointments.
- *Population needs-assessment*: health and local authorities can usefully combine skills and information about needs in different communities and client groups. There is scope to consult clients and communities jointly about their service needs and preferences (e.g. for clients with learning disabilities, see the Welsh experience: Macdonald 1988; Øvretveit and Davies 1988).
- *Home care*: shorter hospital stays and day surgery call for more home care, as well as more primary health care. Health commissioners will need to work with social services to plan and commission home services, especially where nursing and social care overlap.
- *Integrated provision*: there is the potential to form integrated health and social care teams, purchased jointly, at either authority or local levels (see Chapter 9).
- *Decentralized purchasing*: if both health and social services decentralize purchasing in similar ways, this opens the possibility for joint locality purchasing in the future. Locality purchasing managers are an expensive option, but jointly appointed locality purchasing managers are a possibility, and may be able to 'mirror' providers' locality organizations.

The work to be done separately or jointly

The list above helps to clarify areas where there are benefits to collaboration. For a more detailed analysis of work which should or could be done jointly, commissioners can use the model of tasks in the process of commissioning described at the end of Chapter 3, or a model of the commissioning process. Which of the following tasks would be done more cost-effectively if the work or information was shared with a local authority?

- *Technical assessment* of the health needs of the population (local authority housing and other data).
- *Seeking citizens' views* about priorities and services.
- Ensuring that *'silent' citizens' needs* and interests are recognized and upheld in different purchasing decisions.
- Seeking and using *GPs' views* about needs and services in commissioning decisions.
- Formulating local health *priorities*, within national policies and targets.

- Formulating *health aims and strategies*, and a view of the role of other agencies in achieving these.
- *Planning* which services to purchase to meet priority needs.
- *Influencing providers* to plan and establish services so that the services are there to be purchased in the future.
- *Coordinating* planning and contracting with other purchasing and providing agencies (e.g. fundholding GPs).
- *Contract management*, i.e. negotiating and monitoring contracts to reflect the purchasing plan, and organizing payments.
- *Evaluating the impact on health* and the cost-effectiveness of commissioned services and other activities.
- *'Support work'* to the above work (e.g. training, recruitment, office systems).

Closer working with local authorities over some of these commissioning activities can save costs and result in better services. This helps to highlight work other than that done by traditional planning groups where there is benefit to collaboration, and helps us to move beyond a focus on structures. A model which helps to analyse problems in joint commissioning or joint planning groups is the model of levels of work in purchasing at the end of Chapter 3. Many groups fail to get to grips with strategic purchasing issues because their time and attention are taken up during the year with operational provider issues and individual cases. The result is that community care planning becomes a rushed task with little consultation and poor links with need assessment. The model of levels of work in purchasing helps to review the work which is and is not being done by different groups, and to clarify which tasks should be undertaken by joint provider groups. Provider collaboration is one of the subjects of the next chapter.

Degrees of collaboration

Clearly, different types of collaboration are possible and necessary for different purposes. An awareness of the possibilities helps to avoid 'over-collaboration' where it is not called for.

There are a variety of ways of collaborating, ranging from informing (e.g. sending papers or minutes), through consulting, to having meetings to explore issues, clarify options or reach decisions. Sometimes meetings are not necessary, but for some work, just sending papers is not sufficient. The continuum of cooperation shown in Figure 8.3 helps to clarify further which type of joint working is necessary.

Although Figure 8.3 suggests a radical review of current structures, the final point to be made is that, if existing arrangements and staff relations are adequate, it is much better to build on and improve these than to introduce completely new structures, especially if there have not been wide-scale staff changes. Some research (e.g. Knapp *et al.* 1992) and practical

Sharing information	Sharing a resource	Joint purchasing	Consortium	Merger
Population profiles and data, contract specification	Staff, facilities, equipment, same inspection unit, overlapping board membership	Agreed purchasing plan, pool finance for some, or all services	One agency purchases, but each purchaser remains an independent entity	New single purchasing body (e.g. unitary authority)

Figure 8.3   Possible types of commissioner collaboration.

experience suggest that effective joint working occurs where trust and understanding have developed over time. Staff are more realistic about what is possible, have a sound understanding of the weaknesses of the arrangements and have often developed informal ways to compensate for the weaknesses. But can the old arrangements be adapted to the tasks of separate purchasing and provision?

Conclusions: joint commissioning in the future

In general terms, joint commissioning is any form of collaboration between health and local authority social services commissioning staff. Many agencies have joint planning at strategic levels, but, in the future, joint commissioning at locality and care-manager levels is possible. One specific meaning is pooled finance for contracting, according to jointly agreed criteria, at population, locality or individual levels. Future collaboration will depend on how social services develop their commissioning role. Missing from many reviews is a clear statement of the purpose and objectives of commissioning, and of the purpose and objectives of joint commissioning. This in part accounts for the lack of any criteria of success and failure in joint commissioning, or ways of measuring the cost-effectiveness of current or future arrangements.

In a changing situation, chief executives need to identify where collaboration is essential and to mutual advantage, and to set up new working arrangements or develop existing ones to do the work. They need to ask exactly what health and social services purchasers and providers need to collaborate over, to (a) meet the requirements of the reforms, (b) ensure that it is clearly to the mutual benefit of each to do so, and (c) ensure that those most in need are identified and properly served.

Such reviews should start with clarity about the purposes and benefits of collaboration, and develop criteria for forming joint working arrangements. They should include statements about how authorities measure the success of their arrangements and how they will improve their cost-effectiveness.

Reviews need to recognize the many types of collaboration which are possible, and move beyond the old service-planning structures to consider the process of commissioning and where joint working in this process is to mutual advantage. A danger is that authorities will independently de-centralize purchasing and lose control as GP fundholders and care managers use their purchasing power. An urgent subject for joint discussions is how to decentralize purchasing yet also allow both authorities to give direction and pursue joint strategies.

Key points

- The broader the view of purpose which a health purchaser holds, the more important are relationships with other agencies for fulfilling the purpose.
- In a mixed economy of services, provider coordination depends on how well commissioners collaborate, and on agreed commissioning strategies. Commissioning agencies, local authorities and GP fundholders need to establish arrangements to ensure that their plans and actions are at least compatible, and, ideally, further everyone's aims.
- Commissioner collaboration will become even more important with devolved commissioning, i.e. with locality purchasing, more GP fundholders and purchasing by local authority care managers.
- Authority purchasing must ensure stability, but also give appropriate scope and delegate finance for local purchasing. Too much delegation without regulations, together with short-term opportunistic purchasing, can put providers out of business: authorities need to collaborate in decentralizing purchasing and experiment with pooled finance.
- 'Joint commissioning' with local authorities refers to a range of activities, from jointly planning services through to pooling some or all finance for joint purchasing. Where health commissioners have a locality purchasing structure, it can refer to arrangements between health locality commissioning managers and local authority social service providers and purchaser managers in a locality.
- Common problems in joint commissioning groups are: difficulties agreeing health and social care responsibilities and joint priorities; separating purchasing and provision issues and deciding how to coordinate each; defining the horizontal boundaries between different joint commissioning groups to avoid overlaps and gaps; single groups tackling too many levels of purchasing and provider work.
- Before forging new links, health commissioners need to be clear about why they need to relate to local authorities, and about the purposes and benefits of different arrangements. Time is not wasted drawing lessons from past joint working.
- Three sets of ideas are helpful in reviewing collaboration: a model of the commissioning process helps to identify where there is mutual benefit to sharing tasks, skills or information; a model of levels of purchasing

work helps to clarify problems with current arrangements and future purchaser and provider collaboration structures; a model of degrees of collaboration helps to clarify whether a permanent joint group is required or whether other forms of collaboration are more cost-effective.

• For most health commissioners, future collaboration will depend on how a local authority develops purchasing, and its purchaser and provider structures – whether care group or localities predominate. The test of joint arrangements is whether they can manage cuts, as well as proposing areas for development.

9 Developing primary and community health services

Almost a quarter of acute hospital beds will disappear by 1998 and hospitals could be left to provide only a range of outpatient and day care services.
(Report of a consultant's survey of 400 professionals' views of health trends in the UK, *Health Services Journal* 1 July 1993: 6)

Purchasing will lead the provision of health care out of hospitals and into the community, into GP hospital-at-home schemes and hotel hospitals in the community.
(Duncan Nichol, then Chief Executive of the NHS Management Executive, speaking at the IHF conference, London, October 1992)

Introduction

Health purchasers have to plan now for significant changes in the late 1990s: the revolution in health care technology, shorter hospital stays, people living longer and an increase in chronic health conditions. These changes are already leading to an increasing amount of health care being provided outside hospitals in primary health care centres and in people's homes. In many instances the quality of care, health gain and overall costs for purchasers will depend on how well different services cooperate with each other in managing patient care, as much as on what each service does within its own boundaries. In most market systems, purchasers are the only organizations with an overview of the complete care process *and* the responsibility and power to ensure linkages between services, as well as to manage change and develop services outside hospitals.

The purpose of this chapter is to give an introduction to purchasing primary and community health services, and to consider how purchasers can develop these services, where such services are, or could be, better than hospital care. It argues that one way in which purchasers add value and serve their populations is by ensuring that provider services relate to each other and give continuity of care to patients moving between services. It challenges purchasers to clarify their vision of what type and amount of services should be provided in primary care, in local hospitals, and in regional centres. The two issues are, what services are best provided in a primary care setting and how are services best coordinated?

The chapter starts by describing primary care services in the UK, and concentrates on general medical practitioner services. It considers commissioners' role in improving these services and in developing primary health care teams. It then considers other community health services, provided in the UK by NHS community health trusts and purchased as secondary care services by district health authorities. It describes how these services can link with hospitals and with GPs in primary health care teams.

A theme of the chapter is the service which commissioners perform in ensuring coordination between the many separate health services in the community. One way is to require and help to develop multidisciplinary provider teams made up of practitioners from the different services. Because commissioners have a key role in creating such teams – a role they do not have when commissioning hospital services – we consider the different types of teams and how commissioners can encourage cross-provider cooperation. A precondition for such cooperation is that commissioners themselves coordinate their own divisions or directorates to follow a common strategy – the subject of later chapters. This chapter aims to help commissioners to find answers to the following questions.

- *Which hospital services could be provided in a primary care setting without lower quality, or higher cost, and how should commissioners form their views on this issue?*
- *What do GPs and others need in order to be able to provide certain hospital services, and how should we help or encourage them to do so?*
- *Is investing in GP services actually the best way to provide more care in the community: should we be investing in other types of community health services?*
- *How should we help single-handed GPs, and what part should they play in a plan for developing primary care?*
- *How do we tackle the variable quality of primary care and GP services?*
- *How should we develop primary health care teams, with a greater chance of success than in the past?*
- *How can we find out more about community health services: the type and amount of work which different staff are doing in each area, and the costs and effectiveness?*

Changing the emphasis: from hospital to primary care, and from acute to preventative services

The bulk of NHS time and finance is spent on acute hospital services, yet most health care is provided outside hospitals, and people's health often depends on factors other than the health services. A series of government initiatives have sought to move attention and resources away from acute hospital services to primary care and to the prevention of ill health (DHSS 1986, 1987; DoH 1991b, 1992a). One aspect of the community care reforms is to ensure that social care services complement health services outside hospitals, and offer alternatives to hospital care. Sceptics argue that every government emphasizes community care, but none provides the resources to develop services and prevention programmes. In addition, building up long-term prevention and community services will be even more difficult than in the past, with an emerging market system and GP and care-manager purchasing.

It will certainly be difficult for public authorities to carry out *The Health of the Nation* agenda (DoH 1992a), yet also develop market competition and a mixed economy of care, and reduce spending on hospitals to release finance to invest in primary care. One reason for government emphasis on 'stronger commissioning' is that commissioners can, in theory, switch expenditure to develop services outside hospitals and to finance initiatives to prevent ill health. There are assumptions that some hospital services can be provided for less cost in the community, that the savings can be used to improve community health services and that this will reduce demand on hospital services. But the opposite may happen: community services may cost more and increase referrals to hospitals. The notion of increasing primary care services to reduce demand on hospitals may be as mistaken as the post-war idea that demand on the NHS would drop once it had 'cleared up the backlog of illness'. However, building services in local 'polyclinics' may make traditional hospitals redundant.

Whatever the validity of the assumptions, the success of commissioning organizations is measured in part by their progress in increasing the amount and quality of services outside hospitals. This is viewed as a cost-effective way to improve the health of their populations. The relationship between developments in services outside hospitals and health gain is a subject of debate and research, as is whether integrated commissioning organizations are better at the task than separate purchasing organizations. Chapter 3 considered commissioners' activities to improve health in ways other than commissioning services. In this chapter we consider the role of primary and community health services in providing health promotion, diagnosis and treatment, and their potential to host, or to undertake, services traditionally provided in hospitals. We start by defining primary health care and then consider the future role of general medical practitioner services.

Primary care: unlimited potential?

A BMA survey in early 1993 finds that over 30 per cent of London GPs cite extra funds for hospital services as a priority for the next 12 months.
(Health Service Journal 10 June 1993: 4)

A health gain perspective highlights factors which are important to people's health other than health services, but also the role of health services other than hospitals in treating and caring for people and in preventing ill health. There is a view that some hospital services are better provided in primary care settings, and by primary care practitioners, that some services effectively reduce the need for hospital services and prevent illness, and that people find primary care services more accessible than, and prefer them to, hospital services.

These are given as reasons for 'shifting the balance' from hospital to primary care (Pashley *et al.* 1993). But is the limited evidence of the success of some schemes, and of the few treatments and service which have been transferred, enough to support these generalizations and major changes?

Some primary care practitioners cannot and do not want to deepen and widen their role, even with adequate finance and training. They have enough to do to keep up to date with the new drugs, diagnostic methods and treatments for traditional primary care services. Are commissioners expecting too much of primary care services? What is the best way of defining the future role of such services and developing it? Two key questions are asked in Figure 9.1.

The route for commissioners lies between the two extremes of viewing hospitals as expensive anachronisms and scepticism about a wider and deeper role for primary care. Commissioners need to examine carefully:

- which hospital services can be provided in a primary care setting, more effectively, at a lower price and/or higher quality (e.g. consultant outpatient sessions, diagnostic and testing services, minor surgery, therapy services);
- which new services and approaches should be developed in primary care which are cost-effective for health gain objectives;
- how to work with hospitals, primary care providers and others to clarify and develop the potential of primary care services;
- the role of current primary care practitioners in promoting health and preventing illness, and which specialist practitioners are needed for these tasks in a primary care setting.

Despite government intentions to strengthen primary care, spending on family health services has fallen from 33 per cent of total NHS outlay in 1949 to 24 per cent in 1990. The provision of all family health services cost £120 per person in 1990, contrasting with £274 for the hospital sector. Total funding of hospital and community health services will expand by 2.3 per cent in 'real' terms up to '93/4, compared to 1.7 per cent for family health services.

(Davis 1992, summarizing *OHE Health Statistics*, 8th edn)

What exactly are commissioners' expectations?	*Are their expectations realistic?*
Of the needs which GPs can meet, and of the work which they can do?	About GPs' capacity to do more of the same, and to provide new services?
Of primary health care teams?	About what it will take to form effective teams to provide and develop services?
Of GPs as purchasers as fundholders, or in locality purchasing schemes?	Their motivation and ability to take responsibility for devolved budgets? Fundholders' willingness to agree collective purchasing strategies, and their ability to develop hospital services in primary care?
About *transferring finance* from hospital to primary care?	About whether this can be done with a declining purchasing budget, about the speed with which this can be done, and about setting up internal agency arrangements to do it?
About *reducing demand* for certain hospital services?	About the number of hospital services which can be provided in primary care settings, at a lower or the same cost, including the investment costs to do so?
About what *practitioners* can do to improve health and prevent illness?	About the time practitioners will have to do this work, and about how easy it is to develop the skills and attitudes for practitioners to do preventative work?

Figure 9.1 Key questions for defining and developing the role of primary care services.

Primary health care: definition

If we compare definitions of 'primary health care' in other countries with those in the NHS we see that the definitions of primary health care reflect sources of finance for and administration of GP services more than any philosophy of health care. A simple definition is, 'the first point of contact for health services'. In the UK this usually refers to GPs, dentists, pharmacists, and some opticians contracted by a Family Health Service Authority (FHSA), and sometimes community health service staff such as community nurses. Beyond this there are different views about what is and what is not primary care: is siting or provision outside hospital the distinguishing feature? Is a hospital consultant who runs clinics in a health centre providing primary care, or giving specialist care in a primary care setting? Specialist nurses such as community psychiatric nurses are sometimes considered primary health care providers, as are hospital outreach nursing services, and also some hospital accident and emergency departments providing general health services to homeless people and others which are normally provided by GPs.

Primary care may include all of the above, and social services as well. For example, NHS trusts in Northern Ireland manage both health and social services, and some have integrated primary care teams (Øvretveit 1991a). To some extent, definition is less important with integrated FHSA/DHA commissioning organization, which eases the transfer of DHA finance for primary care services. In the future the boundary between primary and secondary care will be determined by what services can be provided in a GP practice or health-centre type setting.

Box 9.1

Primary health care services
Services provided at GP practices and health centres by GPs, practice staff and community nurses. Not community psychiatric nurse (CPN) services or some community therapy services (termed here 'specialist community services') or outpatient consultant sessions (secondary care provided in a primary care setting).

Community health services
Health services other than primary care services, provided outside larger hospitals, paid for from DHA cash-limited finance and contracted by DHAs, integrated agencies or GP fundholders. Includes CPN services. Typically non-hospital health services provided by a community health trust.

Secondary care services
Nearly all hospital-based services, and some specialist services provided in the community (e.g. some community therapy and CPN services), paid for by DHA or GP fundholder finance.

Specialist services
All secondary care services and some community health services.

Community care services
Mainly social services, but sometimes GP and community health services.

The work of GPs

Many people think that they know what GPs do, but we each only get a partial idea from our own and our friends' and relatives' experience of GP services. In the UK, if our GP is near the national average, we are one of 1,900 other people registered with him or her (fewer than 30 per cent of GPs are women), 300 patients being over 75 years old, and 180 less than five years old. If we are average in our use of our GP, we will see him or her three or four times a year. The most common problems are respiratory (usually flu-like disorders) or psychiatric (especially depression). We may be one of the 400 patients our 'average' GP refers as a 'new' outpatient for specialist consultation, or, if we are unlucky, one of the 25 a year he or she refers for emergency hospital admission.

Primary health services are provided by solo GPs and other individual contractors, but more usually in one of three types of grouping: a GP group practice (a private business); a practice team (GPs and their employed receptionists, practice nurse and others); and a primary health care team (PHCT), which includes, in addition to the practice team, community nurses employed by a community trust, and often community therapists and others. The many different disciplines, with different management and financing, have made it difficult to form stable and integrated teams in primary care in the past. More details about general practice can be found in the short summaries by IHSM/RCGP (1993) and NAHAT (1992), and in the next chapter on FHSAs.

Purchasing primary care

Each GP has a contract with the FHSA, which is set at the national level. Each GP is paid according to a schedule for the number of patients (weighted capitation), a basic payment and fees for different services (fees amount to 10–20 per cent of income, a GP 'target income' for 1993 being £36,352).

Use of the term 'purchasing' to describe FHSAs' contracting of GP services is misleading: the 'purchasing functions' of the FHSA are different to those of the DHA, with far less scope for negotiation – the next chapter, on FHSAs, gives more details. However, FHSAs are establishing more formal relations with group practices. Individual GPs, each with his or her own contract with the FHSA, form partnerships or group practices which are small businesses and which establish agreements as a group with their FHSA. FHSAs allocate their discretionary finance for practice staff, premises and computers to improve both solo and group practices. To develop primary care, this finance will be increased (often from DHA sources) and FHSAs will have more formal agreements about what GPs will do in return.

Thus, although FHSAs' influence over individual GPs through their individual contracts is limited, FHSAs are moving to contracts with group practices and, in time, with primary health care teams. This is not easy, not least because of the number of GPs and practices in a district, and because of a confusion between the annual contractual reports, required by the DoH for monitoring purposes, practice reports, which are voluntary and for self-evaluation (Pringle 1990), and business plans, usually for presenting a case for investment finance.

Box 9.2   GPs: further facts and figures

- GP *services cost* £1.9 billion in 1992 (8.6 per cent of NHS spending).
- GP *prescribing cost* £2.3 billion in 1992 (total NHS drugs spending £2.8 billion).
- About 30,000 GPs (12,000 district nurses, 13,000 health visitors).

GP Fundholder 'purchasers':
- About 300 practices in the first wave in April 1991.
- A further 280 practices in the second wave in April 1992, and 600 practices in the third wave in April 1993.
- After April 1993 there were about 1,200 practices in the scheme (6,000 GPs), covering more than 25 per cent of the UK population.
- In April 1994, a further 3,000 GPs became fundholders, covering nearly 40 per cent of the population of England.

Changes in primary care

While there is debate about which hospital services are best provided in primary care settings, there is no doubt that the demand for primary care services has increased and changed, for a variety of reasons. There are changes in the diseases and health problems dealt with by GPs and nurses, with more cancers and degenerative diseases, and more elderly patients and people from ethnic groups with special needs. These changes are in part owing to changes in the population, and in part owing to fewer social and other services.

Changes in hospitals, such as shorter lengths of stay, day treatments and fewer hospital beds, are also increasing GPs' workload. In addition, patient expectations are rising with increased health consciousness and with the Patient's Charter for primary care. Finally, the 1990 GP contract increased the amount of health screening and health promotion activities. Many of these changes were not planned or predicted, but the result is that working in primary care is a different and more demanding job than it was even five years ago. Some workers in primary care feel that there is a potential to take on more work, but that they will need more facilities, staff and incentives to do so.

Most GPs recognize that many of the health problems dealt with in primary care are caused or exacerbated by social and environmental factors, and that there are limits to the impact which health promotion in primary care can have. In 1993, a GP pointed out that

Health promotion work in primary care will have little effect on cutting death rates from major diseases without urgent government action to address economic problems . . . Unless social factors such as unemployment, housing and poverty are tackled, GPs will only be scratching at the surface in their efforts to improve the overall health of the population . . . Advice about diet is no use if people cannot afford healthy food, and controlling stress and blood pressure levels is difficult if people are worried about losing their jobs.

(*Health Service Journal* Report 12 September 1993: 8)

Having questioned the high, and often unclear, expectations which some purchasers have of primary care, we also need to note that there are many GPs, especially some fundholders, who see a much larger role for primary care as being both necessary and achievable:

The general practice of ten years' time will undoubtedly be very different from the practice of today – a health maintenance unit delivering a much wider range of services: such as consultant outpatients, day-case surgery, endoscopy, colposcopy, and many more services. Patients will be referred to the DGH for those investigations which require a piece of equipment which is just too large to be practice-based and for operations which require a degree of medical cover and expertise that the practice just cannot offer.

(Dr Paul Lamden, speaking at the NHS ME's conference 'Purchasing for Health', May 1991)

There are an increasing number of fundholders developing such local services or 'polyclinics', often with no support from purchasers.

Issues in purchasing primary care

Many GPs are unsure about what purchasers expect of them at present and in the future, and want a reconsideration of the core content of their contracts. Many question the value of annual practice reports, and are prepared to consider practice agreements and business plans as a basis for a practice relationship with a purchaser. The Audit Commission has proposed that such agreements could replace the inflexibilities of the GP contract, and give a framework within which purchasers could work with fundholding and non-fundholding practices (Audit Commission 1993b).

Other issues for purchasers include the basis on which they allocate their discretionary resources to different GPs: should they give finance to practices which they feel will make good use of the money, or give it to practices sited in areas of greater need but who may not use the finance to the best effect? Most commissioners are in the early stages of assessing health needs in different areas, and have few reliable needs data on which to decide allocations: an immediate issue is how to bring together DHA and FHSA information about needs and facilities in a usable form (Voss 1993 and Fry 1993 give suggestions and guidance). A further issue is how commissioners can encourage better coordination and communication between practitioners in primary health care teams, where there are teams, and between primary care and hospitals.

Quality in primary care

Purchasers are also concerned about the poor quality of some GP services and some primary health care team services. Apart from a complaints system with effective action, the traditional approach to professional service quality is to ensure high quality inputs. This involves high quality GP training and postgraduate education, checking qualifications before contracting and influencing the choice of new partners in group practices (one practice recently involved patients in appointments). The Royal College of General Practitioners is considering regular reviews and re-accreditation, which could involve FHSAs.

Although specifying and monitoring outcomes in primary care is only realistic for some conditions and treatments, commissioners can make more use of audit in general practice. There are now well-developed systems which GPs can use with their peers or individually (Marinker 1990). In addition, more use can be made of practice audit methods: a King's Fund organizational audit system has been developed for general practice and could be used for external audit, or as a basis for commissioners themselves to develop a commissioner audit system. For the quality of team services, an effective developmental approach is to use a team quality assurance system. One such system was tested and is now used for primary care teams in part of Northern Ireland. The team used the 'Wel-Qual' quality framework to develop with clients and carers a system which was appropriate to their population and situation (Øvretveit 1991a, includes reports from practitioners and managers using the system).

Primary health care teams: a summary

If primary health services are to meet the increasing demand and to develop new services then there is no doubt that stronger primary health care teams are required. My own and others' research has found that many primary health care teams are teams in name only, and that poor coordination and communication between members is the norm, for a variety of reasons (Øvretveit 1990a, 1991a, 1993b). In the past attempts to create or develop teams have largely failed, but some changes now improve the prospects for success, such as the threat or reality of GPs purchasing or employing nurses and therapists, and the availability of new finance. In addition integrated DHA/FHSA commissioning organizations are now more able to create, and are more serious about creating and perhaps contracting,

1 *Membership*: Does the main team base have a list of core and associate members, and are new members given this list with phone numbers for each member?

2 *Population served*: Do all team members serve the same population, whether geographically defined or registered with GPs?

3 *Base*: Ideally all members should have their permanent offices at the same base in adjoining rooms. Does the team have a meeting room which is easy for everyone to get to, with coffee and tea facilities? (Free tea and biscuits, always available at one place, is the most cost-effective teambuilding method there is.)

4 *Roles*: Short descriptions of each person's role, an understanding of each other's role and of when to refer.

5 *Contact and communications*: Times and ways to contact each member, regular meeting times, effective message systems.

6 *Patient index and case records*: A daily updated list of patients currently served by each member, and centralized case records, ideally multidisciplinary.

7 *Review of team services* and performance by higher management and the commissioning agency, at least annually.

(Øvretveit 1993b, p. 184 gives more details)

Figure 9.2 Primary health care teams: a checklist of essentials.

teams and are requiring team working with GPs in their contracts with community units or trusts.

Purchasers' role in developing teamwork

How can health purchasers best ensure that care for each client is co-ordinated across health and social services, between acute and primary care, and between professions within one service? At what point do purchasers cross the 'boundary' and 'interfere' in provider issues? Because team members come from different organizations and employers, purchasers have a key role in forming such teams, rather than contracting one organization to provide an integrated team service and leaving the details up to them. In some cases a largely or entirely GP-employed team may be appropriate, but a purchaser will still need to know about the details of team organization.

Thus purchasers need to know something of the conditions for teamwork, and of which type of team is best for a particular area. We now consider the main types of primary health care team, and Figure 9.2 notes some basic requirements for teamwork.

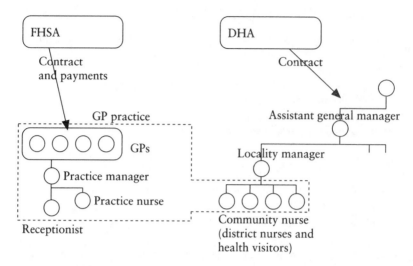

The team may also include therapists, and, if it is a fundholding practice, it will contract community nurses from the trust.

Figure 9.3   The primary health care team combines GP practice staff and community nurses.

Types of team

We now summarize three types of primary health care team (PHCT). The next section of the chapter, on community health services, describes how community trusts can best organize their different disciplines into groups to relate to GP practices, or combine with them to form practice-based PHCTs – either one for each practice or one for a number of practices.

PHCT type 1: two sub-groups, of GP practice staff and community health staff

This first type is the most common, which is where a group practice of GPs and practice staff form part of a larger primary health care team, with another group of community unit nursing staff and associate therapists (Figure 9.3). A key issue is whether the community health service staff serve the patients registered with the GP practice or the patients of a defined geographical area (e.g. a 'locality'). In rural areas, GPs' lists often coincide with the geographical area covered by community nurses because most people in the area register with the same practice. In other areas, different people register with different practices, and if the community staff are organized to serve a population area they will have to relate to two or more practices. Community trusts argue that considerations of staff cover for leave and illness make it difficult to switch from geographical coverage to 'true' practice attachment. Some community trusts create a compromise arrangement, or have a large team with a sub-group attached to a practice and its patients, and a sub-group serving patients in the area registered with other practices (e.g. the Northern Ireland 'patch team' described in Øvretveit 1991a).

On the question of the separate management of practice nurses by GPs, and of community nurses by community trusts, note one community trust's recent approach:

> In the past, the practice nurses have been managed by GPs and the district nurses have been managed by a locality nurse manager. We have identified one nurse – irrespective of background – in each practice to take charge of all nursing services. We as a trust, and the GPs, pass over management and staff to that nurse manager, and they in turn report directly to the principal of the practice.
>
> (Marchant 1993: 33)

The two other primary health care team models noted here are for single-handed GPs:

PHCT type 2: 'hub and spoke'
In this type, GPs are less involved in the team, which is based in a clinic or health centre at a different site from individual GPs' surgeries. GPs refer to and draw on the team for different services, and may come to the team base to run clinics.

PHCT type 3: resource centre model
In the third type, individual GPs remain independent, but are based together in one centre, and relate to a primary health care team based at the centre.

Developing primary care

How can purchasers develop primary care to be able to fulfil a new and extended role? Here we note four practical approaches in different parts of England. The outlines of one practical strategy for integrated DHA–FHSA purchasers were given in a North West Thames Regional document (Pashley *et al.* 1993). This agenda includes creating a single budget and one purchasing team in the integrated purchasing organization (e.g. a directorate of primary care), as well as integrating data for needs assessment. There are a variety of types and sources of data from GPs (see Voss 1993). Methods for gathering these data for public health and commissioning purposes are described in Fry (1993). The agenda also outlines steps for developing providers, for improving postgraduate education and links with hospitals, and for helping to form primary health care teams.

Many of these steps from North West Thames Region follow from the London 'Tomlinson review,' and are also present in the North East Thames Region's approach. However, this latter region views FHSAs as having a more distinct, independent and continuing role. In East London a primary care development agency was established, which directly provided community and family health services, and prepared community services for becoming a trust in April 1995. This development agency was financed for women's services, acute mental health, children's services and care of the elderly, and either provided these services or purchased them (subcontract) from local acute trusts.

There are parallels on a smaller scale in a scheme backed by the integrated Dorset Health Commission. Here the Lyme Community Care Unit, set up by one single-handed GP and a group practice of four GPs, provides a range of health and social care services for a locality of 8,000 people. Community health service funding was transferred to this new unit, which includes a mental health team, a stroke rehabilitation team and a hospital-at-home scheme. There are also plans for this unit to take over all hospital purchasing from the commission:

> The intention from the outset was to provide all possible services in or close to the patient's home, reducing or preventing inpatient stays for all conditions that can be properly cared for by the new powerful and extended community care team . . . resource . . . Transfer is by negotiating differential tariff with secondary care providers which reflects the significantly shorter inpatient stays which become possible with the hospital at home scheme . . . We now operate an electronic record, open to all health care professionals with electronic referral of patients within the unit and the integration of purchasing contracts for secondary care.
>
> (Robinson 1993)

In Wolverhampton, the route to developing primary care is seen to be by the FHSA taking on a 'provider' role. The FHSA and DHA have a combined executive, and the FHSA now manages the new Primary Health Care Unit, which includes community health services and geriatric and psychiatric hospitals. This unit has four primary health care managers, each of whom manages community and primary care services in a patch (Lord 1993). We consider this model and the future role of the FHSA in developing primary care in the next chapter.

Probably the most important practical first steps for any commissioner are to survey practice premises and possible buildings for teams, and to clarify the boundaries of localities to support more integrated GP and community health service provision. Further steps involve forming a view about what services are better provided in a primary care setting, drawing on experience such as that of the Lyme Unit above and the Epsom fundholder 'polyclinic'. Few GPs on their own will be able to take on the range of work and services which commissioners envisage being done outside hospitals. A key issue in developing primary care and community services is to improve integration between family practitioner services and community health services, or establish links in the first place. This is the subject of the next section.

Purchasing community health services

This section gives an introduction for purchasers to community health services and considers how these services can best link or integrate with GP practices. It considers the role of community health trusts in providing health and social care services in the community, and discusses four models for coordinating community health service practitioners in teams and in localities. Moving to a needs-led approach to commissioning means purchasing community health services for a particular area, or client group, or care programme, rather than by discipline (Chapter 3). Commissioners need to know the options open to trusts for 'packaging' and coordinating their services.

Is there a future for community trusts, squeezed between entrepreneurial GPs and expanding acute hospital trusts with their 'outreach' services? Should commissioners encourage merged acute and community trusts, or the absorption of community health service staff in GP practice teams? To do so would appear to improve coordination.

Definition

For the purposes of this book, community health services are defined as 'specialist health services, provided outside an acute hospital, usually by an NHS trust or unit which is independent from hospital services, and is separately contracted by a health commissioner'. Community trusts vary in the range of services they provide and in how they are organized: all provide community nursing services, but some also provide all or some therapy services, learning difficulty services, specialist health services for older people, and some or all mental health services in an area, in the latter case sometimes leasing hospital facilities in a district general hospital to house an acute psychiatric service there.

With GPs employing more of their own nurses and other staff, and hospitals developing outreach services, some have questioned whether there is a future for community trusts, especially small trusts which only provide community nursing and therapy services. Others argue that commissioners should support community trusts as independent providers in order to offer more choice and alternative approaches to service provision, especially as they can offer social care services (but cannot charge for these yet) and integrated community care.

Contracting community health services

To form a view about the role of community health services and trusts, commissioners need more information about the services provided – the type, volume and quality – and need to evaluate the cost-effectiveness of the services (Netten 1993). We noted in Chapter 6 the NSGC 'costing for contracting' project (Reeves 1993), which at present proposes that community health services can be described in terms of five dimensions.

These are: the client group served (e.g. people over 65); the practitioners giving the services (e.g. district nurses, clinical psychologists, a community team); the place of service (e.g. domiciliary, residential, health centre); the health condition being treated (e.g. dementia); and the health activity or procedure being provided (e.g. rehabilitation, injections, psychotherapy). Pilots in Bedfordshire and Hertfordshire show that, in 1994, costing was only possible in relation to the care input (the practitioners giving the service), and more detailed contracting for 1994–5 contracts will have to start with this, and add the setting and condition, and move towards output measures.

Contract negotiations, types of contracts and purchasing for community health services will become more sophisticated, not least because purchasers are putting more emphasis on community nurses' and therapists' involvement in primary health care teams. If there is to be progress in developing primary health care teams, then commissioners must contract community units or trusts to form or develop them. One reason for doing so is that if GPs are dissatisfied with nursing and therapy services to their patients, then they are more likely to consider fundholding. In addition to forming primary care teams, commissioners are turning their attention to developing specialist community teams and services in mental health, learning disabilities, elderly and child services.

Purchasing community health services: what 'packages' to buy

In the past, community services were managed and provided by different professions and disciplines, and sometimes by client-group or care programmes. Commissioners who have gone beyond block contracts may have separate contracts for different discipline-based services, usually covering the whole district. Questions for both trusts and commissioners are: Should some or all contracts with the trust be changed from discipline services to contracts for multidisciplinary team services to an area – should future contracts be for teams not disciplines? If so, which specialist client group teams are needed, where should the boundaries lie between these teams and generalist primary health care teams, and should specialists be 'members' of primary health care teams? How should contracts and service outcomes be monitored for teams, especially primary health care teams?

The following subsection describes some of the options for community teams, starting with a summary of the likely current arrangement. Where does the primary care team end and other specialist teams begin? We start by considering past experience in forming coordinated community services in the UK.

Background: 'patch' nursing and community health service organization

In the late 1980s some community units began to organize their nursing services and other community services on a 'patch' or 'locality' basis.

These geographical areas may or may not have coincided with GP practices or, to be more specific, with where most patients who were registered with one or more GP practices lived. These changes followed the influential Cumberlege Report and the Edwards Report (Wales) on nursing, which were also viewed alongside the 1985 review of primary health care (DHSS 1986). Both nursing reports made proposals for organizing different community nurse disciplines on a 'patch basis', which would also help to develop primary health care teams. A good example of some of these principles in practice is the Norwich model.

Community nursing and therapy services: the Norwich 'patch' scheme
The Norwich approach exemplifies many of the features of schemes elsewhere, is reasonably long-running (started 1984) and reveals the problems as well as the potential for local integrated services. Norwich was divided into GP and geographical 'patches' with populations of between 25,000 and 30,000, as a basis for 'community care groups' (CCGs) of GP services, community nurses (managed by 'patient care managers') and full- or part-time therapists ('community support groups'). These patches are 'closely associated' with other social services and voluntary organizations. For these purposes Norwich (450,000 population, 30 miles by 40 miles) was divided into four sectors and 16 patches.

The aim was to establish a 'locally based network', with the types of professions and their numbers related to the needs of an area, so as to undertake all non-hospital health-related activity. Patches are used to help plan specialist services on a 'bottom-up' basis, by involving staff who know the population and the service deficiencies of the patch. Because of staffing continuity in the area, staff are known to, and have knowledge of, other local services. Although no evidence was given, it was reported that

> Patch populations receive a timely and high quality service, without the duplication of effort and conflict of advice . . . there is better communication and hence more effective use of time and resources where a group of health workers, with common aims, are based together locally and have a continuing commitment to a defined population.

The promise of the scheme was that

> A strong community-based service, as well as being an essential ingredient to high quality primary care, also has a great potential for influencing the ultimate use of scarce and expensive hospital facilities . . . it will undoubtedly have an important effect on the eventual configuration and utilisation patterns of the resources in the hospital sector.

> (Bailey 1987)

If we measure the success of this and similar schemes in terms of reduced demand on hospital services, population satisfaction and impact on health status over the short and long term, then the little evidence there is shows that the impact is limited, mainly because:

- CCGs end up providing health services where there were none, and create demand;
- there are resource problems, full-time staffing for each patch is difficult and split posts reduce integration;
- there is fragmented management, in particular therapists' resistance to 'threats' to autonomy, each with different policies and priorities for district therapy service and each resisting 'role-blurring' with nurses or other therapists.

This and other locality or primary care team schemes have learned that attention to organization, management and professional cultures is essential to more integrated services. There are limits to what can be achieved without substantial changes in these areas. A model currently in favour is for community provider trusts to redirect all or some staff and other staff budgets to locality managers to decide the staff mix: therapy service managers then have to seek income by 'selling therapists' internally to locality managers (Øvretveit 1992b). Locality managers contract directly to fundholders, and subcontract the services which they need from therapists and others.

Before considering four models for coordinating community and family practitioner services, we need to note changes in social service provision, and the potential for closer links with social service teams.

Social service 'locality teams'
Many social service models mix purchasing and provision. The following Essex model is one such (the Berkshire model separates 16 locality purchasing managers from provision):

> Locality teams must be large enough to sustain professional support and supervision. The department is exploring catchment areas covering a population of 40,000 in order to have sufficient workload whilst retaining closeness to the 'local community' . . . will provide a team approach to assessment and care management . . . local teams will be responsible to a Principal Officer and comprise mainly social work and home care organisers with associated support staff . . . Progressively as DSS moneys are transferred it is envisaged that increased purchasing power will be vested in the locality teams.
>
> (Essex County Council SSD, 'Assessment and care management',
> 3 June 1992)

Integrated health and social care provision: Northern Ireland primary care teams
The problems of fragmented management which hampers close integration in many areas are not there in Northern Ireland – at least in theory. The

Down and Lisburn Trust in the Eastern Health and Social Services Board established, in 1991, an integrated patch team of nurses, social workers and occupational therapists, managed by one 'patch manager'. It covers three practices with a population of 16,000. This model is now used throughout the area (reported in Tonks 1993 and Øvretveit 1991a). In practice there are still problems about professional identities and management, but these have been largely overcome using quality methods and philosophies which help staff to focus on patients and to organize their work to avoid quality problems. In the Down and Lisburn Trust there is also the incentive that the community teams are the link to the Trust's acute services: good integration within the team and between the team to acute services is a way of enticing GPs to refer to the Trust's services.

Coordinating community services: four options for community trusts

We started with the question of how family practitioner services could best link with community health services. Yet in the examples we see that not the least of the problems is ensuring coordination *within* a community trust itself – between the different community health service disciplines. The first model below highlights the number of different 'profession-managed' services in many community trusts. This is the first of four models for community teams, described here in order to give commissioners an idea of the different ways in which family practitioner and community health services can be brought together. The first model is an 'open network' of separate professional services, like the Norwich example above. The second and third models show different arrangements for a community trust to coordinate its own staff in a geographical area which is aligned to GP lists, where this is possible. The fourth model introduces local purchasing.

Model 1: local primary care services and separate district-wide services

This is the likely current arrangement in many localities, and is shown in Figure 9.4.

It is possible that:

- all or many of the service disciplines are managed by different managers;
- some services are GP-attached, some health centre based, some covering defined areas and some district-wide.

The drawbacks of this model for health service commissioners are:

- Contracting – who does a purchasing manager or fundholder contact to negotiate a detailed contract?
- Individual care coordination – who ensures that the services are

	District nurses	Community psychiatric nurse (CPN) (probably separate CPNs for acute, elderly, rehabilitation)
GP practice nurse	Health visitors	Learning disabilities community nurse
Client carer	Specialist nurses (e.g. family planning, school nurses)	Community care or rehabilitation team (continuing care) Challenging behaviour 'outreach' nurses and others
		Occupational therapy services Physiotherapy services Dieticians Speech therapists Dentists Clinical psychology Chiropodists
		Social workers Social services staff Voluntary organization staff

Figure 9.4 An 'open' network.

coordinated for a client? GPs are not able to do so for a patient who needs the help of many practitioners, even if there is an agreed system.
• Operational management coordination – who ensures that practitioners in an area are following common policies and practice with regard to issues which should be common across the service (e.g. case records, collecting patient and management data, etc.).
• Planning coordination – developing and implementing plans with knowledge of and cooperation with other services. This is more of a problem as planning becomes more local.

This 'model' is really a list of the different services, but it helps us to understand why coordination and communication are often poor. Indeed, some 'teams' are only lists like this on paper in the community trust HQ, and unknown to practitioners. However, it can be a flexible arrangement if a formalized network is formed, can ensure that scarce professional skills are well distributed across an area, and can ensure high profession-specific standards and better recruitment. In such models coordination is mainly through effective case coordination systems. If a decision is made to develop a network into a more closely knit formal team, or to set one up from nothing, then there are five essentials to ensuring and improving cooperation in such teams (Øvretveit 1993b):

Locality manager or team manager

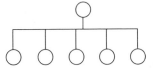

Team members from different professions, fully managed by the team manager

Nurses, CPNs, therapists, and health care assistants
(and possibly social services staff)

Figure 9.5   A locality-managed multidisciplinary team.

- a manager or management group responsible for team performance;
- team accountability reviews, led by the manager or group to deal with team problems, and to ensure that the team fits in with other services and is meeting client needs and purchaser requirements;
- a defined team leader position;
- a team operational policy;
- a team base.

Model 2: locality-managed multidisciplinary teams

At the other end of the extreme to the first model is one multidisciplinary team with a locality manager, who manages all practitioners serving a locality population (e.g. between 25,000 and 65,000 population) (see Figure 9.5). The smaller the locality, the more expensive it is to ensure that the locality has full-time specialists. In practice, some staff (e.g. therapists) are half-time or less, and managed by a locality manager from another locality. In this option, for large trusts with a range of services, separate divisions of mental health, learning difficulty and professional services would only manage hospital and residential services and cross-district 'professional advisors'. Alternatively, there may be generic locality directorates, which manage *all* services in the locality. It is not clear how social services fit in with this mainly 'health' model. Note that this model is for provision only: it does not consider care management, joint commissioning or locality purchasing.

Model 3: locality coordinator model

This model lies between the two extremes of locality management (model 2) and the likely current separate services arrangement (model 1). For a defined 'locality' there is a locality coordinator who coordinates all the community practitioners in the locality. He or she is responsible for developing a 'locality team'. There are different types of locality coordinator roles, with different strengths and responsibilities. In the *first* variation of

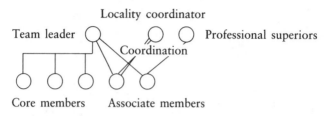

Figure 9.6   The managed-core and coordinated-associate locality team.

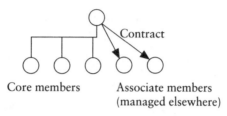

Figure 9.7   The managed-core and contracted-associate team.

this model (Figure 9.6) the coordinator manages core locality staff (e.g. clerks, receptionists, some nurses and health care assistants for the locality), and coordinates other staff associated with the locality who are serving the locality part-time (e.g. therapists, CPNs and social workers). These 'associate staff' are managed by other managers, but there is an agreement as to the coordinating authority and responsibilities of the locality coordinator in respect to them.

In the *second variation* of the model (Figure 9.7) the locality coordinator has a stronger and clearer role with respect to the 'associates'. Associates provide services to the locality under a 'service agreement' between the locality coordinator and the associate's manager (e.g. a therapy head). In time this can become a contract agreement, with locality coordinators paying for associates. This model can develop to one where locality coordinators contract directly with GPs, and themselves assemble whatever combinations of staff they feel they can sell, from within a trust and also by purchasing outside (e.g. private 'alternative therapies' and counsellors).

In the *third variation* of the model the locality coordinator does not manage any staff, but contracts them from other managers. For example, a community services trust delegates a budget to its locality coordinators to purchase services which the trust agreed it would provide for the locality, and locality coordinators could contract directly with GPs and sub-contract the services GPs require.

Note that all three variations of this third model put the emphasis on two factors to achieve local coordination: a formal locality coordinator role with clear authority, and multidisciplinary team working, developed and led by the locality coordinator. All models allow professional management from outside the locality for staff not managed by the coordinator, but temper the strength of such non-locality management with 'service agreements' or 'financial contracts'. In some community units, creating a 'centre coordinator' position assigned to one large health centre is a way to move towards more integrated services.

Model 4: locality purchasing model

The above models are of ways of organizing and managing provider staff (primary community health service practitioners) on a 'locality' basis. The third variation of the last model (the coordinator contracting staff) leads us to the question of locality purchasing and care management. We saw in Chapter 4 that one model of locality purchasing is for a commissioner to have locality purchasing managers for the localities. Their role is to assess health needs for the locality and to propose to the central commissioning organization which services should be purchased for maximum health gain for the locality. They are supported by staff from HQ, and based in the locality, and may have different budgets for direct purchasing for the locality. A variation is integrated health and social services purchasing, possibly with some or all GP fundholder purchasing powers (the commissioning organization can 'sell' a purchasing service to local fundholders, or develop locality purchasing with strong GP links). This model is compatible with joint commissioning.

Summary

None of the models described above in itself provides a method of individual care coordination, or care management, with or without a purchasing element. However, bringing practitioners together in teams makes it easier to develop care coordination methods, and a role of a care coordinator. The latter is a role which could be assumed by any member of a team, as long as a team has clear ways of deciding who takes the role. Formal teams are a precondition for effective individual care coordination, and complement care management.

Existing care coordination arrangements in mental health and learning difficulty teams could be developed into care management, rather than care management being taken out of these teams. A locality team along the lines of the models described would be a good basis for formal care coordination roles and systems which could integrate with GPs and social workers. Further discussion of different teams and care management is provided in Øvretveit (1993b).

Conclusions

One of the great strengths of the NHS which is often not recognized is its GP services. In part this is due to a complex mix of private and public finance and ownership. This mix needs to be retained to successfully develop GP services. Developing primary and community health services are tasks which follow from the aim of cost-effective health gain. Finance invested in primary and community health services can prevent some illnesses, and cure some others at a lower cost than hospital services. With new technology and pharmaceuticals, more hospital services can be provided at a lower cost and higher quality in a primary care setting. With shorter hospital stays, the benefits of hospital care may be wasted if necessary support services are not available in the community. It is for these and other reasons that the UK government has introduced initiatives and requirements which call for improvements and extensions to primary and community health services.

This chapter has considered the actions which purchasers might take to develop services outside hospitals, and the different meanings of the term 'primary care'. It questioned assumptions that most primary care development could be financed from savings from hospital services, that more primary care would reduce demands on hospitals, and that primary care services and facilities had the capacity to take on more and different work without large investments. These assumptions are valid for some services and needs, but not for others. The task for purchasers is to identify which services to develop in collaboration with GPs, community health services and others, and to manage the changes, usually by the politically-difficult method of transferring finance from the hospital sector.

The chapter proposed that cost-effective health gain depends as much on inter-organizational cooperation as on the cost-effectiveness of one service which deals with part of a total patient care episode or part of a health programme. Ensuring provider cooperation is also one of the key services which commissioners provide for patients and for their populations. With a greater variety of, and more independent, providers, and with more pressure for all to pursue their own short-term interests, commissioners have to ensure coordination between providers at all levels. Commissioners are often the only bodies who can take an overview and have the powers to ensure that providers link with each other to give continuity of care for patients. This is part of the value which purchasing adds to the new NHS.

Ensuring provider coordination depends on authorities themselves collaborating, and producing agreed plans which they follow in their contracting, through ensuring good 'vertical linkage' from plans to contracts. It is easier for an integrated DHA–FHSA to finance, coordinate and implement plans for developing coordinated primary and community services. However, to do so it needs good internal coordination between DHA and FHSA functions, especially for relating individual GP practice developments to plans and contracts for community health services ('internal lateral linking').

Two mechanisms for coordinating practitioners and services are multidisciplinary teams and care coordination systems such as individual care management. The chapter highlighted purchasers' role in establishing primary health care teams. In the past many such teams existed in name only, but recent changes, and the need to develop services and prevention programmes outside hospitals, mean that commissioners have to ensure that teams are established and working. Commissioners have to be involved in the details of team organization for teams which involve a number of providers.

Commissioners do not need to be so involved in the details of team organization when all members of the team are employed by one organization, such as mental health or learning disability teams in a community trust. The chapter gave a short introduction to the services and issues in community health services, and described some examples of practitioner teams. It described how these services might be organized and contracted on a team basis for an area rather than on a discipline basis for a district. The four models of community teams need to be considered alongside the three types of primary health care team to examine the options for co-ordinated services in a locality. Other chapters consider how these service provision models can relate to, or mirror, locality purchasing, and the potential FHSA provider role in managing community health services.

Key points

- There are many opinions about the role and scope of primary care in the future, but little evidence about exactly which treatments and services can be better provided in a primary care setting, and about the necessary conditions for doing so.
- Purchasers need to seek out the evidence of successful transfers of hospital services, or of alternatives to hospital services, support and evaluate pilot schemes, and question some of the unexamined assumptions about the pattern of future health care services and the realism of their own expectations of GPs.
- Most agree that existing primary care services need improvement, as do the rules governing their administration. To improve primary health care, priorities for commissioners are to develop premises, examine and improve quality, and help form true primary health care teams to be able to undertake the already increasing workload.
- Some additional finance for developing primary care could come from savings on hospital services and prescribing made with GP cooperation. Integrated DHA–FHSA commissioning organizations may find these savings easier to make and redirect than single authorities collaborating, or even GP fundholders.
- Health gain often depends as much on how well service providers co-ordinate their work as on what each does separately. The best hospital care is wasted if the necessary before and after care is not provided.
- It is through ensuring collaboration between purchasers and coordination between provider services that commissioners pursue the aim of

health gain, and their role as service organizations. An important service which commissioners provide is ensuring that the many different providers outside hospitals link with each other to coordinate their work.

- A commissioning organization has to decide the balance between over- and under-involvement in the details of primary health care teams and specialist community teams.
- Where a team is to be formed from practitioners from two or more organizations, a commissioning organization has to be more involved in the details of team organization than if it contracts one organization to provide a team service (e.g. a community mental health team).

10 Purchasing primary health care and the role of the FHSA

FHSAs are no more simply 'commissioning' bodies than they are simply 'providers', and they perhaps cannot be steam-pressed into existing organizational moulds without compromising aspects of their work and limiting the opportunities available to them.

(Foster 1991)

Introduction

Purchasing primary health care services involves different work and issues to purchasing hospital services. In many countries, secondary and primary care purchasing or administration is undertaken by different organizations, or by different divisions in the same organization. There are different payment systems, regulations and types of relationships with providers in the different sectors. In the future, if purchasers are to retain a distinction between primary and secondary care they will need to do so more on the basis of a health gain perspective than on the basis of a history of rules and regulations for primary care practitioners. Purchasers need to lead a redefinition of the boundaries between primary and secondary care, and reconsider which health needs can be met by primary care and which require specialist services, based either in primary care or in the future equivalent of a hospital.

If the purpose of health gain is better pursued by dealing with primary care and hospital care together, what are the best means for this purpose? What is the best way of coordinating primary and secondary health purchasing work? These are the underlying questions of this and the next two chapters. One aim of coordinating purchasing work is to make it easier for primary care providers, hospitals and other services to coordinate their services. Unless purchasers break down and challenge barriers between primary and hospital care, it will be more difficult for providers to do so. But does this mean forming one organization for purchasing primary and secondary care? In the next chapter we concentrate on the most common coordination method in the UK – through a single commissioning organization or 'agency', with or without a DHA and FHSA merger into one authority.

In this chapter we consider options where a primary care authority (FHSA) and its management remains separate from a DHA. In the UK, purchaser coordination is hampered by many staff not understanding the work and role of primary health care commissioning. The purpose of this chapter is to give non-FHSA staff an introduction to primary care commissioning and to consider the options for the future of FHSAs. It describes the work of FHSAs and their changing relationships to GPs.

The chapter points out the dangers of over-simplistic views of FHSA work, especially artificially dividing functions into 'providing' and 'purchasing' functions. It addresses the following questions raised by purchasing managers:

- *What are the future roles and responsibilities of the FHSA?*
- *What are the future roles and responsibilities of 'primary care purchasing' within an integrated agency?*
- *How will integrated agencies relate to GPs when they combine FHSA and DHA functions: does the agency have one relationship with each practice, or many?*
- *How can we undertake both DHA and FHSA work in the most cost-effective way?*
- *How can we realize the benefits of bringing secondary and primary care budgets under the same management?*

Background

Since the NHS was created, many have viewed the financing and administration of secondary and primary care by separate authorities as one of its weaknesses (e.g. Merrison Report 1979; Harrison *et al.* 1989; Audit Commission 1993a,b; IHSM 1993). In the early 1990s, many saw the formation of separate commissioning authorities for these services as the 'lost opportunity' or 'unfinished business' of the 1990 NHS reforms. They held that 'stronger commissioning' was to be achieved by combining secondary and primary care commissioning for one district, rather than by combining districts to increase their secondary care purchasing power. This former view grew, especially with the greater emphasis on developing services outside hospitals and with more GP fundholders. Integrating the management and organization of a family health services authority (FHSA) and one or more district health authorities (DHAs) in a commissioning agency lays the conditions for developing primary and community care and for closing the gaps between services. In the mid-1990s, the reforms to the top tiers of the NHS made it possible to go beyond management integration and to create a single primary and secondary health care authority (DoH 1993b).

Yet there is another view: that one of the successes of the NHS – the comprehensive and relatively high-quality general medical practitioner service – is owing to it being administered and financed by a separate authority. This 'isolation' prevented finance being drawn out of primary care into hospital services, allowed developments to take place unaffected by other NHS crises and gave the independence, security and support which GPs and others needed to build a system of primary care. It retained GPs as independent contractors and supported GP services as small private businesses, mixed the best of private and public, and protected the GP–patient relationship. This view holds that the 1990 reforms retained and added to these advantages by giving GPs purchasing budgets, administered by FHSAs to ensure their independence. Thus, for some, there are advantages to keeping separate authorities and an argument for separate administrative systems. Is a separate primary care authority and administration a better route for developing non-hospital and preventative services?

In North West Thames and Wessex Regions, a decision about management and administration was made in the early 1990s, and single agencies now exist: the task there is to realize the advantages of a single commissioning agency and avoid the disadvantages. In these regions and elsewhere, a key issue for purchasers in the mid-1990s is recognizing the arguments for and against both integrated agencies and single authorities, and understanding the fears of many GPs and others. One of the difficulties has proved to be a lack of understanding of the role, work and relationships of FHSAs, and not recognizing differences in culture and in ways of working between DHAs and FHSAs. This has also made it more difficult for other authorities in other areas to consider how best to improve collaboration.

In this chapter we consider three types of work done by FHSAs, in order to improve understanding of the work and how it might be combined or coordinated with DHA work. The chapter shows that FHSA relationships with GPs are different to DHA relations with their larger providers, and that there are lessons for the latter from the style and approach of the former. Commissioners need to understand FHSAs' ways of working and the independence of GPs in order to manage transfers to, and developments in, primary care in appropriate ways. The chapter finishes by describing four different future options for FHSAs, and gives examples of FHSAs which are taking a significant 'provision' role.

The FHSA and contracts with GPs

Most FHSA work arises from responsibilities for and relations with GPs, which, in some respects, are similar to their relations with other 'independent primary care contractors' – dentists, pharmacists and opticians. Chapter 9 described the services which GPs provide and changes in general practice. The most important recent events for FHSAs and GPs were the 1989–90 reforms to general practice 'management', the 1990 'contract' (DHSS 1987) and GP fundholding (DoH 1989a,b,c, 1990a).

Background

GPs have always been self-employed and classified as independent businesses. As we saw in Chapter 9, group practices are a collection of independent GP contractors who form a business partnership, which may enter into business agreements with a FHSA, or a bank or any other organization for various purposes. GPs were brought into the NHS in 1948 as independent contractors with nationally set payment rates, administered by the then equivalent of the FHSA, together with general dental practitioners, pharmacists and opticians. The contracting arrangements for GPs are little different now, although the basis for payment and the additional payments for practice improvements and staffing have changed.

FHSAs and GP contracts

In 1990, FHSAs with general managers were created out of family practitioner committees (FPCs) – the shift in terminology from 'committee' to 'authority' corresponded to a shift towards a stronger role. However, 'management' and 'contract' still have a particular meaning for FHSAs, which is different to their meaning for DHAs. To understand FHSA activities, the way FHSA staff work and how integration might take place, we have to understand the nature of the GP contract and FHSA responsibilities, authority and means of influence in relation to GPs.

In formal terms, the responsibilities of FHSAs in relation to GPs are to register practitioners and patients, verify payments, arrange payment and investigate complaints. Their formal authority in relation to GPs covers few areas: their relation with GPs stems from the nature of their 'contract' with them. FHSAs contract each GP as an individual to provide services according to a detailed nationally prescribed standard contract (DoH and WO 1993). 'Contracting' GPs is not the same as contracting a hospital or contracting staff through an employment contract: there is a nationally prescribed contract form and payment schedule, and software which FHSA payment administration uses to pay the contracted individual each month, adjusted quarterly, into a practice business account, from which the GP draws. There is little scope for altering the terms of the standard contract, and the decision about whether or not to contract a GP is governed by a variety of rules and guidelines. The contract is to pay a GP for offering a set of services:

- a basic payment to practice;
- a weighted-capitation payment (based on nationally calculated 'Jarman deprivation' indices, and number of patients aged 0–5, 65–74, and over 74);
- fees for different services.

The 1990 contract introduced financial incentives for GPs to reach targets for immunizing children on their list (£1,800 if 90 per cent of under-twos are vaccinated) and cervical cytology (£2,280 if 80 per cent of eligible women are tested) – GPs were paid previously by item. It also introduced payments for health promotion and other clinics (e.g. child health surveillance and well-baby clinics). Health checks for people over 74 (the sinisterly termed 'over-74s surveillance') are not special payments but are part of the work expected of GPs to care for people over 74 registered with them.

One of the disadvantages of the 1990 national contract is that it allows little flexibility to FHSAs shape local contracts with GPs or group practices to reflect needs in a particular area. As one FHSA general manager noted, 'We can make some progress in service development at FHSA level but the centre must relinquish its hold on what primary care services are to be purchased locally if we are to have a needs-led service' (R. Shakespear, GM, Manchester FHSA, NHS ME 'Purchasing for Health' conference 1991).

Fundholding was introduced in 1991, as well as indicative drug prescribing budgets for non-fundholders. There are proposals to give GPs monthly reports of prescribing costs (prescribing analysis cost data, PACT). Fundholders have an incentive to cut their prescribing costs because they can redirect savings. Some FHSAs have asked GPs to include prescribing targets in their practice business plans. This led to GP concerns that FHSAs could try to bring pressure to bear to reduce prescribing costs by using their other powers to withhold reimbursements for practice staff.

Effect of the 1990 contract on community nursing

The 1990 GP contract led to a clearer recognition of the interdependence between GP practices and community nurses. Because community nurses undertake some of the work for which GPs are reimbursed, GPs in many areas have taken more interest in improving working relations with them. In fact the elusive 'primary health care team' has been brought far closer by cooperation over specific items, such as child health surveillance and over-74 checks, than as a result of years of more abstract arguments for 'closer teamwork'. There are now the conditions for moving to FHSA contracts with primary care teams, of which GPs are part. The previous chapter gave more details about these issues.

In some areas, GPs were being paid for work which DHA-contracted community nurses were doing (e.g. child health surveillance). Community nurses were also undertaking immunizations, which allowed GPs to reach their targets, but GPs could not receive payment because GPs could not claim for what nurses had done. (Fundholders do not get payments for immunizations and clinics done by their contracted community nurses.) Resolving these and other issues often led to better understanding and recognition of interdependence, which often eased the way for GP fundholder contracting of community staff.

How FHSAs relate to GPs

The context surrounding the FHSA–GP relationship helps us to understand how FHSAs work with GPs: by personal contact, influence and persuasion. They can make 'discretionary payments' to improve practices (discussed below) but the scope and amount is limited, although transfers of DHA finance to FHSAs for these purposes could change things. FHSA staff cultivate their relationships with each practice in a variety of ways. An example is a dialogue about why a practice cannot meet screening targets: it may be because of low uptake by women in different ethnic groups. The FHSA may propose to pay for a suitable practice nurse for six months, and to continue funding if the targets are met. At its best it is a productive working partnership. At its worst, the FHSA can do little to improve poor GP practice without formal complaints from the public, and then its actions are limited. The trend is towards more formal contracts between FHSAs and both group practices and primary care teams.

We now turn to a description of the main work of FHSAs, to give agency staff unfamiliar with FHSAs a better understanding of what they do, and to help us to consider how best to integrate the work of FHSAs and DHAs.

The work of FHSAs: three functions

The work of FHSAs in relation to GPs divides into three areas: routine administration, practice development and fundholder services. A large volume of FHSA work can be classified as 'prescribed commissioning work' in the model of levels of commissioning work outlined in Chapter 3.

Administration: registration and payments

This includes:

- assessing GP applications to register as a contractor;
- maintaining a register of patients with each GP;
- receiving forms from GPs for completed items of service, verification and arranging payment;
- reimbursing practices for business rates and rents;
- receiving and investigating complaints.

FHSAs do not proactively monitor and audit standards of clinical practice, but they do monitor premises and performance standards (Chapter 9

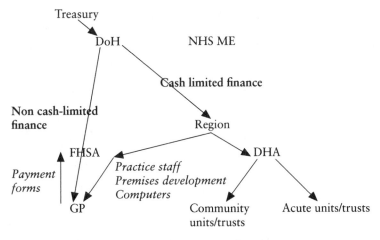

Figure 10.1   Sources and limits to FHSA and GP finance.

considered quality assurance of GP clinical services). Most payments for services covered by the national contract are not cash-limited, and are made automatically by the FHSA to GPs, after they have submitted FHSA-verified forms. At present prescription expenditure also is not cash-limited for non-fundholders, although there is an indicative prescribing budget for each GP.

There is a cash-limited budget for practice development payments (discussed below), which was set for each FHSA by regions from the total regional allocation (see the diagram of finance flows, Figure 10.1). In 1994 this budget was based on 1990 FHSA expenditure on practice staff and premises developments, and, on average, is about 5 per cent of FHSA expenditure. (In 1992, Hillingdon FHSA (240,000 population) made service payments to GPs of £25 million and payments of £1.1 million for practice development.) The sources and limits to the finance to FHSAs and GPs are represented in Figure 10.1.

Practice support and development

FHSAs have for some time employed staff to encourage GPs to recruit practice nurses and to train them, as well as to 'develop the primary health care team'. These training and development services to practice staff are sometimes referred to as FHSA 'provider' functions, although they are not direct services to the public, as are some health education and promotion services managed and provided by some FHSAs.

In recent years, FHSAs have improved their access to and use of information about the populations served by GPs, and about GP performance and standards of practice. They have formed their own public health perspectives, drawing on external GP advisors. FHSAs now have a much better idea of which are the 'poor' practices, in terms of unmet needs of the populations of an area, and of GP performance and standards. This information is used in two main ways: to take the initiative with 'poor practices' and propose and support improvements; and as a basis against which to judge GP business plans and their bids to the FHSA for discretionary practice development finance.

Although FHSAs do influence GPs in many ways, practice staff and development payments are one of the few tangible and direct powers which FHSAs have. One of the meanings of 'primary care purchasing' is to target poor practices and use this discretionary but cash-limited general medical services finance to pay for a variety of services and improvements. The FHSA makes discretionary payments for:

- practice staff (often 70 per cent salary reimbursement (after 1990 it could be 100 per cent), typically for receptionists and practice nurses);
- premises improvements (e.g. payment of interest on borrowed capital through the 'cost-rent scheme', and one-off grants);
- computer equipment.

Most FHSAs have agreed a policy with their local medical committee (LMC) about the criteria for deciding such payments.

Fundholder services

The third area of FHSA–GP work is encouragement and support for potential and actual fundholders. Many FHSAs worked hard to publicize the scheme and support practices in their applications and preparations and in operating the fund. The work of calculating the initial fund budget is considerable, as is the work of setting up payments systems for the FHSA to pay hospital invoices after the fundholder has checked the invoice and passed it to the FHSA for payment (the GPs do not pay directly). The FHSA monitors the fund and does a quarterly 'audit' visit. The Audit Commission does a yearly audit of the fund and a full audit of accounts every three years. Fundholder work continues, although the amount of and enthusiasm for non-statutory work varies between FHSAs.

Some GPs take the view that merging FHSAs with DHAs places their main ally (the FHSA) in the enemy camp: that integrated agencies or authorities will devote little time to encouraging or supporting fundholding as it undermines their role as purchasers. There is no doubt that more fundholders significantly affect both the FHSA and the DHA role, and have made it difficult for some DHAs to deal with unpredicted calls on their finance. For example, with more elective surgery finance in the hands of fundholders, the DHA can no longer reduce elective surgery as one method for controlling expenditure if there is a rise in emergency work or other calls on expenditure.

Developments in fundholding include business managers as full practice partners, and 'multi-funds' involving up to 30 GP practices under a single management team. The latter can in fact make HA collaboration easier by reducing the number of practices to deal with, for example to agree purchasing specifications and strategic targets. An example is 22 practices in Kingston and Richmond (Surrey) which formed a 'multi-fund' in 1994, with an executive board controlling around £40 million (14 per cent of the HA's budget).

Summary: FHSAs and GPs

FHSAs have to undertake a considerable amount of routine work, in addition to their work in relation to GPs. Much of their GP work is also routine essential administration of registration and payments – over 50 per cent of FHSA staff work on these tasks full-time. In this respect an FHSA must provide a quality service to GPs: a precondition for GP cooperation is a fast and efficient payment and administrative service, and integrated agencies neglect this at their peril. One option is for two or more FHSAs or integrated authorities to form a combined payment centre, or even a single centre, like the national Dental Practice Board, which could be organized to give a faster and more efficient service.

In addition to fulfilling contracts with GPs through making the required payments to them, FHSAs make discretionary payments for improvements to targeted 'poor' areas. It is this area of work, based on needs assessment and better information about practice performance, which will grow. This is higher-level FHSA work, which can be categorized as 'situational' or 'systematic' commissioning work, on the model of levels of purchasing in Chapter 3. How much it grows depends on how much cash-limited finance a region redirects from each DHA to the FHSA, and how much a DHA transfers for primary care developments. The amount and type of work for fundholder development and support is an area for debate, and varies between different FHSAs.

Primary care commissioning

'Implementing and Promoting Better Health' described the role of FHSAs as, 'identifying needs, evaluating and monitoring services, planning improvements and allocating resources according to need,' so I therefore find myself somewhat out of sympathy with those who say FHSAs are not truly purchasing Authorities – I have no doubt that they are.
(An FHSA General Manager at the 1991 NHS ME Conference 'Purchasing for Health')

The detailed steps needed to separate the providing, purchasing and commissioning functions of FHSAs may make the purchaser/provider split in HAs look like child's play.
(Joan Higgins, Professor of Health Policy and Chair of Manchester FHSA)

If FHSA contracting is mostly administering GP contracts, then what does 'primary care purchasing and commissioning' mean? Should the commissioning role of FHSAs be developed and should FHSAs be retained? Should primary care commissioning be combined with secondary care commissioning in an integrated authority, or in an integrated agency?

In the next two chapters we concentrate on integrated commissioning agencies, with and without authority merger. In this section we consider the meaning and purpose of primary care commissioning, and the future options for FHSAs which continue as independent authorities with their own executive organization. Many believe that a single purchasing authority for family health services, hospital and community health services is the best way forward for NHS commissioning. However, there are other options which retain a FHSA, and these are not just paper options: some are being pursued in practice. There are many arguments for a separate FHSA and for developing its 'provider' role. The 'merger option' – of management or of authorities – is by no means a foregone conclusion. Neither is full FHSA–DHA management integration in a joint agency: some agencies do not have a joint chief executive (e.g. Harrow and Brent in 1994), and are keeping most FHSA functions separate. Each area will need to examine whether effective collaboration can be achieved without the expense and upheaval of merger, but to do so, all need to understand the arguments for and against separate primary care commissioning, separate FHSAs and separate FHSA management. We consider the issues and options shortly, after addressing the 'problem of terminology'.

Defining 'primary care commissioning'

A problem in considering the options for FHSAs and in learning from other authorities is different understandings of the meaning of 'primary care commissioning' – both what it describes at present and what it could mean. Discussions about the role of FHSAs, forms of collaboration, the structure of integrated agencies and negotiations with providers are also hampered by different usage of the terms 'primary', 'secondary' and 'community services', which can refer to siting, who pays or who employs (see Appendix 1). This book uses the terms as in Box 10.1.

There are different definitions of the 'provider' and 'purchaser' functions of the FHSA. One definition is that the provider functions are those services managed by the FHSA and provided to the public, such as GP registration and health promotion services, and services to GPs such as practice support. Another definition of provider functions encompasses these and the financial payments function, and defines the purchasing functions as planning and development activities (Lord 1993). How one defines these

Box 10.1

Primary care contracting
Contracting of GPs and other independent contractors, according to nationally set terms and conditions, and arranging payments to them after they have provided services, as set out in national agreements. Also includes FHSA registration of practitioners and patients. Most FHSA work is 'primary care contracting' work.

Primary care purchasing
All the activities needed to decide and pay FHSA *discretionary finance for practice development* (the general medical services' cash-limited allocation for reimbursing practice staff salaries, training, premises improvements and computers). Includes needs assessment for deciding development, practice assessment, receiving and prioritizing bids from GPs, consulting LMC and deciding allocations and monitoring expenditure.

Primary care commissioning
Includes primary care purchasing work for practice development, but also work to secure finance and allocate it through contracts and other means to develop and purchase a wide range of services in a primary care setting. For example, negotiating, receiving and using revenue and capital finance from a DHA to develop primary care services to reduce hospital use. Needs assessment and planning for 'commissioning' is broader than for 'purchasing' because more services and needs are considered.

Primary care provision
Services provided by GPs and their practice staff, health promotion and education outside hospitals, but *not* practice training and development support by FHSA-employed staff.

Primary health care services
Services provided at GP practices and health centres by GPs, practice staff and community nurses. Not community psychiatric nurse (CPN) services or some community therapy services ('specialist community services'), or outpatient consultant sessions (secondary care provided in a primary care setting).

Community health services
Health services other than primary care services, provided outside larger hospitals, paid for from DHA cash-limited finance, and contracted by DHAs or joint agencies or GP fundholders. Includes CPN services. Typically non-hospital health services provided by a community health trust.

Secondary care services
Nearly all hospital-based services, and some specialist services provided in the community (e.g. some community therapy and CPN services), paid for by DHA or GP fundholder finance.

functions depends in part on how one views the purchaser–provider split in primary care commissioning, a subject which we consider below.

Issues in examining the future of primary care commissioning and FHSAs

The purpose of primary care commissioning

The book has argued that NHS commissioning has tended to be driven by provider issues and immediate practicalities, and should be shaped more by a view of the purpose of commissioning. It proposed one view of commissioning as health gain within resources through contracting services and other actions. The book also recognized that, in organizing commissioning, there must be a tension between the arrangements which arise out of the past and the current situation, and the arrangements which follow from a more idealized view of commissioning. Here we are concerned with the advantages or otherwise of dividing commissioning into primary and secondary care commissioning. In theory there is an argument that such a division in commissioning is unnecessary and harmful to the purpose of health gain. In practice there are many arguments for continuing the current division and for building bridges. If we accept the division for practical reasons, then three of the many questions which arise are:

- What is the purpose of primary care commissioning?
- What is the scope of primary care commissioning and where do the boundaries between it and secondary care commissioning lie?
- Do and should FHSAs have a provision role as well as a commissioning role?

One way to define the purpose of primary care commissioning is to adapt the general definition of NHS commissioning put forward in Chapter 3: 'the purpose of primary care commissioning is to make the best use of available finance to improve health and prevent illness, by influencing other organizations to contribute to these ends and by contracting primary health services'. As with other definitions, this relies on a definition of primary care services to draw the boundaries between primary and secondary care commissioning. If we use definitions which are closer to the day-to-day work of commissioning we see that there are wide areas of overlap between the two, as in the definition of tasks referred to in the quote at the start of this section: 'identifying needs, evaluating and monitoring services, planning improvements and allocating resources according to need'. Many views of the purpose and work of primary care commissioning reflect models of secondary care commissioning.

The purchaser–provider split in primary care

Another approach is to build a view of primary care commissioning from an understanding of current FHSA work and relations. This approach involves examining the meaning of a purchaser–provider split in primary care. A purchaser–provider split in secondary care is defined by a change from management to contractual relations, competition between providers for income through contracts, and a change from a managing role to a purchasing role for the new purchasing body (Chapter 2). This chapter has shown that some FHSAs manage health promotion services and staff providing a development service to GPs. In addition, that there has always been a purchaser–provider split between independent primary care contractors and primary care authorities.

The purchaser–provider split in primary care differs from that introduced into secondary care in four important respects. First, FHSAs 'contract' individual practitioners through a prescribed national contract, which allows no scope for negotiation. Second, in general providers do not compete for contracts from FHSAs, and FHSAs have little choice of provider. However, there is scope for FHSAs to reach local agreements or contracts with GP practices to provide specific services. Third, the discretionary resources which FHSAs can allocate are limited, and many are already committed, for example by a past agreement to fund a practice nurse. Fourth, FHSAs are responsible for helping to establish, and then overseeing, GP purchasing funds for secondary care.

The purchaser–provider split in primary care is of a particular type, and the purchasing role should not be developed at a pace or to a degree which damages the strengths of the current arrangements. Markets for primary care services differ in important respects to those for secondary care services (Chapter 2). Apart from protecting primary care finance, a strength of the current arrangements is that they have mixed many of the benefits of private ownership and independence with public financing and regulation. The national contract and other regulations have provided stability and security for GP services.

There is now the opportunity to allow FHSAs more flexibility in the GP contract, and to increase the powers of FHSAs to make discretionary payments to practices to allow FHSAs to relate resource allocations more closely to needs assessments. The future of primary care commissioning lies in developing current arrangements and relations with individuals or collegial groups, rather than imposing a conception of a purchaser–provider split suited to purchasing from large institutions and another type of market. Are the concepts of purchasing and provision in their usual senses helpful for thinking of the future of FHSAs? Are DHAs anyway moving closer to the 'FHSA type' of relations with providers – towards persuasion and partnership rather than adversarial contractual relations?

These observations about the meaning and purpose of primary care commissioning help in deciding how to organize the work, and whether or not a separate FHSA should be retained. We return to these issues in the next two chapters. In the remainder of this chapter we consider options for FHSAs, some of which involve a significant role in managing services, and note criteria which can be used in assessing the options for FHSAs in a particular area.

The future role of FHSAs: some options

The four 'foster' options

An early and influential paper outlined four options for FHSAs (Foster 1991).

Model A: dynamic status quo
This model corresponded to the situation in Wales and in most parts of England between 1990 and 1993, with FHSAs separately accountable to RHAs, and separate management and organization. Some advantages cited in the Foster report are: a clear and distinct 'voice' for family health service planning and developments; the combined efforts of two organizations in key areas can result in a higher level of investment; a constructive and competitive tension; and not disrupting the new relations of trust which are being built with GPs. The only disadvantage cited is a lack of clear separation between current commissioning and 'provision management' functions, something which the three other models are said to address.

Model B: integrated purchaser, and separate provider FHS unit or trust
This model is of an integrated FHSA–DHA commissioning authority or agency, contracting or managing a family health services unit or trust, undertaking current FHSA 'provision management'. This unit or trust would 'include' (but really contract) all GPs, dentists, opticians and pharmacists, and all community nurses and other community services, or it could compete with community units or trusts to provide community health services. The report cites the strengths as being integrated purchasing and separation of FHS provision management.

However, in the light of the discussion above, there are questions about the viability and meaning of 'provision management' by an FHS unit or trust, and questions about the need to force a purchasing–provision separation in FHSA functions. It also introduces an unnecessary layer of bureaucracy (Wilson 1990), could lead to primary care financing being redirected into more visible secondary care if finance is cut, rather than the reverse, and may result in community nurses becoming directly employed by GPs. The latter could result in small and specialized community services with no appropriate management, which then become managed by the FHSA.

Model C: unified FHSA–DHA commissioning
This is the closest to the integrated agency model, although it is not clear whether Foster's model involves authority merger. The advantages cited are: single needs assessment and information management; single 'commissioning/contracting policy with outcome targets applicable to all health care'; provider accountability to one body; economies of scale; and simpler relationships with local authorities and other bodies. Disadvantages are: less creative tension between the FHSA and DHA; GP opposition; more

organizational change; and less clear separation between FHSA 'commissioning and provision management functions'. A variation with a GP executive committee is discussed in Starey *et al.* (1993).

Model D: the primary health care authority (PHCA)
In this model the PHCA assumes responsibility and finance for purchasing (or managing) community health services, as well as current FHSA responsibilities. It differs from model B in retaining a separate DHA for purchasing secondary hospital care, and in having a less clear purchaser–provider separation than the FHS unit or trust. In areas with widespread GP fundholding, the DHA role would decline and could be taken over by the PHCA, as could social care purchasing.

City and Hackney FHSA proposed purchasing and managing community health services in 1992 (this affected the North East Thames Region's review of FHSAs). The outcome was a decision to form, in April 1994, a directly managed FHSA unit (a 'primary care development agency') for primary and community services. This unit took over community services provided by acute trusts. The FHSA continued to hold GPs', dentists' and pharmacists' contracts, but operated with a reduced role (Alan Bennett, FHSA manager; see also *Health Service Journal* 15 April 1993: 4). Wolverhampton has a similar arrangement with a primary health care unit, but also a combined DHA–FHSA purchasing health executive (Lord 1993).

Assessing the local options for an FHSA

The future options for an FHSA depend on the current purpose and work of an FHSA, as well as views about how best to develop primary care commissioning and services, and to link them to other services. FHSAs, DHAs and others in each area will need to define the options for further exploration. These include: a separate FHSA; an integrated DHA–FHSA agency retaining separate authorities; or a merged FHSA–DHA(s). These options can be judged against the following criteria:

1 Potential for formulating and implementing a health strategy for health gain.
2 Protection of primary care finance, and ease of adding to this finance.
3 Protection of purchasing finance for GP fundholders.
4 Potential for 'shared purchasing' with GPs.
5 Running costs of the option, and the cost of change.
6 Effectiveness of arrangements for undertaking the three sets of current tasks identified in the chapter:
   • patient and contractor registration, and payments services;
   • developing primary care services, and their links to hospital and community services;
   • FHSA encouragement of, support to and overseeing of GP fundholders.

7 Possible FHSA purchasing of primary care related community care.
8 Possible FHSA 'service provision', including managing a health promotion unit or a community health service provider unit as a transitional management arrangement to prepare for trust application.

Where a decision has been made, the above criteria can be used to decide future collaboration and organization arrangements.

Conclusions

The NHS has a unique opportunity to reshape primary and secondary care boundaries and relations. Purchasers have a key role in leading these changes to reflect the local needs of their population. To date, primary care commissioning in the NHS has grown out of the work of FHSAs and conceptions of the purchaser–provider split in secondary care commissioning. In the future, primary care commissioning also needs to be shaped by a view of the purpose of commissioning and by an understanding of the nature of primary care services. Without this, discussions about future arrangements in a particular area may become dominated by short-term and political considerations, and the opportunity will be missed.

DHA staff and non-executives do not always understand how FHSAs operate, as is apparent in some conceptions of FHSA 'purchasing' and 'providing' functions. Understanding FHSA work and culture is important to deciding how DHAs and FHSAs can best collaborate, or how FHSA tasks are best organized within integrated agencies, or authorities, and to making the most of mergers. One of the aims of this chapter was to convey to non-FHSA staff an idea of the work of FHSAs and their relations with independent practitioner contractors, so as to contribute to identifying areas for closer cooperation or integration.

The chapter defined primary care commissioning as most current FHSA activities, not just GP contracts, payments and discretionary practice assistance. It noted how the term 'primary care purchasing' was sometimes used to describe the circumscribed but discretionary work of agreeing practice assistance payments for GP group practices. 'Primary care contracting' can mean the latter, as well as GP contracts. The chapter argued that the term 'primary care purchasing' is unhelpful for describing current contracting and payment of GPs, because it suggests that FHSAs have more choice and flexibility than they do over which GPs to contract and what to contract them for. Calling payments to GPs a 'provider' function can also be misleading for those who do not understand FHSAs' relations with GPs, but it does emphasize that most FHSAs recognize that they are first and foremost a service organization.

The chapter described the three main types of FHSAs' work: registration and payments, primary care development, and fundholding support. In undertaking this work, FHSAs have different relationships with GPs: in the first their relationship with individual GPs is governed by a detailed 'national contract'; in the second they may form agreements with group practices; in the third they undertake a monitoring role, although practice support for purchasing may overlap with support for developing provision. FHSAs have little discretion and powers to make changes to contracts which follow from their work of needs assessment. Yet viewing FHSAs as mechanical payment and administration bodies does not do justice to their present role or to their potential. The priority is to develop a needs-led commissioning role with powers to make changes. But this has to be done in a way which builds on the strengths of the past system, not in a way which introduces adversarial contracting and competition or more bureaucracy for GPs.

There are other options for FHSAs, apart from authority merger or delegating management to an integrated agency. Transitional management of community services is one alternative, with a stronger provider role for FHSAs. In assessing options for a particular FHSA, important criteria are which option would strengthen the primary care commissioning role, allow development of primary care services in a way which is related to needs and improve their links with hospital and community services?

Key points

- The strength of the UK primary health care service is in part due to its separate financing and administration. Future health purchasing needs to take account of and build upon these arrangements, as well as on existing relationships with GPs.
- The three types of FHSA work need to be organized in different ways: registration and payments; primary care development and discretionary financing; and setting up and monitoring GP fundholders.
- Conventional concepts of purchasing and provision are unhelpful for thinking about the future role of FHSAs and current FHSA functions. The terms 'primary care purchasing' and 'primary care provision' can be misleading and need to be defined if they are to be used in discussions.
- FHSAs have few formal powers in relation to GPs and limited discretion to shape agreements with group practices to reflect their assessment of needs. The 'market' for primary care services and 'contracting' regulations are different to those for secondary care services.
- To develop primary care services and relate to GP fundholders, commissioners need to build on FHSAs' relations with GPs, and FHSAs' experience in influencing and working with GPs. FHSAs operate through persuasion and partnerships, and have a different culture and concept of management to DHAs.
- Primary care commissioning and primary care services would be strengthened by increased resources, by allowing more flexibility in individual GP contracts and group practice agreements, by inviting tenders for some services, by performance reviews and by improving information about needs and services.

- DHAs and FHSAs will need to examine whether effective collaboration can be achieved without the expense and upheaval of merger. To do so, all need to understand the arguments for and against separate primary care commissioning, separate FHSAs and separate FHSA management.
- Models where FHSAs take over the management of community health services are one way to assist primary and community provider integration, especially for areas with many single-handed practices.
- There is immediate scope for coordinating DHA community service purchasing with FHSA practice development, not least to develop primary care teams for their key role.

11 Integrating primary and secondary health purchasing

Introduction

It is common to have different systems and organizations for purchasing or paying for hospital services and for primary health care. In part, this is due to historical and political reasons and to physician payment systems which are still important. In many countries, health purchasers are co-ordinating or integrating purchasing for primary and secondary care and overcoming traditional and often arbitrary boundaries between these sectors. One reason is to lead developments in primary care and respond to the changing role of hospitals. Combining secondary and primary care finance can make it easier for purchasers to develop preventative services and to encourage some hospital services in primary care settings. In the UK, coordinated purchasing is one means for pursuing the purpose of NHS commissioning.

Yet some primary care practitioners and managers are concerned that merging finance could mean that primary care budgets are 'raided' to save the hospital sector. This has not happened in Scotland and Northern Ireland, where integrated health boards manage primary and secondary care finance. Neither has it happened in England and Wales, where FHSAs and DHAs have cooperated more closely since the 1990 reforms, and where more are forming integrated commissioning agencies. It is national regulations rather than authority merger which protects primary care finance, as we saw in Chapter 10. However, it is also true that up to 1994 there was little evidence of finance from secondary care being used to fund primary care developments, outside the UK GP fundholder scheme. Although all are agreed that primary and secondary care commissioning need to be coordinated, there are different views in the UK as to whether integrated commissioning agencies are the best means, and whether primary and secondary care authorities should be merged.

In Chapter 10 we considered options for primary care commissioning where FHSAs develop their role separate to DHAs. In this chapter we consider different ways of coordinating primary and secondary care commissioning without merging, but mostly we examine the arguments for merging and the details of how to carry out a merger. The purpose of the chapter is to help UK commissioning managers and authority non-executives to review their progress in making closer links or in merging DHA and FHSA work, staffing and systems. It also reports research into the merger process with seven UK integrated commissioning agencies during 1992–4, which will be of interest to health purchasers outside the UK. The chapter does not consider ways of linking DHA and FHSA commissioning with GP fundholder commissioning of secondary care, which was discussed in Chapter 4.

The chapter starts by outlining the advantages of integrated agencies. It derives from these a set of criteria against which commissioners can judge whether to combine previously separate functions, as well as a set of intermediate objectives for managing a programme of integration. The chapter then describes the different ways in which DHAs and FHSAs have formed integrated agencies. It finishes with a summary of approaches to integration and a list of practical considerations. Appendix 5 gives a checklist for judging progress in integration. The questions raised by commissioning managers and addressed by this chapter include the following.

- *How do we and others judge whether an integrated purchasing agency is better than any other arrangement – what success criteria should we use to decide when or what to change?*
- *Which primary and secondary purchasing functions should be merged, how and at what pace, and which should remain organizationally and physically separate?*
- *How should 'joining' be managed and reviewed, both across director-ates and within them?*
- *How do we create a single agency identity, and a culture which is capable of dealing with continuous change?*
- *How do we form and pursue common agency policies and ensure that we all convey a consistent message to different external bodies, especially GPs, local authorities and providers?*

Below we consider the background to the increasing collaboration between DHA and FHSA commissioners and to the decision to form integrated agencies in some regions. Forming a new organization out of two and integrating processes and cultures is never an easy task. In the examples we consider, the merger problems were compounded by FHSAs not having a clear purchaser–provider separation, and by the statutory governing authorities remaining separate. In all cases, there is a point beyond which closer working between two organizations falters because there is no agreed and shared vision. In theory, a shared vision is necessary to decide agency structure and processes, but in practice most agency management arrangements were decided without a shared vision.

One view is that there should be no change to current separate DHA and FHSA organization and siting without good reason (the 'conservatives'). Another is that radical and fast change reduces uncertainty and makes the most of the opportunities, with cross-directorate linking making up the details (the 'revolutionaries'). In between are the 'moderates' and 'pragmatists' who combine some DHA and FHSA functions in one or more directorates, and approach integration through project teams and matrix organization for specific tasks and areas of work. The diagrams of seven agency management structures in Appendix 2 give examples of all these approaches and show the main management divisions ('directorates') and cross-linkages between directorates. Even though there are big differences between agencies, many problems are similar and each can learn from and help others to resolve the problems. Some of the issues and questions for DHAs and FHSAs are listed in Box 11.1.

Box 11.1 Merging: issues and questions

Success and objectives
- Which of the responsibilities and objectives of each authority are shared, and which are not common, or in potential conflict?
- What are the short- and long-term objectives of merger?
- How should and will the success of merger be judged by different stakeholders?

Common vision based on needs
- How important is a common DHA–FHSA vision of the range of services in five years for a successful merger?
- If there is a vision, is it based on adequate information about needs and services?
- How can a better common view of needs and a common vision of services be developed by a new integrated agency, especially where FHSA activities are grouped separately in the directorate structure?

Merger implementation
- Specifically, which activities should be fully integrated, over what timescale, and how and why?
- Which areas of DHA and FHSA work should be managed and organized separately and why?
- Does the new agency structure replicate divisions in provider services, and, if it does, how can the agency organize itself and commission in a different way to encourage cooperation between providers?
- What are the different structures and processes for cross-directorate working?
- Should the agency be sited on one base?

Integration, sharing, combining, merger, or take-over?

In England and Wales, forming a joint agency to carry out DHA and FHSA purchasing is, for some districts, a natural progression from collaboration in the 1980s and joint appointments in the early 1990s. For others, there is little history of joint working or knowledge of each authority's role post-1990. For a few there is a record of competition, and a suspicion on the part of the FHSA that integration is in fact 'merger by acquisition' or 'take-over', rather than 'merger by combination'.

Sensitivity surrounds the choice of terms used to describe the formation of an executive agency to serve an FHSA and one or more DHAs. 'Merger' suggests full integration and implies authority merger; 'integration' or integrated agency suggests fuller integration than that which often exists, and indeed may be appropriate. This book uses the term 'integration' to describe the *process* of forming an agency, but does not assume a particular end state. FHSAs and DHAs are separate authorities with different statutory duties, and a variety of other models apart from joint agencies or a single merged authority are being developed across the UK, as was described in Chapter 10. Some view the new agencies as an experiment, and the next two years as a probationary period for agencies to prove their worth.

The purpose of integrated purchasing agencies

Commissioning for health gain

The NHS review of the late 1980s revived the earlier 1974 and 1982 reorganization arguments for a single health authority. Some thought that the 1990 reforms were a missed opportunity, and that GP fundholding undermined the advantages which could follow from integrating DHA and FHSA activities. During the first years of the reforms the ideals – of improving the overall health of populations over the longer term by using finance in flexible ways – were pushed to one side by short-term crises and the speed of change. The market simulations of the 'rubber windmill' (Liddell and Parston 1990) and 'care kaleidoscope' confirmed some people's view that acute services would continue to dominate agendas, and that redirecting resources into community and primary care would be difficult.

These concerns were not reduced by fears about the community care reforms, and by late 1992 the prospects for developing primary and community care appeared gloomy. However, during 1992 another view emerged, which was that the future NHS should be 'primary care led', with 'primary care led purchasing of secondary care' (e.g. the July 1992 NAHAT symposium on DHA/FHSA developments). This view was fuelled by a growing realization that GP fundholding was here to stay and making its mark, and that practice-sensitive and locality purchasing appeared to be one way forward for DHAs.

Vision of the range of services to meet health needs

Although there are questions about the concept of a 'primary care led' health service (Chapter 9), it does draw attention to the pattern of future services which are required for cost-effective health gain and reasserts the long-term agenda. It is also clear that only larger DHAs or joint DHA–FHSA agencies have the capacity to form a view of and realize comprehensive health care for populations, and to preserve principles of equity. It is in these respects that authority commissioners differ from GP fundholders, but have yet to win public recognition of the service which they provide and support for their role as 'champions of the people'.

In practice, many integrated agencies are not formed with a shared and well-developed view of the health needs to be met and the range and type of services which are the most cost-effective way to meet them, over the short and long term. Normally agencies have specific objectives concerned with economies of scale and general statements about combining primary and secondary care financing, such as those listed in Box 11.2. Many of these objectives are intermediate objectives – requirements which are thought to be necessary for the more general purpose of commissioning. However, in some cases they are not derived from, or related to, a shared overall view. It is true that one of the purposes of an integrated agency is to develop a combined view of needs and of the services required in the area. However, closer links or mergers do have to be based on an outline shared view to begin with: FHSA and DHA managers and non-executives have to spend time working through different understandings of the purpose of commissioning and views about types and range of services. Otherwise cooperation is only driven by short-term practical and economic considerations, which can lead to later problems.

Box 11.2   Objectives of integrated commissioning agencies

Generally the objective is 'integrated primary and secondary care commissioning'. Approaches vary from limited collaboration, to full reorganization with DHA and FHSA functions mixed in each directorate. The aims are:

- economies of scale;
- best use of scarce skills and staffing;
- to develop competition and choice between and within hospital, community and family health services;
- aligned geographical boundaries for assessing needs and planning;
- contracting across primary, community care and hospital services;
- to develop GP and community consultation and relations;
- to counterbalance GP fundholding to pursue strategic health gain aims;
- to develop integrated locality purchasing and provision;
- planned transfer of finance from acute to primary and community care.

The objectives of merging: why merge?

Merging FHSA and DHA management

The arguments for FHSA–DHA collaboration and merger are stronger than for merging DHAs to form larger DHAs. Some DHAs are too small to be viable with more GP fundholders, but 'small' DHA–FHSA agencies are another issue. The prevailing wisdom that larger DHAs or consortia are necessary and inevitable should be questioned, and is increasingly challenged by successful examples of GP fundholder purchasing. Larger DHAs can be insensitive to local population preferences and GP views, and are perceived by some as an irrelevant, expensive and unnecessary tier of management. Whether locality purchasing combines the best of large and small purchasing is yet to be decided, and depends on the model adopted.

Generally the objective of FHSA–DHA merged agencies is 'integrated primary and secondary care commissioning'. Later we consider in more detail specifically which FHSA functions and activities should remain separate from those of the DHA, which should be fully merged, and which are debatable and organized differently in different agencies. Here we consider the arguments for, and the objectives of, merging FHSA and DHA management, drawing on UK research into collaboration and the reasons advanced within the North West Thames Region for creating seven commissioning agencies. Readers are invited to question whether each of the following is a necessary precondition for cost-effective purchasing for health gain in their area (i.e. is each an obvious 'intermediate' objective?).

Economies of scale

The objective of reducing costs through economies of scale is one reason for a combined FHSA–DHA agency. As for merged DHAs, these economies are in buildings, staff costs, single departments for secretarial services, personnel and other support services, and through buying and running one office and computer system. However, there are some activities, such as most FHSA finance and administration, which do not 'mix' or give opportunities for economies of scale, even though they can be combined with DHA activities under one manager.

Scarce skills and staffing

For some commissioning work, both FHSAs and DHAs need the same type of specialist skills and staff. Merging makes it easier to attract and make the best use of scarce skills for needs assessment, strategic planning, community care, public health, evaluation, information technology and public relations. There are different views about how well some specialist staff can span both FHSA and DHA activities.

Contracting

FHSA contracts and relations with providers are different to those of DHAs. However, merged agencies make it easier to coordinate primary and community care contracts and development plans. Merged agencies are more able to influence both GPs and community trusts than separate FHSAs and DHAs.

Competition and choice
Merged agencies are better able to increase choice of services because they can more easily encourage services in primary, community or acute settings. Although smaller merged agencies have less scope than larger ones to create competition between similar providers (e.g. acute medical specialties), they have an advantage over DHA-only commissioners in being more able to encourage competition between different *types* of providers: for example, helping GPs to provide some secondary care in primary care settings, or helping community trusts to work with GPs to create alternatives to hospital care. This can reduce costs and increase patient choice; such services are often more popular with patients and carers.

Aligned geographical boundaries
Common FHSA and DHA boundaries (and also local authority boundaries) make it easier to share the work of assessing and planning services. They are a precondition for assessing needs.

Assessing needs
Merging needs assessment makes it possible to combine the epidemiological data and expertise of the DHA with those of the FHSA and its database and practice profile information. This can help to strengthen the sometimes weak link between needs assessment and deciding which services to purchase, where there is choice.

Planning
As for needs assessment, there is great scope for sharing information, staff and activities in planning, and for fully merging primary, secondary and community care planning. The reasons are to create a vision of a comprehensive range of services and a strategy and tactical plan to bring this about.

Joint 'contracting'
One objective of a merged FHSA and DHA agency is to ensure that hospital and community care contracts are coordinated with incentives to GPs. Organizing to achieve this coordination is easier, but not automatic within a joint agency.

GP and community consultation and relations
One objective of merger is to build stronger links with GPs, and to develop better ways of consulting with and involving GPs in purchasing. A combined FHSA–DHA agency is better able to do this than separate authorities consulting over different issues, although whether one staff member

per area should 'represent' both DHA and FHSA is another matter. The same applies to consulting the public over primary, community care and acute care issues which can be viewed together.

Counterbalance to GP fundholding

One less frequently mentioned reason for merging DHA and FHSA management is to organize and provide alternatives to fundholding, and more strongly to influence GPs who are fundholders. However, some GPs feel that putting 'fundholder support' in the agency that stands to lose from more fundholders means less time and finance for developing fundholders.

Integrated locality purchasing and provision

In some areas where there are conterminous boundaries with local authorities, merging makes it easier to carry out joint commissioning with a local authority. With aligned boundaries, there can be closer collaboration over needs assessment, planning services, contracting and quality monitoring for many services and client groups. In the longer term there is potential for collaborative, if not joint, locality purchasing by a local authority social services department and an FHSA–DHA, which could also correspond to locality provision. These organizational conditions make planning and creating community alternatives to hospital care much easier.

Planned transfer of finance from acute to primary and community care

Joint FHSA–DHA agencies make it easier to plan and coordinate investments in primary care to coincide with reductions in acute services, to ensure that services come 'on-stream' as others are reduced.

Criteria for judging merger success

In North West Thames, the above objectives and reasons gave 'second-order' criteria against which the success of mergers was judged. The main criterion for judging whether and how to merge is how the arrangement will contribute to, or detract from, the purpose of primary and secondary care commissioning. This gives the 'first-order' criterion of improvements to health status for the cost, but these are more difficult to measure, and are concerned with agency performance *per se*, rather than the merger itself, which is a means to an end. Appendix 5 gives a checklist for reviewing progress in identifying opportunities for integration or in undertaking integration. Examples of indicators of the success of mergers are:

- no disruption of the commissioner's operational services to independent contractors (mainly GPs), and improvements to the quality of these services (e.g. faster, lower error rates, lower cost);
- GPs' level of satisfaction about consultation, and number of complaints;
- ordinary people (and GPs) being able to explain what their joint commissioning agency does for them, and why it is necessary;

- lower administrative costs;
- fulfilling the corporate contract with the region;
- no conflicting messages to outsiders, e.g. telephone answering, public relations responses to immediate crises and strategic planning relations;
- staff in the agency being able to explain the reasons for merger, how it furthers the purpose of NHS commissioning and improves the services which commissioners provide to the population and others.

Problems in merging

Some of the problems in merging include making the most of, and combining:

- different views in FHSAs and DHAs about the future range of services;
- different understandings of the definitions and philosophy of 'management', 'contracting', 'primary care', etc.;
- differences in culture and ways of working with providers;
- differences in staff and non-executives' background.

Other problems included:

- deciding the role of chairs and non-executives, and any transitional arrangements to a single merged authority;
- judging what and how to merge, and how fast to do it (merger strategy);
- integrating computer and office systems;
- deciding how to handle relations with GPs, fundholders and others in the future and during merger.

We now consider the practical issues of closer working and merger.

The methods of merging in North West Thames, UK

Although the general model of an integrated agency was similar for all the North West Thames authorities, there were differences in how each carried out a merger of FHSA and DHA management. Some of the factors accounting for the differences in approach were size (their populations range from 240,000 to 990,000), whether DHAs were also merged (e.g. Hertfordshire's three DHAs into one), the authorities' involvement in London provider reconfiguration, the number of GP fundholders and FHSA history and strategy (e.g. providing health promotion). However, across the North West Thames Region during 1991–4:

- there was broad agreement that a joint agency was the most cost-effective way of organizing the work of the DHA and FHSA, and that no DHA or FHSA work would remain outside the management boundary of the agency;
- for statutory purposes the FHSA had a named general manager, who was either the agency chief executive or a director within the agency

who combined this function with another, usually as 'director of primary care';
- all agency directors served and reported to both authorities and were accountable to the agency chief executive.

In general there were two approaches to merger: the pragmatic and the radical.

The pragmatic and the radical approaches to merger

The 'pragmatic' approach is to identify and integrate different activities and functions, at a pace with which staff can cope and as the advantages become clear. This approach often retains separate FHSA management and activities within one agency management division or directorate, such as an FHSA or primary care directorate (e.g. Ealing, Hammersmith and Hounslow, with over 30 per cent of the 220 staff dealing with independent contractor payments and registration). Collaboration is developed through staff in that directorate working with staff from other directorates on different tasks and projects, and through some common services: for example, pooling some or all secretarial, personnel and information support services. There was a view that at this stage the FHSA payments function could not be contracted out to a non-statutory agency.

The 'revolutionary' approach is driven by a vision of full integration, and creates a structure in which many or all agency directorates undertake both FHSA and DHA work. This approach tackles cultural and other differences 'head on'. We will see in the next chapter that cross-directorate working is essential in each approach, but is carried out and developed in different ways.

Ways of merging

We now list some of the ways in which DHAs and FHSAs in North West Thames carried out their mergers, starting from the immediate and practical issues and moving to the longer-term issues which had to be considered or planned for at an early stage.

Moving to one base
Some agencies moved staff and equipment from one or more authorities to one base or a new base. Others were assessing the costs and benefits of such a move.

Planning and changing management structure: appointments and staff changes
New appointments had to be made within directorates and staff transferred to take up their new positions. This involved on average about 30 per cent of senior staff changing jobs within one agency or transferring to

another – in one agency all but one director and many first-level staff were changed. For all the North West Thames agencies this process started in the autumn of 1992 and was largely completed by the summer of 1993. In effect this meant that each agency was not able to initiate and pursue many significant new developments until late 1993. Some agencies have one chief executive, others have an FHSA general manager in addition to a DHA chief executive. (Appendix 2 shows the management structure of all the agencies.)

Sharing information for needs assessment
By 1993 some agencies had started sharing information for assessing needs, and others have a longer tradition of FHSA–DHA collaboration in this area. Pooling different types of information was possible and useful for needs analysis and for examining locality options. The information used was of practice profiles, epidemiological studies, analyses of OPCS data and analyses of provider demand and activity information. Some types of sharing are hampered by an inability to link FHSA and DHA computer systems, and to link these with hospital, primary care and community service computer systems. Networking and common systems is an area for further development, but most agencies have FHSA–DHA projects to improve their needs information for the short and medium term, sometimes with local authorities. These projects usually cross-cut public health, strategy, and information directorates.

Collaborating to assess needs
Some public health staff and FHSA staff have gone beyond sharing information to undertaking joint projects or working closely to assess needs for a locality or client group. There is scope for collaboration or full integration in assessing needs.

Joint planning
The first agency health strategies produced in the summer of 1993 were fairly rushed, but most agencies showed a coordinated DHA and FHSA approach – this gave a basis for more integrated planning over the coming years. Even with an integrated agency, there was a need for closer co-operation in planning developments in different areas, and for taking account of the effects of one authority's planned actions on another's and on providers. Agencies differ in their view as to whether and how to link with local authorities for planning, and arrangements for community care planning remained unchanged for most in the autumn of 1993 for the 1994 community care plans.

A common approach to influencing and contracting providers
There is no point in joint or integrated planning if both do not carry through the agreed plans into contracts and ways of influencing providers. There are two 'linking' issues: 'vertical linking' of plans to contracting; and

'lateral linking' of different providers through incentives and contracts (e.g. GP premises improvement to give room for new community staff which the DHA is to contract from a community trust).

Agencies have to speak with one voice to all providers and coordinate their relations with providers. There were situations where, without knowing it, staff from one commissioning directorate were negotiating or influencing a provider to do things which undermined what staff from another directorate were trying to achieve with another provider.

Cross-directorate working

In all the agencies, forming effective cross-directorate working was a key method for integration. Informal 'lead' roles for different tasks were all that was necessary for some tasks, but all soon developed more formal project management (e.g. for planning, or for moving to a new base). Agencies were developing policies and approaches to project management. However, in the first year, formal and systematic cross-directorate working was poorly developed in all agencies: we consider these issues in the next chapter, on purchaser organization.

Integrating accounting

There were immediate benefits to combining statutory accounting arrangements, but agencies found limits to the scope for integrating other financial functions, apart from areas such as agency staff payroll. Arrangements for finance staff support to directorates differed between agencies.

Integrating and developing IT systems

Savings were made by centralizing computer support staff and/or contracting for computer software, hardware and expert services. Agencies found that setting up an integrated system or networking current systems took a considerable time. All agencies were involved in careful planning, and some have tight project management for schemes in progress.

Integrating human resource services

Most agencies created one personnel and training department. They saw this as an obvious area for savings, but, perhaps more importantly, a common human resource department was thought to help in the development of a common agency culture and identity.

Integrating office services

Many agencies formed one office support service to manage secretarial staff and provide administration and supplies. Agencies found that changes for secretarial and office staff needed to be handled carefully to build their morale and loyalty to the new agency. This was not just because their services are essential to agency working, but because some were finding that secretaries sometimes conveyed a poor public image, some not knowing the name of the new agency. Stories were told of telephonists who had never heard of the new agency, and of GPs and others being connected to the hospital manager on whose site the agency was based, which undermined the public relations work being done by other agency staff.

GP relations

One of the early priorities for the new agencies was deciding how to relate to and involve GPs in different commissioning activities. The pragmatic approach was to continue developing the existing FHSA and DHA links and mechanisms, with reviews of these to check for duplication, consider improvements and ensure coordination. The radical approach was to create new structures and processes for relating to GPs to deal with both FHSA and DHA issues. At the time of writing, little evidence was available about how these different methods were working. Much can be learned from different agencies' approach to GP relations, which in part depends on their approach to locality purchasing.

Fundholder policy and relations

Agencies had structures for relating to GPs as actual or potential fundholders which were different to those for relating to GPs in their role as referrers and providers. Whether they can and should be combined depended on the agency's policies on fundholding and view about collaborative or 'shared' purchasing. This was an area for early attention by directors and their senior staff.

Although there were differences between the North West Thames agencies in their approach to merger, they all faced similar issues. Sharing problems and solutions proved an important feature of the purchaser development programme (Øvretveit 1993h). One of the conclusions for others considering or carrying out mergers is that forming networks for sharing and reviewing experience can be of great value.

Examples of merger

Up to 1993 North West Thames was the only region to plan and develop systematically integrated agencies across a region. Although Wessex Region formed six health commissions during 1992, progress was less rapid because of lack of conterminosity. However, collaborative links or integrated agencies were also formed in other areas, often on the initiative of local managers or non-executive members rather than by region. The following examples draw on the author's and others' research between 1990 and 1994 to show different approaches to merger.

From their work in 1990–1, Ham and Heginbotham (1991) reported DHA mergers and DHA–FHSA cooperation in Ealing (300,000 population), Manchester (450,000), Chester/Wirral (500,000), Buckinghamshire (700,000), East Sussex (720,000) and North Yorkshire (720,000). A research study by Ashburner (1993) reported two different approaches to FHSA–DHA collaboration: a shire integration and an inner London approach.

In the latter the FHSA took the view that primary care developments needed to be launched before further joint working with the DHA. In the shire integration, Ashburner reported tensions and concerns about the FHSA being taken over, and growing scepticism about whether finance would be transferred for developing primary care. A joint purchasing executive was formed first, with the two chief executives having dual membership of both HAs, and occasional joint strategic meetings of the two authorities. One of the lessons was that partial integration was not possible, not least because of the uncertainties for staff. 'The FHSA's initial policy was to be very cautious . . . It was believed that with cooperation at the top the integration of lower levels would follow . . . progress was rapid . . . There is a point of no return between joint working and integration. Partial integration was viewed as untenable, neither one thing nor another' (Ashburner 1993).

Experience elsewhere

Stockport
Stockport is a 295,000-population merged DHA–FHSA agency, conterminous with the local authority. Unlike the shire integration studied by Ashburner, the process was pragmatic, rather than radical and revolutionary.

> Our method was a natural, organic and unthreatening process . . . We believe it to be preferable to amalgamations which start from the top and then proceed (or don't proceed!) downwards – amalgamation by paper-clip . . . The amalgamation started as the sharing of specific functions – information planning and health strategy management. From there it grew and progressed steadily towards amalgamation at a natural but accelerating pace. This method prevented a take-over of either authority by the other.
> (Stockport HA summary document, January 1993)

The Stockport approach is of interest for a number of reasons. Because Stockport has a relatively small population it has relatively few purchasing staff. Yet the agency was also concerned to develop locality purchasing. To do this it developed a way of combining geographical, functional and care group dimensions of purchasing in its joint structure. There are six sectors (50,000 population), with a health strategy manager for each, who spend half their time on sector purchasing issues and half on leading strategy for a care group. The other grouping in the joint agency structure is a functional grouping of directors as described in Chapter 4. Their experience was that gradual 'amalgamation' in a 'natural' way did work, and that there was no real need to combine chief executive posts, although they will when the FHSA general manager retires.

Doncaster

Ham *et al.* (1993) describe Doncaster as one of the first areas to move from cooperation to formal integration arrangements. In July 1991, the two authorities appointed a joint chief executive, then formed an integrated management structure and produced a joint health strategy and investment plan. Integration was assisted by moving to a single base and by good relations between chairpersons (who continued in their authority chairing role), and between non-executives and executive directors of the two authorities, which held informal joint meetings.

Dorset

Another early merger was the formation of a Dorset commissioning agency for a newly formed DHA (from two DHAs) and one FHSA. Some of the lessons from their experience include: the need for a clear timetable and targets for savings; close transition management; clarity about direction and expectations; and developing chief executive relations with chairs and non-executives. After the merger, the lessons for others were the importance of creating a new identity and jointly owned business agenda, stopping competition and references to the past, setting achievable early successes, developing external relations and investing in staff development (I. Carruthers, IHSM conference presentation, 1992). The Dorset experience helped in the formation of other health commissions throughout the Wessex Region during 1993. As with Doncaster, a single base was important, but so was a formal joint structure for the non-executive directors: the Dorset Health Commission is made up of five non-executive members from each authority as well as the two chairs and the chief executive. In this merger one chair took the lead role in overseeing the joint agency arrangements.

Bromley

Early in 1991 Bromley undertook a joint commissioning project with the local authority and voluntary organizations which led to a joint FHSA–DHA executive. The force bringing the DHA and FHSA together was reported to be: a recognition that they both had some common objectives and similar problems, both needing more information about service effectiveness and needs, and both wanting to form a clearer view about long-term health objectives and work on a joint strategy (Dean *et al.* 1992). There were initial suspicions about balance of power, a lack of understanding of each other's role and functions, and a concern that community and primary care would not get the attention it deserved.

Wolverhampton

The previous chapter described the Wolverhampton FHSA 'provider' role. Wolverhampton took a different approach to many in separating the 'purchasing' and 'providing' responsibilities of both the DHA and FHSA, and forming separate joint arrangements for each. The FHSA 'purchasing' responsibilities were combined with those of the DHA in a health executive, chaired by the DHA chair. The FHSA general manager manages the DHA community unit as well as FHSA 'provider' staff in a combined 'primary health care unit', which is chaired by the FHSA chair. There are a number of joint committees for the DHA and FHSA non-executives, which deal with purchasing and provision.

Conditions for cooperation or merger

Although there are a variety of approaches, we can draw some general conclusions about the conditions which make purchaser cooperation or merging easier. These include:

- A shared view of the purpose of NHS purchasing and of the part to be played by primary and secondary purchasing. Time is needed for FHSA and DHA staff and non-executives to form an agreed initial view, and a vision of the pattern of services and shifts in resources which follow from this view.
- An understanding of the advantages to the purchasing organizations of closer cooperation and a belief in the benefits of this for the health of the population.
- Conterminous boundaries: changes to authority boundaries or DHA mergers are often necessary to move beyond informal cooperation between one or more DHAs and a FHSA.
- Good relations between DHA and FHSA chairs, non-executives and executive directors, especially where merger is not imposed by region. Although personalities play a part, this is more a matter of building trust between the DHA and FHSA over time. This involves developing mutual understanding of each other's work and problems, often through a variety of joint projects and working groups.
- Opportunity for either the DHA or the FHSA to draw back from further integration at certain critical stages. This helps to reduce concerns about one organization taking over another.
- Staff sharing the same base or bases.
- Effective communications and dialogue – knowing what each other needs to know, exchanging the right amount and type of information, and developing systems and meetings for communication which are cost-effective.

The learning and problem-solving potential

One advantage of national and local variation is the potential to learn from each other. For example, agencies which keep primary care management and development separate from acute and community care purchasing can learn from purchasers which combine primary and community care within a directorate and vice versa. Purchasers can learn about the advantages and disadvantages of different structures, and about ways to create closer collaboration from the experience of purchasers which have different management arrangements and different sizes and types of authorities. Appendix 2 shows the different management structures of the North West Thames agencies and the next chapter considers the advantages and disadvantages of different structures.

Summary: approaches to integration

We can summarize the different approaches to integration described above in three ways: first, by noting the variety of methods agencies have used to integrate FHSA and DHA staff and functions; second, in terms of a continuum of collaboration; and third, in terms of four models of organizational integration.

Integration through a combination of methods

Agencies integrate DHA and FHSA work in a variety of ways:

- by developing a shared vision and strategy for NHS commissioning, for health in the area and for services;
- by developing a common set of values and culture;
- by identifying and jointly conducting tasks which both authorities must undertake (e.g. needs assessment);
- by bringing together different DHA and FHSA work in each directorate, or having one manager managing both DHA and FHSA staff at a lower level;
- by formal cross-directorate project teams, or staff with joint accountability to two directors' directorates;
- by 'harmonizing' management policies, procedures and style;
- by integrating systems (e.g. computers and databases);
- through staff-centred activities, both formal (e.g. common training) and informal;
- through common support services.

All these measures help to realize the cost-effectiveness and advantages of a single agency.

Continuum of integration

The second way of summarizing different approaches is in terms of a continuum of degrees of cooperation, from exchanging information to full integration (see Figure 11.1). This continuum can apply across a DHA and FHSA, or to a single area, such as: single tasks or projects (e.g. a new computer system); areas of work or functions (e.g. needs assessment or public health). A further issue is the level of the directorate within which degrees of cooperation to integration occur (Chapter 3).

Sharing information	*Sharing a resource*	*Joint purchasing*	*Consortium*	*Merger*
e.g. population profiles and data, contract specification	e.g. staff, facilities, equipment, overlapping team membership	Agreed Pool finance for purchasing some, or all plan services	One agency purchases, but each purchaser remains an independent entity	New single purchasing body

Figure 11.1 Possible types of commissioner collaboration.

Models of integration

Figure 11.2 summarizes different approaches to combining DHA and FHSA work and roles. These models represent: stages in increasing integration which some DHAs/FHSAs have passed through; current arrangements for joint or combined working. Some agencies combine aspects of two or more of these models.

The four models in Figure 11.2 represent aspects of agencies' different approaches to integration – in some cases successive stages. The first shows collaboration between DHA and FHSA staff over specific projects, and the second over joint appointments. The third is where most or all FHSA work is organized within an 'FHSA directorate', and the fourth is where most directorates undertake DHA and FHSA work. There are other models of cooperation rather than an integrated agency, such as the purchaser and provider model pioneered by Wolverhampton (Lord 1993) (see Chapter 10). In the next chapter we consider the different ways in which agencies have grouped functions within directorates.

Lessons from integrating purchasing

The following list summarizes some of the experience of agencies in terms of lessons for successful integration.

- An agreed concept of health gain and vision of services in five years helps to decide the best FHSA and DHA merger arrangements to achieve the vision.
- A joint agency structure serves further to refine and carry out an agreed vision.
- Cross-directorate working is critical to agency success – do not underestimate the staff training and organization development work needed to set up such arrangements and make them effective (see next chapter).
- Promote joint working in the first year by agreeing and focusing on a few short-term joint targets.

Model A: Shared projects and information

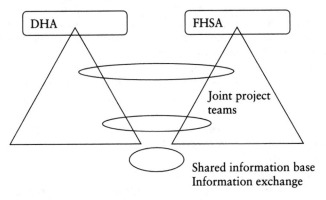

Model B: Joint appointments

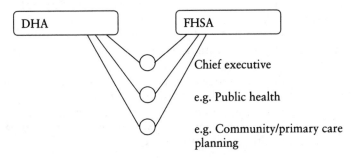

Model C: FHSA directorate (one joint agency for both)

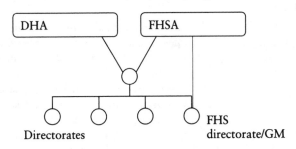

Model D: Combined directorates (one joint agency for both)

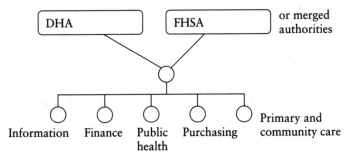

Figure 11.2 Models of cooperation and integration between DHAs and FHSAs.

- Morale suffers unless people recognize what they can achieve and have achieved with few resources, rather than only measuring themselves against grandiose long-term objectives.
- Understand how others judge the success of merger and the value of the agency: many GPs by better FHSA payments and registration services, some by primary care developments, i.e. the speed, amount and targeting to areas of need.
- Clarify the type of relations the agency needs with GPs and decide how to coordinate different directorate relations with them, or establish unified relations with each with one agency contact.
- Agree a shared meaning to terms such as 'primary care commissioning' and 'secondary care' to decide responsibilities and to avoid confusing outsiders.
- 'Details' are important, e.g. a new image is destroyed by staff who have never heard of the name of the agency.
- Time and money can be saved by agencies helping each other to identify and solve problems: the variations and dissimilarities between agencies are a strength for doing this.
- Make use of theories about and methods for managing change which help to bring about effective and speedy integration.
- Recognize that integration and the agency are means to an end. Keep the end result to the forefront: the new agency is a service organization for achieving health gain at the lowest cost.

Conclusions

There are good reasons for having a separate system for administering and paying for primary health services. However, as both FHSAs and DHAs develop their purchasing role in the UK, the need for closer collaboration becomes unavoidable. This is especially so if each sees the purpose of commissioning to be cost-effective health gain, rather than just contracting services. Collaboration can save costs, ensure coordinated strategies and enable commissioners to lead changes in the pattern and balance of services.

There are many ways of improving collaboration, and each authority has to decide which is the best way for the circumstances in its area. Where authority boundaries are conterminous, a popular way of improving collaboration is to form an integrated commissioning agency as an executive body for one or more DHAs and an FHSA. This is a step short of merging primary and secondary care authorities and their finance. Authorities have formed such agencies in different ways.

For many agencies an aim has been to develop primary care services through coordinated planning and the transfer of finance from secondary to primary care. Whether agencies are successful in developing primary care, at the lowest cost, depends as much on a shared vision of health and of health services in the future as on the practical steps they take to bring together functions performed by the two authorities.

Drawing on their shared vision for commissioning and services, DHAs and FHSAs can define their objectives and reasons for merging. These objectives give criteria against which merger progress and success can be judged as the merger is carried out. For purchasers considering the degree of collaboration or what, when and how to merge, there is much to be learned from other purchasing organizations. Approaches to mergers in North West Thames and elsewhere can be summarized in terms of: specific methods, such as joint appointments or joint project teams; a continuum of integration; and four models of integration. These models and examples help purchasing managers to assess the type of cooperation and integration in their own area or agency, and to judge their own progress towards closer working.

Key points

- The purpose of public health purchasing – cost-effective health gain – calls for close cooperation between primary and secondary purchasing, and for continual redefinition of the boundaries between the two.
- One method for increasing cooperation between primary and secondary purchasing is to form an integrated purchasing agency, which combines health authority staff and finance which were previously separate. This can also increase cooperation between authority commissioning and GP fundholder purchasing.
- Mergers between DHAs and FHSAs should be driven by a shared vision of the purpose of integrated commissioning and of the range and type of services to be developed. Intermediate merger objectives should be derived from this agreed view. Forming an integrated agency helps to develop and refine the shared vision.
- 'Merger' is not always the best term to describe some models and the different ways and speeds of joining DHA and FHSA activities. Some FHSA and DHA activities will and should remain organizationally and perhaps physically separate.
- The process of integration is hampered by different cultures and attitudes in DHAs and FHSAs, which are reflected in different usage and meanings of terms. Conventional concepts of purchasing and provision are unhelpful for thinking about the role of FHSAs and current FHSA functions in joint agencies.
- Agencies have integrated DHA and FHSA work in the following ways:

  - moving to one base;
  - planning and changing management structure – joint appointments, grouping DHA and FHSA work in one or more directorates;
  - cross-directorate working;
  - sharing information for needs assessment;
  - collaborating to assess needs;
  - joint planning;

- deciding common approach to influencing and contracting providers;
- integrating accounting;
- integrating and developing IT systems;
- integrating human resource services;
- integrating office services;
- developing a common policy towards and relationships with GPs, co-ordinating how different parts of the agency relate to GPs as providers and as fundholders or having one member of staff relate to a group of GPs for a number of purposes.

- Many agencies are taking a pragmatic approach to integration: in their initial structure retaining most FHSA work in one 'primary care directorate', and actively identifying opportunities to unify work and tasks. A few take a radical approach, with most directorates combining DHA and FHSA tasks. All are developing cross-directorate working arrangements.

 **12** **Purchasing agency organization**

The future of public service management is 'lateral management' and this is nowhere more evident than in the emerging service sector of health purchasing management. Already, inside their own organizations, managers are working with flatter and more flexible structures. The abilities to work with their own teams and other departments will be extended to working across boundaries with staff in other organizations. With increasing service diversity and an enabling role, the purchasing manager's key task will be coordination: success will depend on skills in creating unifying frameworks and vision, in deciding when formalization is necessary, and in influencing, conflict resolution and diplomacy.

Introduction

Health purchasing is a new activity and we are still developing an understanding of what the work is, of the purpose of a purchasing organization and of the nature of the service which purchasers provide. One result is that structures for organizing purchasing work vary between purchasers and are changing. However, we see in this chapter that there is one constant for purchasing managers: the need to manage across internal and external organizational boundaries. We see that a central feature of purchaser organization is cross-directorate working, and that managers have to be able to establish structures to ensure that this happens, and to ensure that they and their staff have the skills for 'lateral management'.

The aim of this chapter is to help purchasing managers to improve their organization, and to report the findings of research into the organization and management of integrated NHS commissioning agencies. Forming one agency to manage primary and secondary health commissioning does not, of itself, ensure that purchasing for both sectors is coordinated. Agencies need a variety of methods and structures to ensure coordination and that the benefits of an integrated agency are realized. Purchasing managers have to coordinate their work and plans with other purchasers, not least with GP fundholders.

This chapter describes how primary and secondary care commissioning is organized within integrated agencies, and alerts managers to issues of organization which were neglected in some agencies in 1993–4. The chapter is also of relevance to managers working in other types of purchasing organizations because it deals with the general issues of how to group functions in directorates (or divisions), and how to organize cross-directorate and project team working with matrix structures. It addresses the following concerns of managers.

- *If purchasers have broadly the same aims, why are there such big differences between how they are organized?*
- *How do we ensure that the different parts of the purchasing organization which need to are communicating and collaborating, without unnecessary paperwork, delays and meetings?*
- *How should purchasing functions be grouped, and at what level should appointments be made? Have we got our directorates right?*
- *How can we ensure that work which spans directorates is identified, responsibility for projects is clarified and tensions between directorates are managed?*
- *What are 'project management' and 'matrix management' and how do we make them work?*
- *What are non-executive directors accountable for, what is their role and how can we involve them more?*

A commissioning organization is a means for undertaking work in pursuit of a purpose. We start by considering how organization should follow from a conception of purpose, and how organization itself helps to develop a collective view of purpose. We then briefly consider the role of non-executive directors and boards and structural methods of integration. Initially, chief executives of commissioning organizations grouped work within directorates on the basis of their views about purpose – how they defined these groupings and the levels of work in directorates are the subjects of the fourth section of the chapter. The decision about horizontal grouping is not so critical if there are effective cross-directorate working arrangements. Two formal arrangements are dual accountability and project teams, which we consider in the section on matrix structure.

In addition to directorate grouping and cross-directorate structures there is a third aspect of commissioner organization: cross-project coordination. All commissioners have many project teams working at one time, many of which have overlapping responsibilities: we consider an example of four mutually dependent projects in one agency. The chapter describes ways to coordinate cross-directorate project teams so that they contribute to each other. It considers how to 'organize for synergy' to ensure that the final result is greater than the sum of the projects.

DHA–FHSA agencies are created on the assumption that they are better able to fulfil the objectives of each authority than two separate executive organizations. We do not consider agency performance in this chapter (see, for example, Boles 1993; Ham 1993a). However, one aspect of performance is the progress an agency makes in integrating and coordinating DHA and FHSA work where there is benefit to doing so. A final section summarizes the chapter in terms of criteria for judging how well and how quickly purchasing managers are integrating DHA and FHSA work in commissioning agencies. These are reproduced as a checklist in Appendix 5.

Before considering the relationship between purpose and organization, we note some general principles which are relevant to understanding and reviewing purchaser organization.

Organization: general points

In the following we view organization as how work is divided between people (roles and tasks); how people relate to each other, and the stable patterns of interaction between them over time. Organization is not something which exists outside of what we do, or separate from us – it is what we do, and how we think about relating our work to other people's work. How a purchasing agency is organized *is* how people currently decide the work which they or their staff will do, how they plan and timetable it, and how they link their work with others. Structure is both the lines of management accountability on charts and the recurring patterns of interaction between people. In this sense there is no formal and informal organization: organization is what people do, and the charts may or may not give a good representation of what people do and how they relate to each other.

To divide up work and to help people see where they fit in, it is useful to describe and represent organization. There are different ways of describing – the most common is a chart with positions, a description of the work of the position and ways of showing how the positions relate. Most chief executives in the seven North West Thames commissioning agencies drew up such reporting charts (Appendix 2), but there was a tension between these diagrams and their written descriptions. The written descriptions of organization put more stress on lateral and cross-directorate relationships and matrix structures than on the hierarchical management relationships. One of the aims of this chapter is to contribute to purchasing managers' search for appropriate and simple ways to describe the new types of organization they are creating, without ignoring fundamental principles of management and the experience of other service organizations.

Purpose and organization

We return again to the question of the purpose of health purchasing. To create a new organization and to improve organizational effectiveness, it is necessary to have some conception of the purpose of an integrated purchasing agency and of its work. Yet a clear and shared view of purpose is something which develops and changes over time. Chief executives in the North West Thames Region based their initial organization on a view of the purpose of the agency, and of the work to be done, but they all stressed that the structures were to be revised and flexible. All recognized that developing a view of the distinctive purpose of the agency, and one which was shared, would take time. Box 12.1 notes the difficulties in forming a shared understanding of purpose, and the perils of organization not being linked to purpose and the work to be done.

Box 12.1   The 'chicken and egg' of purpose and structure: which came first?

Form follows function
Effective organization must follow from a clear and shared view of purpose and the work to be done. High cost, inefficiencies and poor performance can always be traced to vague or multiple purposes, and to conflicting views about the work to be done.

Current form influences function
Many organizations are built on the foundations of old ones. The way an organization is structured influences the type of strategy it produces, and its view of its purpose.

Current form preserves old function
Structure should balance the tension between the past and the future – all too often structure is a conservative force, making the future unthinkable or unimplementable.

The purpose of integrated agencies

We saw in Chapters 3 and 11 that the purpose and work of DHA commissioning is poorly defined and evolving, as are the purpose and work of FHSAs. What, then, of the purpose of a single agency, formed to carry out the work of one or more DHAs and one FHSA? To some extent, deciding that there will be joint DHA–FHSA commissioning agencies in North West Thames helped to define the purpose and work of commissioning by combining primary, community and secondary care. However, it added a further complexity as there were a greater variety of views among DHA and FHSA staff and members about the purpose of a joint agency than there were elsewhere about a single DHA or FHSA commissioning organization.

Implications for organization and management

Although, in theory, purchaser organization should follow from definitions of purpose and work to be done, these definitions are poorly articulated and need more practical experience for their development. Beyond a certain point theorizing without practice becomes sterile and misleading. In practice, commissioning organization is based on a combination of factors, including a view of future purpose and work, but also politics, personalities, history and provider structures. Further, the way an agency is organized influences the view it has of its future purpose. For example, an agency which renames the FHSA executive organization as a 'directorate of primary care', and does nothing else, is predisposed to produce a view of its purpose which perpetuates the division between family health services and other services – unless matrix structures are able to counterbalance this.

Before we move from purpose to organization, we need to note three points. First, there is a need for greater clarity about the specific health outcomes which a purchaser is trying to achieve for different people. Second, a clearer view is needed about whether, or how, an integrated agency is better able to achieve these end results than any other arrangement, such as single authority organizations or developed GP fundholding. Most of the advantages of an integrated agency listed in Chapter 11 were defined in terms of more cost-effective processes for commissioning, rather than in terms of health end-results. Purchasing managers and researchers need to examine whether certain purchasing processes do result in the expected benefits for the population. Third, with a clearer statement of why integrated agencies are more cost-effective for achieving health end-results, there is less of a problem in measuring short-term performance in terms of speed and appropriateness of integration. This is because the links between the means (integration) and the ends (cost-effective health gain) are more clearly understood. In 1993–4 there was little evidence that the extra, often unspecified, health benefits to the population which many believed would come from integrated commissioning agencies were worth the costs and time of reorganization.

Summary: purpose and organization

The general point of this section is that clarity about purpose and objectives is necessary for improving organization and measuring performance, but to develop a clearer view one has to have some form of organization in the first place. Although clearer shared definitions of purpose are necessary, at this stage these definitions will not come from more concentrated thinking. Rather it is action and then reflection on experience which will help to define purpose. Where purpose is unclear, the best tactic is to take a first definition, act and then review.

One implication for purchasing managers is that they have to build in time and processes to ensure that reviews of purpose and organization happen. Chief executives and health authorities in the UK produced initial statements of mission, purpose, values, priorities and targets for purchasing agencies, and based their organization on these conceptions, at least in part. They have emphasized flexibility, and that the structures will be reviewed and changed. Whether this gives sufficient stability in chaos, and whether more formalization would help, is the subject of later parts of this chapter. The chapter now turns to practical issues of organization and integration.

Governance and structural issues in integration

Governance and executive structures

An issue which emerged in 1993 was governance structures 'above' the executive management structure of a purchasing organization, in particular the role of authority non-executives as individuals and as a collective, and the accountability of health authorities. Examples are the relationship between authorities and higher bodies such as the regional offices of the NHS management executive, and the formation of non-executive member groups to address cross-authority subjects, such as policy in relation to GP fundholders. There is a set of important organizational issues of governance, rather than of executive management, which we note but do not consider in detail here.

A first issue is the conceptual distinction between executive functions and the functions of health authority non-executive directors as a group. This distinction helps to answer the questions: what value do or could non-executives add to NHS commissioning; and what difference should they make? Analyses of the work of authority governing boards and the work of the executive in commercial organizations give some limited help, but there are problems with the analogy. The primary purpose of the latter is to protect the interests of shareholders, and they are accountable to and appointed by shareholders. The performance of some boards in representing shareholders in the UK in recent years has proved disappointing, and is another reason why the commercial model is not the best model for a public sector purchasing authority.

It is true that one purpose of health authorities is to represent and serve the interests of people in the area, but they are also responsible for ensuring that government directives and policies are observed, and they are appointed by and accountable to the Secretary of State. This reflects the tension noted in Chapter 3 between purchasers' role as service organizations for their local population, and their role as organs of a national service. One task which arises from the latter role is to ensure that long-term programmes are carried out in the interests of the nation. In simple terms we may define the distinctive functions of health authority members as twofold: independent oversight of executive actions in order to give additional accountability; and to provide guidance on values, priorities and the ends to be achieved.

Clarity about the functions of non-executives helps with the second set of practical issues concerning the tasks and roles of chairpersons and non-executives. Questions include: what should they be doing; what is the right balance between interference in executive work and insufficient involvement in authority business; and which committee structures are required? Answers to these questions and to the questions of what type of training and information they require should follow from an analysis of their distinctive role.

A third set of issues concerns the governance structure for new combined DHAs and FHSAs. How many non-executives should there be in a combined authority? How is it possible to ensure that the professional advice which has proved important to FHSA work is available to combined authorities? How should authorities be structured in a way which allows greater local accountability? The last question has been addressed but not in relation to combined authorities, and the other questions have not been addressed by the author or others at the time of writing. Further discussion may be found in Ferlie *et al.* (1993) and examples of members' roles in integrated agencies in Ham (1993b).

Structural methods for integrating DHA and FHSA work and staff

An early lesson for the North West Thames purchasing agencies was that forming one agency to manage DHA and FHSA work and staff did not, of itself, ensure day-to-day collaboration or cooperation. Agencies needed a variety of methods and structures to ensure coordination, especially where the agency created an 'FHSA-type directorate'. Chapter 11 described the different approaches to merger and summarized these in terms of models of integration. Below we note three structural methods for integrating, and then consider the third in more detail: how agencies group work and management in directorates, which are the first level of commissioner management structure. Unless otherwise stated, the chapter refers to the seven integrated purchasing agencies in North West Thames where the research was undertaken.

Shared base (one or more sites)

One base for DHA and FHSA staff helps communications and to form a common culture and makes the important informal links between directorates far more likely. This can help to counteract any professional or functional 'inwardness' which may arise from grouping staff in one directorate. Some locality models do not need a local base.

Joint appointments

Joint appointments are one way in which DHAs and FHSAs collaborate. Across England and Wales there are joint posts at different levels and for different functions. In the North West Thames agencies, all chief executives and most directors are joint appointments, and accountable to the FHSA and DHA(s), with an employment contract with the two (or more) authorities. There are different views about whether staff below these levels should have an employment contract with one authority or with the two or more authorities which an agency is serving.

An FHSA is required by statute to have a general manager. This role is taken either by the agency chief executive (e.g. in KCW), or by one of the agency directors, such as the 'director of primary care' (e.g. in Brent and Harrow). In the latter the director is accountable to FHSA and DHA(s) and to the Chief Executive. In theory, conflicts of accountability or conflicts of view about family health services and fundholding are possible, but in the first two years no chief executives or directors reported any, or thought it likely.

By management within one directorate
All agencies combine DHA and FHSA work in one or more directorates, or have a support function which encompasses work that was previously organized separately. Early on, most agencies grouped some or all of both DHA and FHSA work for the following areas under one manager or director: information, finance, human resources, business support, public relations and communications and public health.

The most common approach for primary care commissioning is model C in Figure 11.2, where the agency, in effect, renames the FHSA executive organization as a 'directorate of primary care'. For most, this is only a starting point, to ensure no disruption to routine but essential, FHS administration. All agencies rapidly defined 'primary care commissioning' work and ensured that staff involved in this work liaised with other directorates.

Some, for example Hillingdon, combined DHA community planning and development work with FHSA work in one 'directorate of primary and community care'. In forming their sub-directorate structures, a number of agencies moved to model D (Figure 11.2), where all or most directorates combined DHA and FHSA work, and the distinction began to have less meaning: for example, finance staff working on DHA and FHSA accounts, information specialists developing common systems and serving all directorates, or public health staff in a number of directorates. In some cases this involves staff with dual accountability, (part- or full-time) to two directors or managers in different directorates, a subject discussed later.

Directorate structure

All purchasing organizations have to consider how best to combine tasks and work within different divisions or directorates (their primary, or first-level, division). Where authorities are considering or undertaking merger their decision about grouping is more complex because it involves identifying FHSA and DHA tasks and work which should be combined, and those which do not need to be.

In North West Thames, all seven agencies defined the boundaries of their four to six directorates in different ways, encompassing different work and functions. Ham (1993b) also reports four different agency directorate structures. Are these differences significant, and what can others learn from how one agency groups its work? There are two views. The first is the view of most chief executives and many directors of purchasing: how work and staff are grouped in directorates is irrelevant; this grouping is only a convenient way to represent a management structure, which is fundamentally different to those of the pre-reform NHS authorities. There are and should be no boundaries between directorates, and cross-directorate project teams are the main vehicles for organizing work in the agency. The second view is that of some directors and of the author, that directorate structure and management are important, and that functions and work which have to be coordinated and which require staff with similar expertise should be within the same directorate. Cross-directorate working will take time to evolve and staff need clear management during a time of change. We return to these views after first describing and comparing the differences between agencies.

Grouping and level of work

How should an agency define directorate structure or 'group' work within directorates? How should a directorate divide work within the directorate in terms of level and type? These were two of the early questions which purchasers faced, and which they are frequently reassessing. Most tried to strike a balance between:

- discipline/function (e.g. public health, finance, quality, information);
- finance source/service sector (acute (medical specialty), community (care group or discipline) and primary care contractors);
- the contracting cycle or process of needs assessment, strategy and contracting;
- geographical dimensions.

Usually one dimension predominates in an agency's structure – the most common are grouping by discipline/function, and service sector. Surprisingly, in North West Thames no structures were based on analyses of work processes, which is a common approach to commercial service organization design (Edvardsson *et al.* 1994). This may be because of the variety of 'customers' which an agency serves, and its primary population orientation. However, service process analyses will be increasingly used to improve organization within, or across, directorates where there are clear customer service purposes to be carried out (e.g. GP payments).

A striking feature of commissioning agencies is that many tasks and projects cannot be undertaken within the boundaries of a directorate, however one defines the directorates: most activities span two or more directorates. This is not an organizational curiosity, or something which staff discover when trying to get something done, but is fundamental to the nature and purpose of health purchasing as a service, as we see later. How to organize work across directorates and how to maintain clear management and flexibility are critical issues for purchaser success.

Representing structure

Grouping into directorates is related to the issues of how to represent the new types of structures which purchasing organizations are developing. Some argue that representing structure in a conventional management chart (as does Appendix 2) is misleading: that it suggests strict boundaries between directorates, with a hierarchical structure and a static organization. There is no doubt that cross-directorate and cross-authority working is a key feature of each agency's formal and informal organization, and that the diagrams are poor representations of the variety of mechanisms which agencies are developing. Further, each agency's structure is continually changing, with new posts and reporting relationships being formed. Most chief executives have represented their structure by diagrams other than the conventional charts, and some have matrix charts to summarize reporting relationships and other aspects of organization.

There are, however, two advantages to highlighting management structure in the conventional way. First, it draws attention to the need for clear definition of posts and managerial relationships: this chapter later notes the consequences of not doing so and the problems which have occurred because of unclarity about management. Clear lines of management do not detract from or weaken matrix organization, but are essential to effective lateral management. Second, it allows agencies to compare their structures with others and to consider possible improvements to their organization.

Comparing structures

The value of comparisons is that they help us to question taken-for-granted assumptions. Through comparison we can see how others do the same thing differently. It helps us to consider whether there is another, better, way. Here we compare differences in directorate groupings. For example, one agency combines all FHSA and DHA finance functions in one directorate, while another takes the view that some FHSA finance functions are so different that they cannot be combined in this way. Another example is discovering ways to coordinate work, such as commissioning community and acute service, by comparing how one agency coordinates this work within a directorate with how another coordinates the same work across directorates: the latter may in fact coordinate work better than the former.

An analysis of directorate groupings in integrated agencies shows that there are four areas of difference between agencies. Purchasing managers can consider how their organization compares and why, in their organization, work is grouped in a particular directorate.

1 *Organization of FHSA work in an agency.* Some agencies started by forming an 'FHSA-type' directorate. Others combined FHS work with DHA community service purchasing work in a 'primary and community care' directorate. How this work is organized is both the cause and the

effect of how people define 'primary care commissioning' and the FHSA 'provider role'.

2 *Commissioning community and acute services.* Some combine these in one directorate, some have them in separate directorates (e.g. Hillingdon in Appendix 2).

3 Whether *contract management* is within the appropriate directorate (e.g. community health contracts in a community commissioning directorate), or whether all contract management is brought together in one contracting or purchasing directorate.

4 Whether *operational contract management* is brought together with health *strategy* in the same directorate.

There are other points of comparison, in terms of which work is grouped within different directorates (Appendix 2). Do strategy and contracting need to be in the same directorate, and do primary, secondary and community commissioning need to be in the same directorate? Different agencies have different answers. At present there is insufficient evidence to judge whether different groupings of staff and work within directorates are significant, or whether the boundaries are largely irrelevant. It is likely that both are true: that some staff and work must be placed together within the same directorate for effective coordination and control, and that other staff and work can be placed anywhere as the work will be mostly cross-directorate.

Level of work

The second issue in directorate structure is how work is divided between levels within a directorate: the vertical rather than the horizontal dimension of structure. Questions not explicitly considered in early discussions of agency organization were the expected level of work output of a directorate, and levels of work within the directorate (see the model of levels of commissioning work in Chapter 3). These questions do need to be considered if we are to understand some problems which arise and to develop solutions. An example is how to organize management structure for different types of locality working: what level of work should be undertaken by locality managers or teams, and which model of 'decentralization' should be adopted? The main levels of work issues are:

- What is the level of output expected of the directorate and the level of work of the director role?
- Are there posts at appropriate levels below the director and people in the posts to allow the director to operate at the level required?
- Does the level of work capacity of the person appointed to the post match the level of work of the post?
- Is the level of work of all the directorates the same?
- Are directorates in fact operating, for whatever reason, at a lower level than they should be?

There are few organizations which do not have to grapple at some time with issues of the levels of work of their divisional groupings, the levels of work of posts in a management structure within a division, and the capability of people appointed to these posts. Further discussion of these issues can be found in Jaques (1989) and Stamp (1989). Levels of work within directorates are also important for constructing effective matrix structures and teams.

We noted earlier two opposing views of the importance of directorate grouping and formal organization. To date there is not enough evidence to judge whether a particular type of structure is best for specific purposes or circumstances, or what accounts for the differences, apart from the initial views of the chief executive. Neither is there evidence to judge how important directorate structure is to agency cost-effectiveness, with or without effective cross-directorate coordination. However, it is clear that whichever way an agency groups work and staff in directorates, it must have cross-directorate working arrangements – we now consider what these are and how to make them work.

Cross-directorate coordination

Most purchasing managers and their staff work in project teams. Most members of the team have a 'dual accountability' to the project team leader/manager, and to their 'home' manager. Staff not in teams may find themselves working for, or assigned to, a manager in another directorate. The two main cross-directorate working arrangements in purchasing organizations are project teams and posts with dual accountability to two managers in different directorates. This section describes these two aspects of 'matrix structure' and considers how to make such arrangements work.

Box 12.2

Matrix structure: an organization combining line management with project team management, where team members have a dual accountability to their line manager and to a project manager.

Both dual accountability and project teams may be temporary (e.g. a time-limited working party or a three-month 'secondment') or permanent (e.g. regular meetings of the directorate team, or 'dual reporting' in a job description). The arrangements also differ in their degree of formality – in terms of whether, or how much, they are specified. The art and skill of management is to decide how much to specify and agree, and how much to leave open.

Dual accountability: the first element of matrix structure

A man cannot serve two masters

Men and women in modern organizations have proved this Portuguese proverb to be wrong. Working for two bosses is a necessary and successful element of purchasing organization structure – as long as people are clear which manager is accountable for what and the authority of each. However, some agencies use the terms 'outposting', 'attachment', 'secondment', 'dual reporting', and many other terms to describe the same or different arrangements for staff management and accountability to managers in different directorates. This often leads to confusion in a three-party relationship, which is an inherently problematic relationship, and which goodwill only overcomes if the arrangement is temporary.

One source of problems can be reporting to two managers at different levels. Agencies have different posts with dual accountability, each post set up to do work at a different level. Typically people in such posts are accountable to either two directors or two deputy or assistant directors (e.g. the Financial Planner in Brent and Harrow agency (Appendix 2), who is accountable to the Financial Planner (Brent) in the Finance Directorate and to the Harrow Assistant Commissioning Director). Problems can arise when the person is accountable to a manager in one directorate who is at a different level to a manager in another directorate (e.g. a post accountable to a chief executive and to an assistant director; or to a director and to an assistant director in another directorate).

Often the dual accountability arrangement is only for the staff member's involvement in a project team, and describes his or her accountability to the project team leader and to the 'home' line manager (discussed below).

Problems and solutions: agency policy

Most managers have experienced problems when they have 'jointly managed' someone. Most have learnt that the meaning of terms such as 'secondment' and 'outposting' is not self-evident, that people understand different things by these terms, and that some description and specification is necessary. The issues are:

- how to decide whether staff on a *short-term* 'secondment' to a project team need a formal agreement about dual accountability to the project team leader and to the seconding manager;
- whether to take a risk and assume that a *verbal agreement* of the details between the parties is sufficient;
- how much *detail* to give in a written description of the arrangements.

One of the common problems is the staff member not being able to decide priority between work allocated by both managers. The solution to this and to other issues is for the agency to have an agreed standard set of arrangements. This is an acceptable balance between not specifying arrangements and each manager having to agree and specify his or her own arrangements. It also ensures that the agency has a consistent approach which everyone understands.

These dual accountability policies should cover: the authority each manager needs in relation to the staff member, to meet his or her accountability (e.g. to assign work up to x hours per week); the amount and period of time for which the staff manager is working for the 'non-home' or line manager (e.g. full-time for three months, or part-time, two days a week, for an indefinite period). Some organizations also define different arrangements for accountability to managers working at different levels, and whether the staff member is working directly for the 'borrowing' manager or more closely with that manager's staff, as a colleague.

The fundamental principle is that all should be clear as to who is the manager of the staff member, what this means, and the authority and expectations of the other manager. (Appendix 3 in Briefing Paper No. 5 for North West Thames agencies describes 'outposting', 'attachment', 'secondment', and 'dual accountability' to help agencies define a standard set of arrangements.)

Some work and staff should be managed entirely within one directorate; other work and staff are inherently cross-directorate. One innovation in purchasing agency organization is forming a separate 'pool' of staff who always work on cross-directorate projects. Special management arrangements for these staff are required, such as one permanent manager who is responsible for their support and development.

Project teams: the second element of matrix structure

All agencies have tasks or programmes spanning two or more directorates and use project teams to coordinate each task. This is the most common coordination and integration mechanism in purchasing organizations, and may also involve staff from other organizations, such as a local authority or region, for some or all of the life of the project. Project teams are formed where there is a need for:

- clear accountability for the results of work which spans directorates or departments;
- creative ideas or proposal generation, involving inputs from different disciplines;
- control, e.g. implementation of a project to schedule involving different contributions (IT implementation, moving base, etc.).

There are many varieties of project team. Directors form project teams using staff from other directorates. Staff can be members of one or more project teams, as well as of their 'home (directorate) team' (e.g. when 'attached' rather than 'seconded' to a project: the more projects they are members of, the less they can contribute to each and to 'home' directorate work; they end up in meetings all the time, with too much paperwork). In addition, project teams can be made up of staff with different levels of capability, as well as of staff with different accountability and time allocation to the project leader (e.g. seconded to the project full-time for a limited period, outposted, attached or a department subordinate of the project leader). As a general rule, the greater the mix, the more difficult it is for the project leader to achieve his or her objectives.

Types of project team

These types can be defined according to the accountability and authority of the project leader or manager and of the 'home' or line manager, such as a director. For simplicity the following four definitions of type of project team assume that all members of the team are there on the same basis – often teams involve members with different accountabilities to the project leader.

- *'Coordinated project teams'*. In these teams the balance of authority is with directors or their managers below them: directors retain managerial authority, but project coordinators have 'monitoring and coordinating' authority to negotiate staffing, schedules and changes of plan with directors where necessary. The project coordinators link the work of the team with other teams and higher management.
- *'Overlay matrix team'*. In these there is an equal balance of authority between directors and project leader. Project members have dual accountability, and active involvement with both the project and 'home' directorate work (e.g. 'Task forces').
- *'Secondment Team'*. Here the balance of authority is with the project leader. The 'home' directorate ensures professional updating and standards of the project team member, who is seconded, often full-time for a temporary period, to the project, and the project leader takes on most management responsibilities. A variation is where a director is the project leader, drawing on staff seconded or attached to the project from other directorates.
- *'Contracted team'*. The project leader 'buys' staff from other directorates, or from outside the agency. The project leader does not have management responsibilities, and staff in the project are there under contract.

Some project teams are a mixture. An agency's matrix management structure will have a number of each of these types of team. It is sometimes necessary to distinguish core and associate team members, and to agree the length of time for which temporary members are to be seconded (Øvretveit 1993b). Box 12.3 lists some of the more common problems in project teams which are poorly organized.

Box 12.3   Common problems in project teams

These include:

Inefficiency: too much time in meetings, unclear accountability, poor staff time allocation, too much paperwork. Poorly chaired meetings and poor project leadership.

Conflict between managers: project manager needs staff time, but line manager needs staff for departmental work.

Stress and insecurity: conflicting priorities for the project leader, who often has departmental responsibilities as well, or for the team member.

Unclear responsibilities and accountabilities: for line managers where the matrix is imposed without their involvement – losing power as well as staff time.

Project drift: where there is not sufficient oversight of project leaders – accountability of project to one point or group.

All purchasers have part of their organization with a traditional hierarchy for routine work (e.g. GP payments/registration), and organize other work through project teams. Project teams or 'matrix management' are already a way of life for many purchasing staff, some of whom feel that the question of which directorate their manager is in is fairly irrelevant. Certainly many purchasing staff will need to be able to work in, or lead, project teams and judge priorities and time allocations to different projects. In the first two years, senior managers in the North West Thames agencies underestimated the staff development and organizational arrangements which were needed to make project teams successful. It became clear that staff needed specific skills to work in this way, and had to be selected for their ability to work in these flexible structures. Their managers often did not recognize the time which their staff needed away from their 'directorate work', and that project work could take priority.

It was not long before the traditional solutions of late nights and weekend work were not enough as both project work and directorate work increased in the agencies. Chief executives and directors had to set priorities to reduce some of the conflicting demands, and began to specify secondment and other formal arrangements. In time agencies revised their original informal approach and recognized that project teams had to be carefully structured and that they needed a variety of types of team for different types of projects.

Project leader skill development and role definition

Probably more than anything else, the success of a project depends on the ability of the project team leader to form a team and make it work.

Usually interpersonal skills are more important than technical skills for project leaders, even in highly technical projects. As well as training for project management, project leaders need a clear brief, or to know how to develop one and get it agreed. For any sizeable project, they need a clear statement of their role, and authority and accountability in relation to other team members. This can be specified using one or more of the types of dual accountability listed above. In addition, performance reviews should include their work as project team leaders and their results. Project leaders looking for practical and quick guidance will find the documents on project management available from the NHS ME Resource Management Programme especially helpful (e.g. *Milestone Management*).

Box 12.4   Conditions for matrix structures to be successful

Does your purchasing organization have these? Which does it need to avoid problems or deal with current problems? Which are not likely to produce benefits for the time invested?

- Clear *project brief*, expected outcomes, milestones and time targets.
- Defined *project leader role*: their responsibilities, accountability and authority.
- Match authority (or power) to accountability.
- Clarity about any *change* to line managers' role: their responsibilities, accountability and authority.
- Involve *line managers* in deciding the general approach and specific standard arrangements.
- Ensure that performance *appraisal and reward* systems reinforce the responsibilities of project leaders and project members.
- Avoid having a project member who is the manager of the project leader.
- Avoid *mixing* staff working at different levels in one project unless the project leader is experienced, skilled and capable.
- Agree the *time* allocation of each project team member, and how to deal with work priority conflicts.
- Define *ground rules* and procedures for different types of project teams (especially when other organizations take part).
- Criteria and *guidelines* for when to set up and finish a project team, and which type for which tasks.
- Ways to ensure all project leaders and project team members know who their *manager* is and how their performance is assessed.
- Sufficient and appropriate *training* for project members, line managers and project leaders (especially in chairing meetings, leading teams and conflict resolution).
- *Overall* structure and process to manage and coordinate project teams (e.g. top team reviews).

Identifying opportunities for cross-working

A final arrangement for coordination to be mentioned here is staff with a responsibility to identify opportunities for cross-directorate working, and to make proposals for arrangements for collaboration, better communications or specific projects. Purchaser chief executives and directors have this responsibility, with purchaser boards and meetings being the main process for identifying cross-directorate issues. Boards can often make more use of critical path methods to identify how projects relate, oversee progress and set priorities.

In addition, staff in corporate development or other support directorates are well positioned to identify overlaps or opportunities for cross-directorate working, and need to have this task as an explicit responsibility. Purchasing managers need to encourage staff to identify work which overlaps with, or relates to, other directorates' work, and to make it easy for them to liaise with others working on similar issues to save time. This requires that staff have some understanding of the work of other directorates and of the projects in progress at any time.

Summary: formalization without fossilization

Chief executives and directors in integrated purchasing agencies are paying more attention to coordination as they recognize that an agency alone is no guarantee that DHA and FHSA work is integrated when it needs to be. (Appendix 5 outlines how agencies can judge how well they are integrating and coordinating work and staff.) Purchasing managers need to be able to choose and define the particular working arrangement they need. They will need to specify certain arrangements, such as dual accountability, project leader roles and types of project teams. Rather than constraining flexibility, specification defines the limits and expectations and this allows staff to apply their skills more freely within the defined area.

This is not to suggest that everything should be defined, but that each purchasing organization should have, for example, five to ten standard arrangements and protocols for dual accountability, project leadership and project team working. Managers can then call upon a standard arrangement which all understand: it is not sufficient to assume that all know what is meant by 'matrix working', 'attachment' and other terms, or that 'people will work it out as they go'. Such arrangements are central to the work and success of purchasing, and purchasing managers cannot afford the misunderstandings, conflict, duplication and time-wasting that often happens when these arrangements are not carefully defined.

The chapter now turns to the second coordination issue: how to ensure that the many projects under way in a purchasing organization are themselves coordinated, whether they are within or across directorates.

Cross-project coordination

We must be able to see how it all fits together, and work at making sure it does.
We must construct an organization that keeps highlighting the links to us when we do not see the links.

(Jenny Griffiths, Chief Executive, Hertfordshire Health Agency)

Organizing for synergy: how agencies add value by coordination

Hertfordshire commissioning agency had four projects in progress, all of which overlapped: decisions made in each affected decisions made in all the others. Each project spanned disciplines and departments, and coordinating one project was no easy task. It was even more difficult to ensure that the four projects were coordinated in relation to each other, especially as the agency had no experience in this area or structures for doing so. It is common for other purchasers to have 15 to 30 major cross-directorate projects and project teams working at any one time. Many deal with overlapping issues, which also overlap with tasks and projects being undertaken within directorates. This work has to be coordinated to avoid duplication and to maximize potential synergy.

This section elaborates these points by taking the Hertfordshire example and showing how the four projects overlapped: projects on locality purchasing, health investment strategy, GP fundholding and integrating contract management. We noted earlier that many agency tasks were interconnected – this section shows why, and how agencies can ensure that they recognize the connections and coordinate different projects in relation to each other. Failure to do so means lost opportunities, wasted work and not realizing the potential mutually reinforcing effect which can come from relating initiatives. It can also lead to competition between project leaders, for example to be the first to make decisions, which set the options for others – project teams tend to do this rather than passing the decision to higher management to assess the consequences for all projects.

Recognizing connections

The agency we take as an example identified the following key issues and work for the next 12 months.

- Managing within a purchasing budget: keeping within cash limits by ensuring that provider activity does not exceed the finance to pay for it.
- Improving relations with providers from 'adversarial' to 'partnership' and recognizing mutual dependence.
- 'Getting alongside' GP fundholders and developing collaborative purchasing.
- Bringing non-fundholders into purchasing by fundholding or an agency alternative.
- Developing a local dimension to commissioning.

- Developing a health investment strategy.
- Integrating all contracts, contract management, budgets and accounts from three health authorities into one agency management system.
- Integrated information strategy and systems development.
- Integrated approach to quality, with cost of poor quality and practice variations on the agenda.

The connections between the tasks are apparent just from looking at the list: the progress of work in each affects progress in others, both in time and in closing off or opening up options for another area. If we now note the outlines of the vision which the agency was developing we can see the links more clearly. The vision in broad terms was of a primary and community care provider focus, with primary care led purchasing of secondary care. In addition a *shift* of provision from secondary to primary and community care (and self-care), and of resources from treatment towards care, prevention and promotion.

The connections are as follows. Steps towards this vision involve investment in primary care, which in turn requires control of secondary care, to shift finance. This in turn requires close cooperation with GPs (who will benefit from the primary care investment) and with social services. All can be helped by a joint DHA–FHSA approach, but one which is also locally sensitive. Investment in primary care has to target the populations most in need, which requires that these are identified, and that there is political support for shifts in finance and services.

Linking work programmes

The four initial work programmes in the agency were designed to move towards this vision. The following shows how the programmes related, and how important it was for the agency to coordinate them.

A *framework for locally based purchasing*
This project was to define a framework for:

- GP liaison (fundholders and non-fundholders);
- involving other primary health care team members;
- community involvement in commissioning;
- outlet for information;
- involving the voluntary sector.

It was politically necessary to show exactly how the new agency would be more locally sensitive.

Developing a health investment strategy
The strategy makes the vision tangible by defining end results and the steps to get there. The health investment strategy was to drive the development

of primary care, reduce secondary care expenditure and redirect resources to areas of greater need. Building this strategy and continually refining it in the future was to be influenced by locality arrangements and proposals from the third project.

A new approach to GP fundholding and a new role for the agency with many GP fundholders
The agency had to establish new relations with GP fundholders (one of the highest number of fundholders in the UK) and with all GPs. It had to convince GPs that the new agency recognized and wanted purchasing to be driven by GPs – whether as fundholders or an agency equivalent. This project had to work out how to coordinate primary care purchasing (not just GPs) to everyone's benefit, and to align with the agency's strategic vision, which included a central role for primary care. Close FHSA–DHA collaboration was needed to agree:

- a shared policy towards fundholding;
- one or more agency models for other GPs;
- an outline of how to develop cooperation between GPs in their purchasing role;
- an approach to primary care development, which recognized and made the most of primary care purchasing.

The agency's aim to develop primary care provision had to link with its approach to fundholding. Showing this link to GPs helped the agency to convince GPs of its change in approach and mutual dependence, and to establish a partnership in purchasing. All three work programmes connected with the fourth.

Integrating contract management
Getting more from the declining DHA purchasing budgets was essential to keeping within cash limits, and to redirecting finance into primary care development. The new agency could get more from the available finance by using its extra purchasing power, and from the economies of a common agency. A key step was a single contracting process, specifications and contract management (including ECR management). This could also save providers money and time, and simplify relations with social services. The work of untangling contracts and establishing new relations had to be in concert with the other three programmes.

Organizing to ensure mutual reinforcement

This example shows the potential for projects to reinforce each other. It also shows the potential for waste and double messages if the programmes were not coordinated and mutually adjusted. The agency had to ensure that each programme leader (and their programme teams) kept in touch with the others and made continual adjustments to ensure that their proposals and actions were in tune with or contributed to the others, and that the chief executive and board kept an oversight of the links between these work programmes, and between these and other issues.

This is an example of something common to all purchasing organizations. Relating different initiatives and organizing to do so as a matter of course is one of the purposes of integrated purchasing agencies. It is how integrated agencies add value to what would otherwise be isolated projects. To do so calls for good communications, without overburdening everyone with information which they did not need.

Synergy-enhancing mechanisms

The example illustrates a general point: that one of the purposes of a commissioning agency is to identify and define the priority tasks, formulate them into programmes of work, and then work to relate different programmes. The interrelation of the four initial tasks (and of them to others) was not just something to be borne in mind. Rather it was something which had to be managed to make the outcome of one project mesh with others and the end result greater than the sum of the four projects. The future success of purchasing organizations depends on how well they identify and progress programmes in a mutually reinforcing way. They must organize to add value in this way. In short, purchasers have to organize to MaRRI ('mutual reinforcement of related initiatives'). Purchasers do this in two ways. First, they ensure that their staff:

• recognize the links between work programmes;
• communicate with others working on related tasks;
• continually adjust their programmes to take account of directions or decisions emerging from other programmes.

Second, they organize to ensure that the projects link automatically, rather than by chance – because staff members working on one project might discover that the decisions another project was making would make much of their work irrelevant. Earlier we considered project management and dual accountability, and how to coordinate staff and tasks within one project. The issue we just considered is how to ensure that all projects and teams are coordinated, and that the interrelations are recognized. The main mechanisms for doing this are:

• a vision shared by all staff of the future pattern of services;
• chief executives, directors and board meetings scanning and updating on programmes;
• critical paths and cross-project linking diagrams and tracking systems;
• project leaders meeting other project leaders;
• support staff with a responsibility to alert others to unrecognized links and overlaps;
• communications systems which link projects and show points of overlap and milestones.

Summary: evaluating purchaser integration and coordination

This section draws on this and the previous chapter to give a framework for purchasing managers, an authority or an external body to assess how well an agency has integrated DHA and FHSA work and staff. It summarizes five areas to consider and criteria for judging performance in this respect. Appendix 5 gives a checklist based on this summary.

The ultimate value of an integrated public health purchasing organization is to be judged by whether it achieves greater health gain, at less cost, and meets stakeholders' requirements better than do two separate authority organizations. Short-term aspects of agency performance, which are thought to contribute to their ability to achieve longer-term aims are: whether an agency combines previously separate DHA and FHSA activities, where there is advantage to doing so, and in a cost-effective way (how to evaluate integration); how well an agency establishes cross-directorate and cross-project working, where this is necessary (how to evaluate coordination).

Evaluating integration and coordination therefore involves making judgements about whether, and how well, an agency identifies work and tasks which should be shared or combined across directorates and projects. It also involves judging how well these are combined. As we saw in Chapter 11, evidence is only just emerging as to which arrangements or approaches are the most successful. Consequently the following framework is based on what evidence there is, but also on the arguments and issues examined in this and the previous chapter. The criteria are based on assumptions that the mechanisms listed are necessary for effective integration, and that integration and coordination are critical to overall agency performance.

Strategies, plans and timetables

A clear and agreed strategy and timetable makes it possible for staff to see how their efforts relate to those of others in different directorates and teams, and is itself an important coordinating mechanism.

Evaluation criteria/questions
• Do all agency non-executives and staff have a shared view of the purpose of an integrated agency?
• Do all agency non-executives and staff have a shared vision of the service pattern which the agency is trying to create?
• Does the agency have a schedule of projects, showing the critical phases of each and the links between them?
• Do different staff relating to different external bodies share and represent the same understanding of the current agency service strategy?

Directorates

Evaluation criteria/questions
• Is the agency moving to, or continually reviewing, the need for shared base(s)?

- Does the agency have criteria and guidelines for deciding whether an FHSA and DHA activity should be combined?
- Have the authorities reviewed the need for a director to act as an FHSA general manager?
- Do all directors report to both authorities?
- Are all agency staff contracts with the two (or more) authorities, rather than with one authority?
- Does the agency review its directorate structure and boundaries in relation to its strategy and purpose at sufficiently frequent intervals?
- Are there reviews of the proportion of FHSA and DHA work managed by each director within each directorate?

Cross-directorate structure

Whichever way an agency groups work into directorates, cross-directorate management structures and processes (i.e. 'matrix management') are necessary for many tasks (e.g. needs assessment).

Evaluation criteria/questions
Linking
- Does the agency have a sufficiently clear and shared definition of 'primary care commissioning'?
- Are there effective structures and processes for linking primary care commissioning to secondary care commissioning work?
- Are there effective structures and processes for linking strategy to primary and secondary care contracting?

Dual accountability
- Does the agency have standard statements of dual accountability arrangements, which define the two managers' accountability and authority?
- Do managers specify dual accountability where necessary using these standard agency statements?
- Are methods adequate for defining the work priorities for staff in dual accountability positions?

Project teams
- Does the agency have standard statements of (a) different types of project teams, and guidelines for when to use which type; (b) project team working procedures, including when and how to disband the team; (c) defined project team leader roles for each type of team?
- Is there an updated list of teams working on projects of over one month in length?
- Is this list reviewed regularly by the board?

Cross-project coordination

Agencies need to ensure that project teams relate to each other where there is overlap. Agencies need structure and processes to identify these overlaps and to ensure coordination.

Evaluation criteria/questions
- Do chief executives, directors and board meetings review all projects together for overlap, at sufficiently regular intervals?
- Does the agency board use critical paths to identify how projects relate, oversee progress and set priorities?
- Are there effective ways for project leaders to recognize overlap with other projects, and ensure that they coordinate when they do?
- Does the agency define support-staff responsibility to alert others to unrecognized links and overlaps?

Staff training for integration and coordination

Many purchasing managers underestimate the skills staff need to take part in or lead projects. People need to understand these new ways of working, and contribute to improving them.

Evaluation criteria/questions
- Is ability to work in or lead project teams one selection criterion for new staff?
- Are there sufficient resources invested in training for project leaders?
- Do all staff have training in project team working?
- Do staff who need to, get training in the different standard agency arrangements for dual accountability and project teams?
- Is the quality of this training regularly reviewed?
- Do all staff have training about the work of different directorates?
- Do staff know how to prioritize between project and directorate tasks?

Conclusions

Organization is a means for pursuing a purpose and undertaking work. This chapter emphasizes the need for purchasing agencies to review organization as staff and non-executives develop a clearer and shared view of purpose. Such a view influences how staff and work are organized, but at the same time the particular way they are organized leads staff to form a particular view of purpose.

If the purpose of public health purchasing is cost-effective health gain then this purpose is often more easily pursued by organizing primary and secondary commissioning work together. Where this is difficult to do, organizations undertaking primary and secondary commissioning need to co-operate to reduce their costs and to coordinate their purchasing. There are many ways of sharing work and staff and of organizing cross-purchaser teams for work which is common to both.

In most areas of the UK there are advantages to forming an integrated commissioning agency or authority. Forming one organization does not ensure that primary and secondary commissioning work and staff are integrated, and there are tasks which do not need to be. One organization gives a framework within which authority non-executive and commissioning managers can bring together staff and systems to realize the benefits of integrating primary and secondary commissioning.

This chapter emphasizes that successful integration and effective organization depend on developing a shared view of purpose and of health care, and on attention to structures and processes. Some NHS purchasers initially neglected formal structure in a concern to mark the radical difference between the new purchasing organization and the old pre-reform authorities. However, moving beyond hierarchy does not mean ignoring structure: quite the reverse. The best service industries know that successful flexible working requires attention to team structures and the more complex lateral management arrangements.

The chapter described four areas for attention in forming and improving the organization of integrated commissioning agencies or authorities. The first was the role of non-executives and the purpose of the purchasing board. The second was how to group functions within directorates. The third was the cross-directorate coordination structures of project teams and dual accountability. The fourth was structures and processes for coordinating projects.

The chapter noted differences between how agencies grouped work in directorates, especially the work of primary care commissioning. These differences may not be significant if agencies are able to develop effective cross-directorate working. Many agency tasks are interconnected, and ensuring that these interconnections are recognized is central to the purpose of an agency. Because coordination is so important, agencies have to organize to make sure that it happens. Some agencies take a risk and assume that staff know what is meant by 'matrix management', or will 'pick up' how to work effectively in project teams 'as they go'. Exhortations to work across boundaries and banning talk of formal structure and accountability do not help staff to change the way in which they work, or to cope with the problems that arise.

In the first year, agencies underestimated the time and attention needed to set up and train staff to work effectively across directorates: there was an assumption that people would automatically take to 'flexible working' in 'matrix structures'. This was one of the main weaknesses of initial agency organization: the chapter described the two key structures of matrix organization and how to make them work – dual accountability and project teams. It argued for a balanced approach to specifying arrangements – that formalization does not mean fossilization. It proposed defining a few key cross-directorate working arrangements and protocols which everyone could draw on, where appropriate, including types of project teams and the meaning of attachment, secondment and outposting.

Key points

- DHA–FHSA commissioning agencies are no more cost-effective than other arrangements, unless they have effective organization to realize the benefits of combining primary and secondary health commissioning.

- Effective organization follows from a clear and shared view about purpose and strategy, but to form such a view agencies need a structure in the first place. Agencies need frequently to review their organization in relation to their purpose and strategy, in order to develop both.
- A common vision and plans are wasted if there is not the organization to ensure that a common approach is carried through in contracting and in provider relations.
- Forming one agency for DHA and FHSA work will not, of itself, ensure that work is integrated: agencies need to organize and encourage staff to identify work which should be combined or coordinated across authorities, directorates and projects.
- All agencies are concerned with bringing together DHA and FHSA work which was previously separate ('integration'), and with how to organize work which spans two or more directorates ('coordination'). Whichever way an agency groups work and staff in directorates, it must have cross-directorate working arrangements.
- The range of work in combined primary and secondary purchasing calls for a hybrid service organization, where some staff are part of a traditional hierarchy (e.g. for routine GP payments/registration work), some only work in time-limited programmes or project teams, and some work in directorates and cross-directorate project teams.
- Clear lines of management and accountability do not detract from or weaken flexible working but are essential to making it happen. Agencies underestimated the training and investment needed to make matrix structures work.
- New skills and attitudes to cross-directorate and project team working also help staff to establish new ways of working and relationships with outside organizations.
- Many projects deal with overlapping issues, which also overlap with tasks and projects being undertaken within directorates. This work has to be coordinated to avoid duplication and to maximize potential synergy.
- The future success of purchasing organizations depends in part on how well they identify and progress programmes in a mutually reinforcing way. Organizing to do this is one way in which to add value to the NHS and serve the populations.

 **13** **The future for health purchasing: financing, competition and values**

Introduction

Public health purchasers are increasingly purchasing health services from private providers, and establishing joint ventures with private and public organizations. In the UK, the differences between public and private purchasing are becoming fewer. Could public health purchasing be done by a private organization, as it is in many other countries? Is this the only way to transform purchasing into a service? Will people buy more of their own health care? How will changes in social values affect, or be affected by, health purchasing?

This chapter looks to the future by considering the implications for purchasers of changes to the financing, management and ownership of providers and of purchasers. It describes the new organizational arrangements which public and private purchasers are creating. It argues that the distinctions between public and private, and between purchaser and provider, are becoming less useful for describing or developing health purchasing in the 1990s. It examines new sources of finance for public purchasing, the question of competition between purchasers, and new types of inter-organizational relationships and partnerships. The second part of the chapter considers how these changes relate to increasing individualism and consumerism, and the implications for preserving public health and NHS principles of comprehensiveness, equality and equity.

The purpose of the chapter is not to argue for 'privatizing' public health systems. Rather, it is to equip public health purchasers with an understanding of the changes, of the options for the future and of the arguments for and against different mixtures of public and private financing and ownership. Staff and managers who have spent their lives working in public health systems and are committed to the ethics and values of such systems are sometimes blind to the alternatives. By refusing to recognize the changes taking place, or even to consider different ways forward, they unwittingly hasten the changes they oppose and lose influence over future directions. It is only by objectively assessing the options that ways can be found to lead political, social and technical changes, and to preserve and promote the principles of public health systems in new forms.

Even in countries which prohibit private health services there is a thriving alternative system. In China there is a large informal economy for both conventional Western and traditional health services and medicines, as there was and is in other communist countries. Nationalized systems like those in the UK and Nordic countries have always coexisted with parallel private purchasing and provision (WHO 1994). In addition, there have always been hybrid private–public services. One of the strengths of the NHS is the general medical practitioner service, which is made up of independent GP contractors, most of whom operate as private business partnerships. It is certain that the NHS would never have been established if a salaried service was the only alternative for general practitioners in private practice. This is not making a virtue out of a political necessity: it can be argued that the strength of the UK GP service is owing to this public–private partnership, and that it is unlikely that a salaried public GP service would have been as successful. Thus, even to describe the UK system as a parallel public and private system is inaccurate – it is a complex combination, and this was before GP fundholders and provider trusts.

This is not to suggest that, in the broad sweep of history, we will see public health systems as a temporary post-Second World War aberration. Rather, many countries have moved into a phase of mixing the best of public and private, dissolving the distinctions and managing the mistakes which inevitably occur. We are moving into a new era in health organization and management, and purchasing managers have a key role in shaping the new health systems.

Beyond the public–private distinction: public ends and private means?

We ask ourselves, 'What is the core activity of the NHS?' It is not the management of hospitals – that is essentially a secondary activity. The core activity of the NHS is to secure a universal health care system available on the basis of clinical need rather than on the basis of ability to pay.
(Stephen Dorrell, financial secretary to the UK Treasury, presenting the government's 'Private Finance Initiative' for mixed public–private partnerships, now possible without Treasury agreement for capital projects up to £10 million)

My company was recently offered the contract to manage in its entirety, including accident and emergency, a city centre general hospital, by an authority

whose faith in social medicine, free at the point of delivery, is unchallenged and unswerving.
>   (Charles Auld, Managing Director of General Healthcare Group, referring to Stockholm County Council at the 1993 Welsh Association of Health Authorities and Trusts conference)

This section of the chapter considers the arguments for and against fully public systems, and whether private providers or purchasers can effectively pursue public health goals.

Means and ends

Part of the debate about the NHS in the late 1980s concerned whether, or how well, private organizations could pursue public ends. This debate is resurfacing again in the UK and in Europe, after more experience of contracting private organizations for both support services and clinical services.

One view is that non-public organizations cannot pursue public ends, regardless of whether they are not-for-profit or for-profit privately owned. To ensure public aims are achieved, it is necessary to have organizations in public ownership, with management under public direction and control and accountable to higher-level state bodies, with staff employed by public bodies. This view holds that regulation and contracts cannot ensure that private organizations properly pursue public ends, and that their private purposes will always override public interests when the inevitable conflicts of interest occur.

Another view is that whether public ends are better served by public or private organizations is purely a question of efficiency: 'Issues of finance should be considered separately from those of ownership and management. Public financing does not directly imply, nor require, public sector management and ownership, and each could co-exist independently of the other' (Lee 1992). This view gathers support from examples where public ownership, control and management has not prevented public bodies from misusing public finance, and from weaknesses in accountability and control of quasi-public organizations like NHS trusts, GP fundholders, and, for that matter, commissioning authorities.

There are two ethical and moral questions: is it right for private organizations to profit from people's ill health, and is it right that private providers should make profit out of public finance, especially if all public providers are privatized? Some argue that the issues are different for not-for-profit organizations and for-profit companies, and for individual private practitioners rather than larger companies.

For services other than clinical health services, much of the debate has been limited to issues of economy and efficiency (see the discussion in Chapter 2 of 'contracting out'). For such non-clinical services one argument is that the question of ownership and profit is irrelevant: the key question is which provider is most efficient and gives the best value for money. The moral and ethical issues of profiting from ill health can be more easily excluded from the debate about non-clinical services. Some argue that, in fact, it is unethical not to use private non-clinical services if they are more efficient, as the savings can be used to buy more clinical care. This argument is also applied to clinical services by supporters of private health care.

There is a third dimension to the debate about public or private means for public ends. In addition to, or perhaps underlying, the moral and economic dimensions there is the political dimension. One aspect of this is public workers' opposition to privatization and competition. In 1990 the NHS employed one million people. In the Nordic countries and in other European countries such as Spain and Italy, national or local government is a major employer. Transferring some or all health provision into full private ownership and management means changing the pay and conditions of employment of a sizeable proportion of the nation's population. Most public sector unions oppose such changes on the grounds of likely unemployment, and that their members will, over time, get worse pay and conditions of employment, not withstanding the European Transfer of Undertakings Protection of Employment Regulations (1981).

The employment considerations lead us to the fourth dimension of the means–ends debate: the implications for a nation's economy of government withdrawal from the provision of health services through ownership and management. For governments wishing to reduce public spending, often to reduce public sector borrowing requirements, full or part privatization is an attractive option: it provides a one-off injection of private capital into the national treasury, can increase capital investment which would not be affordable from public funds and can reduce future borrowing requirements. However, the benefits may only be short term: loss of ownership and control can lead to higher expenditure in the long term. Much depends on the form of privatization and regulation, as can be seen from the privatization of utilities and other industries in the UK and Europe.

In the USA the notion that private organizations can be contracted to pursue public ends is simply not debated. The concern is that federal and state government organizations may expand, and this, by definition for most Americans, would mean inefficiency, unresponsiveness and a threat to freedom, constitutional rights and choice. The question of public ends and private means is more a cultural, historical and political issue than it is an issue of economic efficiency.

In the UK the debate about public or private means for pursuing public ends continues, but has moved on from the contracting out debates of the 1980s. There is renewed debate about what the public ends of both the NHS and the government are in relation to health, and an increasing recognition that the distinction between public and private is less important, in a number of senses. The UK has established quasi-independent providers in the form of self-governing trusts, and quasi-independent purchasing by GP fundholders. Both are considered part of the NHS, but neither is fully public or fully private. These changes and other legislation have made new private–public arrangements possible and more acceptable to the public and to NHS staff. We now consider the variety of types of financing, ownership and management arrangements being developed for purchasers and providers.

Public and private financing and ownership

What are the options for the future, given changing attitudes about private sector involvement in public health systems? The following account summarizes some of the options for ownership, control and financing of health purchasers and providers. We consider these in more detail in the section to follow.

The main options for ownership and control for *health providers* are:

- full public ownership and management control, including public employment of provider staff (e.g. pre-1990 NHS, most of the Spanish system, most of the health systems in the Nordic countries before 1991);
- quasi-independent public ownership and control (e.g. post-1993 NHS, with 96 per cent of providers as NHS trusts);
- private ownership and control, either for-profit or not-for-profit (e.g. North America).

The main options for *financing health providers* apply to capital and revenue finance to pay for the services which they provide. For paying for services, finance can be from public sources, from collective private sources, such as employers' schemes or private insurance schemes, or from individual patients paying directly. Capital can be from public or private sources or a mixture.

Similar options apply for the ownership and control of *purchasers*:

- full public ownership and control (e.g. NHS health authorities);
- quasi-public ownership and control (e.g. NHS GP purchasing funds);
- private ownership and control, for-profit or not-for-profit.

Finance for purchasing services, for either public or privately owned purchasers, can come from:

- public finance sources (e.g. taxation);
- collective private sources (e.g. employers, insurance companies);
- directly from individuals (e.g. part or whole payment).

Figure 13.1 summarizes the main options, which apply for both purchasing and providing health services.

We can see even from this simple summary that purchasers have to think beyond the public–private distinction, if only to understand what is already happening.

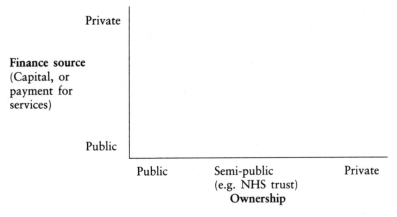

Figure 13.1 A summary of options for financing and ownership of purchasers and providers.

Purchaser financing and ownership

Society becomes more wholesome, more serene, spiritually healthier, if it knows its citizens have at the back of their consciousness the knowledge that not only themselves, but all of their fellows, have access, when ill, to the best that medical skills can provide.
(Nye Bevan 1948, on the founding of the UK NHS)

I am beginning, albeit reluctantly, to consider that alternative sources of finance in much greater amounts will be needed to be introduced into the health care system. The UK does not fall behind comparable countries in the proportion of national income devoted to publicly-provided health care but in the amount contributed by individuals privately or through insurance systems on top of this.
(Professor Chantler, Principal of the Medical Schools of Guy's and St Thomas's Hospitals, speech at BAMM annual conference)

In the UK there has always been private purchasing of private health care and, more recently, private purchasing of health services from NHS hospitals with 'private beds'. The 1990 NHS reforms introduced public purchasing of public and private health care. In this section of the chapter we consider sources of finance for public-owned and controlled purchasing bodies such as health authorities. We also consider questions of competition between purchasers, and of the ownership of purchasing organizations. UK health authority purchasers are having to consider whether to increase their purchasing finance from sources other than public allocations from national government taxation, and whether private purchasers or management teams could bid for contracts to purchase services using public finance. Does the argument that health providers do not need to be in public ownership and control also apply to purchasers?

Sources of purchasing finance

NHS health authorities and GP fundholders are allocated finance to purchase secondary health services out of national finance raised from taxation. Over the years, proposals have been put forward for raising finance from other sources to add to or replace public finance for health services. Here we consider alternative sources of finance for purchasing, rather than finance direct to providers from charging patients, or from selling health promotion or screening schemes to employers.

The main potential sources of future finance for public purchasing are one or a mixture of central or local taxation, private insurance and social insurance (usually by taxed salary payments or 'earmarked payroll taxation'). At present in the UK 82 per cent of NHS finance is from central taxation and 15 per cent from national insurance contributions (HPSSS 1991). The latter is not social insurance in the European sense because there is not a separate national insurance fund for health finance, and people do not have to pay contributions before they can get health services.

The main reasons for reconsidering financing out of central taxation in the UK is the increase in the demand for and costs of health services, together with the government's stated reluctance to increase taxation. It cannot be said, however, that the British public are unwilling to pay more tax to increase funding for health services – there has been little public debate and discussion of the options. Other reasons are the interests of the provider lobby, both NHS trusts and private providers, and of private insurers, although many of these interest groups propose schemes for direct financing of providers, rather than for increasing finance for public purchasing.

One option is to increase private insurance from the current 12 per cent population coverage, by encouraging those who can afford it to take out coverage or to make more use of their insurance. Generally, the British public do not make use of private insurance unless they are faced with a long wait and/or are self-employed (*Which?* 1992; Wiles and Higgins 1992). There are reports of GPs encouraging their patients with private insurance to make more use of their insurance. One way of increasing private insurance coverage is with tax incentives to individuals or employers. However, extending the tax exemption for people aged over 60 years to take out private health insurance to other public groups would introduce inequities and erode solidarity.

In 1993 a number of papers contributed to the debate about future financing of the NHS and health care in the UK. The Institute of Health Service Management reviewed a number of options, and concluded:

> Despite all the obvious advantages, general taxation must be reconsidered as the best option for funding health care. As a source of funding it does not appear to be delivering the likely optimum level of resources for the NHS. The major alternative would be either some form of social insurance or of local taxation.
>
> (IHSM 1993: 45)

The IHSM did not propose abolishing taxation, but suggested considering additional finance from extending private insurance, local taxation, 'top-up' insurance or payments to public purchasers, vouchers, or a health tax like national insurance or employer contributions in a payroll tax. The IHSM proposals imply that much of this finance would be for public purchasing, although the paper does not make the distinction between financing for purchasing and direct provider finance: for example, patient charges could be levied by purchasers or by providers.

Although suggesting a form of social insurance or local taxation the IHSM did not put forward specific recommendations, in part because, 'at present the NHS cannot answer the questions, is health care under-funded or is the money that is available being put to the best use?' (IHSM 1993: 27). There is an argument for not increasing public finance for health services until more is known about how the money is spent and to what benefit, but this may take some time. This argument does not apply to such a degree to increasing private purchasing, or government tax incentives to do so.

The National Association of Health Authorities and Trusts put forward a different view, arguing that a social insurance payroll tax would reduce employment, increase inflation by increasing prices and damage economic recovery and competitiveness (NAHAT 1993a). A qualified proposal was made to consider new charges, as long as it would not discourage patients and collection costs could be kept low. As with the IHSM proposals, distinctions were not made between finance for purchasing and finance direct to providers.

A more radical contribution to the debate came from the European Policy Forum, supported by a private health insurance company (Basset 1993), and can be considered reasonably representative of parts of the private health sector. It proposed increasing the role of private insurers by allowing them to act as purchasers using public funds, and to offer additional 'top-up' schemes to supplement a basic health coverage. People would be able to choose between competing purchasers, licensed and funded by 'district departments'. The proposals are similar to the more recent Dutch 'Simon proposals', which are a modification of the earlier 'Dekker 1988 proposals' (Maarse 1993).

Purchaser competition and ownership

Alongside the debate about financing in the UK, there are proposals to introduce competition between purchasers. In the UK at present the three main types of public health purchasers are not competing in a market for public finance. FHSAs do not compete with DHAs as they are financing bodies for national contracts with GPs. Competition could be introduced between DHA secondary and FHSA primary care purchasers for public finance. However, the arguments and evidence suggest that greater health gain is more likely to be achieved at a lower cost through closer collaboration or integration than through competition (see Chapters 11 and 12).

GP fundholders do not compete with DHAs for public purchasing finance for secondary health services: GPs are automatically allocated a fund from the DHA purchasing budgets if they can prove that they can manage a purchasing budget. In principle, competition could be introduced on a limited basis between these two types of public purchaser, especially if fundholders formed consortia for larger populations. One type of competition is purchasers 'bidding' to serve as purchasers for patient populations. A disadvantage is that if whole populations are transferred between purchasers, there are fewer incentives for the purchaser to pursue long-term health promotion programmes, even if the contracts are relatively long-term (e.g. 5 or 10 years). This disadvantage also applies to dividing off purchasing for some services and opening this to competition, for example by allowing GPs and HAs to compete for finance to purchase mental health or maternity services. Not only does this undermine long-term health promotion, it makes strategic market management even more difficult. There would appear to be more benefits for the population in increased public purchaser cooperation, as in 'shared purchasing' (Chapter 4) and in health authority cooperative strategic contracting (Chapter 6).

Similar and additional disadvantages arise if private purchasers are to compete for some, or all, public health purchasing finance. There are the two problems already mentioned: population transfer problems and lack of incentives for long-term programmes; and difficulties for private purchasers in integrating secondary and primary care purchasing, unless there are radical changes to the reimbursement system for GPs in the UK. These problems are not insurmountable technically, as proposals for purchaser competition in The Netherlands show, but the history and culture of the NHS and the political problems would make such a change unlikely.

There would have to be a convincing case that competitive incentives would produce efficiency savings to pay for the extra cost of administration, and the cost of reorganization. It is unlikely that private interests, even allied with some providers, could persuade the British public and Parliament that the right to choose a purchaser and a health plan would be beneficial. A less radical option is to retain public purchasing authorities and most staffing, but to let contracts for the management of a purchasing agency (Ham 1993b). However, there is little evidence that existing purchasing management skills in the private sector would improve current purchasing, or that private sector incentives would do so. It is by no means clear that this is the best solution to the problems of health purchasing in the UK.

Turning the tables: public purchasers undertaking private purchasing?

There would appear at present to be more disadvantages than advantages to private purchasers competing with public purchasers to act as purchasing agents for public health care. But could the reverse be of benefit: public purchasers managing private purchasing in addition to their existing public purchasing, or themselves establishing a 'top-up coverage' or quasi-private insurance scheme? Could this increase finance for health care and maintain equity?

Consider first the case for NHS public provider hospitals selling health care to the private sector and, specifically, selling NHS 'pay beds' to private insurers. The argument against is that doing so diverts NHS staff and facilities away from NHS patients to private patients. However, although there is some unease and active opposition among NHS staff and the public, the weight of opinion appears to be that the profits from and experience in providing private care increase the amount and quality of NHS services, if the schemes are carefully controlled and managed. The deciding factor is probably specialist medical consultants' interests, and the fact that pay beds do increase consultants' incomes and help to keep them within the NHS.

However, the issues for public providers offering private services are different to those for public purchasers undertaking private purchasing. First, what might the latter involve? Private health purchasing by health authorities or their commissioning agencies could involve acting as a purchasing agent for a private insurance company for some or all health services, and possibly also as a collection agent. The advantages for a private insurer would be that a public purchaser has expertise, information systems and easier access to NHS providers. It would also make dual financing and top-up options easier, especially if the commissioning agency acted as insurance collector. The arrangement could also be attractive to employers with large health plans. It could allow capital investment into purchasing from the private sector for information and administrative systems and a variety of joint ventures. Finally, this could lead to public health purchasers setting up private supplementary insurance schemes.

Although there are advantages, the disadvantages and political difficulties are apparent when we consider the differences between mixed provision and mixed purchasing. First, there is not the same political support for NHS purchasers undertaking private purchasing as there is for NHS providers undertaking private services: consultant support for the latter is strong, yet there are fewer and weaker political constituencies for the former. Political support could come from private insurers, allied with public and private providers viewing this as a way to increase provider financing. Second, there would not be the parliamentary support at present for legislative changes to allow public authorities or their agents to act as both public and private purchasers. The advantages are not clear and there is not the public support for such a change. Third, public purchaser capabilities and staff are currently fully stretched to deal with the NHS changes, and adding staff and resources would only partially ease the problems. Such changes may divert attention from, rather than assist, the more important tasks of improving information for more effective purchasing, hospital reconfiguration and developing primary care. Thus, mixed purchasing by a public body would appear unlikely, unless it became clear that it was an acceptable way for increasing finance for health services.

Summary: purchaser financing and competition

The trend in Europe and in North America is for national or local government to ensure a basic health coverage for the population, with a mixture of providers (public, private not-for-profit and private for-profit) and financed by taxation or a social insurance system; increase the scope for people to buy 'non-essential' health care which is not covered in the basic scheme, usually by paying for private insurance, although often using the same providers as for the basic scheme. In some senses this is the approach in the UK at present, with the NHS and 12 per cent of the population covered by private insurance, often as an insurance against long waiting or for 'hotel' options. With the increasing gap between demand and finance, the financing debate is likely to merge with the rationing debate, and commissioners will need to form a view about which services should be covered by a basic NHS scheme for health gain and equity reasons. Whether commissioners should also become collectors of finance or agents for top-up schemes is another issue which will merge with the debate about accountability, democracy and public involvement in purchasing.

There is a consensus that all options should be explored for increasing finance for health care in the UK. There is less consensus about whether any extra public finance should go to public purchasers or private purchasers, or direct to providers. Most proposals and debates are rightly cautious about any significant changes to financing out of general taxation. It is a cost-effective method of collection and allows equitable distribution and cost-control, even if it ties health expenditure to national economic policy and public borrowing considerations. Further, we know little about whether existing finance is used cost-effectively, or whether the problem is an absolute funding shortfall or just specific shortfalls for certain needs and services.

There is an argument for becoming clearer about cost-effectiveness before increasing public finance, but also a counter-argument that increasing purchaser competition could speed our understanding of cost-effectiveness by giving purchasers more incentives to prove that they purchased cost-effective services. On balance the arguments are against large-scale public–private purchaser competition, against internal public purchaser competition, and for increased purchaser collaboration, especially between primary and secondary health purchasers.

Some limited changes could increase finance for health services. Increasing national insurance contributions by adding specific deductions for defined health care programmes (e.g. waiting list reductions for a range of treatments) might gain public support. This method would share costs between employers and people in employment, and could avoid increased public sector borrowing. Encouraging top-up private insurance for non-essential health care could be done without seriously undermining equity, and without extending tax incentives which would undermine solidarity. Experiments could be undertaken to test private purchasers' ability to purchase for specific services. Finally, there is a need to increase private capital investment into public facilities, in ways which retain planning controls to avoid wasteful duplication and competition. It is to such joint ventures and provider financing and management that we now turn.

Provider financing, ownership and competition

Every year some 550,000 operations are carried out privately – 20 per cent of all elective surgery, 28 per cent of hip replacement operations, and 20 per cent of heart operations.
(BUPA UK, 'Everybody's guide to private health care' 1993)

Before and since the NHS was founded there has been parallel public and private health service provision and, more recently, mixed provision, competition and joint ventures. In 1994, 6 per cent of all acute beds and 15 per cent of operations were in the private sector. This section considers the changes taking place in provider financing, management and competition of which purchasers need to be aware. It is followed by a discussion of the impact of these changes on traditional NHS and public health service values, and of how purchasers can uphold such values and resolve conflicts of value in the new mixed economy of health.

Cross-selling

In the UK, both competition and cooperation between public and private providers has increased since 1991, in addition to the limited internal NHS provider competition. In November 1991, 40 health authorities were reported to have negotiated clinical contracts with private hospitals for 1992 (*Health Services Journal* 21 November 1991: 14) and many GP fundholders are also reported to have contracts with private hospitals. However, it is public providers which have made the larger increase in sales across sectors by selling services to private insurers. This trend is likely to continue as trusts develop their independence and as financial pressures on them increase. It is a trend which public purchasers have to watch closely if they are to maintain equity and access, which is arguably a lesser priority for trusts facing large deficits.

It is also a trend which is worrying private providers, even though it only accounted for about 1 per cent of NHS trusts' income in 1991–2. In the first year of the reforms, NHS income from the 1,063 beds and other services for private patients increased by over 30 per cent to £141 million, or a 13 per cent share of the private market (Laing 1993). Private providers are concerned about 'unfair competition' from the public sector, in part because of the economies of scale in public hospitals, which make them on average 20 per cent cheaper than smaller private hospitals.

Tendering for services

Public purchasers are increasingly inviting tender bids for clinical services from public and private providers. We saw in Chapter 2 that more public providers are contracting out non-clinical support services, and occasionally subcontracting clinical services when they have long waiting lists. The Federation of NHS Trusts has called for competitive tendering for clinical work (*Health Service Journal* 8 July 1993: 5) and the North East Thames Region reviewed three secondary care services for 'market testing': ophthalmology, orthopaedics and ear, nose and throat services. Nottingham HA invited public and private tenders for audiology services (*Health Service Journal* 2 September 1993: 6). At present one of the aims is to use a mixture of tendering and contracting to rationalize secondary services.

The UK government is encouraging purchasers to consider private as well as public services. At a conference on the mixed economy of health care in 1993, the health minister proposed that 'purchasers should show no favouritism in choosing who is to provide health care for NHS patients . . . We want a level playing field.' There are those that hold that it is NHS trusts which are disadvantaged, because of regulations such as restrictions on surpluses, working capital and borrowing, and average cost pricing which prevents prices being related to demand. Further, that if these and other regulations continue for trusts, they will not be able to compete with private services, and the result will be privatization of the NHS. Most private health providers argue the reverse, that the 'playing field' slopes in favour of NHS providers. One press summary reported that most private sector providers believed that they were ignored by purchasers, and that NHS managers and civil servants were distrustful of an increased private sector role (*Health Services Journal* special report, 'Mixed marriages', November 1993).

Private capital and joint ventures

Along with increasing competition there has been increasing cooperation between NHS trusts and the private sector, which has often proved more beneficial financially, and for NHS patients. More types of joint ventures are being established, with government support. For NHS purchasers and providers the main reasons for joint ventures are to gain access to private capital and private expertise and to increase revenue income through profit-sharing schemes. Perhaps the most important is private capital investment into public hospitals and services, but as yet the incentives have not been sufficiently attractive for either the private health sector or the private financial sector. Although NHS trusts have more freedom to sell assets and borrow, many of the pre-1991 restrictions in effect still apply: spending proceeds from capital sales is counted as 'public spending'; schemes of a certain size and type have to have Department of Health and Treasury approval; and they have to prove better value for money, which is difficult with low government interest rates for borrowing from (limited) government funds.

The NHS reforms White Paper (DoH 1989a) proposed sharing the cost of building facilities with the private sector, leasing NHS land, buildings and facilities to the private sector, and private developers building hospitals on NHS sites in return for profits on the sale of NHS land. There was only a gradual increase in such schemes, in part because of the recession, and some well-publicized disasters for the private sector. Although during the 1980s one company had ten successful schemes building private hospitals and day surgery units on NHS sites, the company lost £4 million in one joint venture in the early 1990s. A rival private unit opened first, with reportedly better marketing for the limited private sector market in the area (*Health Service Journal* 3 September 1992: 7).

Notwithstanding the negative publicity, joint ventures were promoted in a variety of ways by government and the private sector. The 1992 government autumn statement proposed that the government would ' "actively encourage" joint ventures with the private sector where these involved a "transfer of risk", and would allow greater use of leasing "where the risk stays with the private sector" and operating agreements with only the lease payments counting as expenditure without capital budgets being cut' (*Health Service Journal* 3 December 1992: 3). This was followed by changes to regulations and further guidance, summarized in NHS ME (1993). Numerous conferences in 1993 and 1994 continued to promote joint ventures, as did one influential right-wing 'think tank' report (SMF 1993). This report proposed six joint venture options for the private sector: leasing private hospitals and equipment to the NHS; building hospitals for the NHS to run ('turnkey projects'); building and operating units for the NHS; operating hospitals under management contracts; offering shared facilities; and increased cooperation in primary and community care services. One of the main proposals was for government to relax capital control procedures to give hospitals more freedom to draw on private finance, as well as to shift spending from capital to revenue to allow the NHS to pay for the running costs of units built and operated by the private sector.

Reported ventures include five proposed schemes between trusts and one large independent provider of acute psychiatric services, which would involve a £10 million investment into the NHS. The private company planned to design, build and open new units, which would be run by either the company or the trusts, or jointly under contract for NHS patients only (*Health Service Journal* 25 February 1993: 8). Another scheme is 'patient hotels', planned, built and managed by the private sector to take NHS patients at a cost which is reported by the NHS Value for Money Unit to be 60 per cent of the usual NHS inpatient cost (company advertisement, *Health Service Journal* 26 August 1993: 21). In another scheme the private company set up a drug preparation unit in an NHS hospital trust, which saved the trust the investment costs of £200,000, and provided low-cost services and income from the sale of services to other hospitals. There are also examples of many non-clinical joint ventures, including 'facilities management' and schemes which 'bundle' a range of support services for external contractors to manage. Rebuilding waste incinerators is one of the more successful types of joint venture, often because private operators have difficulties getting planning permission for new facilities.

Future legislation could make it easier for trusts and purchasers to sell land or assets. Legislation could also keep some existing restrictions, and at the same time make it easier to enter into joint ventures, in effect making this the only route for borrowing, spending and selling. Certainly, joint ventures do offer the potential to increase both capital and revenue finance for providers and for purchasers. However, some controls will be necessary to avoid the duplication of facilities and waste which can occur in unregulated markets. To date, control of capital investment has been one way in which the NHS has planned developments and limited total health expenditure through limiting capacity. Purchasers need to be aware of the options, and also of the risks for providers with whom they contract. Purchasers can make or break many joint ventures and need to weigh up the advantages and disadvantages for their populations. It is likely that joint ventures and subcontracting will increase, leading to arrangements that are far more complex than annual contracting for services from NHS providers.

Summary: beyond the public–private and purchaser–provider divisions

The chapter describes the variety of forms of financing, management and ownership of purchasers and of providers, and shows that market cooperation as well as competition is possible. It shows that purchasers have to think beyond the categories of public–private and purchaser–provider to recognize some of the new possibilities. As a final illustration of this point, we note below one party in the developing health market whose actions cannot be understood or predicted if we hold fast to these categories. Health authority purchasers and integrated commissioning agencies will not be able to reach cooperative agreements with GP fundholders if they think only in terms of public or private, or of purchasers or providers. GP fundholders are quasi-public providers and purchasers. GPs:

- are paid out of public finance as individual independent contractors to provide general practitioner services;
- usually form private business partnerships to provide these services;
- are supported in their business out of public and private funds – many opt to administer a public fund for purchasing either public or private health care;
- may reinvest savings from their purchasing fund into facilities or staff for their practice;
- sometimes combine to form a purchasing consortium.

Other examples of hybrid organizational forms are the City and Hackney FHSA provider trust described in Chapter 9 and the many ventures noted above between health authorities, trusts and private companies and financiers.

Values in future health reforms

The discussion above described some of the changes in the developing 'health market' and pointed to future reforms in financing, ownership and control. These changes and future reforms are not, however, purely matters of economics and organization. Public health purchasers have to consider the values and principles which the public and staff wish to see upheld in purchasing and provision, and whether certain changes would make it more difficult to uphold these values. This book has stressed the importance of viewing methods in relation to the purpose of public purchasing. In this last part of the book we return again to the question of purpose and look at how the changes we have considered either further or detract from the purpose of NHS commissioning. Public purchasers are becoming the main bodies for preserving public health values in an increasingly commercial environment. To set a direction for purchasing in the future, clarity about these principles and about conflicts of principle is increasingly important.

We concentrate on the values of choice and equity for three related reasons. First, choice and equity correspond to two philosophies which are often in opposition: consumerist individualism and collectivist utilitarianism. The future direction of health purchasing is bound up with the current shifts and reconfiguration of political philosophies. Liberal and modern conservative ideologies emphasize individual freedom, responsibility and private property. Markets were proposed as a way of promoting these values and of advancing the common good: choice, individual freedom and competition go together. Socialist ideologies hold that the individual realizes his or her potential through collective action, and advance different forms of collective and cooperative organization and ownership as a way of upholding the interests of individuals as part of society: equity and cooperation go together.

The conflict between these two ideologies is greatest in the fields of health and social welfare, perhaps the last remaining sphere where the Marxist dictum is still widely held: 'from each according to his abilities, to each according to his needs'. The prominence of choice in reforms is a response to growing consumerism, and is connected with right-wing political ideologies of freedom and competition. Choice is a current issue in health reforms because of increasing consumerism and because it is a public justification for market reforms which have other aims, including increasing efficiency and cost containment. Public health purchasers have to manage the tension between these two philosophies.

A second reason to concentrate on choice and equity is a tension between purchasing as a consumer service and purchasing as a public health service for a population. A consumer service responds to consumer views, regardless of the longer-term impact on population health. Purchasers seeking to develop their role as service organizations by increasing patient choice may undermine their public health aims. Third, there is a tension in NHS commissioning between local and national accountability. NHS commissioners are in the contradictory position of being required to seek out and act on local people's views, and also to pursue national or regional policies or government directives which may be in conflict with local views. Local people often want more choice, and government policies often require equity, especially in relation to sustaining a national service. Conversely, government directives may be to increase choice, but local people may feel that doing so results in unacceptable inequities.

One difference between an NHS commissioning organization and a private insurance purchaser is the former's role in ensuring equity. NHS commissioners have to consider equity issues in considering joint ventures, the options for contracting specialties, locality purchasing schemes, ECR policies, priorities and many other decisions. They need to be aware of the different types of equity, of current inequities and of how changes would affect each type of equity, not the least of which is inequity in health. Below we consider different types of equity to enable commissioners to be more precise in assessing the impact of different changes. We also consider different types of choice, and how commissioners can reconcile conflicts between choice and equity. Purchasers can assess the different public and private changes which we considered above in terms of their impact on these different types of choice and equity.

Choice

Almost everyone agrees that people should have more choices in health care, but at what cost? Does more choice cost more, and is it at the expense of other values? In health, is individual choice now more important than equity, and do people wish to put choice above equity if it is not possible to have both? Purchasers cannot ignore these questions – as a service business they have to be in tune with their customers' preferences, as well as with government policies.

To answer these questions we need to define different types of choice and consider which types are most important to most people. Then we can also judge whether some types conflict with equity, and how increasing one or more types of choice affects the health of a population. Figure 13.2 gives a summary of different types of choice.

In the UK many hold that choice has decreased since the 1990 reforms, but this depends on which type of choice we are referring to. The findings to date from research in the UK into patient choice and their criteria are inconclusive. What is clear is that, in the UK: some GPs say that they are influenced by patients' choices of hospital, but patients say that they

---

How does a reform proposal affect a person's choice about: *Before?*   *After?*

To pay
- At time of use
- Of insurer, and of alternative insurance plans

Primary care practitioner/centre
- GP
- Nurse, or other practitioner

Of hospital or specialist

'In-service hotel' choices in hospital
- Private room, menus, television, etc.

Treatment choices, decisions and participation
- Before treatment, to decide treatment
- During treatment, to alter treatment

Choices for a referring agent, and for purchasers
- Physician choice: referral, treatments
- Purchaser choice: monopoly, or many providers

What options are there for each type of choice: two (yes or no) or many choices? Is choice only for some people, or for all?

Figure 13.2 Types of choice.

are not given a choice; GPs vary in the choice they offer to patients; GPs' and patients' criteria are different (Langan *et al.* 1990; Sargent 1991; Mahon 1992); and fundholder patients have more choice than patients of non-fundholders. In addition, the criteria of the purchasing authority or agency are different to those of both GPs and patients. Purchasers' concerns are with cost control, population health, public health aims and long-term changes in types of provision towards more community and preventative services, all of which can conflict with most types of patient choice.

Problems in increasing choice

For choice to be meaningful not only must there be alternatives, but a person must have information about the alternatives. People have to know that they have a choice, that they have a right to ask for information to help them to choose, and to be able to use the information that they get, even if they are not feeling well. Giving more information to help patients to choose is one of the less expensive ways in which commissioners can increase choice. In the UK, the West Midlands Region published waiting times for each consultant and specialty, and there is increasing interest in publishing medical outcome performance, as in the USA (PHCCCC 1992), notwithstanding the problems of interpretation. However, this does not overcome the second problem: difficulties in understanding and using some types of information. Where information about clinical care is available, it is difficult for patients to understand and to use (Sisk *et al.* 1990), although the findings from development projects with computer-assisted treatment information for patients are encouraging. The third main problem, and precisely the reason why purchasers should consider doing more to increase patient choice, is the difficulty in changing professional practice to offer patients more choices and to help them to make decisions.

Purchasers' role in increasing choice

In practice some commissioner decisions and future changes may increase some types of choice for people in a particular social group or geographical area, such as a choice to go to a hospital with a shorter waiting time. If this greater choice is not at the expense of others, then there are few reasons not to allow more choice, even if some health inequities result, for to do so infringes individual liberty. The long-term effects may be that some hospitals which successfully attract more patients expand and others close, thus reducing choice for people near the closing hospitals. Some 'managed care reforms' may increase people's choice of purchaser, but restrict their choice of provider to those selected by the purchasing agency (Enthoven and Kronick 1989). In this instance, purchasing agencies are able to control costs and people may be prepared to trade less choice of provider for lower payments to a purchasing agency: purchasers can do research to find out people's preferences.

In public health purchasing to date, there is no link between patient choice and patient cost. People are not free to pay more for more choices unless they go private. A 'market' does not exist which gives purchasers incentives to find out which choices people wish to pay for. In theory public health purchasers could introduce quasi-private health plans with more choices alongside the public basic schemes, as noted earlier in this chapter. Purchasers have not sought to increase patient choices of treatment or involvement in the treatment process, which is important for some patients. Finally, in practice, people's choice is often restricted because there are few alternative providers, or because there is no information on which to base a meaningful choice.

A consideration of choice in purchasers' decisions and in future reforms raises a number of questions, not the least of which is: why is choice in health care now such an issue? Some argue that the promise of more patient choice at no higher cost is a way to 'sell' market reforms to the public. Competition is linked to choice, for patients or for purchaser contracts or for both – the UK reforms emphasize competition for contracts and hence efficiency rather than patient choice. In the UK the evidence is that some people have less choice of hospital than before the reforms, but patients of GP purchasers may not have to wait as long as previously. In Sweden, more patient choice of hospital and primary care centre has been achieved without higher costs.

However, there are few incentives for public health purchasers to increase choices which are important to people, and providers' concerns are with what wins contracts: evidence of offering a range of treatment or hotel choices to patients is not usually a criterion for winning contracts. The question of what price people are prepared or able to pay for more choice of different types, where choice does cost more, is less easy to answer in public systems. We now turn to the question of whether more choice means less equity in health care.

Equity

The foreword to the 1990 NHS reforms proposal states that 'The NHS will continue to be available to all, regardless of income, and to be financed mainly out of taxation' (DoH 1989a). Most European and US national and state reform proposals aim to reduce inequities. However, there is little analysis of or research into how different public–private combinations or reforms might or do affect equity, or how equity will be maintained with different types of market competition. One of the reasons for having public health purchasing authorities is to uphold equity – something which most people believe is important in health care. Purchasers have to go beyond general statements of principle to show how they have promoted equity in the new system and to assess the impact of proposed changes on equity. This is especially important in carrying out rationing, which people are more willing to accept if it is done equitably.

As with choice, to consider how a particular purchaser's decision affects equity, it is necessary first to define what we mean by equity in health – something which most politicians wisely avoid. One source of confusion is not distinguishing between equality (being equal or the same) and equity (fairness and justice). Often the two are used interchangeably: it is necessary to emphasize the distinction by referring to: 'crude equality', where everyone is treated the same or pays the same, regardless of ability to pay or need; and 'discriminatory equity', where people pay according to their wealth, or receive according to their needs. Most health systems involve both differential payment according to income and differential provision according to need – the proposals for alternative financing of the NHS considered above would affect both types of equity. Figure 13.3 gives a summary of types of equity.

We will not consider all these types of equity here, but just note some general points and different types of equity in payment. To ensure fairness one has to recognize differences and the fact that people are not equal. The debate is usually more about how well or fairly a particular policy recognizes differences than about whether there should be such a recognition: for example, policies for financial allocations to purchasers which recognize differences in populations such as age and morbidity. Usually the term

Of payment by people
- All pay the same, regardless of wealth/income/ability to pay
- Pay according to ability to pay (or pay according to need/use: fair?)

Of resourcing by government
- All areas get the same
- Weighting for current service provision, geography, health status, deprivation

Of service
- All areas provide the same range of services (e.g. comprehensive)
- Different services (decentralization and scope for autonomy)

Of opportunity of access
- Simple: no obvious barriers
- Equal opportunities for all to use, by attention to times, cultures/languages, siting, etc. (up to individual and demand-driven)

Of use
- Simple 'voucher rations' the same for everyone
- Special programmes to ensure equal use of services (e.g. immunization, screening, pre-natal and child health)

Of use according to need
- Distinguish different needs and ensure proactive programmes to target the most in need, or prioritize patients for treatment (e.g. emergency triage) (principle that the most needy should get faster or more intensive treatment)

Of provision according to capacity to benefit
- Same need, but unequal amount/treatment, according to a judgement of likely benefit (utilitarian, invest less where low prospect of benefit)

Of health
- Distinguish different health and ensure proactive health and other programmes to reduce inequities in health (absolutist, invest more to equalize)

1 *'Crude/simple' equality*: same for all, regardless of need (soup-kitchen rations)

2 *'Discriminatory' equity*: according to need, or other criteria of difference – recognizes inequalities to ensure 'fairness and justice'

Figure 13.3 Types of equality and equity in health.

'equity in health' refers to equal health for all – to equality of health. We saw in Chapter 3 that in practice true equality of health is impossible, and is not feasible for purchasers because of the variety of circumstances which affect health over which they can have little influence. *Reducing inequities* in health is a more practical ideal for public health purchasers and one which some have adopted in their conceptions of their purpose.

In practice, however, equity in health has not been the principle which underlies most health systems or many commissioner decisions, not least because it can conflict with individual choice and freedom, and calls for more state interventionist policies than other concepts of equity. Of particular interest to health purchasers at present is how changes in financing, such as provider charges or 'top-up' insurance, could affect equity and differences between fundholders' and other patients' access to services and waiting times.

Equity of payment by people

Like choice in payment, equity in payment can be defined in different ways. Simple equality is where everyone pays the same, regardless of ability to pay or use of health services. Few Western health systems are financed on this basis, although some do involve standard 'co-payments' at the time of use, but these are usually reimbursable for the less wealthy (e.g. $15 per visit to a primary care physician in Sweden, prescription and dental charges in the UK, 'deductibles' in the USA for each 'claim'). The second type is payment according to ability to pay, and systems differ in terms of how much more people pay in proportion to their income or wealth. The third type is where people pay according to their use, and pay more for using higher-cost services. Co-payments have this element, but no public systems relate payment to the resources which the public system allocates to a person's health care.

Equity in payment has to be considered in relation to both payments by patients to a provider at the time of use, and routine payments by people to a fund or in tax to finance health services. Equity of payment according to ability to pay seems to be a principle which current reforms will not change. However, as we saw earlier in the chapter, some proposals, for example in the UK and The Netherlands, consider increasing finance for health services by encouraging more private insurance (IHSM 1993). Such an approach can increase equity by requiring those who are able to pay to take out additional or full private insurance, as long as they continue to contribute to the public service, thus leaving more resources for the less well off. The counter-argument is that, in practice, the best way of ensuring good public services is to make sure the rich and articulate middle classes continue to have a stake in the public system. In practice, reforms to increase finance to public health services through private insurance financing can lead to a 'two-tier' service, as people with more money increasingly seek to reduce their contribution to the public service. Similar issues arise in the debate about reducing or removing rich people's entitlement to a public old-age pension.

Equity issues and commissioning: summary

In summary, many European health systems since the Second World War have pursued equity of resource allocation and of access, and left it to individuals to decide to make use of the service. This is in part owing to assumptions about the causes of poor health and conceptions of individual freedom and responsibility. Behind different views of equity there are assumptions about the causes of ill health being located in individuals or the environment, different views about the freedom and ability of individuals to choose a healthy lifestyle (e.g. poverty), the rights of individuals to choose how they live, views about the responsibility of the individual and of the state for health, and utilitarian and absolutist views about the value of individuals and of life. By being more specific about types of equity, commissioners can make more precise assessments about how their or others' actions will affect access and inequalities in health.

Equity and choice in the future

A trend in health reform in Europe is towards ensuring that all have access to a basic health provision, with the choice to pay more for extra health care coverage. This trend is influenced by the formation of the EC (now European Union, EU) and equalizing entitlements across the EU. It also represents a new balance between the values of equity and choice: many of the types of equity noted above are ensured by everyone having access to the services in the basic scheme and paying into the basic scheme when they can. Choice is increased for those who can pay, by public and private providers offering services beyond the basic scheme, and purchasers competing for subscribers for this 'add-on' scheme. The balance between equity and choice depends on what is covered in the basic scheme, and whether people are allowed to opt out of it.

Equity in health is about recognizing differences and assigning importance or value to differences to ensure that people or communities are treated differently, but in a fair way. As the need to ration public health services increases, so too will concern about equity. Concern about 'fairness' arises not when two patients or communities are treated differently, but when the system does not recognize differences that people feel should be recognized. How the system recognizes and weights these differences is a technical, social and moral issue, and should be the subject of political processes. Market-type reforms and unaccountable purchasers can take these issues out of the political process, with the appearance of being neutral with respect to values. Market reforms in health are not just a question of economic incentives and rewards, but carry with them certain political, cultural and religious values.

Sometimes both choice and equity can be increased: for example, increasing equity of services between different areas can give people in rural areas more choice of providers, but at a high cost. More usually there are conflicts and trade-offs between equity, choice and other criteria such as expenditure and efficiency, and there always have been. Stronks and Gunning-Schepers (1993) recognize that only some constraints can be realistically influenced. They argue, starting from the primacy of maximizing freedom of the individual, that 'the principle of equality in health can only be conceived as a means to guarantee each individual freedom of choice, based on the conception of health as a basic capability. Therefore, only inequalities resulting from an unequal distribution of opportunities to be as healthy as possible, to the extent that this distribution can be controlled, must be conceived as inequities' (p. 109).

Economics-based health reforms and changes to the public–private mix have the appearance of being neutral with regard to values, and of seeking to promote choice for all sectors of society. It is assumed that economic and system changes will produce changes in behaviour, regardless of culture and values in society and in the health care system. Although in Europe there is more recognition that health markets are more complex as systems than other markets, there is little recognition of the importance of social values to health care reform and to individuals' health-related behaviour. There is no doubt that different parties in UK health care are influenced by the new economic incentives, but also that 45 years of NHS culture and certain values mediate these incentives: the NHS model would work differently in the USA, Italy or Poland.

Summary and conclusions

This chapter has considered options for future financing, sources of finance for public purchasing of health services and competition in purchasing. With the increasing 'care gap', the public may be more prepared to support more private and mixed financing. In the UK, the disadvantages of private organizations undertaking public purchasing appear to outweigh the advantages, as do the disadvantages of competition between public purchasers. Nor is there a strong case for public purchasers undertaking private purchasing. The arguments for doing so are different to those for public hospitals selling their services to private insurance companies or employers.

In describing the variety of joint ventures and financing options, the chapter has shown that the public–private distinction is no longer an adequate description of the new organizational forms. It has shown that purchasers need to recognize the variety of inter-organizational relationships and financing options which are possible. In this way they can combine the benefits of public and private to develop health services in the future. It also argued that beyond the purchaser–provider separation there are partnerships of different types, and that short-term contractual and adversarial relationships are to no one's advantage.

Purchasers need to understand their part in an evolving system, compare their situation with purchasers in other countries and contribute to the debate about their future and the future of the health systems of which they are a part. Changes in financing, competition and public–private combinations affect purchasers' ability to uphold traditional NHS and public health values. The chapter has considered the effects of these changes on choice and equity. Increasing certain types of choice can result in poorer population health in the long term, and increase inequities in health. If purchasers are more precise about what they mean by equity and choice, they can better assess the impact of changes which they or others propose.

Chapter 2 showed that the theories and research which have been most influential in 'market reforms' have tended to concentrate on economic incentives, financing and the technical operation of health systems (e.g. Enthoven 1985a), rather than how these changes will affect health. There is a growing recognition that market-type reforms do not solve the problems of health provision, and do not always produce the cost savings which were promised. Further, while debates about health reform acknowledge values as being important, there is typically little analysis of the values implicit in some economic models, or of the values which a reform preserves or promotes, or of how values relate to people's health. In Eastern Europe it is becoming clear that market reforms are incompatible with some social values which people wish to preserve in the health sector. This is also true in some Western European countries, where people recognize that individualism and choice may conflict with other social values, such as equity and solidarity.

The UK is entering a period of debate about the NHS which is similar to that of the late 1980s, but with experience and more knowledge of one type of market system. At the same time, purchasers are trying to give a lead as the 1991 reforms begin to have a real impact. Purchasers' experience and their stabilizing influence mean that they have an important contribution to make to this debate and to the future of the NHS, and need to be aware of the options open to them and to others. Purchasers are one of the few parties whose main role is to keep the health of their populations to the forefront in their decisions and in the debate about the NHS, a debate which threatens to be dominated by issues of acute hospital provision and economics. Purchasers' influence will be greater if they have a clear view about the purpose of NHS purchasing, which also gives a basis for judging different purchasing methods and health policies. Similar points apply to purchasing organizations in the US and Europe. This book sought to draw attention to the relationship between the purpose and methods of health purchasing, in order that purchasers choose methods which advance rather than undermine the strengths of the NHS. Academics often create more questions than answers. Their excuse is that creating the right question is half-way to finding an answer. I hope that this book has also supplied some answers for the emerging discipline and occupation of health purchasing.

Key points

- The public–private and purchaser–provider distinctions are limited in their ability to describe current organizational forms, relationships and financing, and in their usefulness to purchasers for examining future options.

- Purchasing in the future will be in a health system with many public and private providers and purchasers, and using a mix of private and public finance.
- Purchasing finance will come from a variety of sources, and purchasers will enter into a variety of relationships and joint ventures with other purchasers and providers.
- The national and local design of health systems is not solely an economic and technical question of combining incentives, competition and regulation in the right mix. People working in the system interpret incentives, hold values and have a culture which mediates changes in a way that an economic model or machine does not. A rational economic model may be irrational or difficult to implement in the light of social, political and moral considerations.
- New forms of financing and provision can undermine traditional principles of equity, and might not increase choice. All purchasers, but especially public purchasers, have to consider issues other than short-term economics.
- In assessing the impact of future changes, purchasers need to consider the effects on different types of choice and equity.
- NHS purchasers need to be aware of different approaches to financing and competition, with the renewed debate about NHS financing and as a result of comparisons with other nations' approaches to health reform. NHS purchasers have an important role in upholding traditional NHS principles which are still widely held, and in influencing the national and international debate.

Appendix 1
Usages followed in this book

Allocative efficiency: Concerns how much resource should be put into different services for the benefits produced: whether to do something and if so how much to do. A service with a low unit cost (simple efficiency) may be less allocatively efficient than one with a high unit cost, because the relative benefits are less. A service is efficient in this sense if it produces high benefits for low costs (one meaning of 'value for money').

Community care services: Mainly social services, but sometimes GP and community health services.

Community health services: Health services other than primary care services, provided outside larger hospitals, paid for from DHA cash-limited finance, and contracted by DHAs or joint agencies or GP fundholders. Often includes community psychiatric nurse services. Typically, non-hospital health services provided by a community health trust.

Cost–benefit evaluation: Judging the comparative overall economic benefits of interventions for the cost (attempts to cover all costs and benefits).

Cost-effectiveness evaluations: Judging the comparative effectiveness of interventions for the cost (concerned with efficiency and with value for money of different interventions for the outcome). Usually narrower focus than cost–benefit evaluations.

Cost–utility evaluations: Judging the comparative utility of interventions for the cost (often using quality adjusted life years, QUALYs).

Effectiveness: The efficacy of a treatment or service in an everyday setting. A treatment may be effective in a special setting (e.g. a laboratory or teaching hospital) which is difficult to reproduce in everyday situations – it may be efficacious but not effective. Some drugs are efficacious if given at specific times and doses: they may not be effective if they depend on patient self-medication. Some treatments are efficacious but not acceptable to patients. Effectiveness depends on acceptability to providers and patients and patient preferences.

Efficacy: The extent to which an intervention (treatment or service) produces desired outcomes in a controlled setting.

Efficiency: Output for a given input. A service is efficient if it produces the maximum output with the minimum input. Usually measured in terms of 'unit costs'.

Equity and Equality: Concerned with fairness and justice.

- Of provision/resourcing: the same level and types of service should be available to all the UK population (a standard of comprehensiveness of provision).
- Equity of access: equal opportunity to use the health service (e.g. extra resources for rural or ethnic minorities). Consensus around equality of access for equal need.
- Equality of need: those with equal need should receive equal treatment (speed and amount of resources).
- Of health: resources and services should be used to equalize health (thus extra services and resources should be provided to those with poor health).

Evaluation: Judging the value of an intervention or service, compared to none at all or a similar intervention or service.

Joint commissioning: Formal structures for joint working with local authorities.

Justifiable purchasing: Explaining the basis for, and process by which a purchasing agency decides resource allocation and contracts providers.

Locality purchasing: Can mean consulting GPs in a locality about secondary care issues, devolving a budget to a locality manager for purchasing, or an arrangement for involving people in an area in a range of commissioning activities.

Marginal benefits (and costs): How much additional benefit can be gained from an increase in resources, relative to the additional benefit from an increase in resources for another service/client group (purchasing changes are made at the 'margins' – small changes to existing levels of service provision, rather than discontinuing or withdrawing resources completely).

Opportunity cost: The benefits of the second best possible option, which are forgone by choosing the first, best option.

Outcome: The end result of a process (a treatment, service or intervention). 'A change in a patient's current and future health status that can be attributed to antecedent health care.'

Posteriorities: Deciding who or what comes last or receives the smaller proportion of resources.

Primary care commissioning: Includes primary care purchasing work for practice development, but also work to secure finance and allocate it through contracts and other means to develop and purchase a wide range of services in a primary care setting: for example, negotiating, receiving and using revenue and capital finance from a DHA to develop primary care services to reduce hospital use. (Needs assessment and planning for commissioning is usually broader than for 'purchasing' as more services and needs are considered. Thus, this covers most FHSA activities, not just GP contracts, payments and discretionary practice assistance. A narrow definition is only agreeing practice assistance 'contracts' with selected GP practices. 'Primary care contracting' can mean the latter and GP contracts.)

Primary care contracting: Contracting of GPs and other independent contractors, according to nationally set terms and conditions, and arranging payments to them after they have provided services, as set out in national agreements. Also includes FHSA registration of practitioners and patients. Most FHSA work is primary care contracting work.

Primary care provision: Services provided by GPs and their practice staff, health promotion and education outside hospitals, but not practice training and development support by FHSA-employed staff. Sometimes used to describe specialist care provided in a primary care setting.

Primary care purchasing: All the activities needed to decide and pay FHSA discretionary finance for practice development. The general medical services' cash-limited allocation for reimbursing practice staff salaries, training, premises improvements and computers. Includes needs assessment for deciding development, practice assessment, receiving and prioritizing bids from GPs, consulting the local medical committee, deciding allocations and monitoring expenditure.

Prioriphobia: The inability to set and carry through priorities due to an awareness of the suffering which will be caused by denying care and a refusal to value one person's life or quality of life more highly than anothers.

Prioritizing: Deciding which comes first, or relative proportions. Rationing is often done by formulating criteria for deciding priorities, and then allocating resources according to priorities.

Productivity: The output produced (e.g. units per hour from x resources). A person or a service can be productive but inefficient – they may produce more than others, but also be inefficient and wasteful.

Rationing: Restricting supply according to implicit or explicit criteria, in situations where demand exceeds supply. Rationing is a way of relating demand for a service supply where market mechanisms for doing so are inappropriate.

Secondary care services: Nearly all hospital-based services, and some specialist community health services provided in the community (e.g. some community therapy and community psychiatric nurse (CPN) services), paid for by DHA or GP fundholder finance.

Specialist services: All secondary care services and some community health services.

Utility: Satisfaction and benefits derived from a service or product: the use to the consumer.

Utilization: Use of capacity, often measured as an average over a period of time (e.g. bed occupancy, operating room usage).

Value for money: The combination of cost, quantity and quality, compared to another combination, for one intervention or service compared to another.

Variations in usage

Primary, secondary, specialist and community care can refer to:

• the *siting* and setting of the service;
• who *pays* for the service (FHSA, DHA, Local Authority);
• who *employs* the service giver (e.g. a CPN employed by a fundholder gives a primary care service, but when employed by an acute trust gives a secondary care or specialist service).

Primary care services

Can refer to:

• services provided by GPs only;
• services provided by a GP practice/partnership *and* employed staff (nurse(s) and others);
• these services and those of dentists, pharmacists and other FHSA-paid providers;

- these *and* health services provided in a 'primary care setting' by staff employed by a community unit or trust;
- these *and* social service staff who work 'closely' with them.

In other countries primary care can mean all health and social services not provided in hospital settings or by doctors.

Secondary care

Can mean:

- acute hospital medical and 'supporting' services;
- any hospital service (e.g. institution-based learning difficulty services);
- 'specialist' services not normally provided by or in GP practices;
- services purchased by a DHA.

Specialist services

The most general usage is: 'all services apart from general practitioner services' (sometimes called 'specialists in general practice'). The most narrow is 'consultant medical practitioners'. Sometimes all therapists and CPNs are referred to as 'specialists', sometimes only those who are hospital-based.

Community care services

Can mean:

- social services only;
- all health and social services provided outside large hospitals, including GP services;
- community health services purchased by a DHA.

Primary care commissioning

Most narrowly:

- FHSA arranging routine payments for services;
- this plus any FHSA discretionary staff and practice payments;
- everything which the FHSA does (needs assessment, planning, monitoring, etc.) to administer and develop FHSA-paid services;
- this plus placing contracts for community nursing and therapy services (which would include GP fundholders as primary care commissioners).

Test of your use of terms: are district and health visitor nurse services purchased by a GP fundholder, a community health service, a primary care service, or a specialist service, or a number of these?

Appendix 2
Management structures of seven integrated health purchasers

Hillingdon structure

Features

1 Split acute and community commissioning.
2 Integrated primary and community commissioning.
3 All DHA contract management within acute commissioning.
4 Agency director of family and community commissioning also FHSA general manager.

Profile

- Population 240,000.
- Formed from DHAs of Hillingdon, and Spelthorne part of Hounslow and Spelthorne.
- Four GP fundholders in 1993 (14 per cent of the population) – unlikely to increase significantly.
- Director appointments during spring 1993.
- Budget: £71 million for DHA; £30 million for FHSA.
- Staff: 35 DHA; 40 FHSA.
- Boundary now matches London Borough of Hillingdon.
- Considering move to one site.
- GPs: 25 single-handed; 31 in partnerships.

Hillingdon structure

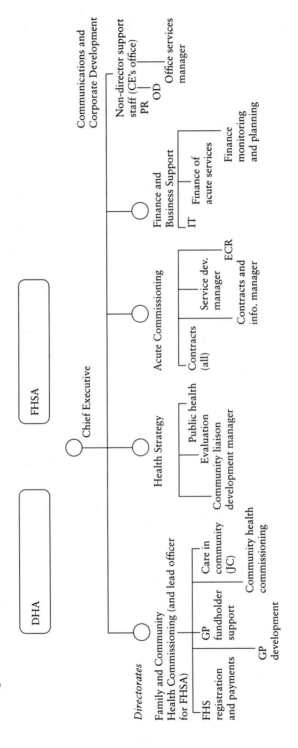

Kensington, Chelsea and Westminster structure

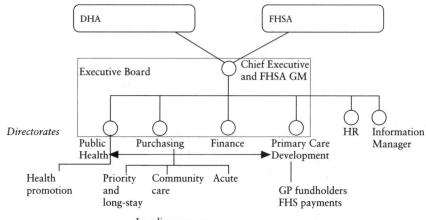

Features

1 Combined acute and community commissioning.
2 Primary care commissioning joint reporting.
3 Chief executive also FHSA general manager.

Profile

• Population 307,000.
• Formed from DHAs of Parkside, Riverside and part of Brent.
• Eight GP fundholders in 1993 (32 per cent of the population) – 216 GPs in total.
• Director of primary care development also FHSA general manager.
• Directorate of purchasing covers acute and community.
• Primary care purchasing manager reports to directors of primary care development and purchasing.
• Large public health research unit.
• Budget: £139 million for DHA; unknown for FHSA.
• Staff: 175 (excluding health promotion).
• Boundary now matches London Boroughs of Kensington, Westminster and Chelsea.
• Common chief executive for DHA and FHSA.
• Four directors are executive members of DHA and normally attend FHSA meetings.
• Considering move to one site.
• Locality purchasing in North East Westminster.

Barnet structure

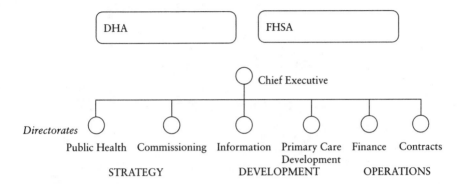

Directorates

Public Health   Commissioning   Information   Primary Care   Finance   Contracts

Development

STRATEGY   DEVELOPMENT   OPERATIONS

Features

1 Combined acute and community commissioning (strategy) and in contracts (operational).
2 Primary care commissioning in separate directory of primary care development.
3 FHSA general manager role combined in agency director role.

Profile

- Population 309,000.
- Boundary matches London Boroughs of Barnet and Harrow.
- Four GP fundholders in 1993 (10 per cent of the population) – 294 GPs in total.
- Barnet and Harrow 'locality' dimensions to directorate organization and work.
- Finance directorate includes FHSA payments work, systems and staff.
- Budget: £99 million for DHA; unknown for FHSA.
- Health promotion unit options.
- Some joint appointments with local authorities.

Brent and Harrow structure

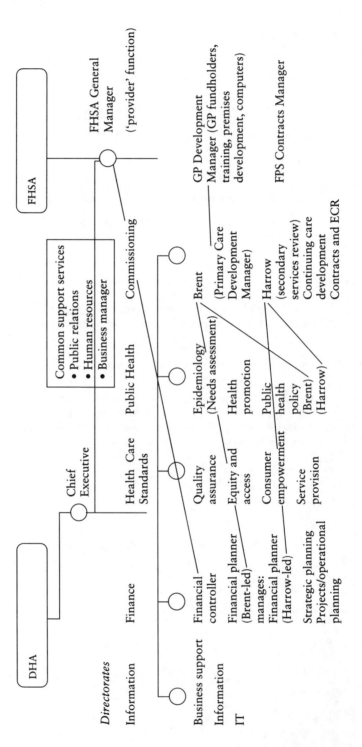

Features

1 Combined acute and community commissioning.
2 FHSA general manager role *not* combined in agency director role.

Profile

- Population 450,000.
- Ten GP fundholders in 1993 (20 per cent of the population) – 328 GPs in total (48 per cent single-handed).
- One site for DHA and FHSA since March 1993.
- FHSA has four functions: FPS contracts; practice development and staff; GP fundholder budgets; strategy and policy for improved provision and quality of FPS services.
- All agency directors have a reporting relationship to the FHSA, but this is stronger for directorates which have taken on FHSA 'purchasing' responsibilities, such as commissioning (for primary care development) and health care standards (e.g. for outreach work).
- Budget: £147 million DHA; unknown for FHSA.
- Staff: 80 DHA; 110 FHSA.
- FPS mostly provider only (managing FPS). Some primary care 'purchasing' responsibilities integrated with other directorates.
- Joint accountability of financial controller to FHSA general manager (for financial functions of FHSA) and to director of finance for other responsibilities.
- Commissioning managers develop GP relations, strategy and joint planning with local authorities.
- Boundary now matches London Boroughs of Harrow and Brent (the Brent part of the old Parkside).
- Structures of directorates have strong Brent/Harrow dimensions.

Bedfordshire structure

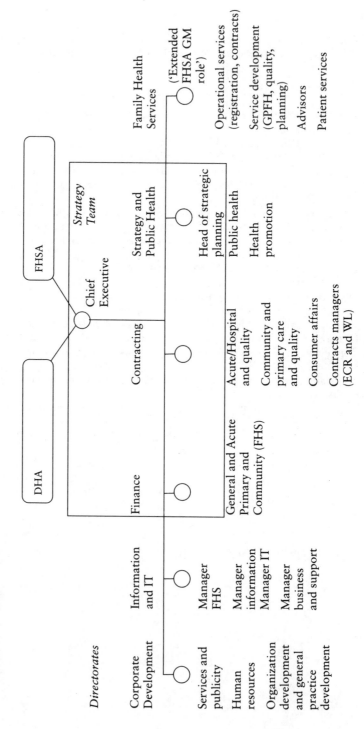

Features

1 Combined acute and community commissioning (strategy) and contracting (operational).
2 Primary care commissioning in separate directorate of family health services.
3 FHSA general manager role combined in agency director role.

Profile

- Population 542,000.
- Fourteen GP fundholders in 1993 (26 per cent of the population) – 294 GPs in total.
- Boundary now matches Bedfordshire County Council.
- North Bedfordshire and South Bedfordshire sites (old DHAs) and north and south aspects to work and organization.
- Budget: £136 million for DHA; £86 million for FHSA.

Ealing, Hammersmith and Hounslow structure

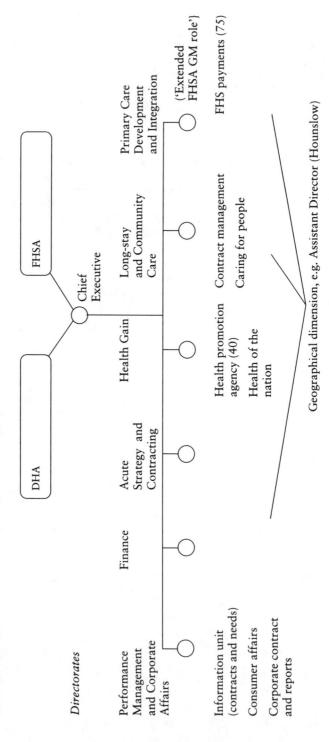

Features

1 Separate acute and long-stay/community commissioning (with operational contracts in each).
2 Primary care commissioning in a separate directorate of primary care development and integration.
3 FHSA general manager role combined in agency director role.

Profile

- Population 723,000.
- Formed from DHAs of Ealing, Hounslow and Spelthorne, and Riverside.
- Seven GP fundholders in 1993 (14 per cent of the population) – 141 GPs in total.
- Structure aims to combine dimensions of *geography* (three boroughs and communities within them), *profession* (e.g. finance, public health directors) and *strategic priorities* (e.g. long-stay and community care, primary care development and integration).
- Budget: £220 million for DHA; £84 million for FHSA.
- Staff: DHA 85; FHSA 140.
- Boundary matches London Boroughs of Ealing, Hammersmith and Fulham, and Hounslow.
- All directors are joint DHA and FHSA appointments.

Hertfordshire structure

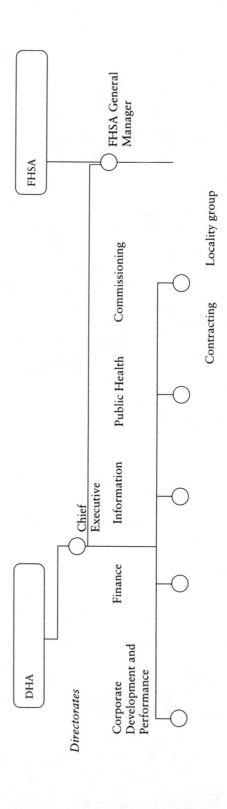

Features

1 Combined acute and community commissioning (strategy and operational).
2 Primary care commissioning in separate FHSA.
3 Separate FHSA and general manager (not combined in agency director role).

Profile

- Population 992,000.
- Agency formed to serve North, East and South West Hertfordshire DHAs (the aim being to merge the three DHAs in 1994) and the FHSA.
- Forty-three GP fundholders in 1993 (43 per cent of the population, estimated to be 75 per cent in 1994) – 150 practices, 25 single-handed GPs.
- Budget: £264 million for DHA; unknown for FHSA.
- Boundary now matches Hertfordshire County Council.
- Four different authority chief executives and sites in May 1993.
- Chief executive appointed April 1993. Director appointments in May–July 1993.

Appendix 3
Profiles of seven UK integrated health purchasing organizations

This appendix gives a profile of seven DHA–FHSA integrated agencies in the North West Thames Region during 1993–4, showing the variations among them and some of the practical issues they faced.

In the early 1990s many UK health authorities combined or formed joint working arrangements. In a number of areas, and especially where the DHA and FHSA boundaries were conterminous, some formed integrated DHA–FHSA commissioning agencies, notably in the Wessex and North West Thames Regions, and in Stockport, Gloucestershire and Doncaster (Ham *et al.* 1993). There are other joint working arrangements apart from integrated agencies, such as the Wolverhampton purchaser and provider agencies described in Chapters 10 and 11.

During late 1991 and early 1992, the then North West Thames Regional Health Authority considered the options for the future configuration of commissioners in the region. The region, together with the eleven district and seven family health service authorities, made a decision to form health commissioning agencies as executive agencies for each FHSA and corresponding DHA or DHAs. During the autumn of 1992, all but one of these agencies were formed, and changes were made to DHA boundaries to make them the same as FHSA boundaries and, in most cases, as local authority boundaries as well.

The rationale for these changes was to integrate the work of commissioning of secondary and primary care services in one commissioning organization, to make collaboration and strategic planning with local authorities easier, to reduce the costs of commissioning by avoiding duplication and by making the most of scarce skills, and to increase the strength of commissioners without creating a large and remote organization.

The commissioner development programme

During late 1992 and early 1993, staff were appointed to the new agencies and began to integrate DHA and FHSA activities, some moving to the same base. At the same time the region, the NHS Management Executive and the agency chief executives commissioned Brunel University to design and run a development programme for the senior staff of the agencies. The programme was based on the Regional Human Resource Department's management development assessment and the researcher's interviews with chief executives and directors, and was adapted to address the issues of concern to agency chief executives and directors as the programme progressed. The programme consisted of on-site workshops and consultancy, Brunel workshops for all seven agencies and a series of briefing papers and conference summaries on the issues which staff wanted to address (Øvretveit 1993h).

The seven agencies

The following gives a summary of the agencies and of some of the issues which each faces. There are many differences between the agencies, between the populations they serve and in how they have each gone about integrating DHA and FHSA work, staff and systems. Their populations vary from 240,000 to 992,000, and include London inner-city, suburban and rural areas. All are conterminous with local authority boundaries, but some cover two or three London Boroughs. The following gives an overview of each for 1994: Appendix 2 gives further details in a profile of each agency, with a diagram of each agency's directorate management structures.

Hillingdon

Hillingdon health commissioning was the smallest agency in the North West Thames Region, with a population of 240,000, and budgets of £71 million (DHA) and £30 million (FHSA). It has the same geographical boundary ('conterminous') as Hillingdon local authority. There is a long history of good collaboration with the local authority, and the aim is to develop locality purchasing with them. In 1993, only 14 per cent of the population were registered with GP fundholders and this is not likely to increase significantly: 25 GPs are single-handed and there are 31 partnerships or group practices of two or more GPs. With the 1 per cent of budget limit for agency running costs, the agency had a relatively small staff of 72 in 1993, but was tackling many of the same demands and challenges as the larger agencies. The four directorates (i.e. management divisions) of the agency are: family and community health commissioning; acute commissioning; health strategy; and finance and business support. Each is headed by a director.

Kensington, Chelsea and Westminster (KCW)

With a 307,000 London inner-city population the KCW agency has a slightly larger population than Hillingdon, but double the budget for secondary services (£139 million DHA), in part because of historical budget allocation for London hospitals. It has significantly more staff (175) and many single-handed GPs, with 32 per cent of the population covered by fundholders in 1993. KCW has a well-developed locality pilot with a nominal purchasing budget for 55 GPs, and is conterminous with the three London Boroughs of the same name. Unlike Hillingdon, acute commissioning and community commissioning are combined in one 'purchasing' directorate, the others being primary care development, public health and finance.

Barnet

The Barnet health agency covers a similar population of 309,000, but has a smaller DHA budget of £99 million, fewer GP fundholders (covering 10 per cent of the population) and even more single-handed GPs (nearly 90 of the total of 196 GPs). Barnet has a key role in London hospital reconfigurations, and, to keep within a diminishing budget, has to oversee substantial rationalizations in local hospitals and contracts. The agency has six directorates, of: public health, and commissioning (the two 'strategy' directorates); primary care development, and information ('development'); and finance, and contracts ('operations').

Brent and Harrow

Brent and Harrow health agency has an urban and suburban population of 450,000 and a DHA budget of £147 million. It is conterminous with the two London Boroughs of the same name and is working to develop arrangements for collaboration with each, as well as having a Brent and a Harrow dimension to its directorate organization. FHSA staff and work are deliberately less integrated into the management structure of the agency than in the other agencies, and this provides an interesting comparison, especially as most of the 80 DHA and 110 FHSA staff are based on one site. The FHSA general manager is accountable to the agency chief executive as well as to the FHSA, and there is a common support services unit. In addition to the FHSA structure, there are five directorates, of: commissioning; health care standards; public health; finance; and information. Relations with GPs is one of the issues for the agency, which has 328 GPs, 48 per cent of which are single-handed; 10 practices are fundholders covering 20 per cent of the population.

Bedfordshire

Bedfordshire health agency was the first of the three agencies with a population of over 500,000 in the old Region, covering the 542,000 population of the County of Bedfordshire. With DHA and FHSA budgets of £136 million and £86 million respectively in 1993, the agency was one of the first to be established and has a history of close DHA and FHSA collaboration. With a rural population and new towns, many issues faced by the agency are different to those of the inner London agencies. Priorities included how to improve relations with the public, the local authority and the 294 GPs, and how best to develop primary and community care. Fundholder coverage was average for the region in 1993, with 14 practices purchasing for 26 per cent of the population. The six directorates are: family health services; strategy and public health; contracting; finance; information and IT; and corporate development.

Ealing, Hammersmith and Hounslow (EHH)

EHH is the second largest health agency in the old region, with a 724,000 population living in the three London Boroughs of Hammersmith and Fulham, Ealing, and Hounslow. An initial task of the agency was to unscramble budgets from the old authorities of Hounslow and Spelthorne, Ealing, and Riverside to form the current £220 million DHA budget (£84 million FHSA). Most of the 85 DHA and

140 FHSA staff moved to one new base in the autumn of 1993. Like other London agencies, EHH is involved in hospital reconfigurations and in improving primary care, including GP facilities and services. There are seven fundholders covering 14 per cent of the population. The agency inherited substantial programmes in community care and long-stay services, and this warranted a directorate of that name, the others being: primary care development and integration; health gain; acute strategy and contracting; finance and performance management and corporate affairs.

Hertfordshire

Hertfordshire health agency is the largest at a population of 992,000 with a £264 million budget, and the last to be formed. It parallels the formation in 1994 of one health authority, conterminous with the FHSA and county boundary, from the three DHAs of North, East and South West Hertfordshire. GP fundholders total 43, covering 43 per cent of the population, and, with more to come in 1994 (67 per cent), improving relations with the 629 GPs is central to achieving any purchasing strategy in the future. Agency programmes began in 1993 with an agency chief executive coordinating projects across the then three DHAs on locality purchasing, health strategy and contracting. These programmes and how they are organized are considered in Chapter 12. The agency directorates are: commissioning; public health; information; finance; corporate development and performance. All these will share work with the FHSA structure.

Stronger commissioning in joint DHA–FHSA agencies

One of the many questions is whether the cost and time of reorganization is worth the health benefits to the population which are believed to follow from integrated commissioning agencies. There are certainly significant differences in how the North West Thames agencies and others in the UK approached closer working, notably in philosophy, organization and cross-directorate processes. These differences in part stem from the different sizes of the new agencies (from 240,000 to 992,000) and their different histories, and from some combining DHAs, as well as carrying out an FHSA–DHA agency merger.

However, in 1993 across the region there was broad agreement that a joint agency was the most cost-effective way of organizing the work of the DHA and FHSA, and that no DHA or FHSA work would remain outside the management boundary of the agency. At that time for statutory purposes the FHSA had to have a named general manager, who was either the agency chief executive or a director within the agency who combined this function with another, usually as 'director of primary care'. In addition, all agency directors served and reported to both authorities and were accountable to the agency chief executive.

Appendix 4
Summary of approaches to locality purchasing

Approach	Size (thousands; total population in parentheses)	Basis
Dorset PATCH	8 to 20 (660)	Citizen identification with a community
North Yorkshire	20 to 40 (720)	Citizen identification with a community Local electoral wards grouped around population centres
Stockport sectors	50 (300)	Epidemiology
East Sussex	100 (720)	Same as district/borough council
South East London	50 to 90 (700)	'Natural communities' (ward boundaries and GP practices, decided with FHSA, LA and CHCs)
Bath		GP practices
North Derbyshire		Local level GP practices Locality level groups of practices
KCW (NE Westminster project)	60 (307)	Old administrative boundary

Sources: Ham (1992b), Johnson (1992)

Functions/purpose	Organization	Other details
Focus for involving the public in purchasing	Groups of localities the responsibility of a PATCH coordinator	PATCHes grouped in areas, with a coordinator for each group of PATCHes
Focus for identifying local health needs For involvement and liaison with GPS	Five or six staff, based in five local offices, relate to localities in their area	
Neighbourhoods (10,000) for needs assessment	A 'health strategy manager' for each sector helps to shape plans and priorities of the central purchasing team	Conterminous DHA and FHSA for some time
Purchasing sensitive to local needs		Three DHAs merge to one
Seek local views about local health issues	Locality coordinator for each	Three DHAs merge to one
Purchasing sensitive to GP views		Nominal budgets for practices Fundholders can be given an 'indicative budget' for non-fundholding services
Purchasing sensitive to GP views		
GP involvement in purchasing	Locality manager	Budget identified

Appendix 5
Checklist for evaluating integration of primary and secondary commissioning

The criteria listed below are for areas highlighted in this book for their importance to successful integration and coordination of primary and secondary health commissioning. A simple way of rating degree of integration is to give a yes/no answer to the questions below for summation to a final score. Another approach which agencies use is to judge the importance 'weighting' of the criterion (per cent) and their performance on the criterion (e.g. 0–5), and then to rate its current priority for improvement (1–3). For example:

Criterion	Current performance	Current priority for improvement
Strategy	(0, poor; 3, OK; 5, good)	(1, high; 2, medium; 3, low)
All agency staff have a shared vision of the service pattern the agency is trying to create	2	1

The value of an integrated agency is to be judged by whether it achieves greater health gain at less cost, and better meets stakeholder requirements than two separate authority organizations. This checklist lists short-term aspects of the performance of an integrated agency, which contributes to its ability to achieve the longer-term aims. These are:

- whether an agency combines previously separate DHA and FHSA activities, where there is an advantage to doing so, in a cost-effective way (how to evaluate integration);
- how well an agency establishes cross-directorate and cross-project working, where this is necessary (how to evaluate coordination).

Evaluation subjects and criteria

Each point carries a value of 1 for 'yes' and 0 for 'no'. (This simple rating method assumes each item is of equal importance. More sophisticated versions have a percentage weighting for each item.)

1 Strategy, plans and timetables

- Do all agency staff have a shared vision of the service pattern which the agency is trying to create?
- Does the agency have a schedule of projects, with the critical phases of each and the links between them?
- Do different staff relating to different external bodies share and represent the same understanding of the current agency service strategy?

2 Directorates

- Is the agency moving to, or continually reviewing the need for, bases shared by directorates or DHA–FHSA activities (one or more sites)?
- Does the agency have criteria and guidelines for deciding whether an FHSA and DHA activity should be combined?
- Have the authorities reviewed the need for a director to act as an FHSA general manager?
- Do all directors report to DH and FHS authorities?
- Are all agency staff contracts with the two (or more) authorities (or with one authority)?
- Does the agency review its directorate structure in relation to its strategy and purpose at sufficiently frequent intervals?
- Are there sufficiently frequent reviews of the proportion of FHSA and DHA work managed by each director within each directorate?

3 Cross-directorate matrix structure

Linking

- Would staff say that the agency had a clear and shared definition of 'primary care commissioning'?
- Are there effective structures and processes for linking primary care commissioning to secondary care commissioning work?
- Are there effective structures and processes for linking strategy to primary and secondary care contracting?

Dual accountability

- Does the agency have standard statements of dual accountability arrangements, which define the two managers' accountability and authority?
- Do managers specify dual accountability where necessary using these standard agency statements?
- Are methods adequate for defining work priorities for staff in dual accountability positions?

Project teams

- Does the agency have standard statements of:
  (a) different types of project teams and guidelines for when to use which type?
  (b) project team working procedures, including how to finish the team?
  (c) defined project team leader roles for each type of team?

- Is there an updated list of teams working on projects of over two months?
- Is this list regularly reviewed by the agency board or other coordinating group?

4 Cross-project coordination

- Do chief executives, directors and board meetings review all projects together for overlap, at sufficiently regular intervals?
- Does the agency have an updated critical path and cross-project linking diagram and tracking system?
- Does the agency board use critical paths to identify how projects relate, oversee progress and set priorities?
- Are there effective ways for project leaders to recognize overlap with other projects and ensure that they coordinate when they do?
- Does the agency define support staff responsibility to alert directors and project leaders to unrecognized links and overlaps?

5 Staff training for integration and coordination

- Do all staff have training about the work of different directorates?
- Is ability to work in, or lead project teams one selection criterion for new staff?
- Are there sufficient resources invested in training for project leaders?
- Do all staff who need to, have training in project team working?
- Is the quality of this training regularly reviewed?
- Do staff who need to, receive training in the different standard agency arrangements for dual accountability and project teams?
- Do staff know how to prioritize between project and directorate tasks?

The total score is a measure of current state of integration and coordination, which can be compared with a score in three or six months.

References and bibliography

ACHCEW (1993) *Rationing Health Care: Should CHCs Help?*, Association of Community Health Councils of England and Wales, London.

Allen, R. (1992) 'Policy implications of recent hospital competition studies', *Journal of Health Economics*, 11, pp. 347–51.

Alter, A. and Hage, J. (1993) *Organisations Working Together*. Sage, London.

Appleby, J. (1991) *How Do We Measure Competition?*, NAHAT, Birmingham.

Appleby, J. (1992) *Financing Health Care in the 1990s*. Open University Press, Buckingham.

Ashburner, L. (1993) 'Building blocks', *Health Service Journal*, 25 March, pp. 22–3.

Audit Commission (1993a) *Practices Make Perfect: the Role of the FHSA*. Audit Commission, London.

Audit Commission (1993b) *Their Health Your Business: the New Role of the DHA*. Audit Commission, London.

Bailey, J. (1987) 'Care for the community – the Norwich model', *Hospital and Health Services Review*, September, pp. 219–21.

Bardsley, M., Beveridge, P. and Byrne, G. (1991) *CASPE/Freeman Outcomes Study, Final Report*. CASPE, London.

Bardsley, M. and Streeter, J. (1992) 'The East Anglian regional approach to developing outcome measurement'. Leeds/ESRC June Seminar, from EA RHA, Cambridge.

Basset, M. (1993) *Ensuring Health*. European Policy Forum, London.

Berwick, D., Enthoven, A. and Bunker, J. (1992) 'Quality management in the NHS: the doctor's role – Parts I and II', *British Medical Journal*, 304, pp. 235–9 (Part I) and 304, pp. 304–8 (Part II).

Bevan, A. (1945) 'Memorandum by the minister of health to the cabinet', CAB 129/3, 5/10/1945. Public Records Office, London.

Beveridge Report (1942) *Social Insurance and Allied Services*. HMSO, London (Cmd. 6404).

Blumberg, M. (1986) 'Risk adjusting health care outcomes: a methodological review', *Medical Care Review*, 43(2), pp. 351–93.

BMA (1974) *Primary Health Care Teams*. BMA, London.

Boles, O. (1993) *Effective Health Commissioning*. Purchasing Development, North West Thames RHA, London.

Brooks, T. (1992) 'Success through organisational audit', *Health Services Management*, Nov./Dec., pp. 13–15.

Buchan, H., Muir Gray, J., Hill, A. and Couter, A. (1990) 'Needs assessment made simple', *Health Services Journal*, 100, pp. 240–1.

Bull, A. (1990) 'Perspectives on the assessment of need', *Journal of Public Health Medicine*, 12(3–4), pp. 205–8.

Buxton, M. (1992) 'Scarce resources and informed choices', AMI conference paper, November 1992. HERG, Brunel University, Uxbridge.

Carnaghan, R. and Bracewell-Milnes, B. (1993) *Testing the Market: Competitive Tendering for Government Services in Britain and Abroad*. Institute of Economic Affairs, London.

CEPPP (1994) *Evaluation of Total Quality Management in the NHS – Final Report*. Centre for Evaluation of Public Policy and Practice, Brunel University, Uxbridge.

Coase, R. (1937) 'The nature of the firm', *Economica NS*, 4, pp. 386–405.

Culyer, A. and Brazier, J. (1988) *Alternatives for Organising the Provision of Health Services in the UK*. IHSM, London.

Culyer, A., Maynard, A. and Posnett, J. (1991) *Competition in Health Care*. Macmillan, London.

Cumberlege Report (1986) *Neighbourhood Nursing – a Focus for Care*. HMSO, London.

Davis, G. and Olsen, M. (1985) *Management Information Systems*. McGraw-Hill, New York.

Davis, P. (1992) 'Graphic details about the funding deficit', *Health Service Journal*, 3 September, p. 12.

Dean, T., Rees, M. and Standish, S. (1992) 'A jigsaw for the people', *Health Service Journal*, 20 February, pp. 22–3.

Dekker Report (1987) *Changing Healthcare in The Netherlands, and Willingness to Change*. Rijswijk, The Netherlands.

Demone, H. and Gibeleman, M. (eds) (1989) *Services for Sale: Purchasing Health and Human Services*. Rutgers University Press, New Brunswick, NJ.

Department of Health and Social Security (DHSS) (1976) *Sharing Resources for Health in England* (RAWP Report). HMSO, London.

Department of Health and Social Security (DHSS) (1981) Harding Report, *The Primary Health Care Team*, Standing Medical Advisory and Nursing and Midwifery Advisory Committees. DHSS, London.

Department of Health and Social Security (DHSS) (1986) *Primary Health Care*. HMSO, London.

Department of Health and Social Security (DHSS) (1987) *Promoting Better Health*. HMSO, London.

Department of Health and Social Security (DHSS) (1988) *Health Services Development: Resources, Assumptions and Planning Guidance*, HC (88) 43. HMSO, London.

Department of Health (DoH) (1989a) *Working for Patients*. HMSO, London.

Department of Health (DoH) (1989b) 'Practice budgets for general medical practititioners', Working Paper No. 3. HMSO, London.

Department of Health (DoH) (1989c) *Funding General Practice: the Programme for Introduction of GP Budgets*. HMSO, London.

Department of Health (DoH) (1990a) *The National Health Service and Community Care Act 1990*. HMSO, London.

Department of Health (DoH) (1990b) 'Funding and contracts for hospital services', Working Paper No. 2. HMSO, London.

Department of Health (DoH) (1990c) *Caring for People: Policy Guidance*. HMSO, London.

Department of Health (DoH) (1991a) *Assessing Health Care Needs*. HMSO, London.

Department of Health (DoH) (1991b) *Integrating Primary and Secondary Care*. HMSO, London.

Department of Health (DoH) (1991c) *The Patient's Charter*. HMSO, London.

Department of Health (DoH) (1992a) *The Health of the Nation*. HMSO, London.

Department of Health (DoH) (1992b) *Local Voices: the Views of Local People in Purchasing for Health*. HMSO, London.

Department of Health (DoH) (1992c) *Purchasing for Population Health Gain*. NHS ME, Leeds (unpublished).

Department of Health (DoH) (1992d) 'Guidance on extra contractual referrals', NHS ME Executive Letter 60. DoH, London.

Department of Health (DoH) (1992e) 'Tertiary referrals', NHS ME Executive Letter 97. DoH, London.

Department of Health (DoH) (1993a) *Working Together for Better Health*. HMSO, London.

Department of Health (DoH) (1993b) *Managing the New NHS*. DoH, London.

Department of Health (DoH) (1993c) 'Costing for contracting', NHS ME Executive Letter 26. DoH, London.

DoH and WO (1993) *NHS General Medical Services: Statement of Fees and Allowances to GMPs in England and Wales from 1st April 1990*. HMSO, London.

Des Harnais, S., Laurence, F., McMahon, I. Jnr and Wroblewski, R. (1991) 'Measuring outcomes of hospital care using risk-adjusted indexes', *Health Services Research*, 26(4), pp. 425–45.

Dimond, B. (1993) 'Decisions, decisions: ECRs and statutory duties', *Health Service Journal*, 28 January, pp. 26–7.

Downie, R., Fife, C. and Tinnerhill, A. (1992) *Health Promotion Models and Values*. Oxford University Press, Oxford.

Dunning Report (1992) *Choices in Health Care*. Rijswijk, The Netherlands.

Edvardsson, B., Øvretveit, J. and Thomasson, B. (1994) *Quality of Service – Making it Really Work*. McGraw-Hill, New York.

Edwards Report (1987) *Nursing in the Community: a Team Approach for Wales*. Welsh Office Information Division, Cardiff.

Ensor, T. (1993) 'Future health care options working paper: Funding health care'. IHSM, London.

Enthoven, A. (1985a) *Reflections on the Management of the National Health Service*. Nuffield Provincial Hospitals Trust.

Enthoven, A. (1985b) 'NHS: Some reforms that might be politically feasible', *The Economist*, 295(7399), pp. 19–22.

Enthoven, A. and Kronick, R. (1989) 'Consumer-choice health plan for the 1990s: universal health insurance in a system designed to promote quality and economy', *New England Journal of Medicine*, 320(29–37), pp. 94–101.

Eskin, F. (1992) 'Daydream believers', *Health Service Journal*, 10 August, pp. 24–5.

Ewles, L. (1993) 'Hope against hype of "Healthy Alliances" ', *Health Service Journal*, 26 August, pp. 30–1.

Ferlie, E., Ashburner, L. and Fitzgerald, L. (1993) *Board Teams – Roles and Relationships*. NHS Training Directorate, Bristol.

Foster, A (1991) *FHSAs – Today's and Tomorrow's Priorities*. Yorkshire Health, Harrogate.

Frankel, S. (1990) 'Total hip and knee joint replacement'. Epidemiologically Based Needs Assessment Project. Health Care Evaluation Unit, University of Bristol.

Frankel, S. (1991) 'Health needs, health care requirements, and the myth of infinite demand', *Lancet*, 337, pp. 1588–90.

Freemantle, N., Watt, I. and Mason, J. (1993) 'Talking shop – research into purchasing developments', *Health Service Journal*, 17 June, pp. 31–3.

Fry, J. (1993) *General Practice: the Facts*. Radcliffe Medical Press, Oxford.

Glennerster, H., Matsaganis, M. and Owens, P. (1992) *A Foothold for Fundholding*. King's Fund Institute, London.

Greenshields, G. (1992) Reported in the *Health Service Journal*, 11 June, p. 12.

Haggard, L. (1990) 'Making the team work', *Health Service Journal*, 12th April, p. 558.

Ham, C. (1991) *The New National Health Service*. NAHAT, Birmingham.

Ham, C. (1992a) 'Local heroes', *Health Service Journal*, 19 November, pp. 20–2.

Ham, C. (1992b) 'Locality purchasing'. HSMC Discussion Paper 30, Birmingham.

Ham, C. (1993a) 'Dial "M" for Management', *Health Service Journal*, 1 March, p. 27.

Ham, C. (1993b) *Partners in Purchasing*. NAHAT, Birmingham.

Ham, C. and Heginbotham, C. (1991) 'Purchasing together'. King's Fund College Purchasing Papers, London.

Ham, C., Robinson, R. and Benzeval, M. (1990) *Health Check: Health Care Reforms in an International Context*. King's Fund, London.

Ham, C., Schofield, D. and Williams, J. (1993) *Partners in Purchasing*. NAHAT, Birmingham.

Ham, C. and Spurgeon, P. (1992) 'Effective purchasing'. HMSC Discussion Paper 28, Birmingham.

Harrison, S. (1991) 'Working the markets: purchaser/provider separation in English health care', *International Journal of Health Services*, 21(4), pp. 625–35.

Harrison, S., Hunter, D., Johnston, I. and Wistow, G. (1989) *Competing for Health*. Nuffield Institute, Leeds.

Heginbotham, C. (1993) *Listening to Local Voices*. NAHAT, Birmingham.

Higgins, J. (1993) 'Merger on the orient express – FHSA/DHA merger', *Health Service Journal*, 26 August, pp. 29–30.

HM Treasury (1991) *Competing for Quality*. HMSO, London.

Hopkins, A. (1990) *Measuring the Quality of Care*. Royal College of Physicians, London.

Hoyes, L. and Le Grand, J. (1991) *Markets in Social Care Services*. SAUS, University of Bristol.

HPSSS (1991) *Health and Personal Social Services and Charity Statistics*. HMSO, London.

HSMU (1992) *Caring for the Community in the 21st Century*. Greenhalgh & Co., Macclesfield.

Hunter, D. (ed.) (1991) *Paradoxes of Competition for Health*. Nuffield Institute, Leeds.

Hunter, D. (1993) 'Rationing dilemmas in health care'. NAHAT Paper 8, Birmingham.

Hunter, D. and Sykes, W. (1993) 'Sound bites', *Health Service Journal*, 4 February, p. 29.

Hurst, J. (1992) 'The reform of health care: a comparative analysis of seven OECD countries', Health policy studies No. 2. OECD, Paris.

IHSM (1993) *Future Health Care Options*. IHSM, London.

IHSM/HFMA (1990) *Making Contracts Work, the Practical Implications*. IHSM, London.

IHSM/RCGP (1993) 'General practice', *Health Services Management*, February, pp. 21–3.

Illsley, R. and Svensson, P. G. (1990) 'Health inequalities in Europe', *Social Sciences and Medicine*, 31, pp. 223–40.

Jaques, E. (1982) 'The method of social analysis in social change and social research', *Clinical Sociology Review*, 1, pp. 50–8.

Jaques, E. (1989) *Requisite Organization*. Casson Hall, Arlington, VA.

JCAHO (1991) *Transitions: From QA to CQI – Using CQI Approaches to Monitor, Evaluate and Improve Quality*. Joint Commission on Accreditation of Healthcare Organizations, Oakbrook Terrace, IL.

Johnson, S. (1993) *North East Westminster Locality Project Papers*. KCW Commissioning Agency, London.

Johnston, N., Narayan, V. and Ruta, D. (1992) 'Development of indicators for quality assurance in public health medicine', *Quality in Health Care*, 1, pp. 225–30.

Joss, R., Kogan, M. and Henkel, M. (1994) *Final Report to the Department of Health on Total Quality Management Experiments in the National Health Service*. Centre for Evaluation of Public Policy and Practice, Brunel University, Uxbridge.

Kanter, R. M. (1983) *The Change Masters*. Counterpoint, London.

Kerr, R., Lidell, A. and Spry, C. (1993) *Toward an Effective NHS*. Office for Public Management, London.

King, D. and Court, M. (1984) 'A sense of scale', *Health and Social Services Journal*, p. 734.

Klein, R. (1991) 'On the Oregon Trail', *British Medical Journal*, 302, pp. 1–2.

Klein, R. (1992) 'Dilemmas and decisions', *Health Management Quarterly*, xiv, pp. 2–5.

Klein, R. and Redmayne, S. (1992) *Patterns of Priorities*. NAHAT, Birmingham.

Klein, R. and Scrivens, E. (1993) 'The bottom line – accreditation in the UK', *Health Service Journal*, 25 November, pp. 25–6.

Knapp, M., Wistow, G. and Jones, M. (1992) 'Smart moves', *Health Service Journal*, 102(5236), pp. 28–9.

Knight, K. (1977) *Matrix Management*. Gower, Farnborough.

Laing (1993) *Laing's Review of Private Health-care*. Laing & Buisson, London.

Landstingsforbundet (1990) *Some Innovative Projects of Swedish County Councils*. Landstingsforbundet, Stockholm.

Langan, J., Stephenson, A. and Cochrane, D. (1990) 'How big can we grow?', *Health Service Journal*, 6 September, pp. 1320–1.

Lee, K. (1992) 'Competition versus planning in health care', *Australian Health Review*, 14(1), pp. 9–34.

Le Grand, J. and Bartlett, W. (eds) (1993) *Quasi-Markets and Social Policy*. Macmillan, Basingstoke.

Levitt, R. and Wall, A. (1993) *The Reorganised National Health Service*. Chapman & Hall, London.

Liddell, A. (1993) 'No view from the bridge', *Health Service Journal*, 2 September, pp. 24–5.

Liddell, A. and Parston, G. (1990) 'How the market crashed', *Health Service Journal*, 17 May, pp. 730–2.

Long, A. *et al.* (1993) 'The outcomes agenda', *Quality In Health Care*, 2, pp. 49–52.

Lord, D. (1993) 'Integrating the purchasing and provision of primary care: the Wolverhampton experience', *Primary Health Care Management*, 3(3), 8–9.

Maarse, H. (1993) 'The insurer–provider relationship in health care', *European Journal of Public Health*, 3(2), 72–6.

Maarse, H. and Kirkman-Liff, B. (1992) 'Going Dutch', *Health Service Journal*, 24 September, pp. 24–7.

Macdonald, I. (ed.) (1989) 'The organisation and development of the Rhondda Vanguard Service'. MHSU, Brunel University, Uxbridge.

Mckeown, J. (1993) 'DHA and FHSA integrating mechanisms: A discussion paper'. Human Resources, North West Thames RHA, London.

MacLachlan (1992) Article in the *Health Service Journal*, 19 December, p. 26.

Mahon, A. (1992) 'Journey's end', *Health Service Journal*, 3 December.

Marchant, C. (1993) 'Toughing out tendering', *Community Care*, 1 July, pp. 14–15.

Marinker, M. (ed.) (1990) *Medical Audit and General Practice*. BMA, London.

Mawhinney, B. and Nichol, D. (1993) *Purchasing for Health*. NHS ME, London.

Maxwell, R. (1984) 'Quality assessment in health', *British Medical Journal*, 288, pp. 1470–2.

Maynard, A. (1990) 'Creating a health care market: myth or reality', *Journal of Management in Medicine*, 4(2), pp. 93–7.

Maynard, A. (1993a) Article in the *Health Service Journal*, 15 July.

Maynard, A. (1993b) Article in the *Health Service Journal*, 24 July.

Meads, G. (1991) 'Let's have local targets', *Health Service Journal*, 14 January, p. 8.

Merrison Report (1979) *Royal Commission on the National Health Service Report*. HMSO, London.

Mooney, G., Gerard, K., Donaldson, C. and Farrar, S. (1992) *Priority Setting in Purchasing*. NAHAT, Birmingham.

NAHAT (1992) 'Family doctor service', *Health Service Journal*, 9 April, p. 31.

NAHAT (1993a) *The Future Direction of the NHS*. NAHAT, Birmingham.

NAHAT (1993b) *NHS Purchasing for a Healthy Population*. NAHAT, Birmingham.

NCEPoD (1993) 'Report of the National Confidential Enquiry into Perioperative Deaths, 1991/92', NCEPoD, London.

Netten, A. (1993) *Unit Costs of Community Care 1992/3*. PSSRU, Kent University, Canterbury.

Netten, A. and Beecham, J. (eds) (1993) *Costing Community Care*. Ashgate, Cambridge.

NHS ME (1992) *Contracts: Setting Practical Directions*. NHS ME, Leeds.

NHS ME (1993) *Public Service, Private Finance: Putting Private Capital to Work for the NHS*. NHS ME, Leeds.

NHSTD (1991) *Purchasing Health Care: Lessons from Abroad*. NHS Training Directorate and Templeton College, NHSTD, Bristol.

OECD (1990) *Health Care Systems in Transition: The Search for Efficiency (Compendium: Health Care Expenditure and Other Data)*, Policy Studies No 7. OECD, Paris.

OPM (1993) *Towards an Effective NHS*. Office for Public Management, London.

Oregon HSC (1991) *Prioritization of Health Services*. Health Services Commission, Portland, OR.

Øvretveit, J. (1986) *Client Participation and Case Records*. BASW Publications, Birmingham.

Øvretveit, J. (1990a) *Improving Primary Health Care Team Organisation*. Research Report, BIOSS. Brunel University, Uxbridge.

Øvretveit, J. (1990b) 'Making the team work', *The Professional Nurse*, 5(6), pp. 284–6.

Øvretveit, J. (1991a) *Primary Care Quality Through Teamwork*, Research Report, BIOSS. Brunel University, Uxbridge.

Øvretveit, J. (1991b) 'Case management and community nursing', *The Professional Nurse*, October, pp. 264–9.

Øvretveit, J. (1991c) 'Why teams fail', in Lindesay, J. (ed.) *Working Out: Setting-up and Running Community Psychogeriatric Teams*. RDP, London.

Øvretveit, J. (1992a) *Health Service Quality*. Blackwell Scientific Press, Oxford.

Øvretveit, J. (1992b) *Therapy Services*. Harwood Academic Press, Reading.

Øvretveit, J. (1992c) *Problems in Purchasing Health in 'Internal Markets' for Health Care*. LOS-Sentrum, Norwegian Centre for Research into Organisation and Management, Bergen University, Norway.

Øvretveit, J. (1993a) *Measuring Service Quality*. Technical Communications Publications, Aylesbury.

Øvretveit, J. (1993b), *Coordinating Community Care: Multidisciplinary Teams and Care Management in Health and Social Services*. Open University Press, Buckingham.

Øvretveit, J. (1993c) 'Purchasing for health gain: the theory, problems and prospects in European health systems', *European Journal of Public Health*, 3(2), pp. 77–84.

Øvretveit, J. (1993d) 'Quality awards and auditing for purchasers of services: towards partnership contracting', *International Journal of Service Industry Management*, 4(2), pp. 74–84.

Øvretveit, J. (1993e) 'Care management and joint commissioning in Hillingdon'. A report to the NHS ME and Hillingdon Health and Social Services (available from Hillingdon Health Agency).

Øvretveit, J. (1993f) 'Auditing for service quality', *Quality Forum*, 19(1), pp. 4–9.

Øvretveit, J. (1993g) *Choice, Costs and Competition in Health Care Reforms*. LOS-Sentrum, Norwegian Centre for Research into Organisation and Management, Bergen University, Norway.

Øvretveit, J. (1993h) *Integrated Commissioning in the NHS*. North West Thames RHA, London.

Øvretveit, J. (1994a) 'Values in European health care reforms', *European Journal of Public Health*, 4(2), pp. 26–36.

Øvretveit, J. (1994b) 'Why TQM failed in the NHS, and what to do about it', report of the fourth 'Quality in Services' international conference, Norwalk, CONN.

Øvretveit, J. and Davies, K. (1988) 'Client participation in mental handicap services', *Health Services Management*, August, pp. 112–16.

Parry, N. and Parry, J. (1976) *The Rise of the Medical Profession: a Study of Collective Social Mobility*. Croom Helm, London.

Pashley, D. *et al.* (1993) *Developing Primary Health Care: A Direction Statement*. North West Thames RHA, London.

Patton, C. (1992) *Competition and Planning in the NHS: The Danger of Unplanned Markets*. Chapman & Hall, London.

Pennsylvania Health Care Cost Containment Council (1992) *Hospital Effectiveness Report*. PHCCCC, Harrisburg, PA.

Pollitt, C. (1990) 'Doing business in the temple', *Public Administration*, 68(4), pp. 435–52.

Pringle, M. (1990) 'Practice Reports' in Marinker (ed.) *op. cit.*

Prowle, M. (1992) *Purchasing in the NHS*. SAUS, University of Bristol.

Rees, A. (1972) 'Access to public health and welfare services', *Social and Economic Administration*, 6(1), pp. 34–8.

Reeves, C. (1993) 'Summing-up: the NSGC "costing for contracting project"', *Health Service Journal*, 10 June, pp. 28–30.

Reinhardt, U. (1992) 'Competition in health care'. Paper for EMHA annual conference, Warsaw, July.

Robiman, R. and Le Grand, J. (1994) *Evaluating the NHS Reforms*. King's Fund Institute/BEBC, Dorset.

Robinson, B. (1993) 'Lyme cordial', *Health Service Journal*, 5 August, pp. 20–2.

Salkever, D. and Bice, T. (1978) 'Certificate of needs legislation and hospital costs', in Zubkoff, M., Raskin, I. and Hanft, R. (eds) *Hospital Cost Containment*, publisher unknown, pp. 429–60.

Saltman, R., Harrison, S. and von Otter, C. (1991) 'Designing competition for publicly funded health systems', in Hunter, D. (ed.) *op. cit.*

Saltman, R. and von Otter, C. (1989) 'Public competition versus mixed markets: an analytic comparison', *Health Policy*, 11, pp. 43–55.

Saltman, R. and von Otter, C. (1992) *Planned Markets and Public Competition*. Open University Press, Buckingham.

Sargent J. (1991) 'Knowing your market', *Health Service Journal*, 14 February.

Sargent J. (1992) 'Charging for health service contracts'. EHMA conference unpublished paper, Trafford HA.

Scheuing, E. (1989) *Purchasing Management*. Prentice Hall/Simon and Schuster, Hemel Hempstead.

Seedhouse, D. (1993) *A Philosophical Review of the NHS*. Wiley, London.

Shickle, D., Verrall, C. and Donnelly, P. (1993) 'Simply sausages?', *Health Service Journal*, 2 September, pp. 30–1.

Sisk J., Dougherty, D., Ehrenhaft, P., Ruby, G. and Mitchner, B. (1990) 'Assessing information for consumers on the quality of medical care', *Inquiry*, 27, pp. 263–72.

SMF (1993) *Opportunities for Private Funding in the NHS*. Social Market Foundation, London.

Smith, J. (1992) 'Ethics and health care rationing', *Journal of Management in Medicine*, pp. 26–8.

Spenser, L. and Macdonald, I. (1989) *MESH: a Report on the Development of Mental Handicap Services in Hillingdon*. BIOSS, MHSU, Brunel University, Uxbridge.

SSI and SOSWSG (1991a) *Care Management and Assessment: Summary of Practice Guidance.* HMSO, London.

SSI and SOSWSG (1991b) *Care Management and Assessment: Manager's Guide.* HMSO, London.

Stamp, G. (1989) 'The individual, the organisation and the path to mutual appreciation', *Personnel Management*, July, pp. 28–31.

Starey, N., Bosanquest, N. and Griffiths, J. (1993) 'General practitioners in partnership with management – an organisational model for debate', *British Medical Journal*, 306, pp. 308–10.

Stevens, A. and Gabbay, J. (1991) 'Needs assessment, needs assessment . . .' *Health Trends*, 23(1), pp. 20–2.

Stronks, K. and Gunning-Schepers, L. (1993) 'Should equity in health be target number 1?', *European Journal of Public Health*, 3(2), pp. 104–11.

Sykes, W., Collins, M., Hunter, D., Popay, J. and Williams, G. (1992) *Listening to Local Voices: a Guide to Research Methods.* Nuffield Institute, Leeds.

Thompson, G., Frances, J., Levacic, R. and Jeremy, M. (eds) (1991) *Markets, Hierarchies and Networks.* Sage/OU, London.

Tonks, A. (1993) 'Making progress – community care in Northern Ireland', *British Medical Journal*, 306, pp. 262–5.

Tremblay, M. (1993) 'Organisational performance and health markets'. Paper presented at the EHSM conference, Warsaw, July.

Van der Ven, W. (1991) 'How can we prevent cream skimming in a competitive health insurance market?', in French, T. and Zwiefel, P. (eds) *Health Economics Worldwide.* Kluwer, Boston.

Von Otter, C. (1991) 'The application of market principles to healthcare', in Hunter, D. (ed.) *op. cit.*

Voss, S. (1993) 'Rich pickings', *Health Service Journal*, 27 May, p. 40.

Wall, A. (1993) Article in the *Health Service Journal*, 19 August, p. 20.

Warren, G. (1991) 'The development of neighbourhood forums in North Staffordshire', *Health Services Management*, pp. 258–60.

Watkinson, T. (1993) 'Contracting models for purchasing', *Health Services Management*, June, pp. 20–3.

Watt, I. (1992) 'Perceptions of quality: the rural dimension', *Management in Medicine*, 4, pp. 26–8.

Weiner, J. and Ferris, P. (1990) 'GP budget holding in the UK: lessons from America', Research report No. 7, King's Fund, London.

Welsh Office, NHS Directorate (1991) *Protocols for Investment in Health Gain.* Welsh Health Planning Forum, Cardiff.

Which? (1992) 'Is it worth going private?', *Which?*, August, pp. 426–9.

Whincup, P. and Zahir, K. (1993) 'Strictly protocol – Haringey ECRs', *Health Service Journal*, 25 March, pp. 26–7.

Whitehead, M. (1992) 'The concepts and principles of equity and health', *International Journal of Health Services*, 22, pp. 429–45.

WHO (1994) *Evaluation of Recent Changes in the Financing of Health Services.* World Health Organization, Geneva.

Wiles, R. and Higgins, J. (1992) *Why Do Patients Go Private?* IHPS, University of Southampton.

Wilkin, D., Hallam, L. and Doggett, M. (1992) *Measures of Need and Outcome for Primary Health Care.* Oxford, Oxford University Press.

Williamson, O. E. (1975) *Markets and Hierarchies.* The Free Press, New York.

Willis, A. (1992) 'Who needs fundholding?', *Health Service Journal*, 30 April, p. 24.
Wilson, K. (1990) 'At the top of the bill', *Health Service Journal*, 25 October, pp. 1068–70.
Winkler, F. (1987) 'Consumerism in health: beyond the supermarket model', *Policy and Politics*, 15(1), pp. 1–8.

Papers in the Brunel North West Thames Commissioner Development Programme series (available from North Thames Region HR Directorate)

Conference Summary, 'Locality Purchasing', Brunel Day 1.
Conference Summary, 'Strategy, Structure and Change Management', Brunel Days 2/3.
Conference Summary, 'Rationing, Effectiveness and Outcomes', Brunel Days 4/5.
Conference Summary, 'Markets, Contracting and Quality', Brunel Day 6.
Conference Summary, 'Commissioning Primary and Community Care', Brunel Days 7/8.

Briefing Paper No. 1, 'Joint Commissioning in Hillingdon'.
Briefing Paper No. 2, 'Locality Purchasing and Providing'.
Briefing Paper No. 3, 'Towards Integration'.
Briefing Paper No. 4, 'Profiles and Structures'.
Briefing Paper No. 5, 'Organising Commissioning'.
Briefing Paper No. 6, 'Justifiable Commissioning'.
Briefing Paper No. 7, 'Market Co-operation'.
Briefing Paper No. 8, 'Commissioning Primary and Community Health Care'.

Index

INFORMATION MANAGEMENT IN HEALTH SERVICES
Justin Keen (ed.)

Health services are set on an inexorable drive for more and better information, and are spending millions of pounds on information technology (IT) in an effort to obtain it. But as the need for information becomes ever more pressing, serious problems have come into focus, ranging from the difficulties of collecting accurate routine data to understanding the role of information in management and clinical processes.

This book seeks to clarify the nature of the problems surrounding information and IT, and point the way to practical solutions. It is divided into three sections: policy overview; views from within the health service; and the views of academic researchers.

Contents
Section 1: Overview: information policy and the market – Hospitals in the market – Information policy in the National Health Service – Section 2: The practitioner perspective – Operational systems – Managing development: developing managers' information management – Clinical management – Nursing management – Contracts: managing the external environment – Section 3: The academic perspective – Information for purchasing – The politics of information – A social science perspective on information systems in the NHS – Information and IT strategy – Evaluation: informing the future, not living in the past – IT futures in the NHS – Index.

Contributors
Brian Bloomfield, Andrew Brooks, Jane Clayton, Rod Coombs, Bob Galliers, Wally Gowing, Mark Harrison, John James, Justin Keen, Andy Kennedy, Rebecca Malby, Margaret Marion, Jenny Owen, James Raftery, Ray Robinson, Mike Smith, Andrew Stevens.

224pp   0 335 19116 9 (Paperback)   0 335 19117 7 (Hardback)